The Remembered Present

THE REMEMBERED PRESENT

A Biological Theory of Consciousness

GERALD M. EDELMAN

Basic Books, Inc., Publishers   New York

Library of Congress Cataloging-in-Publication Data

Edelman, Gerald M.
    The remembered present: a biological theory of consciousness/
Gerald M. Edelman.
    p. cm.
    Includes bibliographical references.
    ISBN 0–465–06910–X
    1. Consciousness—Physiological aspects. 2. Brain—Evolution.
3. Neuropsychology—Philosophy. I. Title.
QP411.E34 1989
612.8—dc20   89–42907
                                                           CIP

To the memory of my parents,

Anna and Edward Edelman

To be aware of a conscious datum is to be sure that it has passed. The nearest actual approach to immediate introspection is early retrospection. The experience described, if there be any such, is always just past; the description is present. However, if I ask myself how I know that the description is present, I find myself describing the processes that made up the description; the original describing is past and it is presumably the new description of the description that is present. To find myself thus landed in an infinite regress is to find myself just where I seem to myself to be. Experience itself is at the end of the introspective rainbow. The rainbow may have an end and the end be somewhere: yet I seem never to get to it.

—E. G. BORING
The Physical Dimensions of Consciousness

I have been accused of denying consciousness, but I am not conscious of having done so. Consciousness is to me a mystery, and not one to be dismissed. We know what it is like to be conscious, but not how to put it into satisfactory scientific terms. Whatever it precisely may be, consciousness is a state of the body, a state of nerves.

The line that I am urging as today's conventional wisdom is not a denial of consciousness. It is often called, with more reason, a repudiation of mind. It is indeed a repudiation of mind as a second substance, over and above body. It can be described less harshly as an identification of mind with some of the faculties, states, and activities of the body. Mental states and events are a special subclass of the states and events of the human or animal body.

—W. V. QUINE
Quiddities

Selection is the very keel on which our mental ship is built.

—W. JAMES
The Principles of Psychology

CONTENTS

PART ONE

INTRODUCTION

PART TWO

THE EXTENDED THEORY

PART THREE

MEMORY, ORDERING, AND CONCEPTS

PART FOUR

CONSCIOUSNESS

PART FIVE

BIOLOGICALLY BASED EPISTEMOLOGY

LIST OF
ILLUSTRATIONS

LIST OF TABLES

PREFACE

All of my life, my main goal has been to understand how I could come to be—to be aware, to sense, and to remember. In pursuit of that goal, I have studied matter, then living forms, and, more recently, the activities connected with mental lives. This last pursuit has often tempted me to speculative excess, a trait, I notice, that is shared by many who have similar personal interests.

During my life as a scientist, however, I have carefully kept to a crafty empiricism. The reasons for this undoubtedly lie in my training in the skeptical bases on which experimental science rests, and in the rewards and protections that this skeptical position affords. But my pride in this habit has diminished over the years. I have come to be less convinced that there is a fundamental distinction among the intellectual procedures of science, of philosophy, and of everyday life. And certainly, I have become more impatient for insights into the origins of mental activity as the gap to personal oblivion narrows.

Impelled perhaps by that impatience, I made an attempt some time ago to formulate an explanation of some basic psychological functions in neural terms. My main focus was on perceptual categorization as it related to memory and learning. I proposed that these functions could be understood in terms of "neural Darwinism"—the idea that higher brain functions are mediated by developmental and somatic selection upon anatomical and functional variance occurring in each individual animal. The key aspect of Darwinism, population thinking, was embedded in the theory of neuronal group selection and was used to explain the manifestations and bases of perceptual categorization—the ability of certain organisms to categorize novelty and generalize upon that categorization as a basis for learning. I proposed that this ability depended critically on two of the most striking features of the brain, its variability and its reentrant connectivity.

I deliberately excluded any extended discussion of perceptual experience—the interaction of memory with the present awareness of the individual animal. The reasons for this exclusion were both methodological and habitual. I felt that perceptual awareness and conscious experience, unlike their antecedents such as perceptual categorization, could not be tested by direct experimental means. Like most of my colleagues, I considered consciousness a dangerous subject.

I took this position not only because of the inherent methodological limitations in ascertaining the empirical bases of consciousness, or because of its rich linkage to complex affective and subjective states, but also because of certain assumptions inherent in the classical notion of the detached scientific observer. Having made this decision, however, I was constantly aware of the compromises and dilemmas that it entailed. In psychology and psychophysics, for example, ignoring consciousness while comparing animals to humans, or taking it for granted in interpreting data, runs various risks that actually endanger reliable conclusions. This avoidance can have unfortunate outcomes: assumption of hidden homunculi, vicious circularity in various arguments, or adoption of an elaborate and sanitary behaviorism that borders on the ludicrous.

After weighing the risks, I became convinced that an extensive attempt must be made to analyze consciousness in terms of its neural origins. Despite its methodological inaccessibility, this issue must be confronted scientifically if psychology is to be solidly based in evolutionary biology. Moreover, a confrontation with the problem of consciousness is certainly required for a better understanding of how science itself is related to the rest of thought and human history.

Although there are many verbal and philosophical accounts of consciousness, there are few if any explicit and principled scientific accounts. An adequate theory of consciousness must contain an explanation of the properties of conscious experience. It should account both for intentionality and for the discriminability of qualia or phenomenal experiences. Such a scientific account should nevertheless be clearly distinguished from philosophical hypotheses, for example, that of mind-body identity.

To qualify as a scientific account, a theoretical analysis of consciousness must achieve four goals: (1) propose explicit *neural* models that explain how consciousness can arise; (2) relate these models to the emergence of consciousness during evolution and development; (3)

relate these models to concept formation, memory, and language; and (4) describe stringent tests for the models in terms of known neurobiological facts, at least in the form of gedankenexperiments, if not ones that can be carried out directly on known living organisms. I have kept these goals in mind in preparing the present account.

In many ways, scientific analyses of consciousness suffer from the same limitations and constraints as cosmological theories: right at the outset, certain manipulations and observations cannot be carried out. Nonetheless, theories of consciousness, like cosmological theories, must at least be consistent with currently accepted scientific interpretations and empirical observations. And like cosmological theories, consciousness theories must rest on a vast body of information pertaining to many levels of organization of matter, some of which are not directly accessible. Patience and a willingness to search for constraints on unbridled speculation are essential to the enterprise.

In the present effort, these constraints are precisely those assumed by the theory of neuronal group selection. This book represents an extension of that theory to concept formation, language, and consciousness. In one sense, therefore, *Neural Darwinism* and this extended theory may be considered a single work. The earlier account had as a major goal the banishment from global brain theory of the homunculus and of the ideas underlying information processing models of the brain. The present work, with its arguments against machine functionalism and for selectionism as an alternative basis for a biologically based theory of consciousness, pursues that goal even more vigorously.

The more fundamental and experimentally accessible TNGS is summarized here to provide the necessary bases for the task of analyzing consciousness. But many subjects and pieces of supporting evidence have been omitted. The interested reader may consult my *Topobiology* for the morphological argument and *Neural Darwinism* for discussions of such matters as detailed synaptic mechanisms, perceptual categorization, and learning.

Two areas have required a rather extended analysis: reentry and cortical appendages. They are presented in the same fashion as they would have been had they been parts of these earlier works. This entails consideration of certain technical matters the nonexpert may wish to gloss over. The presentation of the model of reentry (the RCI model) in chapter 4, while not as detailed as that in the original paper, does require careful working through. The description of cortical appendages (chapter 7) contains specific models of cerebellar, hippocampal, and basal ganglion function. In formulating them, I have risked being accused of indulging in speculative neurology. I have nonetheless attempted to keep the functional aspects of these models well within the known properties of these brain structures. The models, risky though they may be, are intended to reinforce the view that the cortical appendages are temporal organs necessary to the eventual emergence of rich conscious activity. The usefulness of these models is illustrated both in an explicit and anatomically based hypothesis linking attention and consciousness in chapter 12 and in the overall summary presented in chapter 14.

Because any biological theory of consciousness must rest on several such models of brain function, a detailed account of the subject proper does not emerge until the last half of the book, after the necessary foundations have been laid in the first half. I therefore give a preliminary view of the consciousness model in chapter 5. For those who want a summary view of the theory, I suggest reading chapters 1, 2, and 5 as a unit. Readers are also encouraged to look ahead (and particularly to scan chapter 9) to supplement and refine that early view. While chapter 8 provides a basis for a discussion of thinking, inference, and induction, these subjects require a consideration of linguistic issues and matters of social transmission that fall outside the scope of this work.

No scientific theory can expect to explain everything even within a restricted purview. But it should be able to point in new directions, to redefine its subject matter (at least implicitly), to unify observations, to suggest experiments, and to bear on certain philosophical issues that prepare one's mind for further developments. The biological theory I shall describe in this book attempts to do all of these things. Although I have avoided an extensive discussion of the applications of the theory (a task that will require another book), I do attempt to give a few examples of its relevance to perception, action, attention, and memory, as well as to some clinical disorders of consciousness.

Above all, the present essay is intended to provoke thought by scientists about a subject considered in most scientific circles to be beyond scientific reach. To show the feasibility of constructing a brain-based theory of consciousness is perhaps all that can be reasonably expected at this stage of knowledge. On that basis, others may build more firmly when the necessary facts and methods become available.

New York, 1989

ACKNOWLEDGMENTS

This book, the last of a trilogy intended to examine the relation between morphology and mind, has required more help than its predecessors. My colleagues at The Neurosciences Institute, George N. Reeke, Jr., Joseph Gally, and Olaf Sporns, showed mercy and patience in their various criticisms and discussions over many revisions. In addition, Olaf Sporns provided several truly inspired drawings. Israel Rosenfield was a critical but imaginative sounding board and made valuable suggestions about the overall structure of the book. Edward Reed made useful comments providing background in the history of psychology and in child psychology. W. Maxwell Cowan provided his usual penetrating insight into all matters of thought and scholarship in the neurosciences. Semir Zeki gave me important guidance on several questions related to the visual system. I also had the advantage of several extended and lively encounters and discussions with two philosophers: John Searle and Hilary Putnam. They were most generous with their thoughts and, at the same time, relentless in their criticisms. They served as living reminders of the noble reach of philosophy.

Throughout the time I spent on this work, W. Einar Gall arranged matters so that The Neurosciences Institute served as it should—as a scientific monastery and a place for thought and lively exchange. As before, I thank Kathryn L. Crossin for her scientific editing and Susan Hassler, editor of The Neurosciences Institute, for her undeviating efforts and attention to important details.

I have obeyed all of these critics sometimes, and none of them always. I am aware that the results of my efforts remain flawed and that they are my sole responsibility. Above all, I am grateful to these friends and scholars for their companionship and generosity.

PART ONE

INTRODUCTION

1

Consciousness and the Scientific Observer

At the beginning of the modern scientific epoch, a procedure was established and a philosophical position reached, both of which continue to influence scientific practice and everyday life. The procedure was that of Galileo, who removed the mind from nature and simultaneously described a means for relating physical observation to theory.[1] The philosophical position was that of Descartes, whose skeptical introspection led him to conclude that the domain of the mind was not accessible to such scientific inquiry, which was confined to extended things.[2]

Scientific methodology and philosophical dualism for a long time had no need to war with each other. But, as Whitehead pointed out,[3] the mind was placed back into nature with the rise of physiology in the middle of the nineteenth century. This raised a serious question about the adequacy of conventional scientific means in physiological and psychological investigations. In no area is this question more unavoidable than in asking about the nature of consciousness.

With the appearance of Darwin's theory of natural selection,[4] this issue was framed in even sharper terms, although most contemporary philosophers who debated it were unaware of his comments in the M notebook: "Origin of man now proved.—Metaphysic must flourish.— He who understands baboon would do more toward metaphysics than Locke."[5] Before Darwin, the domain of epistemology was associated more closely with matters related to physics and was separated from biology. But with the appearance of the idea of natural selection, the issue of adequacy was joined and a *scientific* confrontation could not be avoided: When and how did mind appear in nature?

Philosophers, of course, have discussed this and related issues from the time of the pre-Socratics to the present day, but not, until lately, against a close backdrop of scientific inquiry. The philosophy of mind was independently pursued along with epistemology, ontology, and the philosophy of language, and in this pursuit Darwin's discovery was largely ignored. Not until William James published his essay "Does Consciousness Exist?"[6] did the accepted division of territory between science and philosophy receive a significant explicit challenge.

Whitehead remarked[7] that James, in asserting that consciousness is a process and denying that it is a stuff, was to the twentieth century what Descartes was to the seventeenth. Each clearly formulated the issue for his epoch. James no doubt considered that consciousness was a property of the organization of the brain and denied the idea of the mind as confined solely to its own world of *res cogitans.*[8] If this latter Cartesian notion were to be accepted, the whole issue of how any knowledge is obtained "of the truly objective world of science," as Whitehead put it,[9] would become a major problem.

One aspect of this problem is reflected in the need to reconcile the worldview of everyday life (the manifest image) and that of science (the scientific image), a problem explored philosophically in these terms by Sellars.[10] Certainly, everyday perception and descriptions of the world are not the same as the formulations of scientific theory, which replace the continuous phenomenal categories of experience with granular states, molecular descriptions, and unusual abstractions. Moreover, as Schrödinger pointed out,[11] our scientific theories *themselves* contain no evidence of sensation, perception, and various phenomenal experiences, nor can they. In general, a proper scientific observer has such experiences but does not admit them into his predictions. And certainly, in most sciences, consciousness itself is taken for granted or at least not defined. For physics this is wisdom, but for psychology it is a headache, for in psychology consciousness cannot be avoided and its definition is by no means easy. Let us make a provisional attempt.

AN INITIAL DEFINITION

Consciousness is something the meaning of which "we know so long as no one asks us to define it."[12] It has been so variously defined that, as an initial gesture, only a descriptive definition is safe. Accordingly, let us attempt such an initial definition of consciousness by listing some of its properties. First of all, consciousness is a form of awareness and is thus a process, not a thing. It is personal (a property possessed by individuals or selves), and, as James observed,[13] it is changing, continuous, deals mainly with objects independent of itself, and is selective in time, not exhausting all aspects of the objects with which it deals.

Consciousness is bound up to some degree with volition and decision. To capture this characteristic and also render some idea of a process that is individual, yet embodies an analogue of the ordering of experience, some authors (for example, Griffin[14]) propose that consciousness is marked by the presence of mental images and particularly by their use to regulate behavior. Consciousness is not, however, a copy of experience, nor is it essential for much of behavior—some learning, many conceptual processes, and even inference can proceed to a large extent without it. (It is not clear, though, and indeed it is dubious, whether the *initial* learning of many complex processes can occur without conscious attention.)

In any case, whatever is in consciousness must have been reflected in prior or current behavior—consciousness is of or about things or events and therefore it relates to intentionality.[15] In humans, it can involve awareness of perception and awareness of action, plans, and intentions. At this point, it may be useful to make a distinction between primary consciousness, which does not embody an extended sense of the past and thus does not smack of the personal but does relate to "mental images," and higher-order consciousness, which in humans is also able to embody a model of the personal (what we shall call direct awareness) and also of the past and future.

Certainly, this initial descriptive definition does not persuade one that one cannot simply take consciousness for granted and proceed with the scientific business at hand. Quine,[16] for example, has done exactly this. By taking a position of philosophical behaviorism and analyzing how language is acquired and used, he has made a good case for the continuity of everyday thinking and that of scientific procedure. This is consistent with the classical picture of the scientific observer, oblivious (at least in his constructions) to his own mind. Let us examine whether this picture is satisfactory for psychology.

THE SCIENTIFIC OBSERVER

So far, we have argued the following case: in providing a description of the physical world that is general and predictive, science has, since Galileo, sensibly relied on a notion of the scientific observer that deliberately ignores or neutralizes matters of the self or of consciousness. This notion has been remarkably successful in physics and in those parts of biology not concerned with the brain as an object of scientific inquiry. The pursuit of such sciences rests on a series of assumptions: (1) the assumption that one does not need to understand consciousness in achieving adequate descriptions and predictions; (2) the assumption that perceptual error and personal bias must be eliminated; (3) the tacit assumption that social transmission and language in scientific practice can be relied on without considerations of either their nature or their origins; and (4) the equally tacit assumption that, although knowledge in a scientific field must constantly be revised and criticized according to the canons of that field, the grounds on which the assessment of the skill of the scientific practitioner rests require no understanding of his mental state other than that obliged by his actual performance.

The success of this Galilean procedure is remarkable, and even the revision of our view of the meaning of certain physical operations that has derived from the Einsteinian revolution has not obliged us to alter its premises.[17] It is true that relativity theory and particularly quantum mechanics made it impossible to separate the manipulations of the observer from the interpretation of any given system. Nonetheless, the Galilean observer and even the Einsteinian and Heisenbergian observers are all psychologically transparent—they can operate in ignorance of the psychological apparatus of the real human being who is their creator. This is as it should be: in most sciences, a knowledge of this mental apparatus is unnecessary and irrelevant. Indeed, even certain areas in psychology itself (particularly those susceptible to functionalist interpretation) can, with small provisos, be pursued under the same program.

Matters are different in other psychological realms, however. It is striking, for example, that theories of how the brain works and theories of how the mind works have rarely been concerned with the same subjects. Indeed, the gulf that separates these two kinds of theory has for the most part been the one that separates science from philosophy. This is not to say that certain branches of psychology do not touch upon the mental. Nonetheless, they usually take a functionalist attitude toward behavior and do not theorize on the basis *in the material order* of perceiving, feeling, and thinking. This activity seems to have been left to the provinces of philosophy, mainly metaphysics since the Renaissance and epistemology since the end of the seventeenth century.[18]

In the last one hundred years, however, there has emerged a new body of scientific knowledge of such importance that it cannot be ignored even by philosophers. This knowledge has been developed within a vigorous set of biological disciplines variously concerned with the evolution, development, structure, and function of the nervous system, and having as a main item on their agendas the understanding of the human brain.[19] In recent times, it has actually become possible to attempt an understanding of the basis of such psychological events as perception in terms of brain structure and function. In this arena, which expects a strict physical account of such psychological events, the classical Galilean stance is insufficient and any discussion of perceptual experience or memory soon verges on the consciousness of the observer himself, on that of his subject, or on their interaction. To this observer, his own consciousness is a datum but that of others is an inductive extrapolation.

Consider observing a scientific observer confronted with a problem of interpretation in relating brain events to behavior. We may safely assume that he believes in evolution and that he would not deny the following historical sequence: "world" (matter) → earth → living forms and evolution → animals → primates and hominids → social communication → culture and language → science. If we wish to describe psychological events in such an observer, and attempt to base our scientific description on physical events occurring within *him,* we encounter a potential paradox. He (the observer as object of study) is certainly a physical object. In attempting to make an objective description of such an observer, one may remove one's own mind, but one may not remove *his* mind. To account for his behavior *and* his reports, one needs to confront his awareness in terms of an adequate model.

This curious situation is not limited to humans.[20] The neurophysiologist may study perceptual processes of animals with rich nervous systems without assuming that they are conscious. But if he attempts to interpret the results of any of his studies of these animals under such a stringent limitation, he must have recourse to a particular series of assumptions about the nature of stimuli in the physical world as well as about the nature of memory. These assumptions may take the neurophysiologist's own consciousness of perception into account, or they may not. If they take it into account, they will be inadequate unless he has an explicit scientific model of consciousness. If they do not take his perceptual awareness into account, they run two risks: (1) much of the subject animal's (particularly a human animal's) perception might in fact be based on conscious awareness and thus might escape adequate analysis, or (2) the physiologist's own physical description of the world (which is based on his *own* consciousness) may be irrelevant to the manner in which the animal under study partitions *its* response to that world.

Traditional reactions to this problem have ranged widely. Before the advent of modern neuroscience, consciousness was a subject for philosophical debate or qualitative psychological descriptions based on introspection. In some schools of psychology, such as behaviorism,[21] it was placed outside of the scientific program, and considered to be a kind of epiphenomenon. More recently, cognitive psychologists[22] have taken certain functional aspects of consciousness as neurally unanalyzed bases for their studies on human perception and even with a certain degree of success. Such a position does not go far enough, however. Any attempt to account for higher brain functions in terms of the physical organization of the brain itself and of its constituent neurons is confronted sooner or later with the need for a detailed analysis of consciousness based on brain structure.

An attempt to lay the grounds for such an analysis is the main concern of this book. There are many, however, who would still argue that such an attempt is premature. What can be said in response to this judgment?

The Feasibility Argument

Perhaps the first thing to say is that, faced with the problem of consciousness, one has several options. One option is to wait for more facts from the subdisciplines of neuroscience and psychology, gingerly reaching out to note but not to analyze various phenomenological observations on consciousness. Another is to split explanations into two classes: those related to the workings of the brain and its components and those related to psychological functioning and based, for example, on the abstract notion of mental representations.[23] Surely, there is enough to keep one very busy in either of these domains. But even if the practitioners in each domain agree in a token materialist fashion that the mind arises as a result of the workings of the brain, the gap between their explanations of neural and of mental functions remains huge.

Many neuroscientists are at present pursuing one or the other of these options. The option I have elected to take here is different and certainly the most hazardous of all—to construct a scientific theory of the mind based directly on the structure and workings of the brain. By "scientific" in this context, I mean a description based on the neuronal and phenotypic organization of an individual and formulated solely in terms of physical and chemical mechanisms giving rise to that organization. In using the word "scientific," I also mean that a consciousness model based on such a theory must either be testable by experiment or, if not, at least be consistent with other brain models that *are* testable by experiment.

Why make this attempt at this stage of our knowledge? One reason is that it forces us to explore whether currently available brain theories can be extended to include the phenomenon of consciousness. But nested in this goal is a related reason that might be called the feasibility argument—even if many details have to be assumed at our present state of knowledge, it would be inherently valuable to demonstrate that a cogent theory of consciousness can be constructed *solely* on biological grounds. In other words, because consciousness has been so recalcitrant a problem in the history of science,[24] it is worthwhile to consider in what manner it *might* be scientifically analyzed in terms of detailed brain structure and function, whether or not certain details of the analysis are incorrect. That analysis should not only account for how consciousness evolved but also show how it arises as a physiological property affecting behavior.

Even if such a biologically based consciousness theory turned out to be wrong, an attempt to construct it would, I believe, be of value provided it could be shown to be self-consistent. This is because explicit and extensive scientific theories or models of consciousness based on brain structure[25] are rare, and attempts at their construction are too often accompanied by what might be called Cartesian shame. Demonstration of the feasibility of a scientifically based consciousness theory would itself be a spur to progress. Indeed, if the history of science provides any guide, even disconfirmation of a detailed theory based on neurobiological facts might serve more rapidly to prompt alternative scientific formulations.

It is no surprise that consciousness models are rare. They are difficult to construct and, from a conventional scientific point of view, hard to accept. They are difficult to construct because any global brain theory on which they must be based itself requires the incorporation of major theories from a great many disciplines. These include, at the least, physics and the theory of matter, the theory of evolution, and an adequate theory of developmental morphology.[26] Brain-based consciousness models are hard to accept for a related reason. They must rest on a number of other psychological and physiological models, each of which is intricate and subject to error at our current stage of knowledge: models of perceptual categorization,[27] memory, learning, concept formation, and, finally, language. The usual reductionistic simplifying criteria—Occam's razor or a minimal number of assumptions—cannot usefully be applied to any such multilevel global model, which must take into account a large series of evolutionary developments. Furthermore, as is the case in some aspects of physics, the objects and processes of interest that are related to mental activity can be observed only indirectly. Worse still, as we have already seen and will see again in the next chapter, the goal process—consciousness—is elusive and difficult to define.

THE MATTER OF CONSTRAINTS

Given these difficulties, how are we to proceed? What we need is a sufficient set of *constraints* so that, despite the complexity of any proposed biological theory of consciousness, it can at least be made subject to critical queries based on evolution, development, and physiology.

Let us consider a list of such constraints:

1. Any adequate global theory of brain function must include a scientific model of consciousness, but to be scientifically acceptable it also must avoid the Cartesian dilemma.[28] In other words, it must be uncompromisingly physical and be based on *res extensa,* and indeed be derivable from them. According to this view, all cognition and all consciousness must rest on orderings and processes in the physical world. Unlike the Galilean view (which is noncommittal on the issue)[29] and unlike Cartesianism, such a view of brain function and consciousness should be based on a materialist metaphysics and on an epistemology of qualified realism, as I shall explain in the final chapter of this book.

2. If an adequate brain theory cannot be formulated without incorporating a model of consciousness, it is equally true that an adequate model of consciousness can be formulated only *after* much of the function of the brain has been accounted for by a parent global brain theory. This account must rest on a description of neural structures. For example, this book takes as its starting point the brain theory called the theory of neuronal group selection (TNGS).[30] This theory was formulated to account for perceptual categorization and certain aspects of memory and learning in terms of brain structure, development, and evolution. For this theory to be tied to the model of consciousness to be described here, it must be extended to account as well for temporal succession and ordering in memory, and it must concern itself with internal homeostatic states and with appetitive and consummatory processes.

3. An adequate theory of consciousness based on brain structure and function must be an evolutionary theory that is consistent with the principles of development. If we assume (as any such theory must) that consciousness arose as a result of evolutionary processes affecting brain structures,[31] we will not find it likely that such processes emerged precipitously or as a result of a *large* number of radical innovations in neural mechanisms. Consistent with this idea, it would be particularly parsimonious if the various constraints already applicable to the TNGS could be applied rigorously and successfully to a theory of consciousness *with no further assumptions*. Given the emphasis of the TNGS on development, this implies that consciousness can emerge only in each individual of a species having the appropriate brain structure at a certain stage of brain development. If this strong constraint were successful, it would strengthen both the original TNGS and the extended theory.

4. A brain-based scientific model of consciousness should be self-consistent, detailed, and persuasive and yet avoid merely verbal or rationalistic accounts. It is not sufficient, for example, to start with an idea of mental representations in the absence of physical mechanisms.[32] An adequate description of an appropriately formulated scientific model based on brain mechanisms should allow one to close one's eyes and say, "Whatever its truth, if I follow the steps and processes of the model, I can appreciate that consciousness could emerge or result." Given the theory and adequate physical resources, one should be able to envision the possibility of building a conscious artifact.

This set of constraints sharply defines my task in this book: starting with the TNGS (which is itself based on a theory of morphogenesis)[33] to construct a biologically based theory of consciousness. The theory should stay close to the structure, development, and evolution of the nervous system as it relates to the rest of the phenotype; this defines what I mean by the term "biologically based." As we shall see, the proposed theory relies heavily on the extension of notions concerning memory and the brain's response to the succession of events. The TNGS must therefore first be extended to account for temporal succession or sequence.[34] An explicit model must then be built to show that consciousness is a special property emerging from systems of memory and ongoing perceptual categorization. Finally, to account for higher-order consciousness, a brain-based theory of concept formation must be tied to a similarly based account of language and its forerunners.

These are demanding requirements. Their satisfaction entails a new view of the manner in which animals with richly endowed brains deal with the macroscopic physical order. This view must not abandon the Galilean program but must supplement it with new ideas concerning certain neural properties of observers, ideas that have rich scientific and philosophical implications.

Philosophical Issues

Unlike many kinds of scientific inquiry, studies of consciousness cannot avoid facing certain metaphysical issues: to take a scientific position on consciousness is *necessarily* to take a philosophical position.[35] This is so not only because a biologically based consciousness model bears directly on many key questions of the philosophy of mind but also because a globally based brain theory incorporating an explanation of consciousness has widespread metatheoretical consequences in many areas of *scientific* explanation. The relation between the scientific observer and his mind can no longer be sidestepped. Apart from the profound (and perennial) problems of the philosophy of mind[36]—the problem of other minds, and of conscious self-awareness and the related questions of privileged access and incorrigible states—scientific epistemology must confront the issue of consciousness in terms of evolution, development, brain structure, and the physical order as we know it. If that confrontation is to remain in the scientific domain, a dualistic solution or any form of Cartesian empiricism cannot be countenanced.

For all of these reasons, the outcome of an analysis of consciousness must be related to an accumulated body of philosophical investigation. I have not avoided the beginnings of such a task here, despite the fact that my qualifications for it are meager. My efforts may at least persuade those with more formal philosophical skills to correct and extend the views I have espoused.

Without exposing those views prematurely, I may tempt readers who are not brain scientists to stay the course if I simply list some of the general questions that will eventually be confronted in one part or another of this work:

1. Is consciousness inexorably tied to specific brain structures and to individual history?
2. Is consciousness at any level causally efficacious?[37]
3. How do concepts arise on the basis of neural structures, and can they function independently of consciousness?
4. Is there a difference between consciousness in animals possessing mental images but no language, and consciousness in language-bearing animals?[38]
5. How does a biologically based theory of consciousness bear on the interpretation of various mental phenomena—sleep, dreams, hallucinations, action and volition, and, finally, thought and language?
6. Can a machine be conscious, and, if so, must such a machine be a new kind, with capacities not possessed by computers or Turing machines?[39]

7. What impact does such a biologically based theory of consciousness have on our view of the scientific observer?
8. What metaphysical and epistemological positions are consistent with such a theory? How can we reconcile everyday phenomenal views of the world with scientific views[40]—the manifest and the scientific images?

The reasons why such questions are important to a scientific inquiry will emerge in the course of this essay. One reason of immediate pertinence to question 7 comes from a brief examination of the philosophical consequences of the Galilean position. To assume the Galilean position is to assume a materialist metaphysics without *necessarily* assuming any clear-cut epistemological position. This simply does not confront the dilemma posed by Descartes's dualist assumption of two domains—*res extensa* and *res cogitans.* As I said earlier, in much of physics this entails no embarrassment, but in psychology it does. In actuality, by skirting the issue of consciousness, many modern psychologists assume one version or another of an idealist or Cartesian epistemology *in a hidden or unanalyzed manner.* For example, to talk about "representations" in the brain is to make certain hidden assumptions about how a conscious observer catalogs what is assumptively described as "information" in the macroscopic physical order, for example, the categories of things and how they are arranged.[41] The very analysis of such situations, however, depends upon the consciousness of the observer, and the Cartesian dilemma appears once again.

In approaching higher psychological functions like consciousness, brain science cannot avoid the risky confrontation with such philosophical issues unless it wishes to face even greater risks—inconsistency, unexamined premises, and importation of dubious metaphysical positions into science by the back door. The benefits of considering a brain-based analysis of consciousness in philosophical terms would be particularly evident if this analysis resulted in a self-consistent scientific view whose metaphysical and epistemological premises are made explicit.

To summarize, I have suggested that there is much to be gained from an analysis of consciousness based on a detailed theory of brain function that is built in turn on adequate theories of evolution and development. Such a theory not only must be consistent with the physical description of the world but also must account in neural terms for a series of psychological functions, beginning with perception and culminating in an adequate explanation of consciousness. This requires that the theory, however unitary, specify the ordering and connectivity of *several* models, *each* accounting biologically for the different psychological functions considered to be required for the emergence of consciousness.

The risks entailed by this procedure can be mitigated by the use of a variety of constraints. The strongest constraint is that no new evolutionary or developmental *mechanisms* be assumed in advancing from explanations of perceptual categorization[42] to those of consciousness.

As I mentioned at the beginning of these remarks, I agree with Quine[43] that common knowledge, scientific knowledge, and philosophical analysis are continuous or at least intersect with one another at many points. What science offers that is special is a methodology based on constructive skepticism and a means of control and prediction. Attempts to build a scientific theory of mind and consciousness in such terms face even stricter limitations than theoretical attempts concerned with, say, the structure of matter. Attention must be paid to these limitations without denying the existence of phenomena or abandoning the goal of producing a sound global brain theory that includes consciousness.

Such an effort is no different for psychology than the attempt to construct a self-consistent cosmology is for physics.[44] Without a self-consistent theory in each of these domains—cosmology and consciousness—modern science and the human institutions it affects will at best embody only partial explanations of the state of affairs accessible to us as aware, thinking beings.

In the attempt to describe the physical world, scientific procedures assume an impartial human observer whose mind is removed from nature and whose sensation, categorization, and motion are only *implicit* in his scientific theorizing. As Schrödinger pointed out,[45] physical theories assume the existence of an observer without including or accounting for his perceptual capabilities in any of their descriptions. An adequate theory of consciousness should allow us to understand better the strengths and limitations of this procedure. The split between epistemology and psychology and between physics and biology has not yet been repaired. This task is incentive enough to take even a few halting steps toward constructing a biologically based theory of mind, a naturalistic theory based on evolution that would allow epistemology to be pursued directly within psychology itself.

2

Proposals and Disclaimers

This is not a work of philosophy but rather an attempt to construct a scientific theory. However, as I hinted in the preceding chapter, there is something special in trying to formulate a scientific theory of consciousness. Although the Galilean observer may consider his consciousness as given and transparent, the scientist studying consciousness obviously cannot do so. By taking on the issue squarely, he also takes on a number of unavoidable difficulties. It is my purpose in this chapter to consider what these may be, and what may be done about them.

In doing so, I cannot avoid certain philosophical problems. Nevertheless, my main purpose is, as I have said, to consider how to proceed scientifically. The scientist studying consciousness may, like his Galilean counterpart, presuppose the reality of the material world. But in addition, he must explicitly assume the reality of conscious experience and consider how this experience can have discriminable properties. It is his task to explain these properties and discover their evolutionary and developmental origins.

Let us begin that task with a short consideration of nonscientific definitions of consciousness in ordinary language.

FURTHER DEFINITIONS

In the preceding chapter, we made an initial attempt to show that consciousness has various levels of definition. As an extension, let us consider ordinary-language usage, if only to restrict our scientific definition more stringently and help us to refine it. Natsoulas[1] has applied the various entries in the *Oxford English Dictionary* as a reference for a comprehensive psychological excursion on the definition of consciousness. The first entry, *consciousness*₁, is related to the idea of "joint or mutual knowledge," not at all the notion of private states that is usually implied. *Consciousness*₂ refers to "internal knowledge or conviction"—a cognitive relation to oneself, a witness to one's own deeds that is related, as Natsoulas suggests, to Mead's idea of the social origins of consciousness[2] as an internalization of some generalized other.

The next two definitions, *consciousness*₃ and *consciousness*₄, are central to any neurally based theory. *Consciousness*₃ is "the state of being mentally conscious or aware of anything." This is taken to be the most basic idea of consciousness, underlying all other senses of the term. It includes perceptual awareness as well as more complex states in the case of *Homo sapiens.* In the present essay, I call this kind of consciousness "primary consciousness" and consider it to be fundamental to all other kinds.

*Consciousness*₄ is "the state or faculty of being conscious, as a condition or concomitant of all thought, feeling, or volition; the recognition by the thinking subject of its own acts or affections." Natsoulas[3] suggests that we are *noninferentially* aware of our perceptions, thoughts, or mental episodes—that, with consciousness₄, we have direct awareness. While direct awareness resembles perceptual awareness in being noninferential, it differs, first, in being about mental episodes (which themselves do not require consciousness to occur) and, second, in *not* involving sense organs and receptors. The term "higher-order consciousness" as used in this book has direct awareness as its foundation.

*Consciousness*₅ is defined as "the totality of impressions, thoughts, and feelings that make up a person's conscious being"—the whole set of one's mental episodes, considered by one as a unity (whether that is so or not). *Consciousness*₆ the *Oxford English Dictionary* defines as "the state of being conscious regarded as the normal condition of healthy waking life." This defines a general state, perhaps similar to that implied by the "intransitive" use of the word "consciousness" as suggested by Malcolm.[4]

Clearly, all forms of consciousness go beyond perceptual categorization, which is itself an unconscious process. It is important to notice that none of these dictionary definitions *explicitly* calls upon the capacity for speech or language. Here, we shall consider consciousness₃ as primary (not requiring language) and deal with all other cases as "higher order." While I shall take primary consciousness (consciousness$_3$) to be fundamental, I consider that consciousness$_1$, consciousness$_2$, consciousness$_5$, and consciousness$_6$ (in humans) all depend upon language. Consciousness$_4$, the beginning of higher-order consciousness, requires concept formation[5] if not language, and particularly requires self-concepts as seen first in a primitive form in great apes.[6] These qualifying and defining remarks suggest that there are orders as well as degrees of consciousness and that, in its higher orders, consciousness can ultimately involve social interactions and notions of self as distinguished from other objects in the world.

It is also relevant to notice that none of the ordinary-language definitions is very explicit about how consciousness is defined operationally. Undoubtedly, this has to do with the curious asymmetry it possesses as a "process in isolation": to each individual his own consciousness is a datum, but that of others involves an inductive extrapolation. That extrapolation is based, as the dictionary definitions show, on a series of commonsense, linguistic, and social observations, none of them very sharply delineated but as a collection reasonably persuasive. For scientific purposes, however, we may do better by attempting to define the scope of our theory.

THE SCOPE OF THE EXTENDED THEORY

No one will deny that consciousness in all its forms is difficult to define operationally in terms of strict criteria. At the same time, very few people deny the reality of phenomenal experience. How does one proceed from the initial "Jamesian" definitions we gave in chapter 1 and from those in the preceding section? One way is to define the scope of the theory to be proposed. In this way, should the terms and interactive statements of the theory prove useful, they may also help refine the various definitions of conscious phenomena. Obviously, one must also suggest ways in which portions of the theory can be evaluated or tested as compared to competing theories.

I propose to list baldly the aims of the extended theory presented in this book. While this list hardly covers all of the ranges of subject matter implied by ordinary usage, I shall attempt to be more rather than less inclusive in respect to primary and higher-order consciousness. This will at least have the virtue of stating what we must account for, even if we fall short of meeting our aims. I will not expatiate on this list, but the reader may refer to it as he peruses the various chapters. (Particularly relevant chapters are noted after each item.) After presenting the list, I shall mention some *general* means by which we might test the theory; specific proposals follow in later parts of the book. The reader should keep in mind that the proposed theory is a biological one. Although psychological phenomena are of the utmost importance in formulating descriptions and tests, the ultimate basis for an adequate explanation is taken to be the actual workings of the nervous system in a given phenotype, considered at all levels of organization and as a product of evolution.

After these cautionary remarks, we may proceed. The extended theory must do the following:

1. account for consciousness both as a product of evolution and in terms of morphology (all chapters)
2. account for the various forms of consciousness as processes explainable in terms of certain activities of the brain (all chapters)
3. show how consciousness may emerge in the course of individual development, accounting for the transition from primary consciousness in biologically defined individuals to higher-order consciousness in individuals with a concept of self (chapters 9 through 11)
4. account for its individual character in animals or its subjective character in humans (chapters 9, 11, 12, and 15)
5. account for its continuity as well as its changeability (chapters 7 and 11 to 13)
6. account for its dealing with objects independent of itself (intentionality) (chapters 3 to 5, 8, and 12)
7. account for its role in the ordering of subjective experience (chapters 7, 11, 12, and 14)
8. account for its selectivity and its relation to attention and salience (chapters 3, 4, and 12)
9. account for the efficacy of consciousness in regulating behavior and actions and for its capacity (in humans) to regulate itself in terms of direct awareness ("metacognition") (chapters 11 and 12)
10. account for its dependency on the activities of multiple parallel brain regions, activities that themselves can never become accessible to conscious awareness (chapters 3, 4, 7, 8, 12, and 13)
11. account for the failure to be conscious of signals in specific modalities or of memory after certain brain lesions, even though tests of performance indicate successful processing of the same signals or of memory in these modalities (this chapter and chapter 13)
12. account for the existence of unconscious states that can be called up to awareness, as well as the dissociability of constructs of the self (hysteria, "multiple personalities," etc.) (chapters 12 and 13)
13. account for the various forms of consciousness—for example, those that

emerge in relation to immediate perception, to images, and to the onset of linguistic capabilities (chapters 5, 6, and 9 through 11)
14. account for the discriminability of various kinds of phenomenal experience (qualia) (this chapter and chapters 9, 11, and 15)
15. relate certain diseases of consciousness, such as schizophrenia, to the theory (chapter 13)
16. relate the premises of the theory to those of sciences that have no need for its explicit descriptions, as well as to scientific heuristics and to various philosophical concerns (chapters 14 and 15)

This daunting list sets our task. Before turning to that task, we will do well to mention what kind of evidence we can accept, given the curious and often reflexive problems posed by the existence of consciousness. This kind of evidence is different in a scientific venture from what it is in a philosophical one. We must, nevertheless, proceed to examine evidence from all possible sources *provided it does not conflict* with known scientific laws of physics, chemistry, and biology. Although rigorous definition and refinement are always in order,[7] the most appropriate times to apply them are after several rounds of evaluation and adjustment have occurred between theory and experiment.

The theory can in general be evaluated by examining its self-consistency with currently testable neurobiological hypotheses; by comparison of anatomy, development, and evolution for homologous structures and functions in animal species and humans; by psychophysical and psychological tests; by pharmacological and ablative experiments (whether deliberate or, as in humans, through accidents of nature); by comparisons of descriptive reports by subjects or patients to their performance; by comparison of human performances with performances of animals that can sign, such as chimpanzees; and even by gedankenexperiments. In other words, in a subject like this, where pioneering efforts are needed, I believe we should be as open as possible to various lines of evidence, however disparate they may be.

SCIENTIFIC ASSUMPTIONS

To make such an effort, we must begin with some assumptions. The first assumption is that, in describing conscious states, we accept modern physics as an adequate description for our purposes of the nature of material properties. Let us call this the *physics assumption*. Physics provides a set of formal correlations of the properties of matter and energy at all scales. While physics does not contain a theory of the phenomenal *scene* or even of the names of macroscopic objects, it does account more or less well for their interactions within that scene. For a conscious animal, the most important physical property of the material order at the macroscopic scale is spatiotemporal continuity. No conscious animal could long ignore that property and survive, either individually or during the evolution of species. We shall make some speculative remarks about this at the end of the chapter.

Our second assumption is that consciousness is a phenotypic property that arose during evolution (the *evolutionary assumption*). This implies that the acquisition of consciousness by certain species either conferred fitness directly or provided the basis for other traits that enhanced fitness.

The physics assumption and the evolutionary assumption taken together with the acceptance that individuals are conscious, each in his own way, generate a number of difficulties. The two main difficulties are these:

1. How can an *objective* account be given that is consistent with the existence of conscious phenomenal states or qualia?
2. If we take the position of the evolutionary assumption (which, as biologists, we must) that consciousness arose as a result of natural selection, how can we deal with the probable existence of conscious states in our immediate prelinguistic precursors and, indeed, in any animals other than ourselves?

To answer these questions satisfactorily from a scientific standpoint, we must recognize what we can and cannot do. We must therefore consider some further allowable assumptions of a scientific account of consciousness and also the restrictions on such an account. In doing so, we will find it profitable to consider both of the above questions more or less at the same time. Let us begin with the problem of giving an objective account of intentionality that is consistent with phenomenal states.

PHENOMENAL STATES

In ordinary parlance, phenomenal states may be considered to be "how things seem to us" as human beings. They make up the collection of various personal or subjective experiences, feelings, and sensations manifested in different modalities that constitute or accompany awareness. They are discriminable properties of conscious experience—otherwise known as phenomenal properties, "raw feels," or qualia. Such properties extend over a wide range of conscious experiences, and they can include successive or simultaneous responses to many different sensory channels. Nonetheless, they are parts of a more or less well defined mental "scene," each with different degrees of definition. This scene can range in quality and apparent clarity from the apperception that one is merely "being conscious" to a sharp concentration on one or a few features of a particular perceived object, emphasizing one modality (visceral, gustatory, haptic, etc.) over another. In general, however, this scene appears unitary or holistic; indeed, it may maintain properties of a mental image and show characteristics consistent with the modality upon which that image is based. In the presence of an object, that image may be extremely detailed, constituting perceptual experience. In the absence of an object, it may be more diffuse, constituting imaging or imagination supported by memory. The phenomenal scene and qualia are almost always accompanied by feelings or emotions, however faint, and in general by a more or less definite sense of spatiotemporal continuity or extent and duration. The detailed sequence of qualia is, above all, highly individual, resting on a series of particular occasions in one's own personal history and experience.

If qualia can range from sharply defined perceptual experiences to vague "tones of feeling," how useful are they in any description of mental life? Some philosophers, such as Dennett,[8] have in fact disallowed them as useful descriptions in any account. Others, such as Searle,[9] not only do not disallow them but consider them the main elements to be explained by an adequate theory of consciousness.

Given that we do not disclaim the existence of qualia, the difficulty is simply put: a *phenomenal* psychology that can be shared *in the same way that a physics can be shared* cannot be constructed.[10] What is available as a datum to one individual is not available in all its details to another individual observer except by induction. Not only is an individual's consciousness a matter of fleeting private history, but interventions designed to probe an individual's qualia may change them. And although he may report his experiences to an observer, that individual's messages or verbalizations will always be partial, imprecise, and relative to a personal context. Moreover, many unconscious and nonconscious processes that are unavailable to an individual's phenomenal awareness may affect his subjective experience.[11] While such an individual may have his own "private theory" of consciousness, that theory cannot, given the unavailability of controls to other observers, be a scientific theory.

We are confronted with a dilemma. Like intentionality, phenomenal experience is a hallmark of consciousness, but it is a first-person matter—the only external criterion for it is the direct or indirect report of a person. While each of us is sure of having phenomenal experience, it does not seem to be consistent[12] with the formulation of a completely objective or causal account, for example, the kind of account called functionalism, which we will describe later.

Is there any escape from the dilemma? There is certainly mitigation: while we cannot be precise about another person's *particular* feelings or sensations, we can *correlate* our own phenomenal experiences with those of others verbally and under certain observational restrictions. This is perhaps not much different from the relativistic predicament we find ourselves in when we attempt to translate one language into another.[13] There is an inherent ontological relativity in meaning and reference even in "objective" discourse, and that relativity requires constant refinement and criticism. While the situation is even worse in reference to conscious states, it is perhaps not completely hopeless. What seems to be needed is a set of restrictions related to reports and also one further assumption in addition to the physics and evolutionary assumptions. Let us first consider the matter of reports.

PROBLEMS OF REPORT IN HUMANS AND ANIMALS

Humans are in a privileged position. While they may not be the only conscious animals, evidence suggests they are (with the possible exception of chimpanzees)[14] the only self-conscious animals. They are the only animals with the ability to model the world free of the present, to report upon, study, and correlate their phenomenal or subjective states, and to relate them to physics and biology. Of all the animals available for study, humans currently provide the best canonical referent because their subjective verbal reports, their actions, and their brain structure and function can *all be correlated,* at least in principle. That correlation can be checked for self-consistency, and at least some parts of it can be subjected to experimental test.

By contrast, animals (again with the possible exception of chimpanzees) can only be *inferred* to be conscious, and that inference can be arrived at only by correlating morphology and behavior. Such an inference is not made simply by scoring the reactivity of animals; it also rests on the hypothesis that their behavior is regulated by some kind of mental image.[15] This inference is obviously always at hazard, and it can only barely be buttressed by behavioral, evolutionary, and morphological evidence.

Humans and animals are biological individuals with unique genetic and experiential histories. Whether they can report phenomenal experience or not, the fact is that all such individuals, both human and animal, are "locked in" with respect to their phenomenal experience. Actual mental states can be experienced directly only by a single individual. Moreover, two individuals cannot continuously share the same succession of mental states identically. This is as true of humans, who, as persons with language, can have subjective states and self-consciousness, as it is of animals, which show biological individuality but cannot report subjective states.

We find ourselves in a curious predicament. Humans can deliver reports to one another (however unreliably) about their conscious states. But animals lack language and so cannot report to a scientific observer. Yet our evolutionary assumption suggests that there are animal forerunners to human consciousness. To make progress, we would do well to compare various phenotypic and neural counterparts among humans and animals. Obviously, if we could determine the anatomical basis and functional role of consciousness in humans, and could demonstrate that animals possess similar structures and functions, this would provide additional grounds for the belief that they, too, are conscious.

REFERENCE STATES FOR THE THEORY

Given our predicament, what may we expect to accomplish in a theory of consciousness? First, we may use human behavior and reports as our best available reference states for comparison. Second, we may consider how consciousness arose in evolution as a result of a series of morphologic events and compare those events with human morphologies. Third, we may provide a set of neural models consistent with observation and experimental data from these two arenas. Fourth, we may test the various assumptions of these models at all levels for consistency with experimental and clinical evidence. Finally, we may consider our conclusions in the light of certain philosophical issues concerning intentionality, meaning, and semantics, and the possibility of reliable human communication. (All the other items are related to the issue of reliable correlations of phenomenal reports.) Let us explore some of these matters here, mainly to orient the reader. They will require the rest of the book to explore in sufficient detail.

In the present theory, in addition to making the physics and the evolutionary assumptions, we will *assume* that phenomenal states or qualia (sensations, raw feels, and the like, constituting collectively "what it feels like to be an X") all exist in conscious humans, whether considered as scientific observers or as subjects. We will describe these states in third-person terms, that is, in terms of a variety of property correlations—discriminability, modality, intensity, continuity, temporal and spatial properties, and so on.

In making this *qualia assumption,* we will distinguish between higher-order consciousness and primary consciousness. Higher-order consciousness (including self-consciousness) is based on direct awareness in a human having language and a reportable subjective life. The more basic primary consciousness is present in all humans and is perhaps also present in some animals as biological individuals. Primary consciousness may be considered to be composed of certain phenomenal experiences such as mental images, but in contrast to higher-order consciousness, it is supposed to be bound to a time around the measurable present, to lack a concept of self and a concept of past and future, and to be beyond *direct* individual report.

The assumption that primary consciousness exists in animals is thus tentative at best, for, in the absence of linguistic report, the ability to make correlations between behavior and phenomenal states is severely weakened. But if that assumption is made, certain correlations of behavior with salience in a complex scene can be undertaken by an observer and then checked for consistency by interpretations of physical constraints, morphology, and behavior. Among the various behaviors, that which is related to conceptual categorization is perhaps the most important, particularly as it concerns behaviors involving imitation and the reaction to novelty (see chapter 9). A morphological criterion can also be applied to the means that an animal possesses for categorization. According to the TNGS, the world is not ordered like a tape for a Turing machine or a universal computer. It is reasonable to assume that an animal confronting such a world could not be primarily aware if it lacked the neural morphology able to support a rich categorization of novelty in a complex scene.

In addition to assuming that normal humans have self-consciousness and subjective experience while certain animals at best have primary consciousness, we shall consider the possession of primary consciousness to be a *prerequisite* for higher-order consciousness and self-awareness. This requires that we explain first how primary consciousness arose on the basis of morphologic evolution and then how higher-order consciousness evolved subsequently. The qualia assumption thus carries with it a number of subordinate assumptions that cannot be neglected.

This research program has a number of inherent weaknesses that result both from the nature of the subject and from the three major assumptions we have discussed. Although our ability to check primary consciousness is highly constrained, we must build first a theory of primary consciousness and then a theory of higher-order consciousness, recognizing at the same time that the possession of the latter kind of consciousness by humans may impede reports on the nature of the former. This implies that, experimentally, our best hope is to check the phenomenology of consciousness at the strongest point (the human) and proceed back down to animals. The order of the experimental enterprise is thus exactly opposite to that of the theoretical one.

THE HUMAN REFERENT

Let us examine a few examples to show the heuristic value of examining consciousness in humans as a reference. For humans, we can correlate personal reports, psychological tests, experiments of nature, results of trauma, disease and surgical interventions, and data from pharmacological experiments and brain scans.

Neuropsychological observations offer a singular opportunity to test theories of consciousness in terms of modality-specific loss, and effects of disease on memory, language, and skill. A good example is provided by the studies of Schacter and colleagues,[16] who have singled out a striking set of dissociations that are similar across a variety of neuropsychological syndromes. In certain syndromes, a patient who does not have conscious access (explicit knowledge) sufficient to perform a task may nonetheless perform that task if it can be posed so as to tap the apparently impaired function in an implicit manner. This dissociation—near normal implicit knowledge with severely impaired explicit knowledge (including perceptual awareness)—has been seen in certain patients with amnesia, blindsight (the ability to distinguish visual stimuli although blind in the pertinent part of the visual field), prosopagnosia (the inability to recognize faces), dyslexia, aphasia, and hemineglect (the loss of the ability to attend to the egocentric side of space contralateral to a damaged hemisphere). Moreover, in anosognosia, some patients can deny defects even when presented with direct evidence for their existence.

Amnesics show skill learning and priming effects on performance even though they have no explicit (i.e., conscious) knowledge or awareness of these skills. Patients with blindsight[17] can not only locate objects in the blind part of their visual field, but this performance can also influence responses to stimuli present in the intact field. There seems to be dissociation between implicit and explicit perceptual knowledge in such cases. To take a different syndrome, prosopagnosics appear to have implicit knowledge of faces that they do not recognize explicitly. Such implicit knowledge is not accompanied by a phenomenal experience of familiarity like that experienced by normal individuals. Moreover, certain dyslexics can read without awareness—these subjects claim to be unable to identify words but can choose objects from a target array when presented rapidly with words in an intact visual field. In aphasia, things are not quite so clear-cut, but there is evidence that some aphasics have greater knowledge than they can consciously put to use. In regard to hemineglect,[18] there is evidence that information present in the neglected field can affect the patient's overall performance in various tasks.

In anosognosia, there is occasionally a case such as that reported by Bisiach[19] in which there was a remarkable *alteration* in conscious verbal report amounting almost to confabulation but with no evidence of global confusion. His patient had left hemiplegia and left hemianopia after a sudden right temporo-occipital-parietal hematoma. He was anosognosic to both of his deficiencies but was not intellectually impaired. When questioned about left-sided tasks, he claimed to have performed them despite the fact that his paralysis prevented such tasks. When his left hand was placed in his right visual field (carried in the hands of the examiner), he claimed that all three belonged to the examiner. When queried about the discrepancy, he replied with flawless logic, "A hand is an extremity of an arm. Since you have three arms, it follows that you must have three hands."

There was no evidence of disorder of the speech area, which was neither impaired nor disconnected but rather, according to Bisiach, "misfed." This case suggests that conscious behavior based on language can be altered by removal of sources of nonverbal signals. Other patients with anosognosia show that they actually have selective knowledge of their deficit or can describe their affected bodily parts as shriveled or altered while denying paralysis of the parts at the same time (see chapter 13).

Schacter and his colleagues[20] point out that in implicit-explicit dissociations the majority of patients do not have total access to implicit knowledge, and they also caution that any conclusion that there is a lack of explicit knowledge is based on inference from subjective verbal reports. Nonetheless, the deficits are not global disorders of consciousness and are domain-specific—in domains outside the defect, the patients behave normally. These workers do not believe that the disorders arise from language impairments or response biases. They point out that the manifestations of implicit memory in amnesics are too diverse to be explained by loss of a particular memory system with a capacity for "conscious remembering." They also believe that the postulation of multiple memory systems in these various dissociative syndromes—one for implicit knowledge, one for explicit knowledge in each domain—is tenuous. Instead, they suggest that (1) conscious or explicit experiences of perceiving, knowing, and remembering depend on the functioning of a common mechanism; (2) this mechanism interacts with a variety of processors handling specific types of information; (3) in the various cases, specific modules are disconnected from the "conscious mechanism." *Conscious awareness of a stimulus thus would depend on mechanisms different from those that process the various attributes of that stimulus.*

I have considered these neuropsychological issues at some length to show that even in the absence of experiments, extraordinary information about mechanisms of consciousness may be obtained by observation of humans. Moreover, with the development of improved scanning techniques, this evidence may in time be linked to functioning anatomy. These examples show the usefulness of taking the human subject, deficiencies and all, as the canonical reference for any robust theory of consciousness. In fact, as we shall see in chapter 13, the theory to be proposed here can go a long way toward explaining certain domain-specific, implicit-explicit dissociations that are based on brain damage.

Obviously, it is language that provides us with the major tool in reporting phenomenal experience and its disorders to one another. It is also language that tempts us to explain consciousness in causal terms similar to those we use in our other scientific constructs or in rational terms like those we use in mathematical or computational theories. This brings us to back to some more methodological and philosophical matters. They relate to the qualia assumption and particularly to the question of whether we can construct an explanation of subjective experiences on the basis of verbal report. They are particularly concerned with some fundamental difficulties of strictly causal or functionalist accounts of consciousness.

The Insufficiency of Functionalism

The results of scientific inquiry are often couched in lawful (nomothetic) descriptions. Scientists tend to admire those descriptions most that have the greatest generality—relativity theory, Pauli's principle, natural selection, and so on. It is therefore tempting to consider whether one might not aim for a scientific description of consciousness that partakes of such generality. Carried very far, such a temptation leads to proposals that consciousness is a property of matter. At another level, consciousness has been considered to be the result of a functional process, describable in a fashion similar to that used for computers.

This quite attractive idea is shared by many thinkers. It is therefore useful at this point to bring up a set of difficulties for theories of consciousness based on notions of functionalism.

In its most explicit and most sharply interpreted form, functionalism assumes that psychology can be described adequately in terms of the functional organization of the brain—much in the way that software determines the performance of computers. Functionalism is concerned not only with functions performed by various systems but also with *relations* between their components, particularly as they *cause* other relations to take place. Functionalist theories are indifferent about the particular instantiation of a system, and they deal in abstract terms with such relations.

In the seminal work of Putnam[21] that stimulated much of the subsequent analysis, mental states were supposed to be defined in terms of Turing machine states. Turing defined a certain abstract class of automaton and showed that any member of that class can compute any of a large class of functions. (All but a few special-purpose computers are Turing machines.) A Turing machine is a finite-state machine with an infinite tape that can write in a given square on the tape either a 0 or a 1, and that can shift one square (containing one such digit) to the left or right. It has instructions containing conditions and actions, and it carries out an action if a particular condition is satisfied. The condition is determined by the symbol on its tape and the state of the machine, and a given action is any one of the four described above, after which it shifts to the next state specified by the program. A so-called universal Turing machine can simulate any Turing machine.

One of the assumptions of Turing machine functionalism is based on the idea that an algorithm or an effective procedure may be executed by any universal Turing machine. The very existence of such universal machines implies that the particular mechanism of operation of any one of them is unimportant. What is important for understanding psychology is the algorithms, not the hardware on which they are executed. Thus, according to this view, what the brain does may be described by algorithms. An analysis known as Church's thesis suggests that, if any consistent terminating method exists to solve a given problem, then a method exists that can run on a Turing machine and give exactly the same results. For problems that *can* be solved consistently in a specified finite amount of time, a Turing machine is as powerful as any other entity that can solve the problem, *including the brain.* According to this analysis, either the brain is a computer or the computer is an adequate model for the interesting things the brain does.

In a trenchant recent analysis,[22] Putnam has repudiated his original and other dependent models. His central point is that psychological states ("believing that p," "desiring that p," etc.) cannot be described by the computational model. We cannot individuate concepts and beliefs without reference to the environment. The brain and nervous system cannot be considered in isolation from the world and social interactions. Their states cannot be simply identified with any software description, and functionalism, construed as the idea that propositional attitudes are equivalent to computational states of the brain, is not tenable.

It should be pointed out that Searle[23] has also been a strong critic of the functionalist position. His opposition has been based on the idea that no purely computational specification can provide sufficient conditions for thought or for intentional states. His argument (which applies to higher-order consciousness) is that computer programs are defined strictly by their formal syntactical structure, that syntax is insufficient for semantics, and that, in contrast, minds are characterized by their having semantic contents. The rejection of functionalism implicit in this position is obvious. Moreover, Searle maintains that, inasmuch as consciousness can be identified in humans with intentionality accompanied by subjective experience, by definition no organism could have intentional states if it lacked subjective experience. Certain functionalists (possibly the majority)[24] restrict their claims to statements that avoid subjective or phenomenal properties. Clearly, Searle would reject their claims (rightly, I think) as having no bearing on the origins of consciousness. It is not clear, however, whether his arguments can be extended to animals with primary consciousness.

Another argument against functionalism, also specifically directed toward humans, is related to Putnam's picturesque claim that "meanings aren't in the head."[25] This notion is based on Quine's ideas of meaning holism and the ontological relativity of meaning and reference.[26] Meaning, as Putnam puts it, "is interactional. The environment itself plays a role in determining what a speaker's words, or a community's words refer to." Such an environment is open-ended and admits of no a priori inclusive description in terms of effective procedures. These arguments concerning semantics and meaning are particularly important for any theory of consciousness (such as the present one) that takes as its canonical reference human phenomenal experience and the ability to report that experience by language.

From an independent biological position based on the analysis contained in the TNGS,[27] Reeke and I[28] have also rejected machine functionalism or, as we called it, "instructionism." An analysis[29] of the evolution, development, and structure of brains makes it highly unlikely they could be Turing machines. This is so because of the enormous individual variation in structure that brains possess at a variety of organizational levels. A simple calculation shows that the genome of a human being is insufficient to specify explicitly the synaptic structure of the developing brain.[30] An examination of the means by which the brain develops indicates that each brain is highly variable. Moreover, each organism's behavior is biologically individual and enormously diverse, whether or not that organism can register or report subjective experiences. We also argued that an analysis of both ecological and environmental variation, and of the categorization procedures of animals and humans, makes it highly unlikely that the world (physical and social) can function as a tape for a Turing machine.

THE SUFFICIENCY OF SELECTIONISM

These arguments suggest that functionalism or instructionism[31] is an insufficient basis for a scientific theory of consciousness. We need a theory that rejects the notion that brains and consciousness are based on Turing machines. At the same time, it must be consistent with evolution, population thinking, and biological individuality while accounting for the "Jamesian" properties[32] of consciousness that we described briefly in the last chapter. The theory should allow phenomenal properties based on values to emerge in each biologically variant individual. It should take account of the ability to categorize a variety of real-world states without prespecification or instructionism. The conditions assumed by the theory should allow the development of semantic capability in each human individual. Moreover, the theory should take account of social interaction and learning in an open-ended manner to yield changes in consciousness and subjectivity. Consistent with the evolutionary assumption, the theory should also consider conscious and phenomenal states as causally significant.

The theory I shall describe appears to go a long way toward establishing an adequate explanation of consciousness within the above limits. It does so for a number of reasons. It is a population theory, that is, it claims that brains operate by selection upon variance at several levels. Such a process leads to differential modification of synapses and the selection of particular neuronal groups on the basis of individual experience in an open-ended world or environment (see chapter 3). Selective systems such as those embodied in the TNGS involve *two different domains of stochastic variation* (world and neural repertoires). The domains map onto each other in an individual *historical* manner (see chapter 14). Neural systems capable of this mapping can deal with novelty and generalize upon the results of categorization. Because they do not depend upon specific programming, they are self-organizing and do not invoke homunculi. Unlike functionalist systems, they can take account of an open-ended environment.

The theory accounts for categorization of signals from the world on the basis of selection from various neural maps linked by a critical process called reentry. This process also allows an organism to carry out spatiotemporal correlations (see chapter 4). A key premise of the theory is that each animal carrying out categorizations by selection has an *individual* history based on the behavior of such systems and on the motor exploration of an open-ended world. Neuronal group selection operates effectively only against the background of inherited and evolutionarily determined *value systems* governing adaptive survival. Such systems include homeostatic regulators, endocrine loops, various sensorimotor biases, ethologically defined action patterns, and so on (see chapter 5).

Because of these properties, such selective systems require specific constraints in order to operate effectively. But unlike functionalism, selectionism requires *no prespecification* of categories or previously defined effective procedures. Moreover, selective systems can lead to the emergence of semantically defined states within hominids in a speech community without requiring large numbers of genetically pre-specified syntactical rules (see chapter 10).

These are large claims, and to go much further at this point without describing the details of the theory itself would not be very profitable. But a few more remarks about the limitations of *any* neurally based theory may not be amiss. I limit my remarks to three points.

The first concerns the issue of whether any biological theory is suffi-cient to account for the emergence of qualia. Since we have taken the human to be our only sensible referent, we cannot be sure unless we can use the theory to design an artifact capable of the same reliability of report as a human. If we could design such an artifact, it might report qualia and we would, of course, then have to confront a number of problems related to the isomorphism of its structure with the human. This goal is clearly out of reach at present. It is more probable that an artifact based on the extended TNGS can be built to have *primary* consciousness. A test of such an artifact is described in chapter 9. Unfor-tunately, however, even if it passed that test, the inference that it had phenomenal experience would very likely be no more sound than the one we can now make about cats and dogs.

Given the "locked-in" state, the canonical reference we have taken to be the conscious (indeed, self-conscious) human, and given that a human can experience phenomenal awareness as subject and scientific observer (the qualia assumption), we cannot claim logical sufficiency of the theory or take a "God's eye" view. But we can insist that we avoid the difficulties of functionalism by invoking selection and then search-ing for evidence to disconfirm it. One can never *prove* sufficiency in a scientific theory, for, as such, it is always incomplete and loose-jointed. If the theory's conditions are met, however, and yet if in any artifact or any particular empirical instance evidence of consciousness does not appear, the theory can be suitably adjusted.

The second point has to do with whether artifacts designed to have primary consciousness are *necessarily* confined to carbon chemistry and, more specifically, to biochemistry (the organic chemical or chau-vinist position). The provisional answer is that, while we cannot com-pletely dismiss a particular material basis for consciousness in the liberal fashion of functionalism, it is probable that there will be severe (but not unique) constraints on the design of any artifact that is supposed to acquire conscious behavior. Such constraints are likely to exist because there is every indication that an intricate, stochastically variant anatomy and synaptic chemistry underlie brain function and because consciousness is definitely a process based on an immensely intricate and unusual morphology. (This conclusion is based on our evolutionary assumption.)

The third point is the most speculative of all. I owe it to discussions with my colleague George Reeke. It is that the nature of the physical world itself imposes commonalties as well as some very stringent requirements on any representation of that world by conscious beings and on the qualia accompanying such representations. Some of these requirements include spatiotemporal continuity, and a property Reeke calls zoomability, as well as a set of requirements having to do with consistency between parts of the world. "Zoomability" refers to the fact that, whatever the mental representation of the world is at any one time, there are almost always very large numbers of additional signals linked to any chunk of the world.[33] These must be accessible via *continuous* paths in any such mental representation. One might argue that such properties are inconsistent with a fundamental *symbolic* representation of the world considered as an *initial* neural transform. This is so because a symbolic representation is *discontinuous* with respect to small changes in the world and does not meet the zoomability requirement. On the basis of these speculations, one might guess that "what it is like to be aware" will in every instance have to be compatible with a continuous representation. This hardly begins to deal with phenomenal experience in all its glory, but it does suggest some grounds consistent with the Jamesian properties that we will account for in the extended TNGS.

In this chapter, we have made three assumptions essential to a scientific account of consciousness: the physics assumption, the evolutionary assumption, and the qualia assumption. We have taken the human state as our reference. We have claimed that, while each of us recognizes his phenomenal experience as evidence that he is conscious, we are "locked in"—a complete transmittal of our states of awareness is not achievable. Nonetheless, we can communicate our phenomenal states through language and correlate them with morphology, brain structure and function, and action.

At present, the analysis of consciousness in human beings is the best we can achieve—no other species of animal or artifact meets as many conditions for successful correlation. Nevertheless, we must account for how structures leading to the emergence of primary consciousness in animals could result in the evolution of higher-order consciousness. This places us in the somewhat paradoxical position that the system least open to test is the fundamental one from the viewpoint of evolutionary biology. To make our case, we must adopt a combination of theoretical, morphological, and behavioral criteria and then make various comparisons with the human. The question I will address in the rest of this book is, What structures or biological capabilities must a biological theory posit to give a scientifically satisfactory explanation of consciousness without assuming a homunculus or taking a classical functionalist position? To answer this question, we must begin by reviewing the original TNGS.

PART TWO

THE EXTENDED
THEORY

3

Neural Darwinism

One would have to search assiduously among the mounting number of studies in the burgeoning area of neuroscience to see any serious mention of the subject of consciousness. And although there are numerous neurobiological studies on various aspects of perception,[1] relatively little can be found that is both explicit and general about those relations between the physical and the sensory order[2] that lead to awareness.

This curious state of affairs may be attributed to the fact that science proceeds with a characteristic methodological modesty, avoiding systematic attack on subjects that are too unformed, vague, or complex. But, almost certainly, it is also attributable to the weariness that neuroscientists feel about the verbal analyses of philosophers, as well as about the often fantastic theorizing in everyday life and in theology that matters mental seem to provoke.

There is another, more down-to-earth reason for this avoidance—as I have already mentioned, it is difficult even to imagine detailed theories relating certain fundamental psychological functions required for consciousness (such as perception) to actual brain structure and function. One of the earliest attempts, the *Project for a Scientific Psychology,* by Freud,[3] was in fact abandoned by him and not even published in his lifetime.

The outstanding early effort in this arena is that of James, whose *Principles of Psychology*[4] ranges from anatomy and physiology to philosophy. This monumental work treats consciousness as a legitimate scientific subject and considers that it is attributable to brain structure and function. But, aware of the limits of brain science in his day, James directed most of his efforts toward correct functionalist interpretations, rather than toward the construction of extensive brain models. One of

his penetrating observations was that conscious mental events are continuous and successive in nature, a fact that must be accounted for in
any scientific model of consciousness.

More recently, a notable materialistic theory of brain and behavior
was put forth by Hebb in his book *The Organization of Behavior.* [5] This
theory proposed to account for important psychological functions such
as perception, attention, and learning in terms of the organization of
neurons into so-called cell assemblies after exposure to various stimuli.
Cell assemblies were constructed by a synaptic rule (now called the
Hebb rule): any two cells that had a synaptic connection and were
simultaneously activated became linked as a result of the strengthening
of that synapse. To account for temporal ordering in mental processes,
Hebb suggested that such cell assemblies were in turn linked into so-
called phase sequences of assemblies that could be activated in succession. Unlike James, Hebb avoided explicit discussion of the topic of
consciousness, but he was obviously aware of the central importance of
succession and temporal ordering in psychological function.

Although Hebb's theory was very influential in pointing up the need
to relate psychological function to brain function, it was not strongly
supported by subsequent empirical findings. These findings made it
unlikely that the environment could *directly* cause structures like cell
assemblies to form (a process called "instruction" in the TNGS). Moreover, as illustrated in the work of Hebb's colleague Bindra,[6] the cell
assembly theory could be used to explain too much, often in a fashion
beyond falsification. Nonetheless, Hebb's theory was valuable because
it provided psychologists, if not neurophysiologists, with a useful way of
thinking about several psychological matters that would otherwise have
remained unrelated to brain structure.

A little over a decade ago, I became interested in the problem of
framing an adequate global brain theory[7]—one that would take comprehensive account of evolutionary, developmental, neurophysiological, and psychological evidence. Above all, I was concerned with the
issue of perception, which I took to be at the very center of any such
theoretical attempt. I was particularly struck by two observations: that
for the perceiving animal in its early behavioral encounters, the world
did not come divided into prearranged categories; and that in all species, but especially those with richly developed nervous systems, the
brains of animals show a great deal of individual variation. The resemblance of these observations to certain others in evolution and immu-
nology suggested that, in adapting to an unlabeled world full of novelties, the brain may act by a process of selection upon variance rather

than by instruction. The facts suggested that it might be profitable to apply population thinking to the brain. Population thinking takes individual variances to be "real," that is, to provide significant bases for modes of selection driven by competition and stabilized by some form of heredity (or changes maintained over time). The results of selection would be reflected by differential reproduction or differential amplification of particular variants in a population. As a useful metaphor, I called this application to the nervous system of population thinking (an approach invented by Darwin) "neural Darwinism." Of course, I expected that the mechanisms by which diversity was generated and selection occurred in somatic neural function would be quite different from those of evolution.

The TNGS that developed from these ideas was a fairly extensive effort to apply population thinking to the nervous system, and it proposed a series of explicit mechanisms for the selection and coordination of neural responses. Nonetheless, its major focus was on perceptual categorization, memory, and learning, all of which are neural forerunners of consciousness. In the interests of empirical testability, its reach was deliberately constrained and conscious perceptual experience was not explicitly considered. I did, however, suggest the feasibility of analyzing perceptual experience. The present work is an attempt to realize that aim by constructing a theory of consciousness.

Obviously, it will be necessary to describe the TNGS before considering its application to consciousness. In this chapter, I will therefore review the TNGS in summary form and draw attention to some neurally based selective recognition automata constructed to explore its behavioral consequences. The principles and mechanisms of this theory provide the major means for formulating an account of consciousness based on brain structure and function (the so-called extended theory). My main task in the first part of this book is to show why this brain theory as applied to consciousness must, like evolutionary theory, invoke selection from variance as a central tenet. I also wish to show that such a brain theory, although materialistic, cannot rely solely on the metatheoretical assumptions of physics but must add in certain neural properties of the observer, as was outlined in the last chapter.

GLOBAL BRAIN THEORY

Even if consciousness were not a critical concern and even if boundless empirical evidence were available, we would need a global brain theory to connect descriptions of neural structure to those of psychological function. For example, the current explosion of activity in neuroscience has given us many new insights into the molecular and cellular biology of the nervous system. We have also witnessed a vigorous resurgence in cognitive psychology and in areas related to artificial intelligence. Yet, a very large gap remains in our understanding of the biological bases of psychological phenomena. On the one hand, no amount of detailed description of channels, synapses, and neuroanatomy appears likely to lead directly to an understanding of perception. On the other hand, we must confess to a certain uneasiness with the algorithms of cognitive scientists and the constructions of psycholinguists, all pursued in neglect of the detailed neural mechanisms that almost certainly underlie the phenomena that these workers propose to explain.

It is unlikely that the gap between these disciplines will be filled simply by further observations in their respective domains. What is needed is a sufficiently broad-ranging theory that can connect their subject matters, as well as a new means of simultaneously visualizing at many levels the complexities of behavior, the phenotypic properties, and the neural interactions of an individual animal.

The formulation of such a theory was prompted by two notions that at first glance seem unrelated:

1. The world of stimuli available to a newborn animal does not exist as prior information simply to be manipulated according to a set of rules, similar to those followed by a computer executing a program. While the real stimulus world obviously obeys the laws of physics, it is not uniquely partitioned into "objects" and "events." An organism must contain or create adaptive criteria to develop information allowing such a partition. Until a particular individual in a particular species categorizes it in an adaptive fashion, the world is an unlabeled place in which novelty is frequently encountered.[8]

2. Individual nervous systems (particularly those of vertebrate species) show enormous variability. This important characteristic was explicitly noted by Lashley,[9] who with rare restraint offered no explanation for it. Variability occurs in both space and time at many levels: molecular, cellular, anatomical, physiological, and behavioral. Despite the commonality of neural structures within a species, the degree of variability in each individual far exceeds that which could be tolerated for reliable performance in any man-made machine. Yet characteristic species behavior can be described, and this behavior is obviously adaptive or current species would not have survived.

Together, these two notions suggest that neither the world nor the nervous system is what it appears to be. For, according to most alternative descriptions,[10] the world is sufficiently unambiguous in its categories and the nervous system in its arrangements that we may profitably consider even the initial interactions of an organism with its world in terms of functionalism and information processing (see chapter 2).

The TNGS disputes this view. It argues that the ability of richly endowed organisms to categorize an unlabeled world in an adaptive fashion arises from two interactive processes, the first as a result of selection during ontogeny at the level of anatomical variance to form networks, and the second at the level of selection of variant populations of synapses to form functioning circuits in maps. In other words, the world becomes "labeled" as a consequence of behavior that leads to particular *selective* events within such neural structures in each animal. This process leads to the formation of relevant perceptual categories and to the association of behaviors with certain constellations of those categories in an adaptive manner. Such selective events act upon preexisting variation at each level of neural structure.

As is detailed elsewhere,[11] the TNGS is grounded in fundamental biological notions of speciation and morphogenesis. A major strength of the theory is its ability to reconcile the complexity of the CNS with its rapid emergence both phylogenetically during evolution and somatically during development. Above all, the TNGS is a theory of perceptual categorization—one that relates this fundamental psychological process of categorization to neural functioning.

MAJOR UNRESOLVED ISSUES IN NEUROSCIENCE

Before describing the TNGS in terms of its specific mechanisms, I want to examine briefly a number of observations that can be nicely explained by a selectionist point of view. These observations pose enormous difficulties for the contrary view that the world is like a computer tape (full of "information") and that the brain is a computer (a device like a Turing machine that is able only to carry out preestablished procedures or algorithms). The observations are summarized in table 3.1 and have been documented in *Neural Darwinism.*[12] Together, they suggest that, at the level of their finest connectivity, rich nervous systems like those of vertebrates cannot have precise, prespecified, point-to-point wiring and that, in general, uniquely specific connections do not exist. Not only are the majority of connections not functionally expressed at any one time; there are temporal fluctuations in the

TABLE 3.1

*Some Challenges to an Information Processing (or
Functionalist) Approach to Neuroscience**

Precise, prespecified, point-to-point wiring is excluded.

Uniquely specific connections cannot exist.

Divergent overlapping arbors imply the existence of vast
   numbers of unidentifiable inputs to a cell.

The majority of anatomical connections are not functionally
   expressed.

There are major temporal fluctuations in maps: unique maps in
   each individual; variability of maps in adults dependent on
   available input.

Extensive generalization in object recognition can occur in
   species without the need for language.

There is a unitary appearance to the perceiver of perceptual
   processes that are in fact based on complex parallel
   subprocesses.

Concepts and beliefs cannot be individuated without reference
   to the environment.[a]

Syntax is not sufficient to generate semantics.[b]

Phenomenal states (qualia) are "program resistant."[c]

The world is not like a computer tape, and the brain is not a
   Turing machine.[d]

[*]See G. M. Edelman, *Neural Darwinism.*
[a]See H. Putnam, *Representation and Reality.*
[b]See J. R. Searle, *Minds, Brains, and Science.*
[c]See K. Gunderson, *Mentality and Machines.*
[d]See G. N. Reeke, Jr., and G. M. Edelman, "Real Brains."

physiologically detected boundaries of the neural territories and maps[13] to which these connections contribute.

From the point of view of function, two other observations deserve notice. First, individual animals (even those in species without language, like pigeons) are capable of a remarkable range of perceptual categorizations and generalizations. Presented with a few examples of novel shapes (say, that of fish), pigeons can respond to large numbers of unique shapes in the same class.[14] Second, in animals *with* languages (and indeed, probably in all vertebrates), objects and many of their properties are perceived as having a unitary appearance; yet these unitary perceptions are the consequences of the parallel activity in the brain of *many different* maps, each with different degrees of functional segregation. Many examples could be cited; a striking case is the extra-striate visual cortex, with its different areas[15] mediating color, motion, and form, each in different ways (see chapter 4). I have already discussed the last four items of table 3.1 in chapter 2.

Collectively, these observations argue against the traditional view that the brain is prima facie an information processor and that the world is a source of signals providing *information* to that processor through a communications channel. What such an information processing view would require in order to account for the observations in table 3.1 is an elaborate series of codes (explicitly shaped to the variance in each individual) designed to extract the signal from the noise or prevent it from being lost in the unpredictable anatomy. It would also require an elaborate means of labeling or of tagging mapped information so that it could retain its identity as it traversed various parts of the nervous system in parallel, only to come together again asynchronously in a particular center. In a parallel distributed neural system (such as that of the visual cortex), this tagging would be required in order to account for categorization and generalization and for the unitary decisions they would require. The information processing view would further need to show how these various codes could actually be used to carry out such perceptual categorization, the key process by which an individual can treat certain nonidentical objects or events as equivalent.[16]

Given the variance of neural systems and the complexity of the world, coding procedures would not only have to be adaptable and elaborate but also be likely to consume most of the signaling band width of the system. There is no evidence for such extensive codes or labels, and a noncircular reconciliation based on functionalism of the issues embodied in table 3.1 has not emerged. An adequate theory to account for perceptual categorization may have to be constructed without reliance on the ideas of information and coding.

BASIC MECHANISMS OF NEURAL DARWINISM

It is just such an account that the TNGS attempts to provide. It explains in neural terms the processes of perceptual categorization, generalization, and memory, and it shows how their interactions can mediate the continually changing relations between experience and novelty that lead to learning. The TNGS proposes three mechanisms: *developmental selection, experiential selection,* and *reentrant mapping.* Each mechanism acts within and among collections consisting of hundreds to thousands of strongly interconnected neurons called neuronal groups.[17] Neurons in a group tend to be more highly interconnected anatomically and to have changes in their synaptic strengths that differentially enhance responses of other neurons in that group. While the various structures of neuronal groups in different parts of the brain are based on local anatomical patterns, such groups are dynamic entities whose characteristics are affected by their developmental and functional history and by the nature of the signals they receive at any time.

Before taking up the nature of neuronal groups in detail, let us briefly consider each of the fundamental mechanisms (figure 3.1).

DEVELOPMENTAL SELECTION

During development, the local connectivity of neurons in any brain region undergoes diversification. Although, in a given species, particular neuroanatomical regions have characteristic morphologies, the dendritic and axonal arborizations in such defined anatomical structures are subject to enormous individual variation and overlapping connectivity. Neither the number nor the variance of these structures could be specified beforehand by the genetic code. Instead, structural diversity during development results from epigenetic regulation of cell division, migration, death, and process extension, as well as of neural activity itself.[18]

The evidence suggests that individual somatic diversification in the face of species constancy is a consequence of elaborate control loops regulating the expression of cell adhesion molecules (CAMs) and substrate adhesion molecules (SAMs).[19] These molecules, which interact with neuronal surfaces, in turn affect cell dynamics and interactions at particular neural sites. The level of expression and the temporal pattern of appearance of these molecules is characteristic of a given area and is more or less precisely regulated. As I have outlined elsewhere,[20] there are various genetic and epigenetic constraints on the expression of these molecules that lead to selection for the overall patterned anatomy within a species. Nonetheless, because their regulation is a *dynamic* process that affects cell movement and process extension, the action of these morphoregulatory molecules inevitably results in local neuroanatomical variation at the finest ramifications of axons and dendrites.

This obligate epigenetic generation of diversity leads to the formation of *primary repertoires* consisting of large numbers of variant neuronal groups (or local circuits) within a given anatomical region. The

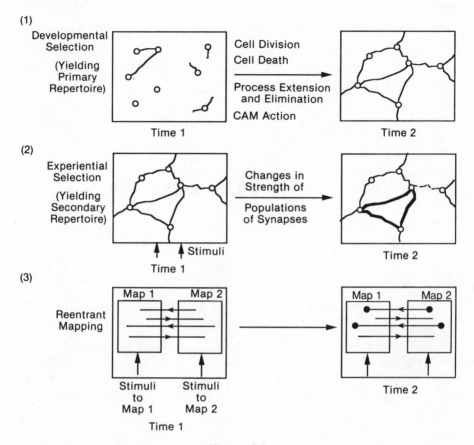

Figure 3.1

Three fundamental mechanisms in neuronal group selection. (1) Developmental selection occurs as a result of molecular effects of CAM and SAM regulation, growth factor signaling, and selective death to yield variant anatomical networks in each individual, the primary repertoire. (2) Selective strengthening or weakening of particular populations of synapses as a result of behavior leads to formation of variant circuits, a secondary repertoire of neuronal groups. The consequences of the strengthening of synapses are indicated by bold paths; weakening, by dotted paths. (3) Reentry, a process by which linkage of maps occurs in time through parallel selection and correlation of neuronal groups in different areas receiving disjunct inputs. This process provides a basis for perceptual categorization (see figure 3.3). Dots at the ends of the active reciprocal connections indicate parallel and more or less simultaneous strengthening of synapses in reentrant paths. Strengthening (or weakening) can occur in both intrinsic and extrinsic (reentrant) connections. The designations "time 1" and "time 2" refer to earlier and later times within each pair of panels but are not related to times across pairs marked 1, 2, and 3. It is important to note that 1, 2, and 3 are not always sharply segregated in time. The processes may overlap, and in some cases (particularly in so-called critical periods) synaptic mechanisms can play a key role in determining anatomy and the primary repertoire.

detailed evidence that developmental anatomy derives its variance from CAM and SAM action has been presented elsewhere,[21] and I refer the interested reader to those descriptions. It is useful here to note that although synaptic changes can and do occur during such anatomical development (see figure 3.1, panel 1), the main contribution of such changes to perceptual categorization occurs later during experience.

It must not be thought that the selective events during formation of the primary repertoire involve *only* the elimination of cells or synapses or the regression of populations.[22] As Cowan[23] rightly assessed the process, it involves dynamic multistage events that can also create *new* interactive populations. In *Neural Darwinism*, I made clear that eliminative or stabilizing selection was not an adequate or sufficient basis for a selective theory of brain function.

EXPERIENTIAL SELECTION

After most of the anatomical connections of primary neural repertoires have been more or less fixed, certain neuronal groups are formed as a result of synaptic alteration. Although some of these are relatively fixed, during behavior particular functioning neuronal groups are dynamically selected by the action of various signals and mechanisms of synaptic change. This selection occurs among *populations* of synapses,[24] strengthening some synapses and weakening others, a process that leads to the formation of *secondary repertoires.* The consequence is that certain circuits and neuronal groups in such repertoires are more likely to be favored over others in future encounters with signals of similar types (figure 3.1, panel 2).

Experiential selection does not, like natural selection in evolution, occur as a result of differential *reproduction,* but rather as a result of differential *amplification* of certain synaptic populations. The rules that govern the pre- and postsynaptic changes in experiential selection do not, however, act to convey information from a single presynaptic neuron to a single postsynaptic neuron as in the Hebb rule.[25] Instead, they act heterosynaptically[26] on neuronal groups and thus act on *populations* of neurons. This activity involves statistical signal correlations rather than the carriage of coded messages. Because of the particular geometry of connections within and between groups (figure 3.2), a great variety of such correlations can arise. Nonetheless, if they are to serve adaptive behavior, these correlations must at some early stage reflect certain key properties of signals arising in the real world. This is accomplished by reentrant mapping.

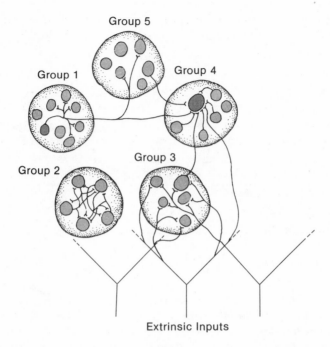

Group 5

Group 1

Group 4

Group 2

Group 3

Extrinsic Inputs

Figure 3.2

A highly schematic diagram of some of the properties of neuronal groups and their connectivities. The diagram is taken from Neural Darwinism *(figure 7.8, p. 199), where it was used as the basis for computer simulations showing how presynaptic and postsynaptic rules interacted in populations to yield changes in synaptic efficacies. Here, the point is simply to illustrate some aspects of intrinsic (within group) and extrinsic (between group and group, or group and input) connectivities. Five groups (dark outlines) are shown with some of their cells indicated. Each group illustrates a different aspect of the connectivity. Group 1 illustrates that each cell contacts cells in its own group and in other groups. Group 2 illustrates the dense intrinsic connectivity of groups. Group 3 illustrates that each group also receives inputs from a set of overlapped extrinsic inputs that can be selectively stimulated. (In general, such inputs extend over distances of many cell diameters.) Group 4 shows that each cell thus receives inputs from cells in its own group, from cells in other groups, and from extrinsic sources. These representations are obviously schematic—groups differ in size (ranging perhaps from 50 to 10,000 neurons) and in actual connectivity, as determined by the local neuroanatomy of the areas in which they are found.*

REENTRANT MAPPING

Although the categories of various signals arising in the world are not fixed prior to neuronal group selection, sampling of signals as events in the world must follow the physical laws governing spatiotemporal con-

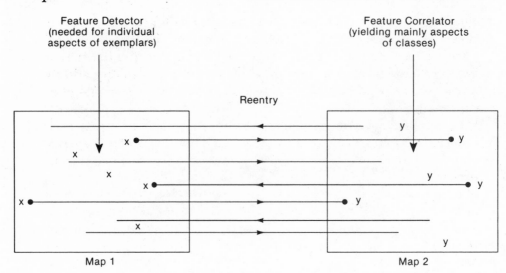

Figure 3.3

Diagram of one kind of classification couple using reentry. Neurons—those in the visual system, for example—can act as feature detectors. They map on the left (map 1) to some higher-order lamina in the brain. Other neurons—for example, those related to light touch on a moving finger—can act as feature correlators, tracing an object by motion. These neurons map to another lamina (map 2) as shown on the right. The two maps project onto each other by reentrant connections, locally distributed and making synaptic connections in each map, so that groups in one map may excite groups in the other. x's and y's represent synaptic domains or populations undergoing changes in synaptic strengths as a result of input signals from feature detectors or correlators. Filled circles represent strengthening of synapses on reentry, coupling such domains in parallel within a particular time period. A classification couple allows the parallel independent sampling of disjunctive characteristics present in the stimulus; because of the reentrant connections, these characteristics can be connected in the responses of higher-order networks. In this way, certain more general characteristics of an object representation can be connected with other, more particular characteristics. As a result of the reentrant signaling, and by means of synaptic change (filled circles), *particular patterns of responses in map 1 will be associated with patterns of responses in map 2. Generalization can occur on signals from objects not encountered before through responses to combinations of local features or feature correlations resulting from the effects of previous disjunctive samplings of signals from similar objects. Reentry in a classification couple thus links various patterns to each other across maps and also links responses to present inputs to previous patterns of responses. (The notion of a classification couple is a limiting case: for real nervous systems, there is every reason to suspect that, in general, more than two maps interact to form classification n-tuples.) Reentry is not simply feedback: it involves parallel sampling in multiple paths from various mappings and can vary statistically in both time and space, as we shall discuss in chapter 4.*

tinuity. This requires the generation of maps relating sensory receptor sheets to particular regions of the nervous system. But because of local variance in neural structure and connectivity and in the statistics of synaptic change, specific tags or labels are *not* available to specify any given map position, as they would be specified in a computer representation.

To coordinate the interaction of receptor sheets and maps with each other, a process by which distributed activity within mapped areas is correlated over time, the TNGS proposes instead that mapped regions exchange signals by reentry (figure 3.1, panel 3). Reentry is a process of temporally ongoing parallel signaling between separate maps along ordered anatomical connections. Reentrant signaling can take place via reciprocal connections between maps (as seen in corticocortical, corticothalamic, and thalamocortical radiations); it can also occur via more complex arrangements such as connections among cortex, basal ganglia, and cerebellum. A striking example of a reentrant system is seen in the functionally segregated areas of the visual system.[27] (We consider such arrangements in detail in the next chapter.)

Signaling in either a phasic or a continuous fashion across reentrantly connected maps permits temporal correlations of the various selections that occur among neuronal groups within these maps. These correlations are driven initially by the signals arriving at primary cortical receiving areas from stimulus objects at a given time and place; selections in all higher-order maps related to the presence of an object are correlated through reentry with these primary areas.

PERCEPTUAL CATEGORIZATION

With these essential mechanisms in hand, we may now confront the fundamental question addressed by the TNGS: how can a selective system give rise to perceptual categorization and generalization? Perception is the adaptive discrimination of an object or event from background or other objects and events. Generalization refers to the treatment, within any given context, of a more or less diverse collection of such entities as equivalent. The TNGS proposes that any nontrivial categorization must arise through the operation of at least two separate channels carrying signals to maps (compare figure 3.1, panel 3, with figure 3.3). Each channel (for example, a sensory modality or submodality) independently samples a particular stimulus domain.

After multiple encounters with a stimulus, particular patterns of neuronal groups will be selected in a mapped area. Following such selection, similar signals in each neuronal channel can preferentially activate previously selected neuronal groups in the repertoires of a neural region to which that channel is mapped. But, as is noted in figure 3.3, each of the higher-order maps to which the independent signals go is mapped to the other. Operations in these different maps that are related to the same perceptual stimulus are linked to one another by reentry.

The simultaneous activation by the stimulus of neuronal groups in each map and the effects of previous reentrant activity increase the likelihood of strengthening various distributed reentrant connections between those groups. This coordinate dynamic interaction between maps results in the correlation of the responses to each disjunct sample made by the different channels, each representing separate modalities or submodalities.

In the next chapter, I will describe a detailed model involving recursive reentry among submodalities in more than two maps; here, I consider reentry between two maps only. Such an arrangement connecting two maps (figure 3.3) is called a *classification couple*. [28] As a result of the action of patterns of response in a classification couple, certain features or relations of a stimulus object are probabilistically linked to each other. By the construction of a series of automata on the basis of the theory (one of which is described below), it has been shown that reentrant mapping can lead to limited categorization and generalization of stimuli without the need for prior programming and thus without the presentation of any descriptive characteristics of such stimuli beforehand.

One of the important properties of such categorical selective systems is that, for the most part, there is no unique structure or combination of groups corresponding to a given category or pattern of output. Instead, more than one combination of neuronal groups can yield a particular output, and a given single group can participate in more than one kind of signaling function. This property of neuronal groups in repertoires, called *degeneracy*, provides a fundamental basis for the generalizing capabilities of reentrant maps. I will consider this issue at the end of this chapter, in a brief description of recognition automata. Before that, however, I wish to point out why neuronal groups have been chosen as the main units of selection and how their properties can account for the phenomena listed in table 3.1.

NEURONAL GROUPS AS UNITS OF SELECTION

Although single neurons could occasionally serve as units of selection, the TNGS holds that in general only collections of neurons in groups provide a sufficient basis for the mapping interactions that are central to the theory. Both logic and experimental evidence support the idea that neuronal groups exist. The logical argument is as follows. In the presence of numerous densely connected interneurons in regions like the cortex,[29] it is difficult to imagine a neuron acting as an isolated or individual unit. Indeed, at any time, nonlinear cooperative signaling (excitatory or inhibitory) between neighboring neurons over a certain domain seems inevitable. Given an anatomy like that of the cortex, in which mapping and local connectivity predominate, this signaling seems all the more likely. These anatomical arrangements ensuring local connectivity facilitate the convergence of multiple correlated inputs onto a single functional unit. Furthermore, everywhere in the CNS where specific roles can be assigned to neurons, local mosaic arrangements are observed (ocular dominance columns, blobs, slabs, barrels, fractured somatotopies, etc.). All of these structures receive coordinated input that provides a natural basis for a functional arrangement into neuronal groups. Such an organization into groups facilitates the process of reentry, which, given the lateral spread and overlap of local dendritic and axonal arbors, can hardly be envisioned as occurring from single neuron to single neuron. Finally, group structure most easily accounts for the facts of embryonic development[30] as well as for the plasticity of cortical neuronal function in the adult: the neuronal membership in a group can expand, contract, or alter the group boundaries while simultaneously maintaining reentrant connections. Such properties have been demonstrated in computer simulations of somatosensory cortex.[31]

This brings us to some evidential matters. In maps of the somatosensory cortex of adult owl and squirrel monkeys, alterations of input resulting from nerve sections in the hand or to imposition of particular stimuli lead to changes in individual map boundaries in areas 3b and 1. These changes, demonstrated by Merzenich and his colleagues,[32] occur both acutely and chronically, and regions of a given map assessed before and after the changes show receptive fields having sharp continuous borders with a resolution of no more than one or two cell diameters (60 micrometers). At the same time, however, the arborization of input axons from the thalamus to the mapped areas extends over much wider distances[33] (for a schematic view of these extrinsic inputs, see figure 3.2, group 3). If single neurons were the unit of selection during such events, then given these arborization patterns, one would expect not the continuous regions separated by the sharp receptive field boundaries that are actually found but rather a "salt-and-pepper" effect or a diffuse arrangement of map boundaries.

In each area in which two correlated sets of inputs compete for cortical neurons (for example, those from the glabrous or dorsal skin of the hand), responding neurons segregate into groups that at *any one time* are nonoverlapping and have such sharp boundaries. Of course, as the experiments show, the boundaries and their underlying neuronal groups are dynamically sustained and can change with time under different stimulus conditions. These findings have been explicitly modeled in terms of group behavior[34] and provide strong evidence that neuronal group selection is occurring.

Other experimental findings support the idea that groups come in different sizes, shapes, and types, depending upon their underlying anatomy, developmental constraints, synaptic properties, and inputs. Some groups are more stable than others; for instance, some found in the visual cortex are fixed during developmental critical periods, while some in the somatosensory cortex are plastic. A good example in the visual system is provided by orientation columns,[35] the properties of which fulfill the criteria for neuronal groups: collections of locally and strongly interconnected neurons carrying out a discriminative function developed as a result of selectively correlated input signals (in this case tuning for orientation). In this example, the major plasticity occurs during a critical period in development, a property not generally shown in somatosensory cortex. (A possible exception is provided by the so-called whisker barrels.)

Although different neuronal distributions occur across borders of orientation columns, evidence has been found for cooperative interactions among single neurons within a given column. By the recording of field potentials, it has been shown[36] that after presentation of appropriately oriented visual stimuli there is a dominant 30–40 Hz oscillatory response within a given orientation column. This response is not seen outside the stimulated column, and the potentials revert to uncorrelated activity after removal of the stimulus. The data have been taken as direct evidence for cooperative interactions of adjacent cortical neurons in groups, and a theoretical analysis has recently been presented.[37]

The variability and degeneracy of groups multiply linked by synapses in populations (figure 3.2) are enormous and easily provide sufficient material for selection. It has recently been suggested[38] that, to constitute an adequate selective system, neuronal groups, like organisms subject to natural selection, would have to show Malthusian population dynamics. This is in error: neither natural selection nor neuronal group selection *requires* a growing population. What is required is *differential reproduction* in the one case (natural selection) or *differential amplification* in the other (synaptic selection).[39] Moreover, synaptic selection according to the TNGS does not occur by Hebbian means but instead usually results from the application of separate pre- and postsynaptic rules acting heterosynaptically[40] on synaptic populations. Contrary to the deductions made[41] according to a Hebbian mechanism, neuronal groups do not have to incorporate increasing numbers of cells or lose selectivity in order to act. Indeed, in explicit models,[42] it has been shown that, when the correct assumptions are used, they do not do so.

Instructionist proposals contrary to those of the TNGS—that "individual neurons each correspond to a pattern of external events of the order of complexity of events symbolized by a word"[43]—provide significantly less combinatorial variability. It is clear that the latter notion, an example of the "grandmother neuron" concept, cannot explain categorization without begging the question. Indeed, while particular attributes have been associated operationally with particular neurons by single neuron recording,[44] there is no evidence that any such neuron has its properties *except* as a result of its synaptic interactions with multiple other neurons in a group and with distant neurons by reentry. To prove otherwise would require showing that different *isolated* neurons could respond uniquely to different categories, that similar categories of stimuli were exhaustive of the responses of a neuron of a given type, that a particular individual neuronal response was not adventitious, and that the responses were independent of those of neighboring neurons.

Against this background, we may now reconsider the contents of table 3.1 in terms of the TNGS. The very absence of specific identifiable hardwiring, which causes difficulties for building instructionist or information processing theories based on single neurons, actually provides the necessary bases for neuronal group selection. Overlapping diverging arbors provide appropriate means for maximizing variation while still allowing crude mapping. The presence of silent synapses would be expected after selective events, and the fluctuations seen in maps,[45] and the local correlation of field potentials[46] during activity can be accounted for as signs of neuronal group selection itself. Finally, the presence of recursive and repetitive reentry and the existence of many kinds of classification couples (figure 3.3) would allow the kinds of correlation needed for perceptual categorization with its generalizing properties. (The last five points in the table will be targets for explanation in the rest of this book and will not be discussed here.)

According to the theory, perceptual categorization is fundamental and must occur before extensive learning can take place. This point deserves strong emphasis, particularly because it must not be imagined that categorization by neuronal group selection occurs only as a result of the action of local maps alone. Instead, the theory suggests that categorization occurs because of *multiple* interactions among local maps resulting from sensorimotor activity. This directs our attention to the *moving organism,* actively sampling its environment. This sampling is the source of signals underlying the selective and correlative neural events that build a procedural memory and provide the bases for learning.

CATEGORIZATION, MEMORY, AND LEARNING

As an animal moves, local visual maps of the brain interact with those of other sensory modalities as well as with those guiding motor output. How are all of these maps coordinated to yield perceptual categorization? According to the TNGS, a given classification couple, or even a classification n-tuple, is in general insufficient for this task. Instead, a global mapping (figure 3.4) is required.[47]

A global mapping is a dynamic structure containing *multiple* reentrant local maps (both motor and sensory) that interact with non-mapped regions such as those of the brain stem, basal ganglia, hippocampus, and parts of the cerebellum. The activity of global mapping connects neuronal groups selected in one set of local maps (as a result of the activity of feature detectors) to neuronal groups selected in other sets of such maps (as a result of the correlation of features that is established, for example, by continuity of motion). The concept of a global mapping takes account of the fact that perception depends upon and leads to action. In this view, categorization does not occur solely in a sensory area that then executes a program to activate motor output. Instead, the results of continual motor activity are considered to be an essential part of perceptual categorization. This implies that global mappings carrying out such categorization contain both sensory and motor elements. Neuronal group selection in global mappings occurs in

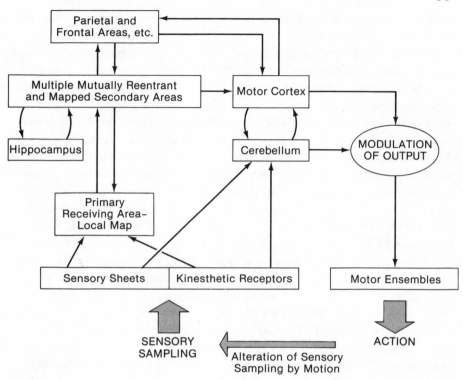

Figure 3.4

*A schematic diagram of some components contributing to a global mapping.
The essential components are (1) sensory sheets tied to separate motor ensembles
capable of disjunctive sampling, such as the retina in the eyes linked to the
oculomotor system, or receptors for light touch or kinesthesia linked to fingers,
hand, or arm; (2) a local mapping of the sensory sheets to appropriate primary
receiving areas, themselves forming local maps; (3) a profusion of mapped
secondary areas for each modality to carry out various submodal responses to
disjunctive samples—these secondary areas are linked in turn to mapped motor
areas; (4) extensive reentrant connections among various maps of each order,
with ultimate reentry back to the primary local map for maintenance of spatiotemporal continuity; (5) subcortical areas (e.g., hippocampus, cerebellum, basal
ganglia) for ordering sequential events or switching output; and (6) appropriate postural or orienting changes via the output of the global mapping to alter
the position and sampling of sensory components of the motor ensemble. Movement of sensory sheets can thereby lead to feature correlation during the time
when these same sheets are carrying out feature detection. A given global
mapping can consist of varying contributions by each of the different components and involves input-output correlation. It is therefore a dynamic structure
that is altered as the sampling by different sensory sheets and its input-output
correlations are changed by motion or behavior. Each alteration can alter
neuronal group selection within the components. Notice that a global mapping
constitutes a distributed system.*

a dynamic loop that continually matches gesture and posture to several kinds of sensory signals.

The process of global mapping (with its accompanying patterns of neuronal group selection and synaptic change) creates a spatiotemporally continuous representation of objects or events. Hence, global mappings constitute a necessary substrate for relating categorization to memory. This function cannot in general be accounted for by the activity of any one small neural region, for, by their nature, global mappings must include large portions of the nervous system. (Of all of the concepts of the TNGS, global mapping based on reentry is perhaps the most difficult. The present short account of the relation of such mappings to memory and learning condenses a large number of ideas. For further exposition, the reader may consult *Neural Darwinism*, chapters 8, 9, and 11.)

Within a global mapping, long-term changes in synaptic strengths will tend to favor the mutual reentrant activity of those groups whose activity has been correlated across different maps during past behavior. Such synaptic changes provide the basis for memory. According to the TNGS, memory in global mappings is not a store of fixed or coded attributes to be called up and assembled in a replicative fashion as in a computer.[48] Instead, memory results from a process of continual recategorization, which, by its nature, must be procedural and involve continual motor activity and repeated rehearsal. Because of new associations occurring in different contexts, changing inputs, and the degeneracy of the neuronal group selection, a given categorical response in memory can be achieved dynamically in various ways.

In this view of memory, the processes of perception, motor response, and associative recollection are intimately tied together by the process of global mapping. In general, rehearsal leads to an enhanced ability to categorize. As new contexts and synaptic associations occur, however, there is continual alteration in global mappings. However, because of the degeneracy of neuronal groups, these alterations can still result in similar or related outputs upon recall. Although an output based on a categorization may be the same, the paths by which it is reached may vary. It is in this sense that memory is considered to be a recategorical procedure. Recategorical memory is discussed further in chapter 6.

Necessary as all these processes are for categorization of an unlabeled world, they cannot serve the adaptive needs of the organism unless learning takes place. In an environment containing unforeseen juxtapositions of events that may affect survival, it is learning, not just perceptual categorization, that ensures successful adaptation.[49] But it is a key point of the theory that learning cannot occur in the face of novelty unless various repertoires undergoing neuronal group selection in global mappings provide a *prior* basis for perceptual categorization in each individual.

Perceptual categorization and memory are therefore considered to be necessary for learning but obviously are not sufficient for it. The sufficient condition is provided by the synaptic linkage of particular global mappings to the activity of hedonic centers and to the limbic system in a fashion that will satisfy homeostatic, appetitive, and consummatory needs. The structural basis for such needs is in general developed through responses to ethological demands during the evolution of a species. In some cases, the appropriate linkages to hedonic centers can occur through synaptic changes in specific circuits, the underlying structure of which is species-specific, as in the circuits underlying bird song. The operation of neural linkages between global mappings and the limbic system can connect categorization to behaviors having adaptive value under conditions of expectancy, that is, under conditions where the set points of the hedonic system are not yet satisfied. Expectancies are the result of categorizations coupled to needs, and learning improves the chances of satisfying these needs.

This view of the relation of perceptual categorization to learning provides an explanation for the adaptive value of neuronal group selection:[50] both evolutionary and somatic alterations in the properties of repertoires of neuronal groups (size, connectivity, synaptic response, degree of variation, etc.) have adaptive value because they increase the opportunities for categorical responses that are required for and enhance learning. Such learning is necessarily constrained, however, by the value systems and homeostatic requirements that have already been selected during evolution for the survival of a given species.

This short survey of the TNGS provides the basis for the construction of the extended theory that will occupy the rest of this book. Before considering that extension, let us turn briefly to some efforts to show the self-consistency of the TNGS.

HEURISTIC MODELS OF SELECTIVE NEURONAL SYSTEMS: RECOGNITION AUTOMATA

Clearly, the ideas of the TNGS (particularly the notion of global mapping) imply that neural activity and psychological responses depend strongly upon specific features of the phenotype in a given species. Psychological functions such as perceptual categorization, memory, and learning are not properties of molecules, of synapses, or even of small numbers of neurons, nor are they general faculties independent of phenotypic change. Instead, they reflect the concerted workings *in each phenotype* of the motor and sensory ensembles correlating neuronal group selection events occurring in a rich and distributed fashion over global mappings.

It is not a simple matter to trace the activity of all of the neurons involved in these mappings or to imagine their sequential patterns even in cases where the activities of individual neurons are known. To some extent, these difficulties can be mitigated by extensive modeling in supercomputers. In an approach called synthetic neural modeling,[51] whole systems or even simple behaving organisms have been simulated. By means of this approach, it has been possible to test the self-consistency of the TNGS through the construction of a series of selective recognition automata.[52] Although these automata are simulated in large computers, their behavior is not programmed. A brief description of one of them, Darwin III, may serve to illustrate how neuronal group selection can operate in a globally mapped system.

Unlike the standard artificial intelligence paradigm,[53] selective recognition automata avoid preestablished categories and programmed instructions for behavior. Instead, they contain networks of simulated neuron-like units; selection and reentrant mapping allow them to carry out simple categorization and association tasks in variant stimulus worlds full of novelty. Although programming is used to instruct a computer how to simulate the neuronal units in a recognition automaton, *the actual function of these units is not itself programmed.*[54] Consistent with selective theories, no specific information about the categories of stimulus objects to be presented is built into the automaton when it is constructed. Of course, general information about the kinds of stimuli that will be significant to the system is built in. (For example, the scale of significant textural features of objects is implicit in the choice of feature-detecting elements that are used.) Such a choice is akin to the specializations built into the receptor organs of each species during the course of evolution.

Darwin III (figure 3.5) is a simulation of a sessile "creature" having a head with a movable eye and a multijointed arm. It exists in a world of moving or stationary objects of different shapes, contours, and textures, and these objects are driven in their motion according to random or systematic paradigms selected by the experimenter and "unknown" to and independent of the automaton. Darwin III combines the recognition and categorization networks of Darwin II (a previous automaton)[55] with a set of motor circuits and effectors that act upon the environment to form a complete automaton capable of global mappings and autonomous behavior.

Motions of the arm of Darwin III can displace objects in the environment, while motions of the eye affect only the "perceived" positions of these objects. The automaton has three "senses": vision, light touch, and kinesthesia (signals from joints in the arm). Because it has motor capabilities and a phenotype, the emergence of patterns of behavior of Darwin III can be scored without knowledge of the activity of its nervous system. In actual tests, however, one may choose to go beyond this "machine behaviorism" and simultaneously observe the stimulus world, the automaton's behavior, and the neural activity (along with synaptic changes) in its nervous system. The ability to observe all three levels provides a number of heuristically valuable insights not so far attainable in other neural models. In the world of such automata, one may avoid the so-called psychologist's fallacy, warned against by James.[56]

Networks in Darwin III are constructed from multiple repertoires, corresponding to functional regions in the brain (figure 3.5). Each repertoire may, like the cerebral cortex, contain several layers of cells, and each layer may have its own rules for connectivity and synaptic modification. Once established, connectivity is fixed, but connection strengths can vary in accordance with a set of rules for synaptic modification that provide the selection mechanisms required by the TNGS. Sensory responses to stimuli occur either on a retina-like input array or on a pressure-sensing array for touch. The simulation procedure generates objects yielding these stimuli and moves them in various ways (random and nonrandom) in order to test the responses of the automaton.

Certain specialized networks in Darwin III reflect the relative adaptive value to the automaton of the effects of its various motor actions and sensory experience. These networks provide the means for the automaton initially to possess "values" prior to experience. Values are arbitrary: in a given example of Darwin III, they have a specific structure and correspond to various kinds of evolutionarily determined characteristics that contribute to phenotypic fitness. Such low-level values are, for example, "Seeing is better than not seeing"—translated as "Increase the probability that, when the retina and its visual networks are stimulated, those synapses that were active in the recent past (and thus potentially involved in the behavior that brought about any increased stimulation) will change in strength." Selective amplification of syn-

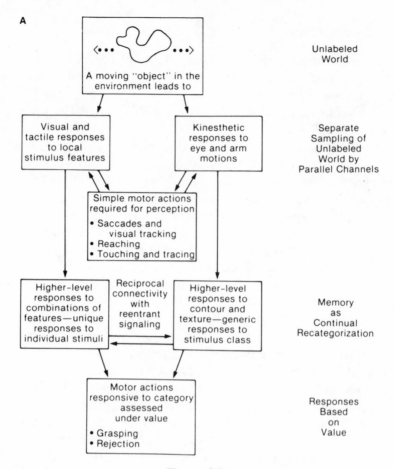

A

A moving "object" in the environment leads to	Unlabeled World
Visual and tactile responses to local stimulus features — Kinesthetic responses to eye and arm motions	Separate Sampling of Unlabeled World by Parallel Channels
Simple motor actions required for perception • Saccades and visual tracking • Reaching • Touching and tracing	
Higher-level responses to combinations of features—unique responses to individual stimuli — Reciprocal connectivity with reentrant signaling — Higher-level responses to contour and texture—generic responses to stimulus class	Memory as Continual Recategorization
Motor actions responsive to category assessed under value • Grasping • Rejection	Responses Based on Value

Figure 3.5

Darwin III, a selective recognition automaton and a representative example of synthetic neural modeling. A: Diagram of functional relations in one arrangement of Darwin III. The box at the top represents the environment, in which an unnamed object is moving about. The remaining boxes represent functions, each of which is subserved by several repertoires of neuronal groups with appropriate interconnections. The arrows suggest causal relations that generally reflect the existence of anatomical connections among the various regions. The two separate major sampling systems (see figure 3.3) of the automaton are at the left and the right, respectively. The result of the automaton's neuronal activity is externally apparent as spontaneous motor activity and as motor activity responsive to its categorization of objects. This categorization proceeds according to internal criteria that emerge because the automaton has biases or values. For example, the value "Seeing is better than not seeing" is expressed in terms of changes in connection strengths in oculomotor repertoires when visual units become more active following eye movements. Note that value does not prespecify categories, but when categories do emerge, it biases the selection of behaviors consequent upon them. Note also that the automaton reflects its experience in more or less stable alterations of connection strengths but does not have coded representations for memory. Instead, memory is a system property

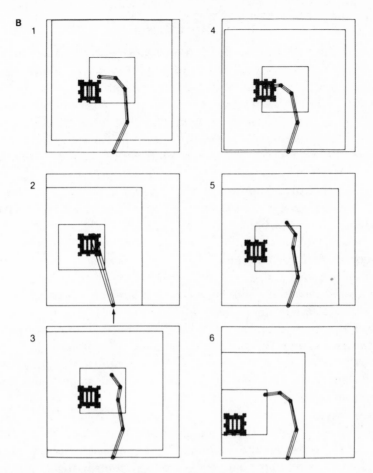

exhibited as an enhanced ability to recognize and categorize objects in classes seen before. Darwin III illustrates the concept of global mapping, according to which there is no specific code or image for an object and no single place in which various parallel processes are organized into a unitary representation. B: *Computer simulations showing responses of Darwin III to a striped bumpy object. The outer bounding square is the "world." The larger, moving inner square represents the field of peripheral vision; the smallest square, the central visual field of the automaton. The automaton has already had experience with seeing and reaching various objects. The successive frames are as follows: (1) the eye moves to center the object, and the four-jointed arm reaches toward it; (2) after touching the object with the last joint, which contains pressure-sensitive receptors, a central reflex straightens the arm, which then "feels" around the object, sending "kinesthetic" signals from the "shoulder" (arrow) to a central neural map; and (3) reentry between this map and a visual map leads to categorization of the object and activation of a rejection response in which a reflex center sends impulses to move the arm rhythmically; see frames 4,5,6. This "rejection response" leads to an adventitious but effective striking of the object, which as a result moves left as it is followed by central vision through visual tracking.*

apses may thus be made to depend on adaptive value as registered by such internal structures, which can bias the responses of synaptic populations. External or explicit *categorical* criteria for amplification (such as those a programmer might provide)[57] are *not* permitted, however.

Perhaps I should emphasize again that the alterations of synaptic efficacy in populations of synapses are not necessarily constrained by just *one* rule.[58] Various rules may operate in different portions of real brains, and this is applicable as well to simulations based on the TNGS. In certain networks, one might arrange, for example, that selection operates to *decrease* the probability of change of synapses involved in adaptively successful behavior.

In Darwin III, pairs of higher-order networks form classification couples (compare figures 3.3 and 3.5). In this example, one network (see particularly figure 3.5, *A*) responds to local visual features. The other responds to kinesthetic features as the last joint of the arm traces contours by light touch (since the low-level value for touch is "More pressure is better than less pressure," this joint will tend to seek edges). The visual and kinesthetic repertoires are reentrantly connected. This reentry allows correlation of the responses of these different repertoires that have disjunctively sampled visual and kinesthetic signals, and it yields a primitive form of categorization.

The behavior of Darwin III can be used to study problems involving motion, perceptual invariance, figure-ground discrimination, and memory. For example, the selection of eye motions leading to saccades and visual tracking may be investigated in systems with an appropriate value scheme of the kind discussed above. After a suitable period of experience with various moving stimuli, the eye of Darwin III in fact begins to make the appropriate saccades and fine tracking movements with no further specification of its task other than that implicit in the value scheme. In a similar fashion, the multijointed arm of Darwin III can be trained to reach for and touch objects that are first detected and tracked by the visual system. This performance entails the coordination of gestural motions that involve the various joints to different extents, and it requires the participation of a whole series of repertoires that perform functions similar to those thought to be carried out in real nervous systems.

The testing of Darwin III carried out so far[59] indicates that after "being born" into a particular environment of moving objects, it will begin to track and fixate particular objects and to reach out to touch and trace them (figure 3.5, *B*). If its reentrant systems categorize a given set of stimuli as an object (meaning "having a contour that is more or less closed"), and if the visual system responds to the presence of certain features such as stripes while its kinesthetic system responds to bumps or rough surfaces, the automaton can activate reflexes that will force its arm to flail, thus registering these categorical responses as an observable output. The combination ("object, striped, bumpy") is decided on by the automaton on the basis of selection. Of course, the neural connectivity calling up the reflex rejection response ("flailing"), which is conditional upon categorization achieved as a result of experience, is built into the anatomy as a higher-level or "ethological" value.

No two versions of Darwin III so constituted actually show identical behavior, but, provided their low-level values are similar, their behavior tends to converge in terms of particular kinds of categorization upon a given value. Most strikingly, however, if the *lower-level values* (expressed as biases acting upon synaptic changes) are removed from the simulation, these automata show no convergent behavior.

Recognition automata like Darwin III serve as heuristic proving grounds for theories that, like the TNGS, are particularly concerned with the understanding of the complex neural bases of psychological phenomena. Indeed, the work on Darwin III provides reasonably satisfactory evidence for the self-consistency of the TNGS. In addition, it offers simultaneous glimpses into the functions of a complex neural system at all levels, from the molecular to the behavioral. Selective recognition automata afford their designers the opportunity to manipulate neural and nonneural phenotypic features as well as environmental stimuli while observing the consequences at each level simultaneously.

It does not seem probable that neuroscience will enjoy a deep view of how the brain functions unless global brain theories and the models that embed them can help us bridge experimental findings in fields ranging from molecular biology to psychology. This is all the more so when we consider how such findings might relate to a model of consciousness. We must in fact consider a *series* of models and processes before attacking the question of consciousness itself. One of the most important is the process of reentrant signaling, which, as we shall see, is of central significance in formulating a model of consciousness. Let us turn to some detailed examples in the next chapter.

4

Reentrant Signaling

Perceptual categorizations and the recategorical processes leading to memory depend critically on reentry. So does coordination between the sensorimotor systems involved in global mappings. It is therefore perhaps not surprising that the brains of richly endowed organisms show a structure unique among all known physical objects. This uniqueness of brain structure may be attributed to its anatomically mapped reentrant connectivities,[1] which occur in enormous numbers. Even in biological systems such as jungles or food webs, where complex parallel dynamics occur in the exchange of signals, comparable *preexisting* structural pathways of this type cannot be found.

Of the mechanisms proposed in the TNGS, reentry is the most critical for an understanding of memory and consciousness. To show the versatility and importance of reentry, I shall consider it here in further detail and discuss a particular model[2] of the process. Although this reentrant cortical integration (RCI) model is based on the visual system, the principles used may be extended to a variety of systems, including those invoked to explain consciousness and language. Indeed, as we shall see in later chapters, primary consciousness is supposed to arise as a result of reentrant circuits connecting special memory functions to those mediating current perceptual categorizations. It is therefore crucial to understand a specific example of reentrant signaling in some detail. Readers who work through the details of the RCI model will have a solid example in mind when considering the role of reentry in consciousness and in processes such as language comprehension. To those who simply want the gist on a first reading, however, I suggest omitting the section on the RCI model.

TABLE 4.1

A Taxonomy of Reentry

	Anatomy				Temporal Characteristics*
	Fiber Pattern		Terminal Distribution		
Type	Registered	Convergent-Divergent	Arborized	Layer-Registered	
Dyadic					
	+	−	+	+	
	+	−	+	−	
$(\text{map}_1 \rightleftharpoons \text{map}_2)$	+	−	−	+	
	+	−	−	−	either 2 or 1,3
	−	+	+	+	or 2,3 or 1,4
	−	+	+	−	
	−	+	−	+	
	−	+	−	−	

Triadic

Parallel   Any combination of the properties shown above, one for each leg
$\text{map}_1 \rightleftharpoons \text{map}_2 \rightleftharpoons \text{map}_3$

Triangle   Any pairwise combination of the properties shown above, one for each
    map_3 leg
   // \\
$\text{map}_1 \rightleftharpoons \text{map}_2$

Mixed   Higher-order anatomies combining dyadic and triadic linkage with the appropriate combinatorial properties as above

Temporal characteristics: 1 = synchronous; 2 = asynchronous; 3 = phasic (intermittent); 4 = cyclic (periodic).

As I mentioned in the last chapter, reentry is a process of temporally ongoing parallel signaling between separate maps along ordered anatomical connections. Generally, such connections are reciprocal and more or less in register. But triangle reentry can occur among three maps or more, and connections between any pair of these maps can be divergent or convergent (see table 4.1, and correlate it with figure 4.1). Reentry can be continuous or phasic and can behave recursively. It is not simply feedback, however, because in any chunk of time, it involves parallel sampling from a geometric range of spatially extended maps made up of neuronal groups.[3] (Feedback involves connection in a fixed path using previous information for control and correction.) Reentry occurs in selective systems in which information is not prespecified, it

A

BASIC COMPONENTS

Registered

Convergent or Divergent

Layer-Registered   Not Layer-Registered

Arborized   Non-Arborized

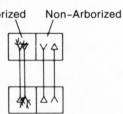

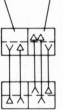

Fiber Pattern

Terminal Distribution

REGISTERED

Arborized

Non-Arborized

Layer-Registered

Not Layer-Registered

CONVERGENT-DIVERGENT

Arborized

Non-Arborized

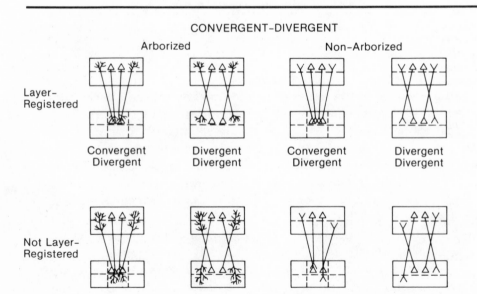

Layer-Registered

Convergent Divergent

Divergent Divergent

Convergent Divergent

Divergent Divergent

Not Layer-Registered

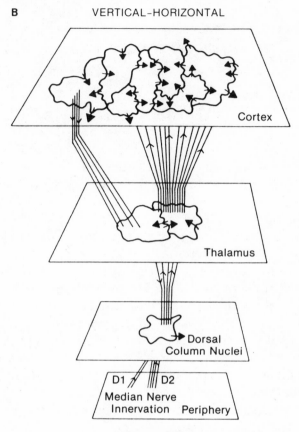

Figure 4.1

A: *Some anatomical patterns showing reentrant connectivity (see table 4.1 for comparison). The functional import of some of the patterns shown here will emerge when we consider the RCI model later in this chapter.* Open triangles *represent cell bodies;* Y *represents axonal terminals.* B: *The vertical-horizontal example is based on the somatosensory system. In this system, alterations in the pattern of incoming signals flowing vertically can lead to alterations of borders in "horizontally" disposed maps (for a discussion of this system, see chapter 3).*

varies statistically in parallel channels, and it is a constructive function, not just a corrective one.

In this chapter, I propose first to discuss some of the types of reentrant anatomical networks that can occur. Although I do not cite specific neuroanatomical examples, every one of the types of connectivity to be illustrated exists in rich nervous systems. After illustrating some possible anatomies, I take up a computer model of reentrant networks dedicated to vision (the RCI model) to illustrate how certain essential functions may be served by processes of reentry.

TYPES OF REENTRY

Because reentry depends on a variety of anatomical arrangements and because it has various temporal properties, it is an enormously diverse process. Given the parallel nature of sampling from mapped regions and the existence of various anatomies, each with particular local synaptic rules, this variety can lead to a large number of ways of combining and recombining reentrant signals (figure 4.1). Reentry can vary statistically or regularly in time and space and, therefore, has components that relate it more to a process of correlation than to signal control only.

As I pointed out in the preceding chapter, specific tags are not available to specify map positions in the brain in the way they are in a computer representation. Yet, neural activity distributed in and between maps must be correlated in time and space. Indeed, for higher-order reentrant correlations to be related to activity in sensory receptor sheets, at least one brain map must be topographic. Other maps in the same modality must be reentrantly connected to that topographic map in order to maintain correlations of the properties that are related to positions of a stimulus object in the world.

Figure 4.1 illustrates some of the kinds of anatomies underlying reentrant activity, and table 4.1 summarizes various combinatorial possibilities. It is, of course, not possible to show the temporal properties of reentry in) a static figure, but it must nevertheless be stressed that reentry is a dynamic process with a variety of temporal properties: periodic (cyclic), intermittent (phasic), synchronous, or asynchronous (table 4.1). This implies that the characteristics of reentry depend upon various latencies and temporal properties of neurons and synapses.

The dynamics of reentry are closely controlled by neuronal group selection and also control that process. This property, and its ability to coordinate parametric changes in vertical and horizontal dimensions of various projections to maps (figure 4.1, panel *B*), gives the process of reentry a central place in coordinating a great variety of neural functions. Such functions range from the registration of maps in early morphogenesis to the synthesis of coherent signal complexes, as we shall see when we consider a computer model of visual processing.

Some of the main *functions* of reentry are listed in table 4.2, which also indicates that certain functions can be modulated by positive or negative changes in synaptic efficacy of varying duration. Reentry in the presence of synaptic change is a powerful means of stably coordinating sequences of signals. At the same time, it can allow quick changes in the procedures by which various connected maps can alter their relative responses to shifts in external signals. When used to correlate the functions of the cerebral cortex with the functions of what I have called organs of succession (see chapter 7), reentry allows moving animals to deal with entire sensorimotor sequences as patterns.

Although I shall not stress embryonic development here, reentry may play a very important role in actually laying down certain neural circuits. For example, the ubiquity and precision of reciprocal corticocortical and thalamocortical pathways raise the possibility that reentrant signaling may actually play a key role during neurogenesis in establishing the final structure of such pathways.

The possibility of reentering signals in a recursive fashion to a lower-order mapped input after they have been processed in several higher-order maps is an enormously powerful way of creating *new* functions. Since this process of recursive synthesis occurs in various successive time chunks, it allows for asymptotic approaches to a great variety of different outputs in complex neural systems. The variety and versatility of these new outputs and their functions are so great that they cannot all be listed in a table such as table 4.2.

This versatility is nicely illustrated in the transactions of the cerebral cortex, an example of which follows. An understanding of the changes seen in this rather simplified model of the visual cortex will be helpful when we take up the role of reentry in consciousness, in chapters 5 and

TABLE 4.2

Some Functions of Reentry

Function	Synaptic Change
Morphogenesis	Yes, + or −
Stabilization of neuronal groups	Yes, + or −
Correlation	Yes, + or −
Association	Yes, +
Filtering, gain control	No
Time delays	No
Resolution of conflict	No
Cross-modal construction	No
Recursive synthesis	No

9. This visual example will illustrate that reentry can functionally link otherwise disjunct maps, resulting in correlation and association of their responses. By such means, reentry can lead to cross-modal construction, to resolution of conflicts in various areas, and to recursive synthesis (the last three items in table 4.2). Cross-modal construction couples two functions, for example, occlusion of objects and object motion in vision. Conflict resolution allows a choice to be made among competing integrations of sensory signals. And, as we have mentioned, recursive synthesis allows signals from higher-order perceptual constructs to be used as inputs for lower-order maps through repeated reentrant signaling.

Let us turn to a specific model of striate and prestriate cortical function in vision to see how such functions may arise. Our main goal in presenting this model is to illustrate how neural arrangements may influence processes important to perception. But it should be kept in mind that the illustration can be generalized to include functional correlations important to concept formation, consciousness, and speech, as we shall show in later chapters.

Cortical Correlation and Integration

One of the most striking properties of the brain is its ability to coordinate and integrate the operations of multiple functionally segregated areas. A good example is seen in visual perception, in which a set of multiple and potentially conflicting signals for motion, shape, depth, and color must be integrated in such a fashion that objects can be discriminated. This discrimination is carried out largely by the visual cortex.

The visual cortex of higher animals is functionally segregated (see figure 4.2) into a number of specialized areas (upward of twenty in the monkey) that are interconnected by a vast system of anatomical connections. Although certain areas, such as the inferotemporal and the parietal, carry out high-order integrations, no single dominant, integrative high-level area has yet been located; rather, every visual cortical area is connected to some subset of the other visual areas. Within each cortical area, cells respond best to one particular attribute (e.g., orientation, motion, disparity, or wavelength), but the same cells may also respond to several other attributes.[4]

The fundamental problem in early visual function is to determine how these distributed, mapped regions containing multiple cell types

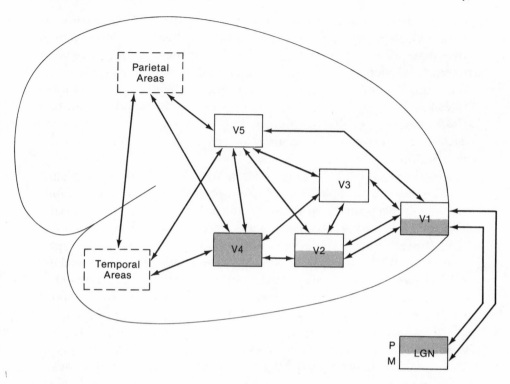

Figure 4.2

Visual areas. Highly schematic diagram of multiple, reentrantly connected visual areas of a primate species. Many of the details of the anatomy, for example termination in various cell layers and distribution of subareas, are omitted. Double-headed arrows *indicate anatomical connections that provide the basis for reentry.* Darkened areas *indicate parvocellular (P) and* lightened areas *indicate magnocellular (M) pathways. (After S. Zeki, personal communication.)*

with specialized but overlapping properties can coordinate and integrate their operations so as to produce a coherent and unified representation of the stimulus domain. This problem is compounded by the requirement that the integrated system must respond to partial, conflicting, or ambiguous stimuli, as is demonstrated by visual illusions and by a wide range of other kinds of inputs. How does the perceptual system compose a scene from such signals?

Several models have addressed this problem of integrating cortical action to yield coherent perceptions. Marr, for example, proposed[5] that the visual cortex computes a series of successively abstracted "sketches" of the visual scene. Marr's model has the virtue of constructing complex system properties from lower-level operations. But this model is strictly hierarchical and does not reveal how individual functionally segregated cortical areas operating in parallel can be coordinated. More recently, several so-called connectionist models[6] have incorporated into their networks a more distributed representation of cortical properties. These models depend upon *learned* associations between visual attributes to modify their connection strengths, however, and are not tied to cortical anatomy. In this respect, they evade analysis of the specifically neural components essential to any biological solution to the problem.

According to the TNGS, neither hierarchy nor specified input-output descriptions with learning are sufficient to deal with the needs of perceptual categorization and memory. Instead, the theory proposes that reentrant signaling acts to coordinate inputs and resolve conflicts between the responses of different functionally segregated maps. Visual reentry allows each mapped region to use discriminations made by other regions (about borders, movement, etc.) for its own operations. This process allows the various responses to aspects of the stimulus world to remain segregated and distributed among multiple brain areas and still constitute a unified representation. Reentrant integration obviates the need for a higher-level command center, or a "sketch." I shall illustrate this briefly by describing a computer simulation of a model of early vision. In the interests of simplicity, I shall not give a detailed account but merely describe the basic procedure and give a few results. Interested readers may consult the original publication for details.[7]

THE REENTRANT CORTICAL INTEGRATION (RCI) MODEL FOR EARLY VISION

The problem I wish to exemplify is embedded in the question, How are the operations of segregated visual cortical areas integrated to produce the basis for a perceptually unified picture of the world? Although verbal descriptions bearing on the answer to this question are obviously essential, they cannot capture the dynamics or details of integration in the visual system. The RCI model represents an explicit theoretical attempt to answer this question by carrying out large-scale simulations of functionally segregated visual cortical areas that are connected by various forms of reentry.

According to the model, the representation of the stimulus world remains distributed among multiple functionally segregated areas, and integration occurs by a process of reentrant signaling along interareal connections. At present, such detailed computer simulations provide perhaps the only practical means of analyzing the enormously complex interactions among multiple networks. For example, the simulations of the RCI model contained about 220,000 units and 8.5 million connections operating dynamically in responses to various signals. It must be kept in mind that this is still only a small fraction of the actual numbers in complex brains and that it is currently not feasible to construct a detailed simulation of even a single visual cortical area. The simulations in the model therefore capture just a few basic properties of each area. Indeed, in the current description, I shall simplify matters even further: only the bare minimum of technical details will be presented.

NETWORK PROPERTIES AND CONNECTIVITY

First, let us consider the visual regions, pathways, and connections that were used as a basis for the model. These may be seen in figure 4.2. Three interconnected areas were simulated whose properties were based largely on the so-called magnocellular pathways in visual areas V1, V3, and V5 (also known as MT) of the monkey striate and extrastriate visual cortex.[8] The pathways through these areas constitute a particularly simple reentrant system in that, besides being directly interconnected, V3 and V5 both receive connections from and also reenter[9] to the same cell layer (4B) in V1. These connections are thus layer-registered, but they are also convergent-divergent (see figure 4.1); reentrant fibers from V5 can potentially influence input from V1 to V3. A similar and symmetric situation exists for reentrant fibers from V3, which could influence input to V5. The overall circuitry in the model proper may be seen in figure 4.3. Units in the model have properties similar to those of neurons, but, unlike previous efforts in models[10] based on the TNGS, no attempt was made to simulate group formation, confinement, or competition. Such units could replace groups in the model because there was no need for the kind of cooperative properties that would require groups. The decision to use units simplified the computation but otherwise did not put unrealistic constraints on the model, the main purpose of which was to explore reentry. By explicit circuit design, a variety of different types of units of different function (dedicated to detecting orientation, occlusion, line termination, etc.) was constructed. These units had electrical activities and synaptic connections, but these connections were not modifiable.

While we will not discuss the actual microscopic circuits used to

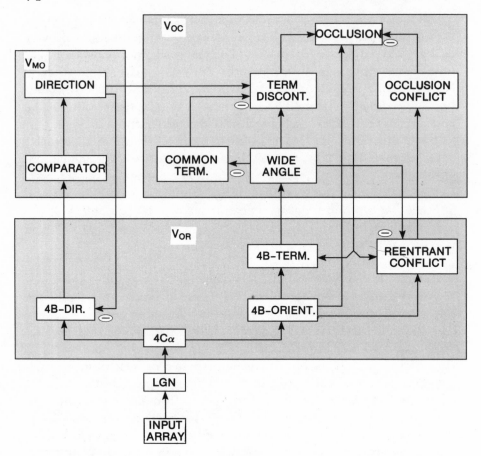

Figure 4.3

Schematic of network connectivity in the RCI model. Major connections between the simulated repertoires are indicated. The three shaded areas indicate the three simulated areas, V_{OR}, V_{OC}, and V_{MO}, which are specialized for orientation, occlusion, and motion, respectively. Repertoires of units (white boxes) in each area are named according to either their dominant function or their closest analogue in the central nervous system. Actual units consisted of circuits designed to carry out each respective function (see table 4.3 for a list). Reentrant connections are indicated between the direction repertoires of V_{MO} and 4B-Dir. of V_{OR}; between the occlusion repertoires of V_{OC} and the 4B-Term. and reentrant conflict repertoires of V_{OR}; and between the direction repertoires of V_{MO} and the termination discontinuity repertoires of V_{OC}. Note that these are not simple feedback loops; while only a single arrow is shown in each direction, reentry actually occurs from many repertoire units in parallel. All connections are excitatory unless indicated by a minus sign. Further repertoire properties and connectivity details are given in the text and in table 4.3.

construct the units with different properties, it is important to list their major properties (table 4.3). Different *types* of units are characterized by the source and the distribution of their inputs and the operations (thresholds, decays, etc.) performed upon them. Multiple units of a given type comprise a *repertoire,* and an *area* consists of multiple repertoires containing different types of units. Several major *pathways* within the system serially or reciprocally connect a number of repertoires in several different areas.

For clarity, many repertoires are named according to the closest analogue in the nervous system. Nonetheless, there is no strict correspondence between the simulated areas and known cortical regions, and the names of simulated areas are therefore based on their major functions, with "V_{OR}," "V_{OC}," and "V_{MO}" designating areas devoted mainly to orientation, occlusion, or motion. It must be stressed that the particular functional properties modeled (e.g., orientation or direction selectivity) are intended only as exemplars: alternative mechanisms to generate these properties are possible, and a completely different set of properties could as well have been chosen.

Thus two warnings are in order: (1) the functions of the three simulated areas V_{OR}, V_{OC}, and V_{MO} (figure 4.3) correspond only roughly respectively to V1, V3, and V5 (figure 4.2); (2) not all of the properties of neuronal units making up each area (e.g., "4B-Orient.," "4B-Term.," "wide angle," etc.) have actually been found explicitly in monkey visual cortex. These functions and units are nevertheless sufficiently exemplary of the known ones to serve our purpose, which is to illustrate by means of the model how reentry works to bring about cortical integration. Indeed, the central point of the RCI model is that, whichever set of functionally segregated properties is modeled, a reentrant mechanism is necessary in order to achieve functional integration. We apply this idea in later chapters to analyses of mechanisms related to consciousness and speech.

To understand the model, we must describe the function of each area and give a minimum description of the arrangement of repertoires within that area. The reader may follow this description by consulting figure 4.3 and table 4.3 in coordinate fashion. The description will provide a basis for understanding the ensuing figures, which actually represent the performance of the simulation.

First, consider the areas. Simulated area V_{OR} contains both orientation units and directionally selective units, simulated area V_{MO} discriminates the true direction of motion of objects[11] regardless of the

TABLE 4.3

Properties of Repertoires of Units in the RCI Model

Repertoire	Major Property	Afferents	Efferents
LGN	ON-center, OFF-surround	Input array	4Cα
4Cα	Orientation selectivity	LGN	4B-Dir. 4B-Term. Reentrant conflict
4B-Dir.	Directional selectivity	4Cα direction	Comparator
Comparator	Compares motion in adjacent directions	4B-Dir.	Direction
Direction	Directional selectivity	Comparator	4B-Dir. Termination Discontinuity
4B-Orient.	Orientation selectivity	4Cα	4B-Term. Reentrant conflict Occlusion
4B-Term.	Orientation and polarity of line terminations	4B-Orient.	Wide angle
Wide angle	Broadens orientation selectivity	4B-Term.	Termination Discontinuity Common termination
Termination discontinuity	Responds to line terminations consistent with an occlusion boundary	Wide angle Common termination	Occlusion
Occlusion	Responds to real contours, occlusion borders, and illusory contours	Termination Discontinuity 4B-Term. (reentrant)	Reentrant conflict
Common termination detector	Detects whether lines with orientations within 90° terminate at a common locus	Wide angle	Termination Discontinuity
Reentrant conflict	Responds to crossings of real and illusory contours	Occlusion 4C-Orient.	Occlusion conflict

TABLE 4.3 *(continued)*

Repertoire	Major Property	Afferents	Efferents
Occlusion conflict	Generates illusory contours between conflicting points found by reentrant conflict repertoire	Reentrant conflict	Occlusion
4B-Term. (reentrant)	Same as 4B-Term.	Occlusion	Wide angle
Direction discontinuity	Responds to differential motion consistent with an occlusion boundary	Direction	Occlusion (motion)
Occlusion (motion)	Responds to occlusion borders based on structure from motion	Direction discontinuity	4B-Term. (reentrant)

orientation of their edges, and simulated area V_{OC} responds to borders[12] due to either luminance contrast or occlusion (the obstruction from the observer's view of one surface by another). Area V_{OC} is able to respond to illusory contours by means of the same neural architecture used for the discrimination of real occlusion boundaries. In addition, this same architecture generates responses to the so-called structure-from-motion illusion (see below) by virtue of reentrant connections from V_{MO} to V_{OC}. These two comments illustrate a central functional consequence of the TNGS: that reentrant connections allow a cortical area to perform similar operations on inputs from different sources, whether "real" or "illusory."

Let us now briefly consider the repertoires and pathways and how they respond to stimuli. Stimuli of various sizes and shapes directly excite the elements of the input array (figure 4.3). The input array (which corresponds to a drastically simplified retina) provides excitation to the "LGN," which contains ON-center, OFF-surround units. The LGN projects to the "4Cα" units of area V_{OR}. Each 4Cα unit receives excitatory inputs from an elongated region of the LGN, and inhibitory inputs from the two flanks of the region. The connection strengths of these inputs are adjusted to give the 4Cα unit a fairly sharply tuned selectivity for orientations. Each 4Cα unit receives two sets of inputs from the LGN, one excitatory and one inhibitory. 4Cα units are also directionally selective because of a mechanism involving temporally delayed inhibition. Directional selectivity depends upon the fact that the inhibitory units are shifted with respect to the excitatory inputs (the direction of the shift determines the null direction [no response] of each $4C\alpha$ unit).

The $4C\alpha$ units of V_{OR} are the source of two different pathways—one reentrantly connected to area V_{MO}, the other reentrantly connected to area V_{OC} (figure 4.3). These connections between V_{OR}, V_{OC}, and V_{MO} follow an anatomical plan similar to that found in the magnocellular pathway in the monkey[13] (figure 4.2). The function of the V_{MO} pathway is to transform the unit responses from a primary selectivity to orientation (found in $4C\alpha$) to a primary selectivity to direction (found in the direction repertoires). The function of the V_{OC} pathway is to detect and generate responses to occlusion boundaries. $4C\alpha$ projects to 4B, which contains several separate populations of units. The "4B-Dir." units are directionally selective and are reentrantly connected to V_{MO}. The 4B-Term. units are specialized for detecting line terminations and are reentrantly connected to V_{OC}. A third set of units, the "4B-Confl." units, receives inputs from both $4C\alpha$ and V_{OC} and serves to mediate conflicts in the responses of V_{OR} and V_{OC}.

TESTS OF REENTRANT FUNCTIONS IN THE MODEL

A general picture is all we can hope to convey; the abbreviated description given here does not, of course, do justice to all of the details. Experience with the model suggests that even a simplified simulation of segregated cortical areas must have a great number of components. But even in the face of this complexity, we must not lose sight of our overall aim, which is to show how reentry links functionally segregated areas with various units of different functions to give an integrated basis for perceptual response.

Tests were carried out to show that units at different stages in the V_{MO} pathway had different degrees of orientation selectivity and directional selectivity for various input signals. Similarly, it was shown that the V_{MO} pathway could respond to occlusion stimuli. The tests for movement involved changing the stimulus in the appropriate direction of movement and noting the response of the network. Reentry over each pathway was carried out in successive cycles after each response was recorded in all repertoires.

One of the main criteria for the functioning of the reentrant circuits was whether the RCI model could deal with both real and illusory stimuli. The requirement that the model give appropriate responses

Figure 4.4

Kanizsa triangle.

to a variety of nonillusory and illusory stimuli provides a severe test of the capacity to integrate multiple functionally segregated areas. One would expect that, in a well-designed simulation, the same reentrant connections responsible for cortical integration are also responsible for the generation of the bases for a number of visual illusions.

These illusions can occur when visual cues that give rise to activation of a particular cortical area indirectly activate other functionally segregated cortical areas through reentrant connections. In certain cases, when used as test stimuli, such visual illusions can reveal the constructive and interactive properties of the system. For example, the Kanizsa triangle (figure 4.4), which has illusory-contour, brightness, and depth effects, shows that the illusory features constructed by the cortex can interact consistently across several submodalities. Illusory contours (variously called subjective, anomalous, or cognitive contours) have been suggested to arise from a certain juxtaposition of local cues to occlusion.[14] Figure 4.5 shows some examples as well as some of the cues for occlusion actually used in the RCI model. In a similar fashion, the development of structure from motion (such as the appearance of borders in juxtaposed streams of moving randomly placed dots) provides the possibility of testing the ability of reentrant systems to deal with dynamic stimuli creating an illusion. A particularly severe test is to use different illusions in combination and search for integrative responses.

Given this discussion, it is obvious that the choice of occlusion as a major property in the RCI model of early vision had a specific motivation: it has been suggested by a number of authors that illusory contours are manifestations of occlusion[15] (figure 4.5). In constructing the model,

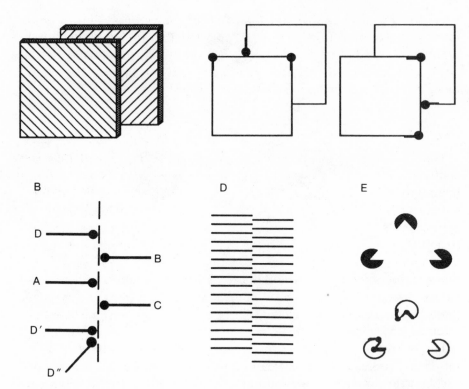

Figure 4.5

Criteria for occlusion and a basic description of the scheme for generating illusory contours. A: Occlusion of one square object by another is indicated by perspective. B: Definition of an occlusion boundary. The dashed vertical line is the presumptive occlusion boundary and circles *indicate line terminations. In the model, it was assumed that an occlusion boundary requires colinear terminations of at least three lines approaching the border from both sides: that is, line A* and *at least two of lines B, C, and D or D'. Lines approaching the boundary at an angle (line D") are also allowed. These same conditions generate responses to illusory contours in the network. C: Cues to occlusion boundaries in the figure shown in A. Circles with stems show line terminations that cue an occlusion boundary according to scheme shown in B. The figure on the left shows the occlusion cues for the "top" occlusion boundary; figure on right shows cues for "right" occlusion boundary. D: Two abutting grids, one-half cycle out of phase, give rise to a vertical illusory contour at their line of intersection. Note that line terminations fulfill the conditions for occlusion given in B. The extreme left and right borders of the figure do not give rise to vivid illusory contours. E: The classic Kanizsa triangle (top; see also figure 4.4). Line terminations (circles with stems) giving rise to the illusory contour forming one side of the Kanizsa triangle (below). Corresponding terminations generate responses to the other two sides. In this case, terminations of both lines and areas are used—a generalization of the scheme in B.*

we therefore assumed that responses to occluding stimuli, illusory contours, and structure from motion are all mediated by the same neural pathway. According to this assumption, structure from motion is actually a form of illusory-contour generation, operating with the same mechanisms, but on a different input submodality. We will illustrate this shortly.

EXAMPLES OF PERFORMANCE

The simulated system was tested with real contours and with illusory contours containing either false cues or potential conflicts with other boundaries, as well as with structure-from-motion cues in which differential motions of random-dot fields were the key stimuli. Finally, a complex combined illusion containing both static illusory contours and structure-from-motion cues was used to determine whether the simulated model could integrate its responses to yield a single, figural synthesis of this input. Inasmuch as at least two different functionally segregated regions (V_{OC} and V_{MO}) were needed to obtain such an outcome, the experiments provided a particularly stringent test of the efficacy of reentrant signaling in cortical integration.

The results of each simulation will be presented in rapid order in a series of figures. The same convention for displaying the activity of various repertoires will be used in all figures. The color plate in figure 4.9, *B* may be considered typical. Eight boxes arranged in a square configuration show the activity of units in the eight directional variants of each repertoire in an area; the relative position of each box in the larger square indicates the preferred *directional selectivity* of that repertoire (i.e., the upper-left box shows the repertoire whose preferred direction is 135°). A dot indicates that the unit at the corresponding position in the repertoire is active, and the size of the dot indicates the degree of activation. (Lines correspond to a series of adjacent dots.) Thus, by viewing the *topographic* pattern of activation in the boxes and comparing the responses to the stimulus pattern, one can immediately judge the fidelity of the network responses.

The simulated system was able to integrate responses to illusory contours (figure 4.6) and could also rule out an occlusion boundary that provided false cues on *conflicts* between a real cue and a possible illusory contour (figure 4.7). When the reentrant connections between repertoires were blocked or cut, these integrations failed and no inhibition of conflicting responses occurred.

One of the most striking properties of the model was the generation of structure from motion, which resulted from cross-modal reentry

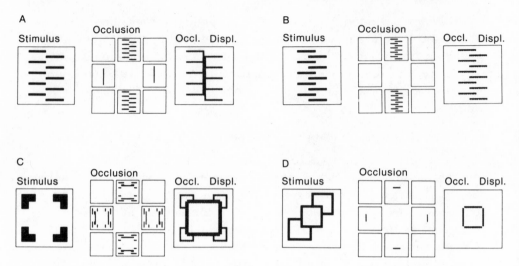

Figure 4.6

Generation of illusory contours. A: Response of occlusion repertoires (center panels) *to an abutting-grid stimulus* (left). *The occlusion repertoires are arranged by orientation preference according to the convention described in the text. The panel labeled Occl. Displ. shows (at a larger scale, for clarity) the superposed responses of all the occlusion repertoires. Note the responses to both the real (horizontal) lines and to the illusory (vertical) contour. B: Responses to a control stimulus in which the terminations of the grid lines overlapped. There are no illusory-contour responses. C: A classic illusory-square stimulus. Responses are generated to the edges of the four corner stimuli, as well as to the four illusory contours making up the square. D: A central square occluding two other squares. Connections from 4B-Orient. to occlusion repertoires (see figure 4.3) were cut in order to show responses to occlusion boundaries more clearly (in this stimulus, the occlusion and real borders are superposed). Only the edges of the central square are discriminated as occlusion borders.*

between the V_{MO} and the V_{OC} areas (figure 4.8). This effect depended upon determination of the direction of motion of random dots by V_{MO} and the response of termination discontinuity units in V_{OC} to local cues from regions of differential motion. Colinear local cues generated responses in occlusion repertoires, and regions corresponding to actual dividing lines between differentially moving dot fields were discriminated. When reentrant pathways were blocked, these effects disappeared.

SYNTHESIS

All of these properties of the simulation suggested that reentry between functionally segregated circuits could yield properties comparable to those observed in various psychophysical and neurophysiological

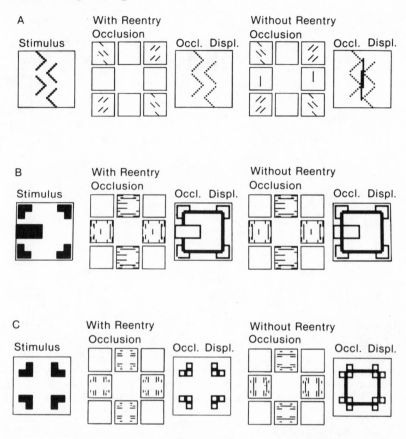

Figure 4.7

Conflict resolution by reentry in the simulated system. A: Responses of occlu-sion units to a stimulus consisting of four angled vertices (occlusion repertoires are all displayed according to the same convention used in figure 4.6). In the presence of connections from common termination detectors. to termination discontinuity units (panels labeled With Reentry), only responses to real con-tours are made. In the absence of these connections (panels on right, labeled Without Reentry), inappropriate responses to vertical illusory contours are made. B: Responses to a stimulus consisting of an illusory square with an occluding rectangle. In the absence of the reentrant connections from occlusion repertoires to reentrant conflict repertoires (right panels), the illusory contour on the left side of the illusory square is constructed. In the presence of reentrant connections (center panels), the illusory contour is censored at positions "be-hind" the occluding rectangle. C: The same elements as in the illusory-square stimulus (see figure 4.6), with the same line termination cues, but rearranged so that an illusory square is not perceived by humans. In the absence of reen-trant connections (right) the networks generate illusory contours. In the pres-ence of reentry, illusory contours are censored between the four corner elements (but not within the corner elements, a special situation not treated in this version of the model).

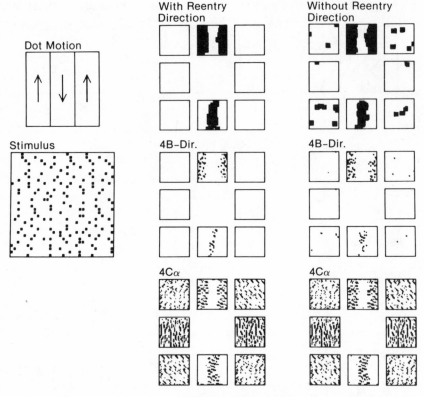

Figure 4.8

Responses of the model to differentially moving random dots. Responses of all units in the 4Cα, 4B-Dir., and direction repertoires are shown (in the presence and absence of reentry; see figure 4.3) after four cycles of a moving random-dot pattern. The stimulus (left) consisted of one-pixel-wide randomly placed dots. Dots in the center third of the display were moved southward, and those in outer thirds were moved northward (see panel labeled Dot Motion) at one pixel per cycle. Panels are arranged by directional preference according to the same convention used in the other figures. The larger receptive fields of directional cells are manifested by the number of cells responding to a single stimulus dot. 4Cα units show a degree of directional selectivity, but many units selective for what are in this case incorrect directions (NE, NW, etc.) are active as well. The 4B-Dir. and direction repertoires respond much more selectively to the direction of motion. Reentry leads to more accurate directional discrimination in that only units selective for the correct direction respond. Without reentrant connections (right), a number of direction units respond incorrectly to dot motion. The responses of units in 4Cα are nearly identical with or without reentry, since 4B-Dir. is the most peripheral repertoire to receive reentrant connections from V_{MO} (see figure 4.3).

experiments.[16] The most critical test of the function of reentry in the model involved the interaction of illusory contours and structure from motion in a combined illusion as shown in figure 4.9.

To succeed, the RCI model would have to synthesize the responses of two separate visual areas in a recursive fashion. The stimulus consisted of three of the four corners used to make the illusory square in figure 4.6. However, in place of the fourth (lower-right) corner of the illusory square, there were two fields of moving random dots: a square-shaped region and an inverse-L–shaped region, which fit together to make a larger square region. As may be seen in the figure, within four cycles of reentry, the units in V_{MO} discriminate the motion patterns very cleanly, and the V_{OC} occlusion repertoires generate responses to two sides of the illusory square. By six cycles, the reentrant connections between V_{MO} and V_{OC} generate responses in the occlusion repertoires to the structure-from-motion contours. These responses are then reentered back to 4B-Term. in the V_{OC} pathway. 4B-Term. repertoires act on these *reentrant* inputs as they do on normal *ascending* inputs from 4Cα, and thus detect terminations of the contours derived both from structure from motion and from illusory contours. The units responding to these terminations then activate the ascending V_{OC} pathway (see figure 4.3). Now, however, there are local (termination) cues for the construction of the remaining two sides of the illusory square, and these remaining contours are in fact produced, as is shown in figure 4.9 (cycle 4). Once generated, the contours are indefinitely stable. When tested on normal human subjects, this construction is indeed perceived as an illusory square. The system works equally well with other directions of motion of the random-dot fields and with other illusory configurations of different shapes (triangles and the like).

The same simulation was carried out under conditions in which the reentrant connections from the occlusion to 4B-Term. units were cut. In this case, the necessary "cross-modal" interactions could not occur, and the bottom and right sides of the illusory square were not generated. The same negative result occurred when the V_{MO} to V_{OC} reentrant pathways were cut. This shows that responses consistent with the illusory figure (very similar to that produced exclusively by the V_{OC} pathway) can be produced only through a *combination* of the action of the direct ascending V_{OC} pathway, the action of V_{MO} repertoires on inputs from the V_{OC} pathway, and the recursively reentered activity stimulated by these structure-from-motion contours. These act on the V_{OC} pathway to create appropriate illusory contours from structure from motion, and the synthesis takes place.

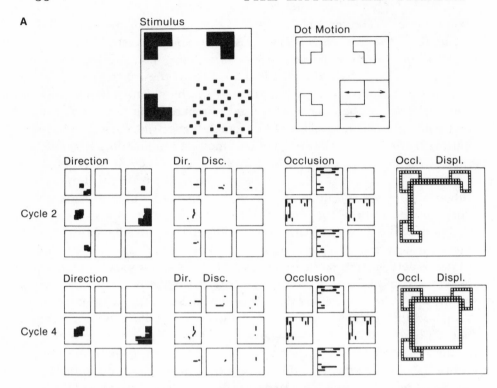

Figure 4.9

Recursive synthesis of a combined illusion. A: *Responses of direction, direction
discontinuity, and occlusion repertoires to illusory contours combined with a
structure-from-motion stimulus. The stimulus consisted of three of the four
corner elements of figure 4.6. In place of the bottom-right corner element is a
random-dot stimulus in which dots are moved at one pixel per cycle in the
directions shown in the panel labeled Dot Motion. By the second cycle* (interme-
diate row of panels), *the occlusion repertoires have generated illusory contours
between the corner elements (see occlusion display for larger-scale view), the
direction units have begun to respond to the directions of dot motion, and the
direction discontinuity units have generated structure-from-motion borders.
By cycle four* (bottom row), *the responses to the structure-from-motion borders
have been reentered back to V_{OR} (see text and figure 4.3), and their terminations have been detected and used by the ascending V_{OC} system to construct
responses to the two remaining sides of an illusory square. These later illusory
contours thus require the prior construction of borders due to structure from
motion. Responses of other repertoires to this stimulus are shown in the actual
display.* B: *Actual network display seen on the computer screen. Responses of
output units in the major repertoires (129 repertoires and 132,096 units) to the
combined stimulus analyzed in A. Small square boxes (blue) indicate individual repertoires; dots within the repertoires indicate activity of units at the*

RECURSION AND THE MULTIPLICITY OF REENTRANT INTEGRATION MECHANISMS

The mechanisms of the reentrant cortical integration (RCI) model provide a unitary explanation for responses both to real stimuli and to a number of visual illusions involving interactions between multiple visual attributes (such as contour, occlusion, and motion). The model takes explicit account of the dominant anatomical feature of the mammalian cortex—the massive systems of interareal corticocortical connections. Although this model hardly begins to capture the actual complexity of visual pathways,[17] it serves nicely to show the versatility and power of reentry in creating a variety of functions as a result of correlations of the properties of maps.

Part of the complexity in studying the coordination of functionally segregated cortical areas by reentry is due to the fact that different reentrant pathways use different integrative mechanisms (table 4.2, compare figures 4.6 and 4.9). The functional properties of several of these integrative mechanisms (the last three listed in the table) were demonstrated in the RCI model by tests of the system in the presence and the absence of reentry.

corresponding positions. Large colored borders demarcate repertoires belonging to the three simulated areas: green for V_{OR}, blue for V_{MO}, and red for V_{OC}. Degree of unit activity is color coded from high to low in five colors: white, blue, green, yellow, and red. The eight panels of each repertoire correspond to units segregated by orientation or direction preference: the position of each panel indicates the preference of its units (e.g., units in the upper-left 4Cα panel prefer 135° lines). This same convention is used in all figures. Activity occurring in the input array because of the stimulus is shown at the bottom center (responses shown in yellow). The panel labeled Occl. Display at bottom right shows (at larger scale, for clarity) the topographically superposed responses of units in all eight occlusion repertoires. The stimulus consisted of three aligned corner elements and two regions of random dots that were moved in different directions (see figure 4.9, A and the text for details) to generate borders due to structure from motion. Through the action of their reentrant circuits, the networks used both structure-from-motion and illusory-contour cues to synthesize a response to an illusory square.

The first mechanism involved the *resolution of conflicts* among the responses of different areas to the same stimulus (or of conflicts within the same area to different aspects of the same stimulus). Such conflicts are unavoidable, given that each area is more or less specialized for the discrimination of particular stimulus attributes. Figure 4.7 contains several examples in which the responses of the V_{OC} occlusion repertoires to illusory contours conflicted with responses to other contours—either real or illusory. The reentrant circuit acted to "censor" the conflicting responses. Another example of conflict resolution involved the reentry between V_{MO} and V_{OR} (figure 4.8). In this case, responses in V_{OR} were inhibited if they did not correspond to the true direction of motion as determined by V_{MO}.

A second mechanism of reentrant integration, *cross-modal construction,* allows one area to use the outputs of another area (which may be specialized for a different submodality) for its own functions. By this mechanism, for example, V_{OC} is able to use differential motion cues determined by V_{MO} to construct structure-from-motion boundaries by reentry (see figure 4.8). A psychophysical analogue of cross-modal construction has been demonstrated by Ramachandran[18] in experiments showing how one submodality can be "captured" by another. For example, Ramachandran has shown that for human subjects, various attributes such as color, illusory contours, and stereo depth can all undergo apparent motion, that is, they can be "captured" by apparent motion.

A third (and most striking) mechanism of integration, *recursive synthesis,* is exemplified in the RCI model by reentrant pathways from V_{MO} and V_{OC} back to V_{OR}. These connections allow the outputs of a higher area to influence the *inputs* that it (or other higher areas) receive from lower areas. More important, recursive synthesis allows constructs derived in higher areas to be recycled to lower areas for use in the generation of additional constructs (where, by "construct," I mean patterned neuronal responses linked to invariant properties in the world).

Recursive synthesis provides one of the most trenchant arguments for the necessity of reentry, for there are situations and responses that could not be explained in any other way. For example, even if units in V_{MO} could *independently* construct responses to structure from motion, some kind of local recursive process would still be required to generate the basis for the contours shown in figure 4.9. This is because structure-from-motion contours must be generated *first* in order to provide the line termination cues required for those illusory contours that correspond to the two missing sides of the illusory square. The most natural implementation for such a recursion, and one totally consistent with the known anatomy, is to let the connections from V_{MO} back to 4B (see figure 4.3) reenter higher-order responses to the illusory contours to act on the early stages of the same pathway.

GESTALT PROPERTIES, EVOLUTION, AND REENTRY

The examples of reentry given in the RCI model indicate that it is possible through reentrant maps to generate integrated responses that could provide bases for certain gestalt properties.[19] This is consistent with Kanizsa's observation[20] that the integrations seen in formation of illusory contours show gestalt properties. At this early level of integration, there is no need to invoke "unconscious inference"[21] or related cognitive notions. Of course, the influence of other neural levels and attentional and contextual factors also play a role in illusions. It is not implied here that early level reentry is their sole basis. Above all, the presentations here are not meant to imply that the responses seen are anything more than a *consistent basis* for those higher-order integrations (see chapter 5) that can lead to actual phenomenal awareness without invocation of a homunculus.

A number of mechanisms of morphologic evolution and development that can account for the appearance and adaptive value of reentrant maps were discussed in *Neural Darwinism* and *Topobiology*. Here, it may be useful to suggest that evolutionary selection for those reentrant arrangements that allow for ordering of partial and complex stimuli in an adaptive fashion might well have provided one of the fundamental bases for gestalt phenomena and *Prägnanz.*[22] Any gestalt patterning that allowed more adaptive actions would have led rapidly to natural selection for particular reentrant circuits and functional segregation. Certain illusions may occur incorrigibly as a consequence of such neural patternings.

It bears emphasizing again that the RCI model is only an example and that it operates at a relatively low level. The major point, for which the model stands as a key example, is that because of its recursive nature and its involvement in global mappings, reentry also permits exchanges of signals in higher-order brain areas. Various higher-order memory systems may be arranged similarly to the early perceptual systems described in the RCI model but obviously with different circuitry. Connection of early perceptual systems, such as those represented in the model, with these higher-order systems would be expected to generate not only groupings of responses of a similar type but also a variety of new integrative mechanisms.

I have illustrated some forms of reentrant signaling by means of a relatively restricted and somewhat artificial example. Whatever the limitations of this particular case, the ubiquity of reentry as a major means for coordination of neuronal group selection in the nervous system can hardly be overemphasized. According to the TNGS, the various forms of reentry are the central mechanisms involved in relating sensory to motor responses in global mappings (see figure 3.4).

At this early stage of the discussion, I am unable to illustrate the temporal properties of reentrant systems (see tables 4.1 and 4.2). But as will be described in chapter 7, in conjunction with the functions of certain cortical appendages (the cerebellum, hippocampus, and basal ganglia), the temporal ordering of reentry provides a main means of developing memory and coordinated motor responses. In systems such as those underlying speech, complex motor cues, sensorimotor coordination, and memory must all interact to yield phonological, syntactic, and semantic structures. Interaction among neural structures at all of these levels must yield a comprehensible output, just as the various visual signals illustrated here in the simulations yielded a coherent pattern. As we shall see in chapter 10, reentry provides a plausible means by which coordination of the perception and production of speech can be achieved.

Most important of all, consciousness itself is proposed to arise as a result of several different kinds of reentrant processes that are related to memory and ordered in time. We therefore have to consider in greater detail both memory and the neural means for ensuring temporal succession. But, at this point in the analysis, it is perhaps useful first to anticipate in summary form how various forms of consciousness may be related to these different processes.

5

Perceptual Experience and Consciousness

In this chapter and in the rest of this book, I explicitly attempt to extend the TNGS into areas related to consciousness, perceptual experience, attention, and thinking. My ultimate goal is to explore some of the human implications of such an extension and even to consider certain areas that are the proper province of philosophy. To some extent, therefore, the theory I finally elaborate here will be unlike its parent, in the sense that it is not as close to experimental test at the neural level. To be properly scientific, however, I will make every effort to warn the reader when I am frankly speculating.

I will first try to show that the TNGS provides the necessary basis for a model of consciousness. Then I will describe such a model of consciousness, but only in the most cursory way and only to provide a framework for the ensuing chapters. But before taking up these tasks, I want briefly to consider the adaptive significance of consciousness.

THE ADAPTIVE SIGNIFICANCE AND NEURAL FORERUNNERS OF CONSCIOUSNESS

Although consciousness is a process, we shall emphasize that it depends upon the particular organization of certain parts of the brain and not upon the whole brain.[1] Nevertheless, to ensure the workings of those

TABLE 5.1

Some Proposed Adaptive Functions of Consciousness

Provides explicit means for relating an individual to its acts and rewards (1°, HOC)

Helps in abstracting, organizing, and lending salience to complex changes in the environment marked by multiple parallel signals (1°, HOC)

Provides a coherent aid for attention in sequencing complex learning tasks and in correcting errors in automatized actions during changing conditions (some 1°, mostly HOC)

Allows long-range anticipation of events and their relation to the past by means of explicit connections to long-term memory (HOC)

Enhances adaptability by permitting planning or "modeling the world" free of real time (HOC)

Permits explicit comparisons of outcomes on the basis of individual values and previous choices (HOC)

Allows reorganization of memories and plans (HOC)

Necessary for linguistic communication (1°, HOC)

1° = primary consciousness
HOC = higher-order consciousness

brain parts upon which consciousness depends, the evolution and prior operation of other brain parts leading to particular kinds of behavior is almost certainly necessary. This subject is taken up at length in chapter 7.

What is the adaptive significance of consciousness[2] itself? As is summarized in table 5.1, both primary consciousness and higher-order consciousness provide means of freeing animal behavior from the tyranny of ongoing events. Without a means of developing a composite "image," relieved to some extent of the immediate flux and variation of signals, an animal would be at the mercy of simultaneous but disparate environmental happenings. In primary consciousness, relief is provided over short temporal intervals—a scene is constructed that involves ordering and succession of perceptual categorizations arising from different sensory modalities and inputs, and their cohesion in a given period of time. This process is also concerned with the relation of signals to the categorization of motor acts. Primary consciousness, as we shall see, permits an animal to regulate the salience of various parts of a stimulus complex in terms of its own individual adaptive needs and, above all, to guide its actions and behavior to reach particular goals.

In higher-order consciousness, the freedom is greater (table 5.1); the emergence of concepts and, later, of symbolism allows the use of memory to develop a coherent picture or an internal model of present, past, and future.[3] It seems likely that complex demands for recognition and action—whether to leap from one branch to another in complex foliage or to recognize a predator by successions of signals over some time period—provided a strong selective force for the evolutionary development of various neural systems that free an animal from the dominance of an immediate driven response.

What kind of systems might these be? The idea that I attempt to refine here is that consciousness is the result of an ongoing categorical comparison of the workings of two kinds of nervous organization. This comparison is based on a special kind of memory, and is related to the satisfaction of physiologically determined needs as that memory is brought up to date by the perceptual categorizations that emerge from ongoing present experience. Through behavior and particularly through learning, the continual interaction of this kind of memory with present perception results in consciousness.

To make this terse abstraction clear, I must describe what elements are *necessary* in order for consciousness to arise, considering the neural structures and functions that lead to these elements. Then I must discuss what additional neural organizations and processes are *sufficient* for consciousness to emerge from experience. I shall list the necessary elements first.[4] They include (1) the ability to carry out *perceptual categorization* on the basis of action and a sufficiently rich set of parallel sensory channels of different modalities, as described in the TNGS; (2) *memory* as a process of continual recategorization, a process that is associative; and (3) *learning,* or acquired context-dependent behavioral change that is based on categorizations governed by positive or negative adaptive value under conditions of expectancy. Learning involves relating perceptual categorization and memory to a definite set of values, linking an animal's past internal state to its present state. Learning must be related to evolved species-specific hedonic, consummatory, appetitive, and pain-avoiding behaviors that reflect ethologically determined values. Such value-dependent behaviors require the operation of specific portions of the nervous system that differ structurally and functionally from those carrying out perceptual categorization. These portions of the nervous system are the basis of the next fundamental requirement: (4) *self-nonself discrimination* by the nervous system as a function that is *biologically based or structurally inherent.* By this I mean that some parts of the nervous system and brain must have evolved to be dedicated mainly to adaptive, homeostatic, and endo-crine functions of the *individual* animal. These functions of the individual animal relate to its immediate needs for survival and reflect evolutionarily selected values that have contributed to fitness. They operate mainly through *interoceptive* neural and chemical signals, in contrast to other parts of the nervous system (such as the cerebral cortex), which are dedicated mainly to the categorization of *exteroceptive* signals arising mainly (but not exclusively) from the world.

These four elements necessary for any form of consciousness—perceptual categorization, memory, learning, and self-nonself discrimination—were all considered in the TNGS (see chapters 3 and 4 and *Neural Darwinism* for a review). But the idea that two parts of the nervous system differ radically in their evolution, organization, and function was not emphasized. A few qualifying remarks may therefore be in order.

In describing the contrast between these two different portions of the nervous system, I shall use the terms "self" and "nonself" in a strict biological sense,[5] not in the personal or psychological sense of "self-awareness," or in the social or philosophical sense of "personhood." In richly endowed nervous systems, these portions must be organized differently but also be in communication. While neural parts of the first kind (e.g., the hypothalamus, pituitary, various portions of the brain stem, amygdala, hippocampus, and limbic system) operate within developmentally given parameters, those of the second kind (e.g., cerebral cortex, thalamus, and cerebellum) operate largely through ongoing exteroceptive sensory interactions with the world, that is, through experience and behavior. The operation of the first set of neural regions is to a large extent ethologically fixed[6] or bounded by genetic constraints and is essential to define self within a species by assuring homeostatic regulation[7] in each individual. The second set operates mainly to define nonself, although, as we shall see, it also contributes by various interactions to the definition of self-boundaries. As we shall also see, the self portion exists to assure the persistent dominance of adaptive homeostasis. It is the discrimination between the self and the nonself portions of the nervous system mediated by the mechanisms leading to primary consciousness that leads to a means for assigning salience to some events over others in a complex scene.

All of these regions and brain functions can operate prior to and independently of consciousness. Their mechanisms and interactions were described by the TNGS in its constrained form in order to account mainly for perceptual categorization (see chapters 3 and 4). Can the theory be extended to account for perceptual experience and awareness as they serve to guide action?

To answer this question, we must consider the *sufficient* conditions for the emergence of primary consciousness. This will require a further description of memory as well as of those neural means (largely in the cerebellum, hippocampus, and basal ganglia) that together with the cortex allow the linkage of a *succession* of sensory and motor categorizations.[8] With such a description at hand, we must then show what interactions lead from perceptual *categorization* to perceptual *experience*—that activity allowing the value-category matching in terms of time or succession which eventually leads to consciousness.

Explicit models for the ordering of movement and sense are presented in succeeding chapters, and they are followed by a detailed description of a model for primary consciousness that depends on them. At this point, I intend only to provide a sketch of this model and to touch on its implications for language and various philosophical issues. This sketch will be elaborated greatly in later parts of the book, above all with descriptions and explicit diagrams representing its mechanisms and with specification of anatomical locations. Nevertheless, even without these details, it is useful to have an initial view of the proposed models of consciousness, particularly to justify the further extensive analysis of some of their neural substrates presented in the next several chapters. Note, at this point, that I shall not explicitly discuss matters of phenomenal experience or the relation between conscious and unconscious processes. These shall be taken up in later chapters.

A PREVIEW OF THE CONSCIOUSNESS MODEL

The main proposal is that primary consciousness arose as a result of two novel evolutionary events. (1) The first event led to the development of special memory repertoires composed of neuronal groups specifically dedicated to storing *past* matchings of value to perceptual categories. Value is generated by homeostatic adaptive brain systems. Perceptual categories are generated by sensorimotor systems (mainly cortical) that are devoted to categorization through motor behavior and sampling of external stimuli (see chapter 3). Most major learning occurs by way of such systems.[9] A necessary basis for the proposed special memory repertoires involves portions of the brain capable of concept formation,

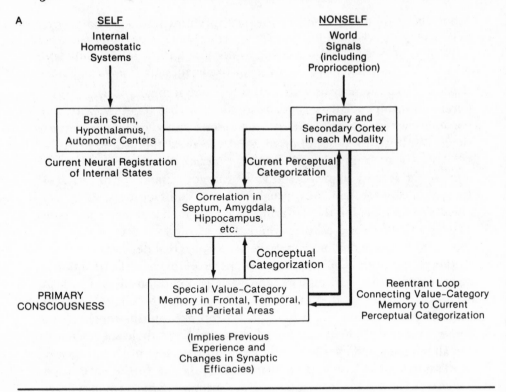

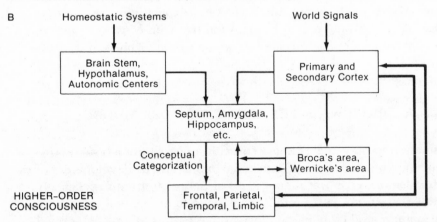

the ability to distinguish objects from actions, and categories from relations (we shall consider concepts in detail in chapter 8). (2) The second evolutionary event led to the development of new circuits allowing reentrant signaling between these special memory repertoires and those *currently* devoted to sensorimotor sampling of the environment for perceptual categorization. The operation of these circuits depends

Figure 5.1

A sketchy diagram indicating necessary and sufficient elements for the various forms of consciousness. A: *Primary consciousness requires (1) perceptual categorization by selective systems in primary and secondary cortices for each modality, (2) memory including sequential as well as temporally unitary elements, (3) learning, and (4) a biological self-nonself distinction. The sufficient elements in order for consciousness to appear are a conceptual system leading to a memory of past value-category associations and a reentrant pathway by which this memory can discriminate current perceptual categorizations (thick lines at right).* B: *Higher-order consciousness begins to emerge when a conceptual system can develop categories related to a concept of "self" (not just to self as a biological individual). It flowers when a linguistic system dependent on social interactions permits a rich semantic and syntactic memory for concepts, and when the conceptual categorizations of such a memory free the animal from categorization in real time only.*

upon the first event, that is, the prior evolution of a system of memory capable of relating value and perceptual category by conceptual means. The key circuits underlying primary consciousness contain particular reentrant pathways connecting this self-nonself memory system to primary and secondary repertoires carrying out perceptual categorization in all modalities—smell and taste, sight, hearing, touch, proprioception.

The extended TNGS proposes that the operation of such a system (figure 5.1) leads to the development of primary consciousness. Clearly, the memory repertoires allowing self-nonself distinctions are not themselves sufficient to give rise to primary consciousness. But imagine that the various memory repertoires dedicated to storage of the categorization of *past* matches of value to perceptual category are reentrantly connected to mapped classification couples dealing with *current* sensory input and motor response. By such means, the past correlations of category with value are now themselves interactive in real time with current perceptual categorizations *before* they are altered by the value-dependent portions of the nervous system. A kind of bootstrapping occurs in which current value-free perceptual categorization interacts with value-dominated memory before further contributing to alteration of that memory.

Primary consciousness thus emerges from a conceptually based recategorical memory (relating *previous* value-category sequences) as it interacts with current input categories arising from the neural systems dedicated to *present* value-free perceptual categorization. It constitutes a *discrimination* of the acquired self-nonself memory from current ongoing perceptual categorizations. This discrimination occurs in parallel across all perceptual modalities. It can alter the relative salience to the animal of particular events in the stimulus domain and help it choose goals and actions (see table 5.1).

In the absence of such mechanisms of primary consciousness, salience in a complex of signals would be determined almost entirely by the dominance of one external event over another in each parallel sensory channel, rather than by the adaptive values of the animal. Previous matchings of those values to categories within a special memory system linked to separate perceptual channels by reentry allow an animal with primary consciousness to direct attention to particular events in a selective fashion that serves its own adaptive needs.

CONNECTING VALUE TO CATEGORY BY REENTRY

By determining values, certain of the repertoires of neuronal groups necessary for consciousness constitute a basis for categorization of a self-nonself distinction. As I have already stressed, the notion of self should not be confused with personhood; as used here, the term refers to autonomic activities that sustain the survival of an individual. Self is fundamentally determined by the signaling activity of areas mediating homeostatic—autonomic, hedonic, neuroendocrine—brain functions. Such areas include brain stem and pontine nuclei, mesencephalic reticular formation, hypothalamus, amygdala, septum and fornix, and their various connections to prelimbic forebrain areas. In contrast, nonself signals are composed of corticothalamic inputs and of cerebellar and hippocampal loops other than those in the fornical path.

In the governance of behavior responsive to threat or deprivation, the major determinant of action and value is the evolutionarily prior set of neural structures that is devoted to homeostatic adaptation.[10] But later in evolution, defined cortical structures arose and added the ability to carry out perceptual categorization as described in the TNGS. As we have indicated, these two sets of structures are organized in very different ways. The emergence of the special memory repertoires devoted to the self-nonself distinction allowed both continual interaction and discrimination between these two sets of neural structures, which are completely different in both anatomy and function. The functioning of the memory repertoires depends upon connecting interoceptive signals (which are primary and relate to value but cannot be categorized in spatiotemporal detail) to those exteroceptive signals that can be categorized in great detail and that happen to be temporally correlated with these interoceptive signals. This results in a value-dominated memory system that associates sensorimotor perceptual categories with value states. When categorized behavior satisfies a value[11] (e.g., by bringing the system closer to set points in hedonic or endocrine systems), the interactions of self and nonself systems lead to altered synaptic efficacies in corticolimbic systems. Such changes provide one of the necessary bases for storage in the special memory, correlating value with category and discriminating self from nonself.

The value-dominated memory reflects on the operation of a conceptual system, that is, a system capable of relational categorization that depends on perceptual categorization but that far exceeds it in generalizing power. In chapter 8, we shall describe the kind of mapping necessary for such a system to function, as well as its loci in the brain. Briefly, we may say here that concept formation depends upon a special kind of connectivity in which the brain categorizes its own global mappings by type—those connected to objects, those concerned with motion, those concerned with hedonic states, and so on. In humans, the loci carrying out these conceptual distinctions (and thus also the special value-category memory functions) are assumed to be in the frontal, temporal, and parietal lobes and the cingulate gyri. Such a system would be inherently capable of classifying perceptual categorizations if it were suitably connected to their various neural sources in the different modalities. That connectivity is a reentrant one, and reentrant loops are the key to the establishment of primary consciousness. The functioning of such a system can determine the relative salience of external events according to internal value schemes. It affects the selection of goals and action patterns and therefore affects behavior.

We may now summarize both the necessary and the sufficient mechanisms and functions that must exist for primary consciousness to arise. This list may be compared with that on page 93, in which only the necessary conditions are listed in a different order. (It is important to note that this list does not account for higher-order aspects of human consciousness.) The mechanisms and functions include (1) neuronal group selection leading to perceptual categorization and memory; (2) a self-nonself distinction reflecting values *already given as part of the phenotype* by the evolutionary emergence of the brain-stem, endocrine, and limbic systems mediating adaptive homeostasis; (3) a cortical–hippocampal–basal ganglia system for categorization of successive events and for concept formation; and (4) an ongoing interaction between the two systems in items 2 and 3, leading to a conceptually based special memory system for value matched to past categories (the neuronal loci of this system will be more fully described later). Learning contributes to this part of the "consciousness loop," and much of this memory system is in fact devoted to learning. The resemblance to the model of learning described in *Neural Darwinism* is not fortuitous. Of utmost significance is (5) a set of reentrant connections between this special memory system and the cortical systems dedicated to present perceptual categorization. The functioning of these key reentrant connections provides the sufficient conditions for the appearance of primary consciousness. As will be described in chapter 9, the cortico-thalamic system and reticular nucleus of the thalamus as well as the pulvinar and the long corticocortical connections are candidate structures for mediation of this critically important reentry.

In the view sketched here, primary consciousness is a process dependent upon the ongoing operation and interaction of a very specific set of brain structures whose functioning requires continuing behavior and a means of ordering temporal successions of events. It is the task of the extended theory to describe the pattern and function of these brain structures in detail, a task to which the remainder of this book is devoted.

PROPERTIES AND TESTS

To the degree that this abstract précis of a model of primary consciousness is correct, it corresponds well with James's notions:[12] it is a process that is "personal" (i.e., related to the biological self) and that is constantly changing (because it is based on inner homeostatic states and on dynamic global mappings); it is continuous (as all reentrant systems leading to categorization must be); it is intentional and concerned with objects independent of itself (i.e., it is based on constant reentry with ongoing perceptual categorization, which itself depends on things); finally, it is selective (as are the perceptual categorizations and the operation of the value systems on which it depends). It depends on volition, inasmuch as it depends on global mappings that involve categorization for actions related to goals, not just the movement of body parts. Through consciousness so defined, memory can affect behavior. And yet, because various systems of memory, categorization, learning, and pattern formation can be embodied in global mappings *separate* from the particular comparisons proposed here to be involved in consciousness, many brain functions of a high order may proceed without it.[13]

The interesting question is what brain functions can proceed only because of it. We shall consider some plausible answers to this question when we take up the actual brain structures that must have evolved to subserve consciousness as well as the crucial issue of scientifically acceptable tests of this proposed model of consciousness. In the meanwhile, the entries in table 5.1 should serve as a reasonable initial list.

The proposed model escapes the homuncular paradox or fallacy[14] for a number of reasons. It rests on an *inherent* (evolutionarily determined) difference in the structures and the functions of the homeostatic nervous system and the perceptual nervous system. The homeostatic system is prior, does not depend upon categorization for its physiological function, and is dominant. Unlike the perceptual nervous system, it is not rich in topographic mappings and its states are only indirectly accessible—they are one of the essential bases of primary consciousness but do not provide its main content. Finally, the primary consciousness model involves a discriminative bootstrapping—the self-nonself memory must be built of *previous* perceptual categorizations by a conceptual system. Only after a considerable amount of experience accumulates can detailed conceptual discrimination of current perceptual categorizations occur.[15]

This complex of mechanisms and functions possesses a number of interesting properties. It relies on a matching of hedonic states to conceptual categories and is thus related to learning. It requires a continual recategorization of these matches in time. But notice that, because of anatomical and functional differences, the discrimination of hedonic states and interoceptive signals has available a much less extensive and fine-grained set of categories than does current value-free perceptual categorization. Indeed, the correlations of categories to hedonic states and value depend upon a many-one relation—the categories from without (including those for proprioception) far exceed in variety and changeability those from within.[16] The generation of a "mental image" (which as we shall see is not at all an actual image in the pictorial sense) emerges as a result of a series of such correlations. That image depends on the reentrant connection of the special value-category memory to cortical systems carrying out perceptual categorizations that have not yet entered that memory or altered the limbic system (although they may do so at later times under particular conditions).

Primary consciousness may thus be briefly described as the result of the ongoing discrimination of present perceptual categorizations by a value-dominated self-nonself memory. Inasmuch as such a memory is built by relating previous perceptual categorizations to values, primary consciousness is accomplished by continual bootstrapping of current perceptual states into memory states. Current perceptual events are recategorized in terms of past value-category matches. It is the *contrast* of the special linkage of value and past categories with currently arriving categories, and the *dominance* of the self-related special memory systems in this memorial linkage, that generate the self-referential aspect of consciousness. Multiple parallel inputs from different modalities are correlated in this fashion, and their salience is altered mainly from within, depending upon previous value-category matches.

We may test the consistency of this consciousness model by asking what it would take to prevent the appearance of primary consciousness or to make it disappear. If no comparison took place between value and past categorizations to form a special memory, consciousness would not appear. This is because the initial contrasting condition between this memory match and present categorical input could not *discriminate* between the "self pattern," arising from ethologically determined systems and expressed as a form of memory, and the present value-free "perceptual pattern," arising from continual sampling of stimuli in the world.

Alternatively, if external stimuli (including some from within the body, such as proprioceptive input) were completely removed, primary consciousness could not appear. Under these conditions, an existing consciousness would be severely affected but might not disappear entirely.[17] This is so because it is impossible to remove all exteroceptive input *over a long enough period* to prevent value-category matches from being stored. Moreover, past value-category matches can interact with perceptual areas mediating imagery. If most current perceptual categorization were to cease (as in sensory deprivation), one would expect consciousness to continue (although its organization would be increasingly jeopardized),[18] depending on the degree of past storage related to value-category matches. On the other hand, if it were possible to interfere specifically with certain reentrant pathways proceeding via the thalamus (if these are indeed among the key routes of reentry; see chapter 9), then primary consciousness would be lost. As we shall discuss in chapter 13, the loss can be domain-specific, dependent on the lesion.

HIGHER-ORDER CONSCIOUSNESS

So far, I have been considering primary consciousness. An animal possessing this early form of consciousness generates a "mental image," or a discriminative correlation that is determined largely by immediate multimodal perceptual categorization but that is nonetheless still largely dependent upon the succession of events in real time. What about the processes required for higher-order consciousness? Here I can only adumbrate some of the analyses set forth in later chapters. Anticipating those discussions, I suggest that, in humans, there is one function the *development of which is required* for the emergence of *most (but not all) forms* of higher-order consciousness and that in turn *absolutely requires primary consciousness.* That function is language, a uniquely human activity in its full symbolic and syntactic manifestations, but one foreshadowed in higher primates such as chimpanzees.[19]

In both species, higher-order consciousness requires the ability not only to form concepts but also to think.[20] It is simply inconceivable that *symbolic* linguistic function with social transmission could be transacted among unconscious humans (at least in the sense of *first* learning to carry out such transmissions). As I shall attempt to show in a later chapter dedicated to the subject, this statement is equivalent to the idea that development of a rich syntax and grammar is inconceivable without the ability to produce *concepts and primary consciousness,* on both of which a subject-predicate relation will ultimately be based.

A model of concepts will be described in chapter 8. This model is based on the categorization by the brain of its own states, particularly those represented by global mappings. The earliest basis for subject-predicate relations is an emerging consciousness of the distinction between *categories* related to the "self" (now using the term in the sense of "personhood")[21] and those related to entities classifiable as "nonself," whether similar (as other humans are) or dissimilar (as all else is). With this ability, we may consider that the beginnings of higher-order consciousness are in place, as may be observed, for example, in chimpanzees. But only with the appearance of true language in a social context can this form of consciousness fully flourish (figure 5.1, *B*).

I shall suggest in chapter 10 that the emergence of true language depended upon the previous evolution of brain centers dedicated to concepts and allowing production of a *model* of the self-nonself distinction that is based on action and that is prior to speech. The concurrent emergence of the vocal tract and brain centers for speech,[22] such as Broca's and Wernicke's areas, facilitated the development of this model of a conscious self acting on things, a model that would be extended enormously during the evolution of hominids.

The key element in this proposal is that the bases for the emergence of meanings, if not all the other components of a grammar, are already epigenetically potential in the sense that, before language, the brain had already evolved areas that carried out extensive concept formation. The evolutionary emergence in hominids of phonological capabilities and of specialized brain areas (including Broca's and Wernicke's areas) permitted semantic bootstrapping and creation of syntactic ordering.[23] The connection of phonology, syntax, and semantics by specialized reentrant memories and their ongoing relation to the areas of the brain responsible for concepts gave rise in hominids to language. With speech, a symbolic means of remembering and altering concepts arose that not only could label these concepts but also could be altered by them in turn.

Without primary consciousness and the subsequent evolution of a model of subject-predicate relations by reentrant interaction of "language areas" with those brain areas subserving conceptual categories, true symbolic language and higher-order consciousness could not be fully realized. When higher-order consciousness was so realized, however, it freed animals from an obligatory dependence upon the succession of events in real time. Such a development must have greatly facilitated planning, which requires the making of distinctions between past, present, and future acts (table 5.1).

At this point, it is important to stress that because human beings have higher-order consciousness, they cannot subjectively experience or reconstruct primary consciousness without the intrusion of some additional components of direct awareness and higher-order consciousness. Perhaps the closest human model of primary consciousness is that possessed by the right brain of certain left-dominant individuals with split-brain surgery.[24] Even in these cases, however, the comparison with primary consciousness is compromised by the previously connected state of the right hemisphere. With higher-order consciousness, however, direct awareness[25] is possible; the left hemisphere of such an individual can, in contrast to the right, mediate such awareness.

This chapter has sought to outline the ideas fundamental to and sufficient for a neuronally based model of consciousness, to list some of the brain structures and functions required for primary and higher-order consciousness, and to show their necessary bases in the TNGS. One of the capabilities essential to the emergence of consciousness is that of recategorical memory; equally important is the capability of temporal ordering and succession. It is on these properties that the continual temporal correlation of inner states and the categorization of outer objects rest. Indeed, metaphorically, one might say that the previous memories and current activities of the brain interact to yield primary consciousness as a form of "remembered present." We shall turn in the next several chapters to the neural structures and functions that are essential for these temporal properties.

PART THREE

MEMORY, ORDERING,
AND CONCEPTS

6

Memory as Recategorization

Given the idea that primary consciousness depends upon a particular memory system (one that connects past categorized values related to adaptive internal states with current categorizations based on exteroceptive signals), it is important to distinguish among various forms and systems of memory.[1] If our viewpoint is correct, consciousness could not exist without memory. But one must keep in mind that the word "memory" has been applied to molecular events, learning events, modality-specific phenomena, and linguistically based abilities. The term "memory" has been employed in so many contexts that it almost loses operational significance. Our task here is not to review or criticize these uses but rather to point out a use fundamental to the TNGS. In this chapter, I will restrict the term to apply to a specific dynamic process that relates memory to structures conferring the ability to categorize. This process is mediated by synaptic change and is not a separate faculty. It is a system property reflecting the structure of the neural system in which the synaptic change occurs.

Whatever its form, memory cannot, I suggested in *Neural Darwinism,* be strictly identified with the short- and long-term changes in synaptic efficacy that together provide its basis. Nor, I argued, can it be identified as a form of precise replicative store based on information from without, as in a computer. Instead, I suggested that, in rich nervous systems, memory is the specific enhancement of a previously established ability to categorize. This ability is procedural, and it emerges from the continual dynamic changes in synaptic populations and global mappings that allowed a particular categorization to occur in the first place. Memory thus arises from alterations of synaptic efficacies in global mappings as a result of the facilitation of particular categorizations or of motor patterns.

GENERALIZATION AND RECATEGORIZATION

We saw in chapter 3 that simulated recognition automata based on the theory of neuronal group selection (such as Darwin II and Darwin III), each comprising systems of classification couples and global mappings, can operate to categorize objects without a prior description or a program. As a result of their interactions with a signal-producing environment, these automata alter their synaptic efficacies and can classify, associate, and generalize at least in a limited fashion. Their performance shows how a dynamic recategorical memory can operate and demonstrates some of the categorizing capabilities of classification couples.

According to the TNGS, categorization of objects and events is relative, depending on cues, context, and salience. Categories are not immutable but can be altered by the current state of an animal. Indeed, one of the most extraordinary properties of animals capable of perceptual categorization is their ability to generalize: after encounter with a few instances of a category under learning conditions, they can recognize a great number of related but novel instances. When changes in synaptic efficacy occur in neural systems such as classification couples (see figure 3.3), they allow the possibility of further refinement or alteration of perceptual categorization. This leads to a form of nonreplicative memory that depends on the dynamics of such associative and degenerate networks. Calling up outputs that were originally the result of a categorization can be facilitated by the action of such a dynamic memory. Moreover, both the accrued associations and the context dependence of this kind of memory can lead to a greater variety of responses and a more rapid recall.

It is important to understand what is meant by calling such a memory "recategorical." This term does not mean the recall of a particular categorical response only in the form it had when it first occurred (although this is not ruled out as a possibility). Recall, under the influence of constantly changing contexts, changes the structure and dynamics of the neural populations that were involved in the original categorization. Recall is the activation of previously facilitated portions of particular global mappings. Such recall can result in a *response* similar to a previously given response ("a memory"), but generally it is one that has been altered or enriched by ongoing changes.

To sum up, recategorical memory is a process involving facilitated pathways, not a fixed replica or code. It is metastable and subject to change. More than one facilitated pathway is involved, and even though a particular set of pathways is subject to change, some subset can yield an output similar to that instituted by an initial categorical response. Of course, to assure a memory at all, the synaptic changes leading to such facilitated paths had to be affected as a result of an earlier categorical process, and their outputs have potentially to be recallable at some subsequent time.

Although a memory so defined is associative and inexact (as a computer's replicative store is not), it is at the same time capable of remarkable degrees of generalization. Such a memory is first engaged through motor acts, and it depends upon them; only later in evolution, with the development of higher-order consciousness, can it lose some of that dependency. The exercise of memory involves continual neuronal activity or firings, and in simple nervous systems such activity is usually associated with behavior via fairly direct (even if multisynaptic) paths. The properties of association, inexactness, and generalization in richer nervous systems derive from the fact that perceptual categorization, the basis of memory, is a probabilistic process, although occasionally it may be exemplary in nature.[2]

Perceptual categorization itself depends upon the continual motor activity that drives neuronal group selection in global mappings. *Neural Darwinism* suggests that this form of selection arose mainly from disjunctive parallel samplings of the world of objects and events by multiple sensory sheets driven through motion. By means of reentrant signaling, different maps separately receiving signals for features or for correlations of features could be connected in time, space, and neural properties and be altered as a result of correlated synaptic changes.

In this manner, the selection of neuronal groups in one map can be coupled to the selection of neuronal groups in another, yielding a classification couple (see figure 3.3). As a result of reentry, new properties and combinations of properties can emerge. Arrays of such classification couples or n-tuples provide the basis for the global mappings that relate sensory input continually to the sampling of signals from the world by means of motor activity (see figure 3.4 for an example). As I have already stressed, a global mapping is the smallest dynamic unit capable of rich perceptual categorization; in chapter 8, we shall see that the formation of concepts is deeply dependent upon distinctions *between* various forms of these mappings.

Alterations of the synaptic strengths of some of the neural components[3] of a global mapping provide the biochemical basis for the procedural memory related to categorization. According to the TNGS, such a memory can be adaptively linked by learning to previous categorizations that were related to the satisfaction of value-ridden aspects of behavior. The activities of hedonic centers and various responses to nociceptive signals provide the basis for the values that, together with memory, result either in unchanged behavior or in an alteration of behavior that leads to learning. As is discussed in *Neural Darwinism,* a change in the direction of learning is very often based on elements of novelty or surprise.[4] Just as perceptual categorization provides the generalizable recognition required for the initiation of learning, so ongoing recategorical changes based on synaptic alterations provide the memory required for its consolidation.

In this view, perceptual categorization, learning, and memory are indissolubly linked, and their operation in general engages the activity of large parts of the nervous system and the motor-sensory ensemble. Through rehearsal, memory results in an enhanced ability to categorize. But because of continually changing inputs with new associations in different contexts, and because of the degeneracy of neuronal group selection, a given categorical response may be achieved in a variety of ways. It is for this reason that one can consider memory a form of recategorization[5]—in various instances of recall, a memory almost never appears completely unchanged.

THE PROBLEM OF ORDERING

Neither the original theory nor simulated recognition automata deal in satisfactory detail with the successive ordering of events in time mediated by the several major brain components that contribute to memory, particularly as it relates to consciousness. The remainder of this chapter considers some properties of these orderings, and the next chapter describes the components responsible for them. Such components must exist to mediate the successive orderings of movements or of memories of events either in short-term sequences or in long-term patterns. The continuous nature of consciousness depends to a great extent upon these orderings.[6]

A review of the neural structures of the thalamus and cortex, which, together with sensorimotor ensembles, form the basis of classification couples, gives no hint how either short-term sequencing of categorizations or their placement into long-term orders might take place. Whatever the role of the thalamus or cortex, other structures are likely to be involved in this ordering process, which is critical for the understanding of consciousness.

What are these structures? I pointed out in *Neural Darwinism* that, prior to the establishment of motor memory, certain aspects of the ordering of smooth sequences of rapid motions depend upon the action of the cerebellum. The book also outlines how the ensuing perceptual categorizations might be linked to ordering in short-term memory by the action of the hippocampus. Moreover, it notes that the basal ganglia are likely to be involved in the sequencing of motor programs. Its descriptions of the functions of these regions are cursory, however, and it does not try to relate them in detail to perceptual *experience*. In the next chapter, we shall provide a more extensive description of models of each of these areas, related respectively to smooth succession in motion, to ordering of perceptual events, and to movement sequences and choice. These models of what I shall call cortical appendages or organs of succession will provide us with the substrates necessary to connecting spatial patterning with temporal change. It is such substrates that make both coordinated action and the flow of consciousness possible.

In preparation for these models, it may be useful to distinguish here between motion-dependent categorization, short-term memory, and long-term recall, all of which are separate components of the ordering problem. In discussing them, I shall emphasize the succession of events; necessarily, this involves notions of time. At this juncture, however, I will not be very precise about temporal matters, distinguishing succession and ordering only within grossly different time frames—seconds, minutes, hours, lifetimes.

The essentiality of smooth movements for perceptual categorization is discussed at length in *Neural Darwinism*. The animal's own speed of movement defines a relatively short time frame. This movement is also the basis of all other means of determining succession in the central nervous system.[7] It provides the main means of feature correlation, of the sampling of signals in varying contexts, and of alteration and refinement of global mappings. When it occurs in actions, movement is not arbitrary but is in fact itself the result of categorizations yielding patterns or synergies. Furthermore, certain sequences are *imposed* upon movements by phenotypic structural characteristics, for example, the succession of joint movements in walking or reaching.[8] The combination of the successive components of various actions obeys certain physical constraints; as we shall propose in the next chapter, this combination also depends to some extent upon cerebellar and basal ganglion activity.

Although the successive character of movements is important in establishing certain perceptual categorizations and is thus essential to the initiation of all forms of memory, it is not a direct element in short-term memory. This is so because short-term memory involves the succession of *sequences of events* over longer time periods than those of any usually executed movement. Its occurrence presumes that a series of categorizations have been made and linked in a certain order, and it therefore requires the activity of classification couples. It also requires a means of linking those combinations in a global mapping of classification couples that actually were active during a particular time period and in the successive order in which they were activated by real events. Only through such linkages can a global mapping (see figure 3.4) be stabilized over time.

All of these considerations suggest that several conditions have to be met in order for an effective short-term memory to be realized: (1) perceptual categorization has to have taken place; (2) the actual order of events or objects in general has to be reflected in a similar order of linkage of categorization events; and (3) the time over which this linkage operates must, in general, be greater than that represented by a simple movement used in any particular constituent categorization.

There must exist a neural means of linking (at least temporarily) a *series* of categorizations effected by a global mapping or by separate global mappings. It is highly unlikely that such a serially ordered linkage could be formed either early within any one of the local maps that contribute to a global mapping or in the cortex alone, particularly given the highly parallel nature of cortical operation and structure.

What seems to be required is a neural structure serially linked to the various cortical components that are themselves reentrantly connected in classification couples. If, after perceptual categorization driven by real-world objects and events initially occurred, the operation of various classification couples could be linked in serial order and their linkage maintained for a certain time by synaptic change, a form of categorical short-term memory would become feasible. I shall suggest in the next chapter that this function of assuring ordered linkage of high-order cortical classification couples and n-tuples, reflecting a memory for succession in real time, is carried out by the hippocampus, which may be considered one of the essential cortical appendages dedicated to temporal succession.

In stabilizing components of global mappings, the activity of the hippocampus alters the nature of categorizations by linking an actual succession of categorized signals over time periods longer than those of the individual completed movements of an animal and its parts. Such an associative yet time-dependent serial linkage certainly would confer an evolutionary advantage: those animals possessing this short-term memory would be freed from the strict domination of immediate categorizations that depend on exterior movements. Without short-term memory, these categorizations would shift, one to the other, in an unconnected manner within very short time frames. Animals capable of short-term memory, however, would avoid this unconnected sequence, permitting them constantly to be involved in rich recategorizations, as various signals shift and times elapse that are longer than that of the decay of immediate neuronal activations.

The functioning of such a short-term memory must rely in part on the connectedness of background events in space as well as on the general relations of objects moving in near space. This cannot be true of long-term memory, which, although dependent for its *initiation* on the mechanisms of short-term memory, must have a different mechanism. A key proposal of the TNGS is that, as a result of a sufficient amount of reentrant activity from the hippocampus back to the cerebral cortex, *secondary* synaptic changes occur in the cortex that relate some of the same neuronal groups that were involved in a given short-term memory. By this means, the associative interaction of such groups in higher-order classification n-tuples would correlate their activity to characteristics of the complex of features, objects, and events of the kind that promoted the original group activity. Unlike the mechanisms underlying short-term memory, however, the changes leading to long-term memory would not *serially* connect the activity of such groups, a function for which the cortex itself appears ill-suited.

We conclude that, to achieve ordering in long-term memory, some conventional means must exist not only of relating its categories to the sequences and repetitions of short-term memory but *also of distinguishing present from past*. As we shall discuss in later chapters, the first of these requirements is met by primary consciousness, in which there is a temporal lag between the interaction of past value-category relations and current exteroceptive categorization. The second of these requirements, however, requires conceptual and symbolic mechanisms provided only by the structures underlying higher-order consciousness. It is important to recognize that such symbolic mechanisms are required *not* for long-term *storage* itself but only for the ability to order events in recollection. Long-term memory of learned responses can itself alter an animal's behavior without the intervention of consciousness.

In addition to conceptual mechanisms (to be discussed in chapter 8), the cortex must control its sequences of output. Is there any evidence that particular neurons are actually involved in ordering events? There is certainly evidence of conditioned readiness to respond by neurons in a variety of areas (table 6.1). The ability to establish and maintain anatomically restricted and complexly interconnected groups of neurons in various regions that are responsive to moment-to-moment sensory input may underlie the performance of activity in a serial order. It provides a mechanism whereby the cortex can antici-pate or prepare for the consequences of its own activity so that the next step in a series can begin at the appropriate moment. For exam-ple, in a grasping motion in the dark, the arm moves forward until tactile stimuli signal the closure of the fist. The role of a system of this sort for controlling attention is described in greater detail in chapter 12, and the contributions of cortical appendages are considered in the next chapter. Analogous mechanisms might similarly play an essential role in controlling the serial or sequential order of even more com-plex mental activity, such as that which provides the basis for speak-ing and reasoning.

Sustained periods of enhanced firing rates of individual neurons (spike trains) have been observed by neurophysiologists in almost every cortical area investigated, as well as in many subcortical locations in which neurons may be driven by cortical input (table 6.1). The period of firing of many of these cells has been found to correlate with the timing of environmental signals or with the behavior of the animal, and hence such cells are thought to have functional significance. The ease with which these neurons are found indicates that they represent a high percentage of the cells in the cortical area explored, and this is sup-ported by studies designed to observe oscillatory or sustained high activity in large neuronal populations (e.g., analysis of EEGs, glucose metabolism, and PET scans).

The previous discussion suggests that, while short- and long-term memories both involve recategorization, they have completely differ-ent ordering mechanisms. Both depend upon neuronal group selection within global mappings and upon synaptic changes in populations of

TABLE 6.1

Sites of Neurons Showing Conditioned Readiness to Respond
(Sustained Enhanced Unit Activity in Anticipation of Future Events)

Anatomical Area	Reference
Motor cortex	Tanji & Evarts (1976)
Prefrontal cortex	Fuster (1973)
Visual cortex	Haenny, Maunsell, & Schiller (1988)
Frontal eye fields	Bruce & Goldberg (1985)
Parietal cortex	Mountcastle (1978)
Temporal cortex	Miyashita & Chang (1988)
Cingulate cortex	Niki & Watanabe (1979)
Somatosensory cortex	Chapman, Spidalieri, & Lamarre (1984)
Basal ganglia	Hikosaka & Sakamoto (1986)
Hypothalamus	Rolls, Burton, & Mora (1976)
Colliculus	Hikosaka & Wurtz (1983)
Dentate nucleus	Chapman, Spidalieri, & Lamarre (1986)

neurons. As I have discussed elsewhere,[9] these synaptic changes are of two different types that differ in the time scale of their stability. Short- and long-term memory must not be simply identified with these types of synaptic changes. The ordering of short-term memory depends upon real-time events as reflected in the input and output of the hippocampus and its associated cortical structures. Long-term memory may involve many of the same *neuronal groups* in cortex as short-term memory, connected after frequent rehearsal by strengthening of synapses in secondary pathways, but its ordering requires a present-past distinction that is dependent upon the structures that lead not only to primary consciousness but also in humans to higher-order consciousness.

In sum, the view of memory taken here is in sharp contrast to the notion that a strict storage of coded information must be precisely replicated or "read out" in memorial events.[10] Instead, it is proposed that memory is procedural and that it is dynamically based on increasingly facilitated mechanisms of categorization within global mappings. This categorization is associative and continual, and it involves constant revision based on action and behavior. This accords well with the idea that short- and long-term memories are not just versions of the same storage of information with different modes of access.[11] Rather, short-term memory is determined by categorization linked in real-time sequences through hippocampal-cortical activity. Long-term memory requires such activity in order to be established, but once established, it is ordered through other means, mainly structures in the cortex that are closely related to those necessary for the development of higher-order consciousness.

I have not dwelt on the fact that the notion of memory as recategorization necessarily implies the presence of many different kinds of memory.[12] This is because memory is a system property and many different neural systems can undergo synaptic change and thus alter their contributions to global mappings. Given that this is so, it is perhaps not surprising that the word "memory" is used in so many different contexts ("motor memory," "semantic memory," "episodic memory," etc.). These terms apply to particular manifestations of the underlying dynamic process involving global mappings. We have already seen that primary consciousness itself requires a memory of value-category successions related to fundamental homeostatic needs. Similarly, we shall see that the development of concepts requires another kind of memory and that language requires still other interactive memory systems for phonology and syntax. One of the major tasks of the complex neural systems underlying consciousness is to *coordinate* the different forms of memory originating in different systems in order to mediate effective action (see table 5.1).

The discussion of memory as recategorization in this chapter has not provided detailed models for smooth motion and its sequencing, both of which are assumed to be necessary for the connection of perceptual categories to serial events. Specific models are also necessary to meet the requirements that space and time be correlated both in memory and in consciousness and that, in carrying out complex actions, specific choices of output follow upon correlations of input. In the next chapter, we will present such models in the course of describing the structure and proposed mechanisms of action of three main temporal cortical appendages important for temporal succession—the cerebellum, the hippocampus, and the basal ganglia. These models were touched on in *Neural Darwinism* but not developed. Because of their central importance to models of consciousness, that deficiency will be repaired here. An adequate description is perforce technical. Those readers who wish to skip the details on a first reading may consult the chapter introduction and the summary of each of the three models before proceeding to the description of concept formation in the next chapter.

7

Time and Space:
Cortical Appendages and
Organs of Succession

One of the most striking features of consciousness is its continuity. Insofar as we shall be espousing the thesis that consciousness depends upon a particular kind of memory and that, in general, memory consists of various forms of recategorization, it is important to inquire how both the *continuity* of perceptual categories and their succession in time can arise even prior to consciousness itself. As was noted in the preceding chapter, we must distinguish succession in real time and succession in the recollected past. The latter depends upon the former and is considered in later chapters. Here, I wish to discuss the origins of succession in real time and describe those parts of the brain concerned with ensuring that succession can be related to significant neural events and, above all, to action. Many of these events are necessary for consciousness to be established but do not contribute directly to it.

The origin of succession in stimuli is clearly motion in space, either of external signals relative to an animal's receptor sheets, or of the whole animal or its parts that bear those sheets.[1] The perceptual categorizations of motion depend very much upon the succession of joint and muscle responses and of gestures that are, in general, themselves smoothly linked and successive.[2] Similarly, the relation of perceptual categorization to short-term memory is also largely a matter of succession of these categorizations or of their features within a certain period of time.

Where is each of these successions, motor and perceptual, handled functionally in the brain? Are there organs of succession? A structural and functional analysis of the cerebral cortex does not support the view that it is a primary organ of succession. Neither the electrical activity nor the parallelism of the cortical sheet is particularly consistent with the support of intrinsic, continually repetitive, serial activity.[3] More likely, it is the interaction of the cortex with certain cortical appendages that yields such activity. Through its topographic maps, the interactive cortex would then provide the necessary relations between time and space.

I consider here models for three of these appendages—the cerebellum, the hippocampus, and the basal ganglia—whose functions are required to account for the unconscious coordination of succession as well as for the continuity of consciousness itself. All of these models contain some speculative components, but each is based on known properties of the respective anatomical areas. The model of the cerebellum relates to the smoothness of motor succession and its singular importance in perceptual categorization. The model of the hippocampus provides an essential part of the successive linkage of perceptual categorizations necessary for perceptual experience itself—particularly that related to short-term memory. The model of the basal ganglia pertains to successive linkages involved in motor planning, choice, and complex acts. Roughly speaking, these successions range from seconds for the cerebellum to tens of seconds or minutes for the hippocampus and basal ganglia. Presumably, still longer successions are handled in the cortex with the aid of one or more of these appendages.

Succession and Smooth Motion: The Cerebellum

To present a model purporting to explain how properties of succession in various movements relate to perceptual categorization, I must review certain aspects of movement that are discussed at greater length in *Neural Darwinism*. First, it is important to stress that the brain deals mainly with *patterns* of movement, more specifically with gestures.[4] A gesture is one of the degenerate sets of all those coordinated movements that produce a particular pattern. A closely related notion is that of a synergy—a class of related gestures. According to the TNGS, perceptual categorization depends upon the metastable neural structures of global mappings that relate gestural movements to sensory signals. Such global mappings are dynamic systems consisting of multiple reentrant local maps that correlate sensory input with motor activity, interacting with nonmapped regions to yield categorizations of objects and events (see figure 3.4). Motor activity as reflected in global mappings leads to the production of synergies,[5] which are essential elements in categorizing certain kinds of sensory input as well as in categorizing movement itself. The result of the combined activities of synergies and tactile and visuomotor coordination is the selection of neuronal groups in such a way as to correlate and link the synergies and their transitions, one to the other.

Because, in forming synergies, sensory sheets are moved in real time, their linkage is a source of feature *correlation* and not just of feature *detection.* In this correlation, the cerebral cortex relates the neuronal groups receiving proprioceptive input from musculotendinous receptors to groups receiving visual and tactile inputs, principally in the parietal cortex.[6] In addition, it correlates the activities of such groups with those representing the combined effects of gestures in regions like frontal motor fields and basal ganglia. But, as I have already indicated, in none of these regions is there a hint of anatomical structures that might smoothly coordinate the sensorimotor components of a synergy in short periods of real time in a feed-forward fashion.

The idea I want to explore here is not new. It is that the provision of this temporal coordination is the main role of the cerebellum,[7] which *together* with the motor cortex (and the spinal cord), contributes to global mappings that allow registration, linkage, and smooth succession of movements. Such a succession is a critical part of the categorization of motion, particularly in novel tasks and situations. It is also an essential part of the workings of the classification n-tuples dedicated to the categorization of gestures themselves.

As is shown in figure 7.1, the cerebellum has a number of remarkable features:

1. It is a highly regular and repetitious structure, the fundamental input and output circuits of which are known.
2. It receives two main sets of inputs, each of which is served by many regions of the neuraxis.
3. It has only one main kind of output cell, the Purkinje cell, the output of

which is inhibitory and which connects to the deep cerebellar nuclei that in turn connect to the cerebral cortex as well as to the spinal cord.

4. It shows a peculiar fractured somatotopy[8] of its sensory inputs from mossy fibers and a zonal arrangement[9] of its second system of climbing fiber inputs. Traversing the regions of fractured somatotopy are long, parallel fibers of the granule cells that are served by mossy fiber inputs.

These features and the evidence that the cerebellum is not absolutely required for the *initiation* of motion suggest that it has a very specific role in timing and reflex gain control during the production of successions of movements, and a role together with the cortex in determining the ordering of outputs to muscles. For such a task, it must clearly have a very large sensory input, and both anatomical and physiological evidence suggests that this is so. Mossy fiber inputs come from spinal cord tracts serving somatosensory roles as well as from vestibular nuclei and the pons. Climbing fiber inputs arising in the inferior olive are in turn related to olivary inputs from the spinothalamic tracts, the dorsal col-

Figure 7.1

Simplified diagram of basic features of the macroscopic and microscopic anatomy of the cerebellum. A: Relations of the cerebellum and brain-stem areas with the cerebral cortex. Multiple cortical areas (including motor, premotor, somatosensory, parietal, and frontal areas) project to the pontine nuclei, terminating in a columnar fashion. Pontine neurons (PONS) give rise to a large mossy fiber projection to the cerebellar cortex, terminating in the granular cell layer (GR). Granule cells send parallel fibers to synapse with many Purkinje cells (PK). Motor cortical, brain-stem, and spinal afferents reach the olivary nuclear complex (IO), which in turn emits climbing fibers to the Purkinje cells. Local excitatory and inhibitory connections within the cerebellar cortex are indicated and described in more detail in B and C. Purkinje cells send out inhibitory axons that reach the deep cerebellar nuclei (CN) and form a termination pattern reminiscent of a columnar or group-like arrangement. Neuronal signals are then transmitted back to the motor cortex via a thalamic nucleus. B: Fine details of the microscopic anatomy of the cerebellar cortex. Emphasis is placed on the geometrical relations between afferents and intrinsic circuits. The topography of the climbing fiber projection results in a subdivision of the cerebellar cortex into sagittal microzones that are oriented orthogonal to the major direction of the parallel fibers of granule cells. The granule cell layer itself appears to be organized in two overlying and rather different mosaics. C: Climbing fiber microzones run orthogonal to parallel fibers and bear no apparent geometrical relation to the fractured somatotopy of the granule cell layer, suggesting that their function involves combinatorially rich interactions with multiple somatotopic regions. Additional abbreviations: BS = basket cell; GO = golgi cells; NR = red nucleus; TH = thalamus; cf = climbing fibers; mf = mossy fibers.

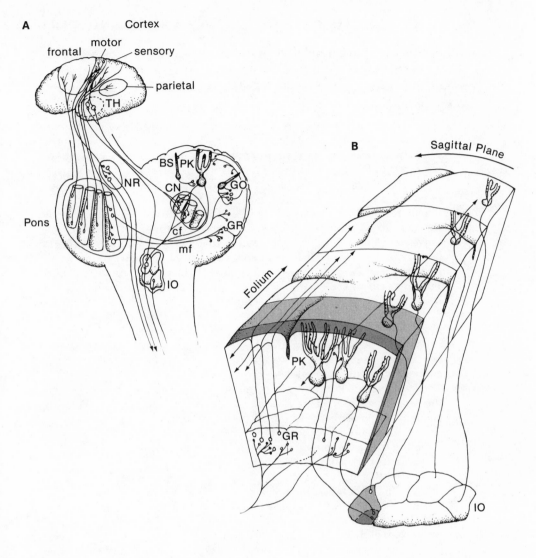

A

Cortex

frontal
motor
sensory
parietal

TH

BS PK

NR

CN

GO

Pons

cf

GR

mf

IO

B

Sagittal Plane

Folium

PK

GR

IO

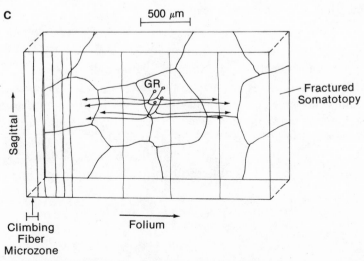

C

500 μm

Sagittal

GR

Folium

Fractured
Somatotopy

Climbing
Fiber
Microzone

umn nuclei, vestibular nuclei, tectal regions, and the motor cortex.

How can such a structure act as an organ of succession? The model proposed to answer this question will first be described for motor cortical inputs and outputs and then be generalized for those of other regions:

1. Activity in the motor cortex initiating a movement is relayed via climbing fibers to Purkinje cells, with powerful stimulatory results (especially in the absence of other modulatory effects). Connections with the inferior olive are involved in sequencing these signals.

2. Somatosensory and particularly kinesthetic activity provide signals through mossy fiber inputs to granule cells to stimulate *particular sequences* of Purkinje cells, emphasizing that the cerebellum is in part a large sensory organ. These sequences are in general unique for each movement and arise because the granule cells link many serially ordered Purkinje cells by their parallel fibers. Such Purkinje cells are more apt to be activated by coactive climbing fiber inputs; the two inputs thus reinforce each other. But because of the existence of fractured somatotopy, granule cells will select a particular sensory region corresponding to a collection of receptors from the skin, muscles, and joints. Such inputs do not extend over large body regions, but in general they show some connectivity within a region.

3. The sequence of Purkinje cell responses corresponding more or less to the sensory sequence is relayed to the deep cerebellar nuclei, where it changes the pattern of output back to the cerebral cortex. This favors the repeated firing of motor cortical neurons activating those muscles corresponding to the movements giving rise to sensory patterns, thus yielding movements that will form part of a motor program.

4. The activity of such sequences reflects the proximodistal order of joint, muscle, and appendicular movements. This activity occurs very rapidly and in general constitutes a feed-forward system for reflex gain control and synchronization.

5. Alterations of the sensory input caused by repeated or altered movement lead to new sequences of Purkinje cell–nuclear-cortical firing, reflecting different parallel fiber–climbing fiber correspondences.

A movement receives its immediate pattern of succession largely as a result of motor cortical activity modulated by cerebellar activity, but it can also be modulated by other parts of a global mapping. The *synaptic* changes that lead to *patterns* of activity corresponding to gestures occur mainly in the motor cortical connectivity, however, not in the cerebellar connectivity, although synaptic changes in the cerebellum can enhance certain modulatory signals. By this means, multiple repeated gestures of a synergy could result in learned motor performance. While the smooth *succession* of movements would still depend upon cerebellar activity, such activity is most critical mainly in the first or early gestures that are performed in a learned act or during the appearance of novelty in the course of a gesture. It is in these activities that alteration in synchronization and reflex gain control would be particularly important.

According to this view, the cerebellum and cortex act together as a classification n-tuple serving to categorize smooth gestures. The cerebellum and its nuclei provide the relations necessary for gain control and succession in a motor program[10] on the basis of the selection of particular inputs related by fractured somatotopy. The cortex provides the origin and succession of the motor signals as well as other modulatory sensory signals that are coordinated in the cerebellum with those from other structures.

This picture of a dynamic loop between cortex and cerebellum can thus be extended to spinal inputs and outputs. Undoubtedly, a major aspect of cerebellar function relates to the monitoring of the amount of activity that results in output from each region of the neuraxis. One of the important features of these functions of the cerebellum is the question of smoothness and minimization of energy expenditure in rapid movements. While the origin of such smoothing is not known, it is a reasonable conjecture that the activity of joint and muscle receptors is correlated with other sensory activity to contribute to the selection of those serial activations of Purkinje cells resulting in efficient movement. Training and repeated activity undoubtedly also contribute, as do the elastic properties of muscles, which can adjust length-tension relationships to smooth trajectories.

One challenging question prompted by this picture concerns the number and uniqueness of patterns established by means of fractured somatotopy[11] through parallel fibers in conjunction with the microzones[12] of climbing fibers. An examination of the available data on the number of different somatotopic patches in each cerebellar folium, on the vast number of parallel fibers, and on the zonal distribution of climbing fibers suggests that each movement would select a virtually unique sequence of Purkinje cell activations. The overlapping nature of the somatotopies, their arrangement in neuronal groups, and the particular peripheral receptors stimulated in a given order make it likely that closely related movements would generally (but not always) pick activation sequences that have some Purkinje cells in common. At the same time, because of the multiplicity of fractured somatotopic representations, a change in body position or postural context for a movement might select a completely different somatotopic sequence, even though the isolated movement itself is very similar or identical to that arising in a different postural context.

Because of the branching and bidirectional spread of parallel fibers and the dense sequential input from their appropriate climbing fibers, there is no simple sequential order of stimulation of a given Purkinje cell in a fractured somatotopic region that corresponds neatly to the spread of a signal along a single parallel fiber.[13] Instead, there is a *combined* interaction of multiple parallel fiber inputs leading to a complex sequence of Purkinje cell stimulations that predispose certain cell *combinations* to be fired by climbing fibers. Nonetheless, these unique combinations would have a temporal relation *to particular sequences* of mossy fiber inputs driven from either the center or the periphery.

As a complex zonal structure, arranged for rapid response to successive sensory inputs and as a result of its selective action, the cerebellum is ideally suited to help "sculpt" a series of cortical or spinal outputs for gestures. In doing so, the cerebellum acts to carry out synchronization and reflex gain control in motor programs, but it is not likely to initiate actual motor sequences.

The present proposal is unlike certain previous proposals,[14] in that the cerebellum is considered to be less a learning device than a modulating device working with cortex to carry out *categorizations.* What they categorize together is the *smooth succession of motions in gestures* and the succession of gestures in synergies, although such successions are unlikely to originate in the cerebellum. This kind of categorization is of particular significance in the selection of spontaneous gestures during motor learning. It is important to emphasize that all such categorical activity is in general prior to and not generally accessible to primary consciousness. Nonetheless, it is the rapid, parallel sensory activity engaging many parts of the cerebellum in different successions that yields the basis of the smoothing of motor activity that is essential to the categorical perceptions leading to consciousness. Most of that motor activity is rapid and reflexive and is carried out in global mappings without conscious intervention. The cerebellum is essential in early motor learning that relates the categorization of gestures to the perceptual categorizations arising from and altered by these gestures. In the sense that it contributes to *feature correlation*[15] in such categorizations, the cerebellum is an indispensable early component in forming the basis of memory and ultimately of primary consciousness. It is obvious, however, that it has no direct role in consciousness itself; indeed, of all the organs of succession, it is the most removed from that process.

SUCCESSION AND SENSE: THE HIPPOCAMPUS

If *categorization* of rapid smooth motor patterns is important for the formation of synergies as well as for perceptual categorization itself, a means for registering the actual *succession of such perceptual categorizations* yielding a short-term memory is even more critical to consciousness and its continuity. There has accumulated an impressive body of evidence implicating the hippocampus in such a role.[16] Here, rather than review that evidence in detail, I wish to make a case for the hippocampus as an organ of succession—one that ensures the ordering of the *perceptual* categorizations that result from global mappings. In doing so, I shall emphasize the linkage of two different kinds of neural structures (those dedicated to internal value or to hedonic stimuli and those dedicated to categorization of outer events), each represented in two main neural loops of the brain. The hippocampus, a major structure in both of these loops, will be discussed here at length. As part of the prelimbic system, the cingulate gyrus is a major structure in the other loop and, as we shall see later, plays an important role in coordinating value-dependent states in a neural model of primary consciousness.

The anatomy and connections of the hippocampus (figure 7.2) underline its proposed role in the succession or timing of sequential processes and the modulation of that timing by adaptive needs, and they suggest a parallel mode of operation resulting from a lamellar organization. This anatomy strongly contrasts with that of the cerebral cortex. As we mentioned in the last chapter and in the section on the cerebellum, although classification couples in global mappings (particularly those of the cerebral cortex) play a primary role in perceptual categorization, the structure of the cortex suggests that it has no direct role in linking categorizations that are successive in time.

One of the main tenets of the model proposed here is that the intersection of various global mappings by the passage of signals from their classification couples through the inner hippocampal loop (figure 7.2) allows for their linkage in a succession reflecting the actual temporal order in which these signals occur. Another tenet of the model is that

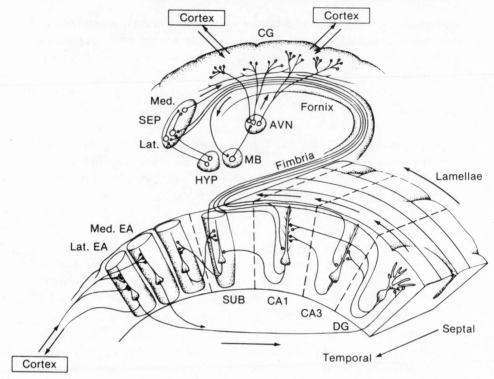

Figure 7.2

Schematic diagram of the anatomy and principal connections of the hippocampus. A large variety of cortical areas connects reentrantly to the entorhinal cortex. The perforant path is the first component in the "trisynaptic circuit" making up the inner loop *of the hippocampus; mossy fibers from the dentate gyrus (DG) to CA3, and Schaffer collaterals from CA3 to CA1 close this loop that leads via the subiculum (SUB) back to the medial and lateral entorhinal areas (med. EA, lat. EA). The connections of the inner loop are oriented approximately orthogonal to the long axis of the hippocampus, forming a "lamellar" arrangement. Connections exist linking individual lamellae horizontally ("association fibers"). Major efferents of the hippocampal formation travel in a massive fiber bundle, the fornix; its postcommissural portion reaches the lateral septum (SEP). The medial septum connects back to the various subfields of the hippocampus, terminating on pyramidal cells in a characteristic pattern close to the soma. Another portion of the fornix contains fibers traveling to the mammillary bodies (MB), which in turn connect to the anterior ventral nucleus (AVN) of the thalamus. From there, fibers reach the cingulate gyrus (CG), which is intimately related to widespread cortical regions (arrows), as well as to other regions of the limbic system, such as the entorhinal cortex itself. The route from the hippocampus via mammillary bodies and AVN to the cingulate gyrus makes up the* outer loop *of the limbic system (sometimes called the Papez loop). Additional abbreviations: HYP = hypothalamus; lat. = lateral; med. = medial.*

this successive ordering is modulated by internal adaptive needs and hedonic stimuli. This modulation occurs as a result of combination within the hippocampus of input from systems receiving hedonic stimuli with input from classification couples in cortical areas.

The proposed model of hippocampal function is based on three assumptions:

1. The hippocampus *does not* carry out categorization but receives inputs from classification couples in global mappings and sends outputs back to those cortical regions whose neuronal groups were originally responsible for the hippocampal input.
2. As a result of its synaptic organization, the hippocampus yields an asynchronous ordering of these sequences of input in time chunks of 100 msec to 1 sec. Because it has a loop structure operating in parallel, however, it maintains an ordering across time of sequences of inputs from cortical neuronal groups over durations of seconds to minutes. This activity, if sufficiently repetitive, organizes and guides the strengthening of *secondary* synaptic cortical connections. These form linkages independent of the hippocampus that in long-term memory can involve many of *the same cortical neuronal groups* that were originally activated in the loop concerned with short-term memory.
3. Such formations can be affected by modulating hippocampal activity through signals from regions subserving internal hedonic states.

The synaptic responses of the hippocampus thus may change not only with changes in categorically related cortical inputs but also with changes in the hedonic states of the animal. We assume, for these reasons, that the hippocampus is one of the regions engaged in the matching of the perceptually significant input from sensory stimuli with subcortical signals arising from centers mediating adaptive internal values and hedonic states. Septal inputs and other subcortical inputs can influence the structure of firing patterns in the hippocampus and thus alter their efficiency in linking global mappings. The hippocampus therefore may play a role in certain specific attentional states (see chapter 12) as well as in the laying down of long-term value-category memory in the cortex.

Consider the structure of the hippocampus in terms of basic elements contributing to this proposed functional scheme (figure 7.2). The intrinsic circuitry embedded in the inner-loop structure links the entorhinal area to the hippocampal subfields and the subiculum.[17] All connections in the inner loop are unidirectional, and there is no evidence of reentry in the basic loop except between the entorhinal area and the subiculum. In marked contrast, the extrinsic connections that link the entorhinal area (and the cingulate) to a large variety of secondary or tertiary areas in the temporal, frontal, and parietal cortices are strongly reentrant.[18] The entorhinal area is small in comparison with these various input and output areas, suggesting the existence of extensive convergence and divergence in the circuitry.

Within the hippocampus proper, the main input from the entorhinal area proceeds from the perforant path into the dentate fascia via granule cell mossy fibers to the pyramidal cells of subfield CA3. These cells send so-called Schaffer collaterals to the pyramidal cells of subfield CA1 (figure 7.2), which in turn connect to the subiculum. The subiculum connects back to the entorhinal area to close the loop. The laminar structure of the subfields is essentially made of a single layer of principal cells in CA1, CA3, and dentate fascia. There is a layering of synaptic inputs on the dendritic trees of the principal neurons: inputs from the septal afferents are close to the cell bodies, whereas those from the sequence arising in the perforant path are on apical dendrites. This account describes what we have called the *inner loop*.

Another set of unidirectional connections is formed by the so-called postcommissural fornical-thalamocortical path. Fornical connections terminating in the cingulate cortex originate exclusively in the subiculum,[19] forming an *outer loop* by reentry from the subiculum to the entorhinal area. Brain-stem and hypothalamic inputs thus enter the septum, which then sends reentrant connections to the entorhinal area. Fornical outputs connect to the mammillary bodies, go thence to the AV nucleus of the thalamus, and then to the cingulate gyrus.[20] Reentrant connections from the cingulate go to the subiculum, as we already mentioned. This outer loop will later be seen to play an important role in the model for primary consciousness.

With this overall anatomical background, we may now look at the fine structure related to sequencing in the inner loop. We are concerned mainly with the lamellar and neuronal group structure of the hippocampal subfields. Collaterals connecting the subfields proceed mainly in one direction, DF→CA3→CA1, defining a lamellar spread.[21] An axonal arbor of a CA3 cell can spread as far as 600 micrometers longitudinally (about 5 percent of the whole length of the hippocampus) and can thus potentially activate CA1 cells in a wide area. Other connections of the so-called longitudinal path proceed along the length of the hippocampus and arborize widely, linking up cells from different horizontal lamellae.

There is a distinct possibility that the hippocampus is arranged in neuronal groups that overlap, are linked by the longitudinal and commissural paths, and are limited in number (about 50–100/cm, a total of 400 in the human). Each such group would respond to signals from a number of other groups in the entorhinal area (deep layer), while the projection back to the entorhinal superficial layers could maintain some degree of registration and topography. It is clear, however, that proceeding from the dentate fascia to CA1, well-delineated group structure would tend to be lost.

Insofar as the entorhinal area is reentrantly connected to the neocortical association areas, and given the size discrepancy pointed out previously, it appears likely that several anatomically distinct cortical areas *involving different modalities* terminate on a given portion of the entorhinal area but nonetheless maintain a crude topography. This results from convergence of input: a neuronal group from any one cortical subfield must be correlated with input from neuronal groups mediating different modalities from different subfields. Such cortical subfields themselves may also be linked by "U-loop" fibers and their synaptic connections; these connections may be strengthened if reentry from the hippocampus is allowed to occur following modulation through the fornical connections.

This picture is in accord with the idea that excitation in a particular part of the entorhinal area passes through the inner hippocampal loop and finds its way back roughly into the cortical region where it started 10–20 msec earlier. It is compatible with the fact that afferent and efferent connections of the entorhinal area are roughly in register. But the connectivity is point-to-area, since any single group in the entorhinal cortex activates cells in the hippocampus, ultimately projecting back to a larger entorhinal area. A regulatory influence from longitudinal and inhibitory connections in the hippocampus may guide the successive signals that reach the cortex from the reentrant output of the entorhinal area.

As a result of the activity of global mappings, a pattern of active neuronal groups in the entorhinal area would activate a certain number of groups in a large region of the hippocampus. Through reentry, a number (but not necessarily all) of these hippocampal groups would be *repeatedly* activated, allowing synaptic change involving long-term potentiation and an integrated response to perceptual input.[22] The number of such cells would be smaller than that originally activated, however, and would correspond to signals occurring in a global mapping within a particular time chunk over which sensory inputs arose in the world.

This set of connectivities results in the successive ordering of reentrant signals back to the cortex, in time chunks of 100 msec to 1 sec, as well as in the ordering across time of reentrant inputs that have *not* been presented in *immediate* succession. The time units of succession are roughly (1) those of cortical excitation patterns occurring in a period of 10 msec, the basis of ongoing perceptual flux; (2) *sequences* of such events from 100 msec to 1 sec, corresponding to integration of perceptual categories; and (3) *chains* of such sequences occupying longer times and related to learning and fixation of secondary synaptic strengths in the cortex.

It is important to emphasize that the ordering of time chunks (i.e., of signals represented in global mappings) is not a simple reverberating circuit. Overlap, divergence of inputs, and mixing of signals prevent such a simple circuit property from emerging. But there is a selectional pattern in time: a topography of signaling emerges from the recycling of signals (through the reentrant connectivity from and to the cerebral cortex) resulting in long-term potentiation (LTP)[23] within the hippocampus.

By this means, the hippocampus could alter the extent of particular global mappings by "carving out" an appropriate subset of reentrantly activated cortical neuronal groups in such mappings. It could also link two different global mappings by becoming a focal region for the overlap in time and in topography of these mappings. After strong repetition of successive signals, supported by modulating input from regions reflecting value and hedonic states (via fornical inputs), activity in the hippocampus could lead to strengthening of U-loop connections between the *cortical parts* of such global mappings. One would thus expect the hippocampus to be involved in attention and learning insofar as these are connected with long-term memory (see chapter 12).

In sum, the hippocampus is proposed as a selective link between parallel and sequential patterns of the global mappings that function to give perceptual categorization (see chapter 3 and figure 3.4). Because of its anatomy, showing a convergent-divergent reentrant loop to the cortex, its susceptibility to metastable synaptic change by LTP, and its concomitant fornical connections related to value, it serves to allow temporal ordering of perceptual categorizations and to potentiate fixation of secondary connections between cortical neuronal groups involved in classification couples. By these means, it ensures short-term memory over seconds to minutes and provides an essential component for the *initiation* of long-term memory.

Our remarks so far indicate that succession is essential to the establishment of consciousness as well as to consciousness itself. In chapter

9, we shall see in detail how the succession of motor and sensory components of perceptual categorization may be related to a special long-term memory system. This system links past value-category associations to present categorized input in such a way as to yield the basis of primary consciousness. Among the elements involved in instrumental actions integrated by these means are the basal ganglia.

SUCCESSION, PLANNING, AND CHOICE: THE BASAL GANGLIA

One of the extraordinary aspects of the planning, execution, and learning of complex motor acts is their mixture of sequencing and concurrency. Motor programs are sets of muscle commands put together before the beginning of a movement sequence. They permit that sequence to be carried out without peripheral feedback and are linked by the motor system into complexes that can be affected by planning, thought, and intention.[24] What governs the outputs chosen as a result of such activity, coordinates the various cortical inputs required, links the cortical responses, assures the necessary attention, and permits a relation to be established between such plans and motivational and hedonic states?

It would be satisfying to say that the activity of the basal ganglia can be related to all of these functions, but present knowledge permits us to relate this cortical appendage only to certain of their aspects with any confidence. The evidence linking basal ganglia to motor plans is reasonably direct.[25] That linking their activity to complex coordinated acts is somewhat more indirect. That linking their activity to motivation and attention is both speculative and indirect.

Before assessing the collective evidence and suggesting a model, let us review the basic connectivity and structure of the basal ganglia.[26] A skeletal diagram of the parts and connectivity to the cortex, thalamus, and brain stem is given in figure 7.3. The neostriatum (caudate and putamen) receives inputs (probably excitatory, involving glutamate receptors) from all areas of the neocortex; those from the substantia nigra to the matrix and patches in the neostriatum are dopaminergic. There is connectivity between these distinctive patches[27] or striosomes (which also contain enkephalin, opiate receptors, and substance P) and the matrix. The caudate sends axons to the dorsal third of the globus pallidus and the putamen to the ventral two-thirds of that structure.

These neurons are GABAergic and are thought to be inhibitory, as are those from the pallidus to the thalamic nuclei. There is a radical convergence in the striatopallidal projection. The pars reticularis of the nigra also sends input to the thalamus (not shown in the diagram).

What is striking about the overall connectivity of this system?

1. The cortical input to the matrix of the striatum is *topographic* (in a somewhat fractured fashion).
2. The striatum connects back only indirectly to the cortex.
3. The striosomes receive input from the prelimbic cortex, nucleus accumbens, and amygdala, *all regions related to hedonic systems.*
4. The body of the substantia nigra sends connections to the mesencephalic reticular formation, the raphe nuclei, and the locus ceruleus, *all regions involved in state control and arousal.*
5. There is a *parallel organization* of the functionally segregated circuits going to and from cortex to basal ganglia to thalamus and back to cortex. This is perhaps the most remarkable recently uncovered feature of the system. DeLong and colleagues[28] distinguish a minimum of five such circuits, each of which receives multiple, partially overlapping corticostriate inputs: the "motor" circuit, the "oculomotor" circuit, the "dorsolateral prefrontal" circuit, the "lateral orbitofrontal," and the "anterior cingulate" circuit. These authors stress that although each of these circuits is open to other adjoining circuits, there is in each a central "closed loop" portion comprising a basal ganglion–thalamocortical pathway that receives input from and terminates within a single cortical area. Similar neural operations are presumed to occur at comparable stages of each of the five circuits.

The motor and oculomotor circuits are the ones about which evidence is most definite. A variety of studies suggest that the "motor" circuit is involved in the control of the scaling of movement amplitude and velocity. The connectivity of this circuit, particularly the putamen, which receives projections from the motor and somatosensory cortices, is consistent with these findings. The "oculomotor" circuit relates to frontal eye fields. This is consistent with evidence that reticular neurons of the substantia nigra are related to control of saccadic eye movements.

The connectivity of the "motor" circuit to the supplementary motor area of the cortex is well documented, and it is clear that basal ganglia are somehow involved in the planning for movement, probably in the choice of types of output. The somatotopy is consistent with the presence of functional "channels" for control of individual body parts. There is an arrangement in the matrix of the putamen of functional clusters 200–1,000 micrometers in extent that may, in fact, be neuronal groups. These dimensions are similar to those of the striosomes, which also may be neuronal groups.

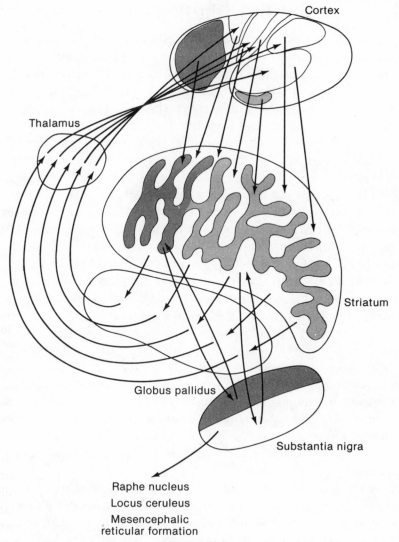

Cortex

Thalamus

Striatum

Globus pallidus

Substantia nigra

Raphe nucleus
Locus ceruleus
Mesencephalic
reticular formation

Figure 7.3

Schematic diagram of the main anatomical connections of the basal ganglia and their relation to the cerebral cortex. Many cortical regions send afferents to the striatum; these afferents are anatomically segregated into two domains within the striatum. The matrix zone receives connections from motor, premotor, somatosensory, and parietal areas; the striosomes receive connections from the prefrontal and prelimbic areas of the cerebral cortex. The striatal matrix projects onto the globus pallidus; from there, axons reach a thalamic nucleus. The loop is closed by an ascending projection onto motor and premotor areas from this thalamic nucleus. Matrix and striosomes both project onto neurons of the substantia nigra and receive a back projection from that structure. The nigra is connected to brain-stem structures as indicated. See figure 12.2 for a model of how the basal ganglia might be involved in regulating motor programs and plans and thus be concerned with aspects of attention.

The two prefrontal circuits and the "cingulate" circuit may serve an important role in connecting parietal and temporal cortical signals mediated by polysensory and visual areas to the motor, premotor, and frontal areas. It is particularly notable that the striate and prestriate visual areas are connected indirectly via the basal ganglia to these more rostral areas of the cerebral cortex.[29] A *dorsal route* goes via V5 (see figure 4.2) to the parietal cortex (area 7a), which connects to the prefrontal cortex (areas 8 and 9) and then to the anterior supplementary motor cortex; area 9 connects as well to the premotor cortex. Parietal area 7b sends fibers to the anterior supplementary motor cortex, the lateral premotor cortex, and the cingulate cortex. The *ventral route* from striate and extrastriate cortex goes to the inferotemporal cortex, which sends projections to the prefrontal cortex (area 8) and the inferoprefrontal convexity, which connects in turn to the ventral premotor cortex.

The central role of the basal ganglia in motion and in the construction of motor plans is made clear in Parkinson's disease, in which the nigral dopaminergic neurons are destroyed.[30] Hypotheses that the basal ganglia are involved in state control and attention[31] are less well documented. But it is an intriguing possibility that striosome-matrix interactions connect limbic circuits related to hedonic states and value to motor-planning events, selecting particular sequences of cortical inputs and outputs by triangle reentry. Indeed, some recent studies implicate the function of the basal ganglia in obsessive-compulsive disorders,[32] particularly in relation to signals that connect the striatum to the anterior cingulate cortex. We will consider this issue at some length in chapter 13.

All of these observations are consistent with the idea that there is at least partial segregation of function in the basal ganglia. Rolls and Williams[33] have accumulated detailed neurophysiological evidence to support this interpretation. They suggest that cortically processed signals may be sent to the striatum, for example, and that the striatum serves to send signals that switch or alter *behavior*, not specific individual motions. Noting that input to pallidal neurons comes from different parts of the striatum, they suggest that the basal ganglia can serve as an associative net. If, for instance, cortical inputs fire particular striatal neurons after categorizing an event and other striatal neurons fired because of postural adjustments, the two events might lead to a strengthening of synaptic efficacy at the pallidal synapses. This could then trigger appropriate sets of motor patterns, and, in this fashion, the basal ganglia can participate in choice—linking appropriate motor outputs to an evolving sequence of inputs.

The foregoing remarks suggest that the basal ganglia may provide a major coupling between sensory responses and motor responses, particularly those involving identity of visual cues for planned action. According to this hypothesis, the basal ganglia may collect signals by reentry from several areas, integrate them in terms of hedonically modulated goals and motivations, and participate in translating cortical activities for coherent action and motor plans.[34] In this view, basal ganglia not only regulate movement in a motor program but also help direct what is to be done according to a motor plan. A growing body of data suggests that the corpus striatum receives segregated (mostly indirect) sensory inputs and that it may serve to correlate various *combinations of these inputs* with the *initiation* of complex motor patterns and behavioral responses.[35]

The connection of the striatum with the amygdala, which projects to the temporal and ventral frontal cortex, and of the ventral striatum to the entorhinal cortex and hippocampus, and the association of the parahippocampal gyrus with the ventral and dorsal frontal areas are consistent with possible relations of basal ganglion activity to motivational states. It is particularly suggestive that these prelimbic structures connect with the striosomes (figure 7.3) and that striosomes project to the substantia nigra, which sends axons to the brain stem—that is, to the mesencephalic reticular formation, raphe nuclei, and locus ceruleus.

An explicit model relating these ideas concerning motor plans and programs to the conscious and unconscious control of attention will be presented in chapter 12. This example will show in detail how one of these organs of succession (in this case, the basal ganglia) interacts with the cortex to give succession and choice.

Some Conclusions

The main conclusion to be drawn from the foregoing anatomical and physiological remarks is that the cerebral cortex does not act on its own to link time and space. Instead, it carries out its correlations of spatial patterns in times governed by the various cortical appendages. It is of some interest to compare the three major organs of succession as shown in table 7.1. Each appendage acts as an organ of succession in its own way. The cerebellum acts in motor adaptations of vestibuloocular reflexes, saccades, and functional stretch reflexes, and it regulates reflex gain control. Concerned with the signaling of errors in movement con-

TABLE 7.1

Neocortex and Organs of Succession

Organ	Time Constants of Major Responses*	Sensory Input	Motor Output	Connection to Limbic System	Relation to Perceptual Categorization	Relation to Motor Patterning
Neocortex	short medium long	direct	+	+ (particularly pre-frontal, frontal)	+	+
Cerebellum	short	direct and indirect	+	0†	indirect	+ +
Hippocampus	short medium	indirect	indirect	+ +	0	0 or indirect
Basal ganglia	short	indirect	+	+	indirect	+

*Short = 10 msec–300 msec
Medium = 300 msec–minutes
Long > minutes
†Connections exist to the hypothalamus.

trol, it does not itself generate motor programs, because, without input, it acts only in 300 msec intervals or less. But it is essential for timing and synchronization[36] of smooth movements and for linkages of responses to novel sensory stimuli. It may be involved in efference copies required to connect rapidly changing body positions, and it may therefore undergo adaptive changes. It is *not* connected to the limbic system in any strong fashion, although its bidirectional connection to the hypothalamus[37] suggests a possible role in the regulation of autonomic centers affecting smooth muscle tone and various visceral centers. It is mainly a sensorimotor transducer, synchronizer, and error corrector. It is important in shaping the motor programs involved in feature correlation and sensorimotor categorization, but it has no direct role in plans connected with motivation.

The hippocampus is important in connecting perceptual responses to the flux of external events, and its responses do extend over time periods longer than those of the cerebellum. It appears very likely that it connects the signal flow from various cortical areas in terms of sequences that regulate the order of perceptual categorizations. It modulates cortical long-term storage in a fashion that may be altered by connections with hedonic and motivationally important areas. While necessary for long-term memory, it is not likely to subserve it; rather, changes in cortical synapses probably serve this role. The successions directly controlled by the hippocampus concern events in reentrant systems related to short-term memory, and thus it acts in time periods up to minutes in length.

The basal ganglia may be involved in choices and initiations of output during planning of successions of motor programs, and therefore their main activity is in short time periods, between 300 msec and several seconds. These structures appear to be important in the linkage of motor programs into behavioral plans by means of connections to premotor and prefrontal areas as well as directly to motor areas. It is very likely that the role of the basal ganglia is conditioned, at least indirectly, by prelimbic inputs from frontal areas and by their connections to the brain stem. Thus, like those of the hippocampus, the functions of basal ganglia are also likely to be influenced by motivational states. Basal ganglia are among the major areas to increase in size during the evolution of the mammalian brain in the therapsid–mammalian transition. They also show major increases in size and representation during primate evolution.

Obviously, the cortex has the major correlative role in perceptual categorization.[38] But only by its linkage to these cortical appendages to form the bases of dynamic global mappings can it truly coordinate sensorimotor interaction in space and time. As we shall see, *distinctions* among the various kinds and functions of these mappings provide major bases for the development of concepts and conceptual categorization. While it is remotely conceivable that perceptual categorization is achieved by the cortex alone, perceptual experience and memory of any duration appear to require the interactive ensemble of the cortex and its appendages. This holds a fortiori for the development of concepts, which are an essential bridge to primary consciousness and to which we now turn.

8

Concepts and Presyntax

The preliminary description of primary consciousness given in chapter 5 linked immediate perceptual categorization to memory. It did not, however, consider in detail another aspect of brain function that contributes essentially to primary consciousness and at the same time serves as the gateway to higher-order consciousness. This aspect concerns concepts and concept formation. Different concepts not only can be linked in particular orders during thinking but also can be *about* orderings. As we shall see, they are intimately dependent on various types of global mappings, and they strongly involve memory and spatio-temporal succession. They are necessary for the formation of the value-category memory, held to be essential for primary consciousness. For this reason, we discuss them now.

Of all the subjects to be considered in formulating an adequate theory of consciousness, that of concepts is the most daunting—concepts are difficult to define, and their existence and neural bases must be inferred indirectly from experimental evidence. Moreover, one is constantly tempted to consider concepts as properties of language.[1] But this is not so—a good case can be made that animals without true linguistic abilities, such as chimpanzees, have concepts and that concepts are acquired *prior to* language. It is important to resist the temptation to think that concepts are merely mental images or (even worse) that they themselves are the "language of thought." Moreover, because the word "concept" is ordinarily used in connection with language and with thought, there is a terminological difficulty at the outset. The term has often been used to apply strictly to situations in which one may talk of truth and falsity. In contrast, I shall use the word here to apply to functions separate from language as well as in connection with linguistic capability, allowing context to guide the discrimination. I feel that this is preferable to introducing a neologism like "preconcept" for the present nonlinguistic usage.

How, then, can we define a concept prior to language? This is a difficult task. An animal capable of concepts is able to identify a particular thing or action and control its future behavior on the basis of that identification in a more or less *general* way. It must act *as if* it could make judgments based on recognition of category membership or integrate "particulars" into "universals." This recognition rests not just on perceptual categorization (although a concept may have a highly sensory content) but, to some degree, *must also be relational.* It can connect one perceptual categorization to another even in the absence of the stimuli that triggered these categorizations.

Concept-forming abilities must allow assessment of the objective consequences of action, must allow generalization from one class of stimuli to another, and thus must be able to assimilate novel content. To succumb to the temptation I just warned against, one might suspect that *if* an animal with concepts could speak, it would reveal its concepts as ontological categories[2]—things, motions, and classes.

The present theory holds that both during evolution and in the individual, concepts precede language and meaning. Concept formation, according to the view I am developing here, precedes semantics. Concepts are driven by the perceptual apparatus, are constructed by the brain, and require memory. They are coherent and can correspond to things and motions. They can be achieved as a result of interactions with the world and other members of a species in the absence of speech. Unlike speech, concepts are not conventional or arbitrary, are not linked to a speech community, and do not depend on sequential presentation.

In their most elaborate form, concepts may serve as bases for image schemata[3] ("object," "motion," "barrier," "container," etc.) summarizing a variety of general physical situations. Concept formation is relational, can be used for identification and further generalization on things and relations in the world, and is therefore a necessary but not sufficient condition for semantics (insofar as concepts in the present usage are considered to be different from words, meanings, and language).

What animals have concepts, and how do we test for them? By the somewhat loose criteria used in the definitions above, it is obvious that, as humans, we possess concepts.[4] It is less obvious but nonetheless persuasive to consider the case of chimpanzees as positive. These animals definitely show the ability to classify and generalize on relations—whether of things or of actions. They can also decide on sameness or difference, make analogies, and assess intentions, guiding their actions by such processes.[5] For example, eighteen-month-old infant apes can demonstrate not only that they can recognize when two objects they see belong to the same category but also that two different objects are organized in the same relation. I conclude that, like humans, they have concepts.

The difficulties are greater in assessing the capacities of other mammals and greater still as we pass to other vertebrates. In the absence of a strict knowledge of brain areas essential for concept formation, and as the distinction between behaviors based on classification of relations and those based on simple stimulus equivalence becomes more difficult, we must hesitate.

Nevertheless, we can make certain surmises on the basis of what we know about behavior, brain structure, and the brain functions that are absolutely required for concept formation. It seems likely that perceptual categorization, long-term memory, and learning are all necessary capacities for concept formation. This implies that an animal able to have concepts must be able to form local and global mappings and behave on the basis of expectancies related to the satisfaction of hedonic constraints. But it is unlikely that the brain areas responsible for such capabilities (the brain stem and primary and secondary cortical areas, at a minimum, as well as organs of succession) are *sufficient* for concept formation.

These remarks indicate that concept formation goes far beyond perceptual categorization. Concept formation requires the capacity to deal with *relations,* a capacity that needs to include many abstract spatial and temporal cues. Above all, these relations are *varied.* They include those based on immediate perceptual categorization, on bodily and external events, on motion in relation to time and space, on feeling, and on memory.[6] The categorizations and generalizations reflected in concepts are much richer, more abstract, and therefore less immediate than those seen in perceptual categorization. They may involve the memory of much earlier or more distant events, various degrees of explicit quantitative difference, analogy (sometimes involving relations of a higher order than simple dyadic ones), and less than immediate reference to various objects. Concepts may involve judgments made in absence—judgments made about classifications of stimuli long past.

All of these conclusions suggest that the ability to have concepts must have required the evolution of brain regions that are capable of these more recently evolved functions but that are nonetheless structurally based on the earlier functions of perceptual categorization, memory, and learning. However, it is not necessarily true that any basically new *microstructure* of the brain had to be developed in order for such a capacity to emerge. One can reasonably suppose that the frontal, parietal, and temporal cortex and the basal ganglia are good candidates to serve as bases for the temporally delayed judgments and actions entailed by the having of concepts and necessary for their generation. If this is true, lobsters and perhaps even birds do not have concepts, but dogs might. The problem, of course, is that while we can test for concepts in linguistic animals like ourselves, and in nonlinguistic animals to which we can sign, such as chimpanzees, the distinction between learning and concept formation becomes more difficult if we cannot exchange signs or otherwise communicate with the subject animal.

On the assumption that brain areas for concept formation include frontal (and possibly temporal and parietal) neocortex and basal ganglia, what *mechanism* may we suppose underlies such a capacity? Can we assume that concept formation would naturally arise from higher and higher orders of perceptual categorization in global mappings, involving the hippocampus and the cortical structures subserving long-term memory? This does not seem likely, for one very compelling reason: the heterogeneity of the categorizations and the range of the generalizations involved in concept formation. As I mentioned earlier, concepts involve various mixtures of relations concerning the real world, memories, and past behavior. It does not seem that simple extension or recursion of the activity of reentrant maps can *alone* lead to the emergence of such new relations.[7]

There is, however, one candidate function that could meet such disparate requirements. This is the function carried out by global mappings, which are dynamic metastable patterns of activity involving mapped classification couples and nonmapped regions (see figure 3.4). Global mappings can emerge from practically any combination of actions, past or present, and insofar as they involve large parts of the brain and various combinations of local maps for different modalities, they can subserve a large variety of perceptual categories. Different global mappings can correspond to widely different things: an object, an action, or a relation between two disparate objects, for example. Moreover, global mappings by their nature involve both spatial and temporal relations.[8]

BRAIN MECHANISMS FOR CONCEPT FORMATION

These observations lead me to suggest an hypothesis on the function of brain structures that are responsible for concept formation: *they are structures that can categorize, discriminate, and recombine patterns of activity in different kinds of global mappings.* It does not seem likely, however, that such structures (let us assume mainly frontal, temporal, and parietal cortex and basal ganglia as candidates) can *directly* categorize or map various global mappings one at a time. Instead, they must be able to activate or reconstruct portions of *past* global mappings according to modality (or submodality), or types of movement, and then by recombination or some comparator function mix or compare them. This implies back reentrant connections from the frontal cortex to other cortical regions and to basal ganglia and hippocampal regions.[9] Such connections must (1) stimulate portions of previous global mappings *independent of current sensory input;* (2) relate movement categories to the spatial references provided by maps with either object-centered or body-centered coordinates; (3) relate pairs or even larger collections of movements in respect to a sensory modality or combinations of modalities, for example, in terms of perceptually categorized object boundaries; (4) distinguish classes of global mappings relating to objects from those relating to movements; and (5) mediate long-term storage of the results of such activities, since concept formation requires memory.

These proposals are motivated by the recognition that perceptual categorizations alone do not allow a sufficient degree of generalization on relations between objects and actions. It is important, though, to add that generalizations from global mappings can be modal or amodal, depending upon the demands of a given situation. If motion is involved, for example, it is conceivable that similar outputs can be achieved from mappings involving different modalities (e.g., vision or touch) as they sample the same output. This amodal response seems to have occurred in the studies of Spelke[10] and her colleagues on infants' decisions on what is an object. Such prelinguistic infants appear to be able to construct *concepts* of cohesion, boundaries, substance, and spatiotemporal continuity either from visual *or* from haptic experiences of moving objects.

It is not clear whether such conceptual activities require topographic mapping in the actual cortical region capable of carrying them out. It seems doubtful that this is a necessary requirement; indeed, such an arrangement might actually hinder the combinatorial properties required of such a cortical region. More valuable would be a form of mapping of the most frequently used cortical local maps *themselves,* so that, for example, all visually related mappings (or all those related to auditory functions) could be connected in a region subserving the categorization of global mappings. This notion requires only that a new cortical area dedicated to concept formation be connected reentrantly to other cortical areas themselves capable of participating in global mappings.[11] Interactions with these areas are not necessarily restricted to corticocortical connections alone; for example, connections via the basal ganglia could provide the necessary pathway for concepts of action based on cortical activities (see chapter 7). Moreover, various connections could serve to relate limbic activities to particular comparator functions of the cortical regions (including cingulate cortex) that are responsible for concept formation.

Through reentry, the frontal, parietal, and temporal cortex may compare the activities of different *combinations* of brain regions composing portions of global mappings. As a result of such internal activity, these cortical areas could give rise to classifications of global mappings as a basis for action. In particular, the function of the frontal cortex could abstract the various consequences of action and store them as synaptic changes capable of *restimulating* common features of global mappings characteristic of different individual experiences. Given this memory and the ability to recombine or compare different portions of global mappings as a function of internal activity, the frontal cortex would be able to support generalization. And because of its connection to the basal ganglia and the limbic system, it *could establish relations among values and categorizations of sensory experiences themselves,* as will become evident when we discuss higher-order consciousness (see also the discussion of prefrontal cortex in the next chapter). Because global mappings and the reactivated portions of such mappings involve temporal ordering and long-term memory, the formation of concepts can also include bases for a generalized notion of succession and of the past.[12]

This proposed model for concepts, in which the brain categorizes its own activities, is obviously highly schematic and incomplete. Nonetheless, it does avoid the postulation of an entirely new kind of brain microstructure to account for the evolution of regions subserving concepts. It also avoids the evolutionarily anachronistic maneuver of postulating a need for language or even a "mental language"[13] to explain the development of concepts.

For this reason, in discussing the possible bases of concept formation, I have deliberately excluded any explanation that requires invocation of linguistic competence.[14] This does not imply that an animal capable of concepts cannot use concepts to make judgments on actions or cannot act as if it had "beliefs." The close tie to memory and value implied by the model suggests the opposite.

Insofar as this notion of concept formation refers ultimately to the finding of identity *in the world*[15] (even if only on the basis of memory), it provides a mechanism for responses based on "ontological categories." Ultimately, although concepts can be highly abstract, they are tied to objects (and actions) in the world, as are the perceptual categories on which they rest. This is so because even the long-term memories used in concept formation require calling back activities in those brain structures (e.g., primary receiving areas or early visual areas; see chapter 4) that were *originally* coherent because they were perceptually correlated with real-world objects. Concepts serve intentionality.

Concepts can override perceptual input while not neglecting it. The most striking case is that of illusions. Illusions are incorrigible; with experience, however, we can detect the incongruities in a perceived situation and even attempt to alter our view of that situation. While early reentrant systems, such as those of the RCI model in chapter 4, can integrate and resolve the complexities of perceptual categorization into a gestalt when presented with various illusions, they cannot escape an incorrigible response. Only with the advent of rich enough conceptual systems can generalizations be built, allowing us to distinguish between appearance and reality.

Before we turn to how concepts themselves might be ordered, we should note again that the theory considers concept formation to be essential for primary consciousness. This brings up a subtle but important point. If consciousness itself were required for or entailed by the formation of concepts (i.e., the ability to deal with the *relations* between perceptual categories even in the absence of perceptual stimuli), this might provide a *sufficient* explanation for the role of consciousness in prelinguistic animals and its selective advantage in vertebrate evolution. Unfortunately, this hypothesis, although possibly consistent with available evidence and theory, is also not clearly compelled by either, nor is it obvious how it can be tested. I shall assume that at least those concepts related to previous actions can be exercised unconsciously, leaving moot whether the formation of new concepts requires primary consciousness.

PRESYNTAX

Concept formation itself is not the same as thinking, deducing, or inducing.[16] Nothing in the model I have described so far implies that concepts themselves can be *extensively arranged* in higher-order structures. It is conceivable, in other words, that an animal can develop concepts but not be able explicitly to carry out analogy formation or similar activities over any length of time (of course, the converse, that such activity requires concept formation, is necessarily true).

To achieve that next order of activity and to provide an early basis for the evolutionary emergence of semantic activities, yet one more capability must have evolved. That capability is a new kind of memory, *one that can place concepts in an ordered relation.*[17] At the point of evolutionary emergence of such a capability, the very early steps just preceding the evolution of language abilities must have been taken. I say this because some form of ordering is required to link concepts to carry out thinking. It may very well be that concept formation and ordering evolved together. A capacity for such ordering is not the same as the syntax underlying a full-blown grammar, however, for such a capacity can be exercised *without* the use of symbols.[18] In other words, a means of simply classifying, distinguishing, and temporally ordering event concepts and object concepts as a special memory would have represented a great evolutionary advance but would not have required symbols and grammar. It requires and builds upon the ability to carry out behaviors in a serial order, however. To distinguish such an ordering capability from the much more recursively refined syntactical bases of language, I shall call it *presyntax.*

While not directly a part of linguistic competence, the ability to carry out presyntax would enable concept formation *eventually* to attain semantic significance in evolution, as we shall see in chapter 10. Following our program of placing strong constraints on our consciousness theory, and invoking only evolutionarily small changes and the principles of neural Darwinism, we might suppose that new reentrant linkages of several brain areas are responsible for the acquisition of presyntax. A candidate might involve areas of the temporal cortex linked to basal ganglia and frontal cortex. If temporal areas were linked reentrantly to frontal areas (and basal ganglia as organs of succession) in such a way that certain *concepts were responded to only in a fixed order,* the basis for a new kind of memory would be in place. This memory—in which, for example, the response to a concept of an *object* must always precede (or follow) the response to a concept of *action*—would provide a matrix for analogy and thus for the first bases of thought. This could be accomplished by a connectivity that was asymmetric; an actual *output* might be guaranteed in such a connectivity, for example, only if the order (object-concept) then (action-concept) were followed. Chaining of such outputs would extend this presyntactical ability.

Of course, the actual anatomical and synaptic bases for such a succession requirement cannot now be specified, but it is not difficult to imagine a connectivity scheme capable of assuring such a succession. For example, certain object concepts may require activation of global mappings lacking hippocampal reentry while other action concepts may require such reentry. A local mapping supporting such a discrimination or differentiation might be present in the frontal cortex. If that were so, a temporal cortical circuit[19] that would achieve output only if frontal cortical stimuli were followed by hippocampal ones would, for example, serve to put presyntactic ordering into place.

The view of concept formation and of presyntax presented here is closely tied through global mappings to the mechanisms of motor and perceptual sequences. Moreover, even if that tie is indirect, the structures underlying any conceptual functions must ultimately be tied to perceptual relations constrained by events in the world and the ability to identify such events. Although language is *not* involved and although elaborate intrinsic rules or fixed orders of mental representation are avoided, it is obvious that capacities for concepts must precede those for presyntax, just as terms precede predicates for linguistic animals. In this account, I have deliberately not considered thought—the building of conceptual theories about the world—in any detail. That is a whole project in itself.[20] But it should be evident that presyntax provides a necessary basis for such an enterprise, one that necessarily also depends upon an analysis of consciousness.

Two questions now face us: How do two domains, those of concepts and those of later-evolving language, relate to each other in terms of brain structure and function? And how does that relation affect consciousness? To frame a provisional answer to these questions, an answer that will lead to a consideration of higher-order consciousness, we must first develop a more detailed model of primary consciousness.

PART FOUR

CONSCIOUSNESS

9

A Model of
Primary Consciousness

Starting with the précis in chapter 5, I attempted in the ensuing chapters to expand mainly upon the *necessary* conditions that must be met in order for consciousness to appear. In this chapter, I wish to consider certain of these conditions in more detail and then discuss the *sufficient* conditions for primary consciousness in terms of a well-specified neural model. The two main neural forerunners of consciousness are neuronal group selection in reentrant maps and the evolutionary emergence of two very different kinds of neural structure and function—one related to interoceptive homeostatic regulation and the other to exteroceptive perceptual processes. As we saw in chapter 7, the exteroceptive functions depend upon interactions of the cortex with the so-called organs of succession, for which we have suggested specific models.

It is obvious from these considerations that a brain-based model of primary consciousness must itself be based on a number of neural models consistent with neural Darwinism. To emphasize this point, I shall briefly summarize the mutual or intersecting assumptions of these subsidiary models in the light of the TNGS. In line with that theory, it is assumed that the world is an unlabeled place (see chapter 3). Perceptual categorization occurs through disjunctive sampling by sensorimotor systems yielding signals to local reentrant maps; these interact to give global mappings that are continually modified by behavior and particularly by movements. The cerebellum and cortex provide a basis for smooth movement patterns or synergies that are necessary to categorization and that are themselves motor categorizations. Short-term memory emerges in terms of successions of categories that depend upon cyclic reentry between various cortical regions and the hippocampus. Portions of the cortex become adapted to classifying different types of global mappings leading to a conceptual memory. Learning arises as a specific linkage between category and value in terms of adaptive responses that lead to changes in behavior. The patterns of internal value and hedonic responses are based on evolutionary selection for homeostatic and endocrine functions mediated by brain-stem and limbic structures in particular phenotypes.

This matching or linkage between category and value is based on two very different kinds of nervous structures and functions: the limbic and brain-stem system, and the thalamocortical system. The first of these systems is related to appetitive, consummatory, and defensive behavior. It includes the hypothalamus, the brain-stem reticular formation, the amygdala, the hippocampal formation, and the septum. It receives a great deal of interoceptive input from many different organ systems and the autonomic nervous system. In general, the neural circuits in the limbic and brain-stem system are polysynaptic loops with a relatively low degree of local topographic mapping, and their temporal responses to input tend to occur in slow cycles. These loops depend extensively on biochemical as well as on neural circuits, and they appeared in evolution well before the cortex and its thalamic connections. Their ongoing function is in general developmentally assured, and it does not depend upon extensive categorization or learning.

The second, or thalamocortical, system is linked strongly to exteroceptors and is closely and extensively mapped in a polymodal fashion. It consists of the thalamocortical reentrant system, the primary and secondary sensory areas, and association cortex. It is strongly linked to the three main cortical appendages, the cerebellum, the hippocampus, and the basal ganglia, and its main functions are correlated with perceptual and conceptual categorization, memory, and learning. Except for its appendages, it has a low number of long polysynaptic loops but is characterized by a highly interconnected, reentrant, and layered local synaptic structure. Adapted to receive a highly dense and rapid series of multimodal signals, it appeared as a later evolutionary development permitting increasingly sophisticated motor behavior.

Given their evolutionary order of appearance and their role in learning, it would appear that cortical systems served to extend the range of adaptive behavior in increasingly complex environments both to reduce threat and to serve appetitive needs. These functions require a

matching of the two disparate neural systems, limbic and thalamocortical, with the emergence of connectivity patterns that serve actions
having evolutionarily selective value, whether they are reflex in nature
or constitute complex ethological patterns. A number of loci are candidates for matching between the two systems: fornix and septal systems,
hippocampus, temporal cortex, forebrain, and cingulate gyrus.

This matching is a critical part of the model for primary consciousness. We shall now consider how it might provide a sufficient basis for
this remarkable evolutionary development.

THE MODEL PROPER

The model has three main components, which I take up in order; I then
elaborate on each, as necessary.

The first component emerges as a result of the evolution of close
linkages between systems mediating concept formation in various areas
(frontal, temporal, parietal, and cingulate cortex) and interoceptively
determined value systems mediated by circuits related to hedonic responses. Such an interaction, supported by limbic circuits connecting to
the hippocampus, amygdala, and cingulate gyri, would have adaptive
value both for conventional learning and conditioning and for species-
specific ethological responses that are highly patterned. Presumably,
the increasingly refined matching between the two systems would extend the range and subtlety of ethologically constrained functions of
foraging, mating, and defense.[1]

The second component of the model is a separate form of memory
emerging as a result of the functioning of these linkages. Unlike simple
perceptual categorization, this cortical memory system would recategorize the combined interaction or carry out a comparison of states of the
two basic systems. It would be mediated by synaptic alterations reflecting the relation between category and value, largely as a result of
learning and *conceptual* change based on perceptual categorization.
Category, which is largely but not entirely mediated by exteroceptive
signals, is determined by behavior in an animal's niche as it receives
environmental signals. Value is mainly *self-determined,* inasmuch as it
is given by evolutionary and ethological constraints related to the phenotype. Nonetheless, some neural elements and synapses determining
those constraints may be modifiable, and value can be altered to some
extent by experience. A detailed learning model based on the reentrant

linkage of global mappings to value systems is consistent with this component of the model for primary consciousness and is described in *Neural Darwinism*.

There would be an adaptive advantage in evolving a conceptually based memory system[2] that correlated the continual ongoing interactions between categorized exteroceptive signals and interoceptive signals that reflect homeostatic needs. Recategorization based on past interactions of the two systems would confer obvious advantages in speed of learning and adaptive response.

Given these necessary components, the third and critical component of the model provides the *sufficient* condition for consciousness to appear. Consistent with the ideas of neuronal group selection, the model proposes that special circuits evolved that carry out a continual reentrant signaling between the second component (mediating "value-category memory") and the ongoing, real-time exteroceptive global mappings that are concerned with perceptual categorization of *current* exteroceptive stimuli *before* they can form part of that value-category memory. According to this idea, there are neuronal groups whose activities underlie accumulated "self-categories," which reflect a previous succession of states that are autonomic, consummatory, and dominant. These groups, responding to major value elements related to survival as well as categorical elements, interact by reentry in real time with other groups mediating novel ongoing perceptual categories. Such perceptual categories can then become incorporated as further parts of "self-categories."

This reentrant interaction between a special form of memory with strong conceptual components (we shall consider its possible loci later) and a stream of perceptual categorizations would generate primary consciousness. Phenomenally, this function would appear as a "picture" of ongoing categorized events or a "mental image." In the brain, there is, of course, no actual image or sketch (even if we consider visual input alone). Instead, primary consciousness arises as a discriminative comparison of previous "self-categories" (which include prior environmentally stimulated categories that were correlated with interoceptive signals) with the current or immediately categorized exteroceptive input. It is the actual physical interaction between the reentrant circuits we have mentioned and the spatiotemporal ordering of current signals from the niche that together determine the "image." An image is, in fact, a set of *correlations* of such interactions with prior memory states. We will return later to this question of the "image" and the phenomenal aspects of consciousness.

Perceptual *experience* thus arises from the correlation by a conceptual memory of an ongoing set of perceptual categorizations. Given that the extended theory is based on the TNGS, the categorizations perforce involve motor acts, and actions and responses are therefore a key part of the model. Since reentry to and from mapped receiving areas correlates the various signals emerging from an object, and since previous categorizations in memory can interact with the outputs of these reentrant paths, there is no homunculus "looking at the image." It is the discriminative comparison between a value-dominated memory involving the conceptual system and current ongoing perceptual categorization that generates primary consciousness of objects and events. Because this comparison involves a temporally conditioned bootstrapping process and a continual growth or alteration of memory, there is no infinite regress, as there is in homuncular models.[3] In effect, primary consciousness results from the interaction in real time between memories of past value-category correlations and present world input as it is categorized by global mappings (but before the components of these mappings are altered by internal states).

A Schematic Representation of the Model

Put otherwise, consciousness is an outcome of a recursively comparative memory in which previous self-nonself categorizations are *continually* related to ongoing present perceptual categorizations and their short-term succession, before such categorizations have become part of that memory.[4]

We may now consider in a diagram (figure 9.1) the form of such a recursive discrimination and take up a number of critical details, including the various anatomical loci for the storage of synaptic changes related to primary consciousness. Abbreviations for various functions are given in the diagram—the letter C standing before a parenthesis stands for "categorization of . . ." and implies reentrant function. Boldface C stands for "conceptual categorization of . . ." I stands for interoceptive input and W for exteroceptive or world input; a dot between symbols means linkage through neural connectivity or synaptic change; further definitions are given in the legend.

As the figure shows, these loci mediate a cumulative memory involving multiple recategorizations comparing previous C(W) and C(I) with the current C(W), leading to a "mental image" or primary conscious-

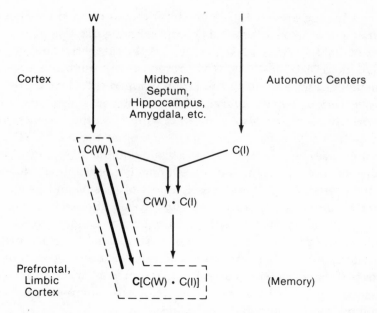

Figure 9.1

Schematic of various interactions in a model of primary consciousness. C(I) is the neural basis for categorization of I, the interoceptive input—autonomic, hypothalamic, endocrine. It is evolutionarily earlier, driven by inner events, mediated by limbic and brain-stem circuits coupled to biochemical circuits, and it shows slow phasic activity. C(W) is the neural basis for perceptual categorization of W, the exteroceptive input—peripheral, voluntary motor, proprioceptive, and polymodal sensory signals—and is mediated by thalamus and cortical areas. It is driven largely by outer events, is fast, and handles many more signals in parallel. C(W)·C(I) represents the neural basis of interaction and comparison of two categorical systems that occurs, for example, at the hippocampus, septum, and cingulate gyri. C[C(W)·C(I)] is the neural basis of conceptual recategorization of this comparison, which takes place in the cingulate gyri, temporal lobes, and parietal and frontal cortex. (The boldface C indicates conceptual categorization.) Synaptic change in each of these areas results in a cumulative special memory based on this categorization. Consciousness arises as a result of reentrant, currently acting connectivity and signaling between $\mathbf{C}[C(W)_{t=n} \cdot C(I)_{t=n}]$ *and* $C(W)_{t=n+1}$*; this is outlined in the dotted box. One must keep in mind that C(W) occurs by means of a number of different* parallel *modalities and submodalities, each with a separate reentrant connectivity; the figure shows only one such connectivity. Vision would be represented by a variety of early (see chapter 4) and higher-order reentrant connections; somatosensory, kinesthetic and proprioceptive, and auditory, olfactory, and gustatory inputs would each project by reentry to appropriate portions of the association cortex.*

ness. The "image" emerges from the play of current perceptual categorizations in real time on the accumulated value-category memory. Note that there are several possible loci for the conceptual recategorization of the combined C(W) and C(I) that have already been correlated in some previous chunks of time to form the postulated special memory system. These loci include the prefrontal, temporal, and parietal lobes, mediating concept formation, and the cingulate gyrus, comprising higher levels connected to the limbic system.

The emergence of primary consciousness depends upon a *difference* in the workings of the two different neural orders—one of which is not strongly mapped topographically and is structured to reflect regulatory changes that are relatively slow, and the other of which is strongly mapped to receive highly dense, rapidly changing exteroceptive input. A fundamental phenotypic and evolutionarily established self-nonself distinction[5] arises, one based on the difference in the categorization of interoceptive signals from functioning organs and the categorization of exteroceptive signals arising mainly from the outside world but also of proprioceptive signals. For this distinction to take place, there must be one neural means of internal homeostatic and endocrine control that is *already* ethologically determined as well as another neural means of perceptual categorization of external signals that *allows for coordination of rapid temporal succession.*

Memory as recategorization plays a major role at all of the neural stages leading to primary consciousness. Recategorical memory occurs for C(I)·C(W) and C[C(W)·C(I)], and this requires appropriate neuronal group selection and synaptic change in the various areas noted in figure 9.1. The emergence of consciousness depends upon the existence of a sufficiently large store in C[C(W)·C(I)]. As is illustrated in figure 9.2, this store accumulates *in time* as previous categorizations are bootstrapped into memory. The step leading to primary consciousness involves a comparison of this memory, which is critically determined by self events leading to C(I), with fresh categorizations of world events C(W) that have not yet been related to value.

Learning, which depends for its direction on value,[6] greatly contributes to the emergence of primary consciousness, which, according to the model, requires experience and is an epigenetic event. The comparison that leads to primary consciousness has Jamesian properties: it is subjective, continuous (because of behavior and reentry), always changing, and about things or events (categories). Although certain subsets of C(I) can serve as C(W), they generally do not.[7]

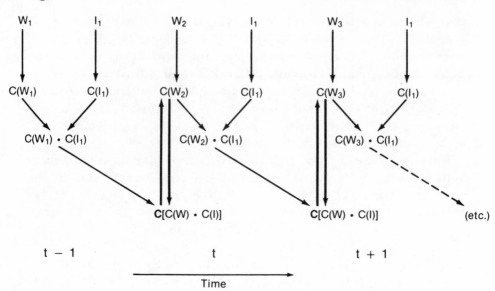

Figure 9.2

A schematic illustration of the interactions shown in figure 9.1 as a function of time. (Symbols are identical in the two figures; subscripts refer to signals.) Because perceptual categorizations in each parallel input channel are driven by action, and because they are in constant interaction with systems carrying out conceptual categorization and the organs of succession, the continuity of consciousness is assured. Reentry, which has a strong temporal and rhythmic character, also contributes to both continuity and change, yielding Jamesian properties. Because the self-nonself distinction is dominant (see figure 9.3), primary consciousness is subjective. Inasmuch as the interaction is with perceptual categorization, C(W), however, its content is concerned with things, movements, and events. It is important to understand that primary consciousness, in any time period, must shift and that, at a given time period, it may or may not be shaped by previous conscious episodes. Indeed, as the diagram makes clear, the actions of systems that can never become conscious always contribute to the process. Note that in the time period illustrated, W signals change rapidly, as indicated by successive subscripts, whereas I signals have not yet changed significantly, as indicated by the same subscript. In an animal with primary consciousness only, the representations in any time period are the experience at that period—obviously, no direct experience of the more remote past is possible.

In this scheme, the categorization C(I) has precedence particularly in respect to output, even though it is much less rich in potential orderings than is C(W). This is shown in figure 9.3. The recategorical memory designated **C[C(W)·C(I)]**, a prime determinant of self in the self-nonself distinction, is accordingly regulated by a number of factors. These in-

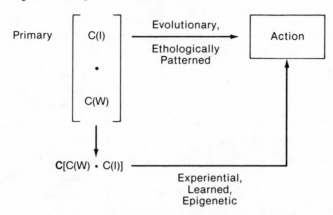

Figure 9.3
Primacy of C(I), which can lead to action independently of **C[C(W)·C(I)]**. *C(I) is evolutionarily prior and is continuous as part of the homeostatic control in the phenotype (symbols as in figures 9.1 and 9.2).*

clude: (1) the strong evolutionary dominance of internal homeostatic events as controllers of behavior, whether through reflexes or through ethological patterns;[8] (2) the strong and extensive coupling to biochemical circuits, particularly those of the endocrine system;[9] (3) the prior developmental activity and *continual* internal input (I) to the brain of all these systems, *more or less independently* of external input (W), which can be gated, damped, or reduced in response to needs related to (I); and (4) the critical dependence of **C[C(W)·C(I)]** on previous C(I).

An additional asymmetry related to C(I) warrants special notice. The interaction by reentry leading to consciousness is between present C(W) and accumulated **C[C(W)·C(I)]** and *not* with C(I). In general, C(I) is nonconscious and not accessible to conscious "imaging"; in any event, C(I) does not reflect extensively mapped structures, as does C(W). Indeed, if this asymmetry were not maintained, primary consciousness (which is based on the *difference* in the nature of internal and external categorizations and on the dominance of the internal) could not arise.

PREFRONTAL CORTEX: A LOCUS FOR C[C(W)·C(I)]

The candidate loci for the value-category memory include the frontal, cingulate, temporal, and parietal cortices. Of these, the prefrontal cortex of the frontal lobe plays the most important role in goal-directed behaviors extending over time, in anticipatory activity, and in attentive control. It has strong reentrant connections with other cortical regions, the basal ganglia, the hippocampus, and the cerebellum.

One of its main functions is to regulate the temporal ordering of connected behaviors. When carrying out this function, it must maintain short-term working memory (see table 6.1), which provides capability for anticipatory set—"keeping a goal in mind." The prefrontal cortex is likely to be essential in the formation of motor plans and their conversion via the basal ganglia and motor cortex to motor programs. As we shall see in chapter 12, when we consider a model for attention, the prefrontal cortex is likely to be concerned not only in the coordinate linkage of successive acts to fulfill a motor plan but also in recognizing novelty. It is concerned with "foresight," choice, and attention.

In an excellent review, Fuster[10] has termed the prefrontal cortex "a mediator of cross-temporal contingencies." This term is applied mainly to the dorsolateral portions of this structure; the orbital and mediolateral portions of the prefrontal lobe appear more functionally correlated with emotional alterations and disinhibition of behavior.

A considerable amount of evidence regarding man and animals has accumulated to support these ideas. Delayed-response tasks, such as one in which, after a delay, a monkey must decide under which of two identical objects food has been placed, serve as a test of the proposed functions of prefrontal cortex. The animal must remember which object concerns the food and ignore inappropriate stimuli. In delayed alternation, the animal must remember the side of the last response and alternately press the right or the left of two buttons simultaneously lit between delays. In delayed matching to sample, the monkey must remember a color (red or green) corresponding to the sample, presented on the top button. After a delay, the two colors appear simultaneously, and the monkey must choose the color of the sample in that trial. The colors of sample (upper) and choice (lower) buttons are changed randomly between trials.

Lesions in the prefrontal cortex result in deficits in performance and learning of such delay tasks, and the deficit depends upon the length of the delay. The deficit is not simply one of short-term memory, because it is not manifested when there is no choice between alternatives, as in remembering only one goal. This is brought out sharply by tests of discrimination reversal in which, after the animal is trained to associate one of two stimuli with a reward, the stimulus-reward association is shifted to the other stimulus. To carry this out successfully requires memory of a current stimulus-reward contingency *and* the ability to suppress the alternative response. Lesioned animals lack this so-called interference control. A reasonable interpretation is that the prefrontal cortex helps coordinate temporally separate categorizations in order to carry out goal-directed actions. To be successful, the animal must have appropriate short-term memory and the ability to control interference, which is an attentional process. Lesioned animals appear to have a defect in presyntax.

The original studies of evoked potential and contingent negative variation (CNV) in human subjects by Walter and his colleagues[11] provide additional support for the view that the prefrontal region plays a role in such tasks. CNV is a slow electrical potential recorded from the scalp in the frontal region. The subject presses a button after two stimuli, one auditory, one visual, separated by a one-second delay. After repeated exposure, the CNV appears and persists during the delay. Many variants of this scheme have supported the interpretation that the subject actually learns of a relation of contingency between temporally separated components in the trial and that the CNV is correlated with this learning.

Prompted by these findings, Fuster and his colleagues[12] analyzed cell discharge in the prefrontal cortex of monkeys engaged in delay tasks. They found evidence of cells showing elevated discharge during the delay mainly in response to a cue and of cells that increased in activity during the delay as choice and motor response approached. We listed in table 6.1 similar findings of cells present in various brain regions reflecting conditioned readiness to respond.

We will briefly discuss human subjects with prefrontal lesions in chapter 13, on diseases of consciousness. Here, it suffices to say that some of the patients afflicted by such diseases cannot properly anticipate or plan the consequences of their own movements and show repeated errors of action even though they are aware of them. The scanning studies of Ingvar[13] and of Roland[14] on normal humans measuring blood flow and metabolic rate in cortex are consistent with this: they definitely show activation of prefrontal areas in the ideation, "programming," and performance of actions.

All of these data support the notion that the prefrontal area is important in certain kinds of short-term memory, anticipatory set, formation of concepts, presyntax, and attentional suppression of interference.[15] While it is necessary for such functions, however, it almost certainly is not sufficient. As we shall see when we discuss the attention model, in chapter 12, in order to achieve success in these functions, activity in this region must be coordinated by reentry with the basal ganglia and many other cortical areas.

I have chosen the prefrontal cortex as an example of an area carrying out $C[C(W) \cdot C(I)]$ not because it is the only such area but because it illustrates many of the relations we have proposed to be necessary for the development of primary consciousness. Its responses can be shown to be connected to situations of reward in which $C(I)$ must be processed. It is closely connected to orbital and medial regions of the prefrontal lobe that are themselves connected to the cingulate cortex. It is involved in relations that are both anticipatory and conceptual. Finally, it depends upon a series of connectivities with motor areas and with organs of succession, such as the basal ganglia, for its central function of mediating the ordered succession of actions based on a goal. All of these properties are ones that require more than the mere seriatim linkage of perceptual categorizations.

The hypothesis prompted by these ideas is that the prefrontal cortex is capable, among other functions, of "classifying" the activity of global mappings made of classification couples from other cortical areas. Acting through synaptic changes and both the hippocampal and the basal ganglion loops, it can help distinguish objects and movements in definite sequences. It is a concept center par excellence.

In the light of our previous discussions, however, it must not be assumed that the prefrontal cortex (or even this cortex together with the cingulate, parietal, and temporal cortex) is *sufficient* for primary consciousness. The essential other element is the key reentrant loop back to $C(W)$. Let us consider some possible candidate structures for this loop.

POSSIBLE ANATOMICAL BASES FOR THE KEY REENTRANT LOOP

In presenting the model, I have already indicated the areas that may be involved in carrying out $C(I)$, $C(W)$, $C(W) \cdot C(I)$, and $C[C(W) \cdot C(I)]$. Before speculating further about the reentrant loop that gives rise to primary consciousness, we will do well once more to collect these assignments to anatomical loci here[16] (see also the legend to figure 9.1). Of course, at this stage of knowledge, these assignments can only be approximate and incomplete. $C(I)$ takes place at the midbrain level through the mesencephalic reticular formation and at the diencephalic level through hypothalamic responses. It receives input from autonomic and visceral systems. C(W) occurs via the thalamocortical systems leading to primary and secondary cortex for each modality and via loops involving the motor cortex as well. The smoothing of responses on the motor side is carried out by the cerebellum. [C(W)·C(I)] occurs in the amygdala, septum, and hippocampal formation as well as in basal ganglia. Finally, C[C(W)·C(I)] is likely to occur as a result of global mappings (involving all of the cortical appendages at one time or another) in frontal, parietal, temporal, and cingulate cortex. In particular, as we have already noted, it must strongly involve the prefrontal areas related to concept formation.[17]

These pathways all participate in reentrant signaling from sensorimotor areas, resulting in perceptual categorizations based on external input. This provides the basis for learning and further alterations of response. But it is unlikely that these *same* pathways are used for the key reentrant process between C(W) and C[C(W)·C(I)] that leads to primary consciousness. To avoid conflict and to allow continuing changes that are not proximately dependent upon consciousness, at least one other pathway seems to be required.

Three (not necessarily exclusive) candidates come to mind. One comprises the long cortical fiber tracts—the dorsal, the medial, and the uncinate longitudinal fasciculi, for example—that connect cortical areas to each other. A second is the medial pulvinar nucleus of the thalamus, which is reentrantly connected with prefrontal, cingulate, and parietal cortical areas and thus can correlate activity in all three. These pathways do not appear, however, to have a structure subject to various levels of control or activation.

Another candidate, more speculative, but less deficient in respect to control, is the thalamocortical and corticothalamic reentrant pathway (figure 9.4; see also figure 12.2, *B*, in which all three candidates are diagrammed in connection with the control of attention). In addition to the pulvinar, most of the nuclei of the thalamus have direct and reentrant cortical projections that are quite specific. Moreover, these nuclei do not connect directly with each other. On the other hand, the reticular nucleus of the thalamus has reentrant connections with each of the other nuclei as well as a more sparse and diffuse cortical connection.[18] Although these synapses with other nuclei are GABAergic and are likely to be inhibitory, they fall onto inhibitory local circuit neurons *in* these nuclei as well as onto neurons that are excitatory for the cortex. Thus, depending on the relative activity of these two kinds of neurons, activity in the reticular nucleus of the thalamus could be disinhibitory or inhibitory for particular pathways, resulting in mutual excitation between the cortex and particular nuclei.

If the activity is disinhibitory, it could link or correlate the activity of corticothalamic connections from one cortical area to the activity of thalamocortical connections proceeding to another cortical area. This correlation would occur through reentrant paths (figure 9.4) mediated by the reticular nucleus and connecting the two thalamic nuclei involved. These paths would relate the activity along particular *combinations* of the reentrant connections between cortex and thalamus. By this means, a separate reentrant path with its attendant correlations could be established between $C[C(W)\cdot C(I)]$ in frontal cortex, for example, and $C(W)$ mediated by primary or secondary sensory cortex.

The operation of the "multiplexing" model based on such indirect linkage of the activity of the various thalamic nuclei via the reticular nucleus does not necessarily exclude simultaneous reentry via corticocortical long tracts to close the "consciousness loop." It is an attractive idea that both pathways and those to the pulvinar can operate simultaneously and synergistically. Inasmuch as the reticular nucleus of the thalamus receives direct input from midbrain areas related to the reticular formation and the activity of locus ceruleus and raphe nuclei, this postulated activity of "multiplexing" by the reticular nucleus could be subject to definite state control. Thus, it would be particularly satisfying if primary consciousness and sleep states could be related by such a mechanism.[19]

For the waking state, there is evidence for the independence of pathways leading to conceptual performance and learning and those mediating consciousness. Among the most striking observations, already discussed in chapter 2, are those concerned with dissociations between so-called implicit and explicit (or conscious) knowledge in neuropsychological syndromes.[20] Patients with syndromes as diverse as amnesia, blindsight, prosopagnosia, dyslexia, aphasia, and hemineglect can perform tasks that tap an impaired function as long as the tasks are posed in a manner that does not require explicit conscious knowledge. A patient with prosopagnosia can reveal familiarity with a given face in tests while having no phenomenal experience of that familiarity. Similarly, a patient with blindsight can locate an object with no conscious knowledge that he has located it. Schacter and his colleagues[21] have pointed out that such dissociations range over a variety of different syndromes and that each is nevertheless domain-specific and selective and does not represent a global disorder of consciousness. Their pro-

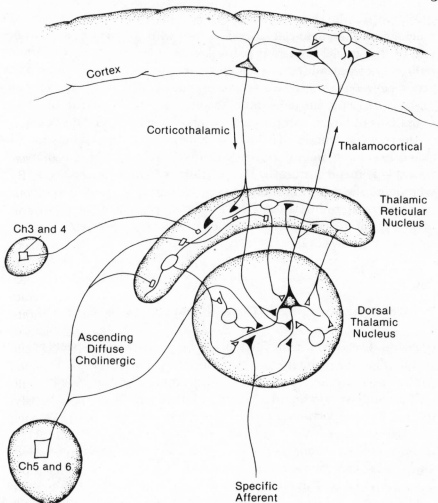

Figure 9.4

Synaptic organization in the thalamus revealing the possibility of inhibition and disinhibition of corticothalamic and thalamocortical pathways. Filled-in symbols (▲ = *cell body,* ◄ = *axonal terminal) represent excitatory neurons;* open round symbols (○ = *cell body,* ◁ = *axonal terminal) represent inhibitory neurons;* open square symbols *represent cell bodies and synaptic terminals of dopaminergic neurons. Ch3 and 4, Ch5 and 6 = nuclei of cholinergic neurons in brain stem and basal forebrain (□ = cell body; □ = axonal terminal).A large thalamic nucleus, the pulvinar (not shown here) may also mediate corticocortical activity (see figure 12.2, B). It is reentrantly connected with all cortical lobes (but mainly frontal, parietal, and cingulate) and has limited subcortical connectivity. The nucleus and the areas to which it is connected are largest and most differentiated in primates. Brain scans show increased pulvinar activity in humans during conscious memory-imaging tasks.*

posal that, despite their domain specificity, these disorders fit a common mechanism of consciousness accords well with the idea that the function of the special reentrant paths proposed here may be directly or indirectly compromised in such disorders (see chapter 13). Such a disturbance in one domain would *not* prevent $C[C(W)\cdot C(I)]$ from operating and carrying out conceptual distinctions, nor would it affect the operations of key reentrant paths in other modalities or domains.

The reentrant model of primary consciousness proposed here implies that considerable neural processing is required before registration of a percept. This is consistent with the findings of Libet and coworkers,[22] who timed the report of such percepts following a stimulus and found a latency of up to half a second. This timing is also consistent with the operations of the cortex in connection with its various organs of succession (see chapters 7 and 12).

PHENOMENAL ASPECTS OF PRIMARY CONSCIOUSNESS

Although I shall comment further on the phenomenal aspects related to the model of primary consciousness in the chapters dedicated to various psychological and philosophical implications, it is worth forestalling any skepticism that might arise in regard to the special or inaccessible properties of qualia, "raw feels," "images," and so on.[23] As we discussed in chapter 2, qualia are the various subjective experiences, feelings, and sensations that constitute or accompany awareness. There, we proposed to choose human conscious behavior and reports as our best reference in comparisons with other species. We *assumed* that qualia exist in humans and pointed out that while we cannot give a precise account of any individual person's qualia, we can correlate their reports and behavior with our own as observers as well as with various measurements. But this is true only of humans with higher-order consciousness—a state that requires the construction through language and social interactions of a concept of the self and the ability to model the past, present, and future.

An animal having only primary consciousness cannot report qualia to itself or others. Indeed, it is possible that the lack of higher-order consciousness imposes a barrier to the development of an explicit conscious memory for phenomenal experience. An animal may have phenomenal experience, and that experience may have an individual, historical character that can affect future behavior, but it is not *subjective* experience—there is no subject or person to make discriminations or reports of that phenomenal experience over time. This is not a denial of the possibility of phenomenal experience. Indeed, with the human as a referent, we may attempt to correlate behavior, morphology, and neurophysiology in an effort to assess the phenomenal states of an animal. But we cannot call such states qualia in the sense that we can call our own states qualia.

We touched on the difficulties of this predicament in chapter 2. It implies that if a consciousness theory is to provide a sufficient explanation for qualia, that explanation must be made in terms of *human* conscious experience. The path we must take is therefore to provide an account of primary consciousness on which an account of higher-order consciousness, including qualia, can be based. This course, forced on us by our present scientific limitations, does not mean that we cannot attempt to *discriminate* possible phenomenal states in other animals with appropriate morphologies. The reentrant discrimination in real time between an internally correlated set of memories (which are conceptual and recategorical) and present perceptual categorizations driven by immediate world events through *different* sheets of sensory receptors and inputs would inevitably lead to discrimination of a series of different perceptual modalities. Each would be a priori differentiable from the other on the basis of the neural structures and dynamics characteristic of it. Accordingly, if a creature that had *only* primary consciousness were capable of reporting (which, of course, it is not), it would admit to registering a *different* "feel" for each different modality within the confines of the present. "Feels" are a result of such discriminations, and each corresponds to a particular set of neural structures and dynamics related to a particular modality. A visual "mental image" is one such kind of "feel."

It is important to emphasize again that despite the primacy of C(I), the density, relationships, and character of such "images" are determined practically completely by interactions with the world and its objects and arrangements. Of course, changes in neural structures can remove or alter components of an "image" (see the above discussion on implicit or explicit knowledge), but they cannot create it de novo without experience. Memory as recategorization in the absence of world stimuli[24] is not the same as consciousness of actual perceived stimuli. We will consider this subject further when we discuss higher-order consciousness, in chapter 11.

We may anticipate some of the ideas presented in chapter 14 by pointing out that attempting a scientific explanation of qualia across species is as speculative as a scientific explanation of why matter exists.[25] Quantum field theory can give us a basis for discriminating various energies and material states, but its equations can only speculatively account for the *existence* of matter. Similarly, a principled brain theory explaining consciousness in terms of neural structures can account for how particular structures allow conscious discrimination. But given a satisfactory explanation of those mechanisms and structures in an individual that allow that individual to experience and discriminate sensations (and, in the case of humans, to report them), no additional communicated scientific explanation is feasible or necessary. It is sufficient to provide a model that explains their discrimination, variation, and consequences. As scientists, we can have no concern with ontological mysteries concerned with *why* there is something and not nothing, or *why* warm feels "warm."

TESTS OF THE MODEL

Primary consciousness as defined by the model has a temporal structure (because of its dependence upon succession and recursion; see figure 9.2), and it is based on highly differentiated neural structures that have specific functions. The model should therefore be falsifiable, or at least testable for consistency, as I discussed in chapter 5. This is true, however, only in a conditional sense. The condition arises from the fact that, because it involves a self-nonself distinction, consciousness is an individual process and that in examining it, an observer runs the risk of committing the psychologist's fallacy as outlined by James.[26] The only criterion for assessing phenomenal experience is the report of an individual,[27] and that is only possible for humans (the qualia assumption; see chapter 2). Therefore, the model must be examined rather carefully for traps and pitfalls, particularly because animals having *only* primary consciousness can yield no direct report and because observations of that function must therefore always be indirect and by induction. Moreover, as we shall see when we consider higher-order consciousness, it is not possible for creatures possessing it (like us) reliably to "intuit" what it is like to possess *only* primary consciousness.

There are two resources available in such a situation: (1) check for consistency with the rest of the available neurobiological data (this is akin to the arguments pursued in cosmology on the basis of available data and theories of current physics); and (2) consider gedankenexperiments on an animal's behavior that might be revealing.[28]

I shall exploit both resources here, discussing further the structural requirements that would, if removed, obliterate primary consciousness or not let it emerge (see also chapter 5). I will then consider certain functional states that emerge from the model and compare them to those that have actually been observed in such states as sleep. I defer discussion of other states (hallucination, dreams, illusions) until we have considered higher-order consciousness. I do this because their corroboration in others, like higher-order consciousness itself, depends almost completely on the individual's ability to report.

According to the model of primary consciousness, a "mental image" should be strongly affected by self inputs and world inputs in different ways, and aspects of each of these inputs should also be strongly time-dependent or sequence-dependent in different ways. But simple suggestions to reduce or obliterate these inputs independently are hard to arrange because of their intricate anatomical interactions or their failure to correspond to accessible body boundaries. For example, sensory deprivation experiments can reduce W inputs (see figures 9.1 and 9.2) to levels very rarely experienced by a waking animal, but cannot reduce those components coming from joint sense and other proprioceptive channels.[29] The reduction that can be achieved does not lead to a loss of consciousness in adult human subjects, but it can lead to severe alterations in *states* of consciousness and to bizarre images, if not hallucinations. Given a reasonable amount of experience, $C[C(W)\cdot C(I)]$ can interact with even slight amounts of W inputs to sustain some degree of awareness. In any case, this paradigm unfortunately cannot be extended successfully to tests of animals lacking verbal capacities. The only possible exception might be a chimpanzee trained to sign; one might observe changed responses to various signing and learning paradigms as a result of sensory deprivation.

It is correspondingly difficult to obliterate all the visceral states of an animal; its survival literally depends on them and generates them. But an indirect test of the model related to the physiology of sleep[30] is conceivable. Sleep may, in fact, be obligatory in organisms with primary consciousness for a number of reasons, the most important being to maintain the match required in conscious animals between the greatly disparate C(I) and C(W) systems of categorization. C(I) is slow, phasic, and temporally coupled to various biochemically different regulatory and endocrine systems. Compared with C(W), it has much lower densities of input, but it may have a much larger cellular energy demand imposed by its linkage to biochemical circuits. The cells, transmitters, and hormones of this system may be greatly subject to metabolic alteration, *particularly when coupled to and driven by those of C(W).* [31]

In contrast, C(W) is fast, parallel, and highly dense in its mapped inputs from a large number of different sensory and memorial systems, probably with a much lower energy demand on target cells per unit of input. This continual requirement for C(I) to match world categories, leading to C(I)·C(W) in awake, alert behavior (see figures 9.1 and 9.2), may result in biochemical alteration and asynchrony in the matching or interaction of neuroendocrine loops. This would result in a failure of adaptive matching—C(W) would "load" C(I) and vice versa or, speaking more correctly, affect the corresponding neuronal groups. Indeed, it is obvious that the matching of such groups to C(W) inputs occurs in sites such as the septum and hippocampus and the cingulate gyrus—one apparently necessary for short-term memory, the other possibly a critical site for mediating in part the memory related to C[C(W)·C(I)].

Sleep may therefore be required in evolution in order to reduce C(W) drive periodically, thus allowing *alternative* C(I) and C(W) systems to be replenished biochemically and synchronized. If so, the model predicts there is an evolutionary parallel between sleep behavior and the emergence of components contributing to primary consciousness.

If the thalamic multiplexing hypothesis is correct, then sleep states known to be correlated with behavior of the reticular nucleus of the thalamus may be informative. Indeed, according to this hypothesis, primary consciousness (and attention) should be strongly affected, or possibly be obliterated, by damage to or bilateral removal of this nucleus or its connections. Another test of the primary-consciousness model is also ablative. Although I inputs, W inputs, and their categorizations C(I) and C(W) cannot be fully removed, one might attempt to identify the sites for C[C(W)·C(I)] by ablation or accidents of nature. Likely sites for such a recategorical memory include parts of the frontal and temporal lobes and the cingulate gyrus. Temporal lobe seizures certainly can lead to a loss of higher-order consciousness, but it is not clear how to test for particular degrees of *primary* consciousness loss in a human subject. Strokes leading to obliteration of the cingulate gyrus should severely alter primary consciousness (particularly various affects) and might indeed lead to unconsciousness and even coma. We have already mentioned the various neuropsychological syndromes that result in loss of so-called explicit knowledge. We will consider these issues related to disease more extensively in chapter 13.

The fact that *all* of these various states may lead to a distortion or loss of primary consciousness points up the difficulty of empirical test in a nonverbal animal—how is one to detect the presence of primary consciousness, let alone interpret the consequences of its loss, if the situation causing the loss leads to larger or multiple changes? Undoubtedly, this difficulty has contributed to the rise of radical behaviorism: insofar as there can be no report of "mental images," the conservative suggestion is to observe only the animal's behavior and its consequences. Moreover, because much of behavior may involve processes independent of those mediating primary consciousness (particularly *after* learning has taken place or novelty been reduced to habit), it has been suggested that there is little point in pursuing occurrences that cannot be directly tested.[32]

At first encounter, there is much to be said for this position. Unfortunately, it is wholly inadequate in any attempt to explain the evolutionary link to verbal animals that obviously know they have primary consciousness.[33] This Cartesian dilemma is "solved" by the behaviorist by denial, despite the phenomenal experience of the individual.

Is there a way around the difficulty? The possibility exists that a pattern of neural activity associated with consciousness in humans will also be found in animals and thus provide grounds for inference. Failing this, can one at least construct a set of gedankenexperiments that will clarify the nature of the difficulty? I shall try to do so here by taking the greatest license—imagining that automata can be constructed that have systems corresponding to those in figures 9.1 and 9.2 and asking, through a gedankenexperiment, how I might conclude that their behavior suggested the presence of primary consciousness.

Let us call a pair of these automata A_1 and A_2 and specify that in all aspects they are identical except for experience. Now imagine that A_1 is placed in a situation where (after some experience in the "world") it can observe only A_2 and not the world situations or larger contexts with which A_2 interacts. A_2 cannot observe A_1 but is continually presented with a rich set of novel situations $(s_1, s_2, \ldots, s_n)$ to which it must adapt. Now imagine further that A_2 *does* adapt to some situations *while being observed by A_1* and that an unperceived human observer can simultaneously see both of the automata, their world, and their behavior.

After some time, remove A_2 from the scene and present A_1 with the same set of novelties $(s_1, s_2, \ldots, s_n)$ and with these situations in different orders. If it proceeds to adapt very much more efficiently than it would have had it not observed A_2, a reasonable conclusion by the human observer would be that A_1 is conscious. The reasoning is that if the succession of situations were diverse and novel enough, one could proffer no explanation of A_1's enhanced performance without including an internal interpretation on its part of A_2's performance. That interpretation would have to have identified A_2's performance *categorically* with some possible performance by A_1 itself. But that identification requires a "picture" of the class of "animal" related to itself, as well as an identification back to itself of behavior observed in A_2, so that imitation of that behavior could take place to improve A_1's performance on initial presentation with novelty.

If A_2 were in fact constructed *differently* from A_1 and if such a performance were to occur, the argument would be strengthened even further. This is so because A_2 would have to, in addition to carrying out its other tasks, transform its observations of A_1 to fit its own situation. In this case, the objection that A_2 is "simply imitating" A_1 and thus is merely "simulating" consciousness is removed.[34]

This intricate and indirect construction (deliberately made in terms of automata to underline our difficulty) reveals how the problem of observation is complicated by the individuality of all forms of consciousness. Indeed, the automaton gedankenexperiment is crude when compared, for example, with the criteria that Lenneberg has laid down to determine whether an ape might learn a language.[35] Only badly controlled observations could duplicate the gedankenexperiment described above in real animals. Nonetheless, the observations of Premack on evidence for intentionality in chimpanzees suggest the presence of primary consciousness.[36] Moreover, the observations of the Baldwin effect, and the propagation of various innovative or imitative behaviors in birds and mammals[37] may also indicate processes relying on primary consciousness.

Curiously enough, it is easier to obtain evidence for the existence of primary consciousness along with higher-order consciousness in animals that have concepts and language[38] (i.e., humans). And language or its neural precursor is required for the robust emergence of higher-order consciousness, just as primary consciousness is required for the acquisition of language. Let us therefore turn next to a consideration in neural terms of how language may have evolved.

10

Language

Language provides a major clue to the emergence of higher-order consciousness—the capacity that sustains direct awareness related to plans. In its fully developed form, higher-order consciousness may be considered an ability to model internal states free of real time (and occasionally also of space)—so that past, present, and future are connected in terms of such plans.

It is not my intention here to develop a complete psycholinguistic theory, and I certainly will not venture into linguistics proper. Rather, I want to show how, in a global brain theory, the evolution and acquisition of language may be related to the previous evolution of brain areas for concepts. This will require some consideration of the special apparatus of speech, of phonology and syntax, and of semantics and language comprehension. The goal will be to sketch a model for the acquisition of speech and language based on the extended TNGS. If I succeed, this will provide a basis in the next chapter for discussing the connection between language and the beginnings of higher-order consciousness.

Obviously, despite my disclaimers, this project cannot be completely divorced from current work on linguistics and psycholinguistics.[1] Nevertheless, it must be distinguished from such efforts in terms of its assumptions. A basic distinction must be made between the present project and Cartesian linguistics—proposals by Chomsky of a universal grammar embodied as a set of rules in a brain module whose functioning is genetically predetermined.[2] Our task will be otherwise—to see whether one can account developmentally and evolutionarily for the emergence of language as an *epigenetic* phenomenon. To do so, I must set out some fundamental premises and then comment on some pertinent aspects of linguistics and psycholinguistics. Following that, I sketch a theoretical proposal for language acquisition based on the ideas of the TNGS.

There are four fundamental premises upon which that sketch rests. The *first* is that a necessary but not sufficient basis for semantics already exists in those areas of the brain concerned with concepts, areas such as the frontal, temporal, and parietal lobes (exclusive of Broca's and Wernicke's areas). Although these areas do not mediate semantics, I assume here that these areas are needed (in addition to Broca's and Wernicke's areas) for the *development* of semantics as well as of syntax. A *second* premise follows from this: Broca's and Wernicke's areas, which are evolutionary adaptations unique to language, are *not* themselves sufficient for the realization of meaningful speech. As various phonological and syntactic mechanisms evolved, they exploited the already existent cortical apparatus related to the categorization of global mappings and presyntax, which provide the brain bases for ordering of gestures[3] in terms of concepts and vice versa (see chapter 8). *Third,* when sufficient phonology emerges (as the result of various specialized evolutionary developments for speech), words and sentences become symbols for concepts, and true syntax can appear. The *fourth* premise is the strongest of all: at that time in an individual when a lexicon is sufficiently developed, the conceptual apparatus may recursively treat and classify the various productions of language themselves— morphemes, words, sentences—as entities to be categorized and recombined without any *necessary* further reference to their initial origins or to their bases in perception, learning, and social transmission.

Before proposing a model based on these premises, we will do well to make several evolutionary, developmental, and linguistic distinctions. It is now reasonably certain that speech is a special and unique evolutionary development in *Homo sapiens.* It seems likely that the major evolutionary adaptations in anatomical structure underlying the capacity for speech were the following.[4] (1) The emergence of changes in the basicranium after assumption of bipedalism that permitted shaping of the supralaryngeal tract and alteration of the vocal folds and their articulation. (2) The associated development of cortical regions (Broca's and Wernicke's areas and the arcuate tract) that were responsible for the production and categorization of phonetic structures that involve coarticulation[5] in speech. Insofar as such cortical regions are involved in the categorization and recategorization of gestural aspects of speech, they also formed the bases for a specific and special memory related to the production and stabilization of phonemes. (3) These cortical structures had to be connected to areas responsible for the planning of motor sequences (premotor cortex, accessory motor cortex, and arcuate sulcus, as well as basal ganglia), to areas for acoustic perception, and to cortical areas (frontal, parietal, and temporal) dedicated to categorizing global mappings as a basis for concept formation.

Notice that such evolutionary developments could have been gradual.[6] Insofar as a selective advantage, however slight, accrued to those hominids who could exchange even a small set of signs and symbols in a coarticulated fashion, the stage would be set for any mutations enhancing appropriate morphologic changes in the brain, or the vocal tract, or in emotional expression, that increased fitness, whether for hunting or mating or the rearing of young.

AN EPIGENETIC THEORY OF SPEECH

With these comments in mind, we may attempt to construct a theory of speech acquisition consistent with the TNGS. This theory assumes that, prior to speech, the brain bases of gestural ordering, of concepts, and of the presyntactical features of thinking were already in place and that the conceptual apparatus already had neural means to distinguish objects and actions (see chapter 8). As phonology emerged in a speech community using sentences as the major units of exchange, the phonemes and parts of sentences could be associated by learning. Utterances corresponding to nouns in a particular language could be associated with objects and those corresponding to verbs with actions. This association provided the beginnings of semantics. As long as there already existed presyntactical structures (see chapter 8) allowing nouns to follow verbs in a defined order (or vice versa) and even if that ordering involved only dyadic arrangements, this assignment of semantic significance would have led to the emergence of a more intricate syntax, particularly as Broca's and Wernicke's areas appeared.

This speech theory proposes that the acquisition of phonological capacities in evolution *provided the means first for semantics and then for syntax to arise by the connection of preexisting conceptual learning to lexical learning.* It rests on assumptions similar to those of lexical functional grammar as formulated by Bresnan and is also consistent with the idea of semantic bootstrapping developed by Grimshaw, Macnamara, and Pinker.[7] In addition, however, I suggest here explicit evolutionary, anatomical, and physiological means based on the TNGS by which semantic bootstrapping is made possible. The major new components in the present proposal, which contrast with these previous suggestions, concern the description of structures supporting concepts and presyntax (see chapter 8) and the provision of a basis for grammar in selectionism rather than in functionalism (see chapter 2). A young infant *already* has conceptual categories[8] that are not defined or originated by semantic criteria, and these categories arise epigenetically from the activity of structures concerned with concepts and presyntax. As Pinker has pointed out,[9] the semantic-bootstrapping hypothesis has received support from data on children's language,[10] which show a close correspondence between syntax and semantics.

I assume that the *evolution* of the ability to use language[11] depends upon a close connection between phonology and syntax and that syntax emerges richly in each individual only after semantic bootstrapping takes place. Moreover, it is important to the present proposal that the conceptual system can deal with newly acquired lexical and semantic items as entities for further categorization.[12] The resultant emergence, interaction, and correlation of syntactic, semantic, and phonological levels[13] by reentry provide a rich basis for the developmental emergence of further syntactic rules and semantic interpretations. This follows from our fourth premise, mentioned in the preceding section. Thus, by these means, newly acquired items can be reassorted and recombined to achieve new meaning. As Pinker has discussed,[14] syntactic knowledge already acquired can also be used to help interpret utterances whose explicit semantic interpretation is otherwise not available. This should lead to acceleration of acquisition as well as to increasing mastery over new linguistic relations.

Such a theory could account for syntactic sequences in a generative manner without already assuming a large number of *preexisting* rules.[15] The theory achieves this by supposing that an initial syntactic ordering or a primitive (such as that present in presyntax) can be expanded by the addition of the activity of Broca's and Wernicke's areas to deal effectively with strings of utterances. This occurs by recursively relating semantic to phonological sequences, generating syntactic correspondences, and then treating such rules in memory as objects for conceptual manipulation. The important neurobiological element in the theory is that *this recursion occurs by reentry among various cortical repertoires.* Thus, the theory relies on the assumption that to build a rich syntax one must already have reentrant structures providing a *conceptual basis* for semantics. According to the TNGS, this conceptual basis is provided by the categorization of global mappings in frontal, temporal, and parietal areas as described in chapter 8. These conceptual bases are the same ones required to build the special memory needed for primary consciousness itself.

In such a system, appropriate cortical and subcortical areas must be linked so that phonological, syntactic, and semantic levels can interact in various combinations.[16] This suggests a need for special memory systems related to words and sentences at *each* of these levels. According to the TNGS, the key element connecting the cortical areas mediating memory for each level is reentry (see figure 10.1). Reentry among the cortical regions subserving the relation of acoustic to phonological categorization, the production of utterances, and conceptualization would act to unite a particular sequence much in the same manner that multiple visual areas (see chapter 4) that are functionally segregated can yield the basis for a particular coherent "image."[17]

This is a fundamental point: in the evolution and acquisition of speech, it is particularly important that memory, comprehension, and

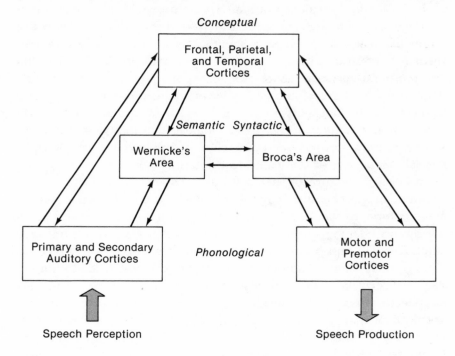

Figure 10.1

Diagram indicating the need for multiple reentrant connectivities subserving phonological, syntactic, semantic, and conceptual functions in order for language to arise. Because of the necessary participation of global mappings (see figure 3.4), perception and production are tightly linked.

production interact *in a great variety of ways*. Reentry provides the means for this interaction. In this fashion, not only do words serve as symbols for already existing concepts but the conceptual system can recategorize such symbols in a context-dependent manner in their relation to other symbols and syntactic order. This addresses the problem created by the fact that often a higher-order structure is needed (just as in planning for motion) to elaborate lower-order sequencing, execution, and interpretation (figure 10.1).

While this theory of language acquisition is based on the evolutionary emergence of special anatomy,[18] it is clear that this anatomy must necessarily have been linked in its function to already sophisticated areas in the brain capable of concepts. The greatest significance of recent work on chimpanzees[19] may be in demonstrating that they are capable of conceptual formulation and thought. Although they can use counters or signs for words, they clearly cannot go beyond presyntax. The key evolutionary step beyond these capabilities was the emergence of Broca's and Wernicke's areas. These provided a special set of recategorical memories related to the means for production and recognition of coarticulated speech sounds. Motor sequencing based on recursive reentrant connections—particularly to the frontal, parietal, and temporal cortices, where global mappings were already categorized in terms of object and action—then allowed the development of a powerful reentrant syntactic system based on epigenesis and semantic bootstrapping. This proposal has biological plausibility. No new biochemistry or radically novel neuroanatomy is required—just additional specialized neocortex dedicated to the task.

An essential feature of such a flexible scheme is the recursive and synthetic property connecting the relative positions and types of utterances to types of concepts in a nested reentrant system (figure 10.2). As we saw in chapter 4, recursive reentry permits a large number of combinatorial possibilities and the emergence of new functions. Clearly, such reentry allows chaining of sequences as well as independent categorization of semantic interpretations on the basis of the order of speech sounds, particularly after a rich enough lexicon has been acquired in a particular speech community. The ordering of nouns and verbs in a syntactic system that arises as a result can, and does, differ in different speech communities.[20]

In the evolution of speech systems, the linkage of the means of sound production to the breath period and to the rhythm of speech was probably particularly important. This temporal aspect of the production of speech sounds was, in all likelihood, correlated with the phasic reentrant signaling of cortical systems yielding correlations among various memory systems. It is possible that the extraordinary coarticulation[21] seen in phoneme production was not simply a later development to make speech more efficient but rather an early *requirement* for effectively achieving a rate of speech consistent with demands for temporal coordination of the reentrant cortical areas mediating the phonological, syntactic, and semantic levels of speech (figure 10.2). Such coarticulated sounds may also have provided a richer basis for the discriminatory pattern recognition by the auditory and speech areas that is necessary to analyze, sequentially emit, and sharply distinguish consonants and vowels. It must have been particularly important that the start of an utterance, at least, and possibly its close, be signaled by means related to the rhythmic production of speech, breath stops, stress, and intonation. Thus, speech rhythm, segmentation, categorization, and reentrant cycling may all have been closely linked in the evolution of the powerful speech specialization.

Given the recursive relation between recombinatorial conceptual capabilities and speech production and recognition, it is perhaps not surprising that an enormous extension of conceptual power rapidly emerged as a result of the evolution of language. The development of reentrant means of linking category formation to an emerging special system of sound production, recognition, and memory undoubtedly played a major role in the evolution of the hominid brain. In this view, language is *not* required for concept formation, which is prior.[22] Nevertheless, the specialization and development of linguistic capabilities implies the development of new means of memory for concepts as well as of an internal mode for relating that memory to other memories concerned with imagery. Meaning per se is not carried in a single module and emerges only as a result of interactions at many levels. The same is true of grammar.

Note that this theory implies that, although the productive means of speech were essential for its evolution, the system, once evolved, was able to provide for comprehension and language recognition in the absence of an individual's ability to *produce* speech.[23] Because the drive to syntactic ordering depends upon concepts, presyntax, and global mappings, *any* available gestural system can be used to acquire symbols and speech. The neural connectivity of motor and sensory systems[24] can account for signing and for the language learning of deprived individuals like Helen Keller.[25]

Clearly, the proposed theory, which is based on a concept system and presyntax, is consistent with the social role of the language learner in

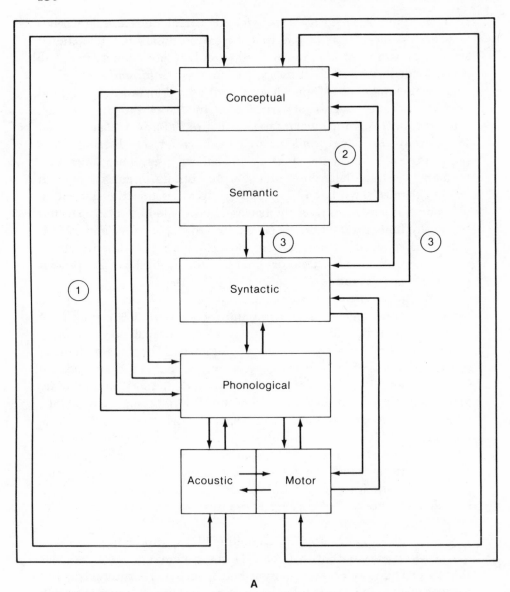

A

Figure 10.2

The strongly nested set of reentrantly connected functions for language. As shown in A, phonological responses can be related (1) to concepts to produce (2) semantic memory via learning. The motor sequencing fixes a syntactic order (3) in the perception and production of phonemes, words, and sentences. Multi- ple degenerate interactions can occur at the different levels. This can lead to cross-modal construction, resolution of conflicts, and recursive synthesis in a fashion similar to (but obviously not identical with) the events for early vision,

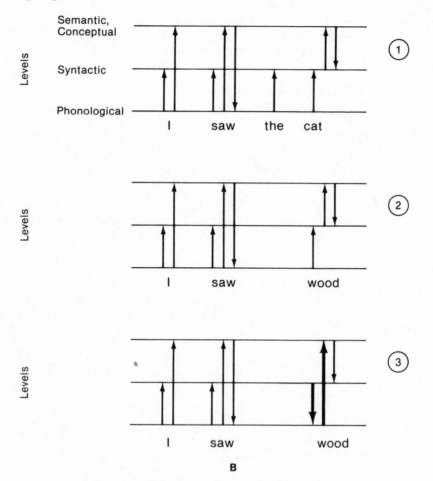

B

discussed in chapter 4 (see table 4.2 and figures 4.7–4.9). *For example, B and C illustrate some possible interactions on isolated presentations of two different sentences and sequential presentations of the same two sentences. These diagrams are only figurative—the actual neurology is not available at present.* Arrows in B *show sequential reentrant activity changing pattern from 2 to 3. Understanding spoken language* (C) *involves serial activity in reentrantly interconnected (◄——►) neuronal groups present in functionally and anatomically distinct cortical areas concerned with phonology (p.), semantics (sem.) and syntactics (syn.). Semantic and/or syntactic ambiguity (e.g., "saw") results in activity in multiple groups; resolution of appropriate alternatives is dependent upon the object or context of the sentence.* □ = *activity of neuronal groups corresponding to subject of sentence;* ● *or* ○ = *activity of neuronal groups corresponding to verb in sentence;* x *or* Δ = *activity of neuronal groups corresponding to alternative objects of sentence.*

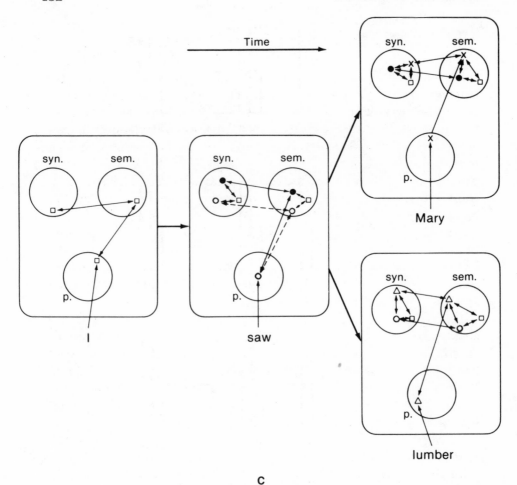

C

a speech community. It also takes account of certain differences between acquisition in child language and in adult language.[26] In the
child, a critical period (possibly as a result of "neotenic learning"[27]) may
allow rapid acquisition of complex categorical memories for lexical,
syntactic, and semantic items. In the adult (i.e., after the critical period),
the use of the conceptual apparatus to categorize an increasingly rich
lexicon independent of sensory input may change the way in which
new meanings and references are made. This may lead to decoupling
of the various levels, phonological, syntactic, and semantic (except in
cases of error) and also force a switch to different, or at least modified,
means of language acquisition.

COMPARISON WITH OTHER MODELS

It is useful to compare this evolutionary and developmental theory of language production and acquisition with certain aspects of more abstract transformational models of language.[28] But first, it is important to emphasize again that certain aspects of the present epigenetic model are closely allied to lexical functional (LF) models of grammar.[29] Such models *assume* conceptual and categorical capabilities. The present proposal explicitly accounts for such capabilities in terms of the reentrant interactions of cortical structure and of the mapping of types of global mappings by particular cortical regions, leading to concepts. This proposal allows us to tie semantics and syntax in a natural way to the phonological capabilities that emerged in evolution, as has been described by Lieberman.[30] The development of these capabilities in turn allowed new and specialized sensorimotor categorical perceptions to appear, as has been pointed out by Liberman.[31]

This synthesis of the TNGS with certain aspects of LF grammar and an adequate evolutionary hypothesis is capable of dealing with various constraints on syntactic mapping that have been discussed by Bresnan.[32] These constraints on language, which were brought to the fore by the seminal work of Chomsky,[33] are (1) creativity, (2) finite capacity, (3) reliability, (4) order-free composition, and (5) universality. In *creativity,* the language user can in principle construct means for characterizing any of the infinite number of possible sentences as grammatical. And yet there are only *finite* sets of words and relations and *finite* storage ability in syntactic systems. A syntactic construction must be judged *reliably* by such a user as well formed or not, independently of context and meaning. Moreover, local grammatical relations can be reliably constructed for arbitrary fragments of sentences, *independent of order,* although such fragments show more possible grammatical relations when free of that order than when they are in a sentence. Finally, Bresnan[34] points out that any string of words must be related to some mental structure and that the procedure for mapping these strings and structures onto a grammar must be *universal.* She suggests that, while not necessarily true, it is an attractive assumption that this mapping procedure is the same as that used normally in *learning* a language. If it were true, this would lead to the conclusion that language acquisition and comprehension interact and reinforce one another.

In the present theory, the creativity constraint is provided by the linkage to cortical conceptual systems that themselves allow enormous combinatorial power *as long as a means for a special memory of new conceptual combinations is provided.* This means is supplied during the emergence of language by reentrant memory systems (Broca's and Wernicke's areas, for example) that can interact with already existing conceptual systems (figure 10.1). The finite-capacity constraint is met to some degree by the notion that memory is a form of recategorization[35] with strong capabilities for generalization. This generalizing power enhances the applicability of a few terms and relations to a very large range of objects and referents. The reliability constraint is related to the fact that the already existing conceptual system can itself treat the productions of verbal strings as a set of objects to be classified. There are thus many *internal* checks in the multilevel reentrant systems shown in figures 10.1 and 10.2. The order-free constraint is more consistent with our developmental assumption that syntax *emerges* from semantics (and, of course, from phonology). As Bresnan[36] argues, this assumption is not compatible with order-dependent transformational grammars. The universality constraint is consistent with the categorization of productions by the conceptual system. Rich conceptual categorization provides a means for apparent universality even in languages in which there are discontinuous constituents—for example, in Dutch, in which verbs are discontinuous from the phrases that contain their arguments.[37]

Such an epigenetic theory of language based on an orderly emergence of phonological and syntactic abilities in evolution is not consistent with the neo-Cartesian notion[38] that human language cannot be related to the intelligent behavior of other species. Although there *are* unique specializations related to speech production, recognition, and memory in the human brain, their evolutionary emergence required no radically new mechanisms.[39] The mechanisms of reentry and the appearance of new cortical regions leading to an enhanced memory for speech, combined with the idea that already existing conceptual capabilities can give rise to the constraints of syntax after the emergence of phonetic means, appear together to be sufficient to allow language to emerge.

The assumption of a language module with innate *genetically* constrained "rules" for language appears improbable for two chief reasons. First, this module would have to specify rules for transformation that would be both extensive and intricate. Second, such a set of rules would have to map in an orderly and complete fashion to brain regions that *already* are capable of leading to concept formation. The alternatives that would result are both unpalatable: (1) the evolutionary construction of an error-free map between a language module and an already existing set of concepts that were developed independently of language and a universal grammar, or (2) the conclusion that concepts are not possible in the *absence* of such a grammar.[40]

It seems more reasonable to suppose that a preexistent conceptual base was followed by a linkage of phonology to syntax by means of semantics. This allows one to recognize a variety of elements: the role both of prior brain structure and function *and* emerging evolutionary developments; the specific relation of speech to anatomy; the epigenetic nature of rule acquisition by an individual in a speech community; the development of special means of linguistic memory that are based on reentry; and finally, the evolutionary continuity of all of these developments under the constraints of the TNGS.

To the extent that it is an evolutionary theory, the present proposal is nativist, but it differs from that of Pinker in that it does not presuppose "the combination of functionalism, cognitivism, and computationalism that dominates modern cognitive science."[41] However, while innate rules are not assumed in the present selectionist account, innate *constraints* permitting emergence of appropriate (and similar) rules are presupposed. Without such constraints, no epigenetic system could function.[42]

The evolutionary emergence of the capacities for language enormously enriches the conceptual power and discriminative power of a thinking animal. Above all, speech allows the development of internal models and conceptual categorizations that can be time-independent as well as of enriched distinctions of the concept of self, leading to personhood.[43] It is these capacities that allow higher-order consciousness to develop.

This short account provides us with the basis for considering higher-order consciousness in the next chapter. It has, of course, been a tacit assumption of the discussion in this chapter that no language could have developed among animals lacking the neural apparatus for primary consciousness.

11

Higher–Order Consciousness

The evolutionary emergence of primary consciousness had the adaptive advantage in that it coherently coupled dominant internal (or individual) homeostatic requirements to multiple parallel categorizations. This linked a variety of modalities to the dynamics required for extended action and exploration of the environment. At the same time, the development of short-term memory that was related to the succession of events and signals further consolidated the evolutionary advantage provided by an integrated "mental image," allowing the assignment of salience to events in terms of adaptive values. But an animal possessing these means is still tied to a frame of the present: although its *behavior* is undoubtedly altered by long-term changes in learning, it has no means of reviewing explicitly its present perceptions in terms of analogues in the past or in terms of anticipated analogues projected to the future. It has no direct awareness (consciousness$_4$; see chapter 5) and is not "conscious of being conscious."

Extensive development of such capabilities requires the evolution of structures that allow a *symbolic* modeling of the self-nonself distinction. Such structures free some part of neural activity from the external drive of current behavior at the same time that this part still retains access to that behavior and its consequences. Only with the evolution of such symbolic structures can there emerge a true long-term memory based on a notion of the *past*. [1] As we saw in the preceding chapter, the neural structures having such properties are also those required for the possession of a true language with syntactic structure and semantic reference. In other words, to become "conscious of consciousness," or directly aware,[2] an animal must have a distinction of self from nonself that is to some degree time-independent. It therefore must also possess structures able to model the effects of past events on the self.[3] At this point, "self" becomes a term referring to such a conceptual model and not just to a biological individual, as is the case for primary consciousness.

It is difficult to imagine how that modeling could have arisen without some form of social transmission involving imitation.[4] By its very nature, moreover, such modeling requires conventional means of reference (based on such communication) that go beyond simple signification. An awareness of the actions of the self and of others in various temporal successions entails a linkage to past action. This, in turn, entails a symbolic representation of past action via long-term memory.

All of these properties are also those needed in the exercise of a true language, although such a language has additional requirements, as we have already discussed. My thesis here is that the development of such a language is itself absolutely predicated on the existence of consciousness—first, primary consciousness, and then the emerging ability to relate various systems of memory to a *symbolic* representation of the self acting on the environment and vice versa. This representation is the essential element in freeing an animal from slavery to present time and its "neural image."

Homo sapiens is the only animal with a true language, although higher primates appear to use individual symbols with some degree of semantic reference (not just simple signification). These primates, such as chimpanzees, lack rich syntactic resources, but they do display some evidence of self-awareness.[5] The emergence of this trait suggests that chimpanzees have at least the beginnings of higher-order consciousness with some capacity for forming a self model in relation to a world model. True language is thus probably not absolutely necessary for the emergence of higher-order consciousness, although it is required for its later elaborations.

In a socially transmitting species in which symbolic systems begin to emerge, there is a fundamental need for a subject-predicate relation, because this relation is central in the emergence of a rich grammar. I have already suggested that the minimal evolutionary requirements for elaborations of consciousness based on language are twofold. First, brain structures dealing with concepts must have evolved to be capable of modeling the distinction between self and nonself in a new sense— one exceeding that of biological individuality. An animal with this conceptual capability must also be able to relate that distinction to any action.[6] This obviously requires linkage of such a conceptual system to primary consciousness and perceptual experience. Second, specialized developments like the larynx, a supralaryngeal airway, and a neural perceptual and production system for phonemes must have coevolved,[7] as was discussed in the last chapter. This emergence was probably gradual in hominids, but it would not have led to language if the first requirement had not already been to some degree fulfilled. As I mentioned in chapter 10, such developments do not appear to require an extensive remodeling of a brain already capable of primary consciousness and concept formation. Rather, they imply certain additions that were then linked by reentry to existing structures. Those early structures related to verbal expression and recognition must have evolved into what we now recognize as Broca's and Wernicke's areas.

THE CONCEPTUAL SELF AND FREEDOM FROM THE PRESENT

It is not obvious whether the requisite repertoires of neuronal groups having to do with the *conceptual* emergence of the self-nonself distinction emerged in the frontal or in the temporal lobes or in both. But such a distinction clearly must have preceded the evolution of actual "speech areas." It is valuable, in any case, to list the further requirements to be met by repertoires able to carry out the conceptual self-nonself distinction:

1. They must be able to categorize the process of primary awareness itself. This in turn requires their anatomical relation to the special memory system carrying out value-category distinctions, as well as the development of a means of connecting such a memory system to models[8] of self via the portions of the brain mediating concept formation. This must have required the ability to delay responses, a key function that seems to reside in the prefrontal lobes[9] (see chapter 9).
2. Such self-categories must have had the opportunity to emerge by comparison and discrimination through social transmission.[10]
3. A conceptual self-category must be stable and therefore must accumulate. It can arise (as in the chimpanzee) but cannot develop further without being freed to some extent from current activities and their distractions. Successful development of this trait requires a means of long-term storage of relations that are symbolic, standing for states of memory that are related to communication with other individuals of the same species.[11]

In this view, higher-order consciousness cannot emerge fully without the activity of a special memory system to carry out self-nonself distinc-

The apparent universality of grammar, as observed by Chomsky,[18] can more likely be explained by the epigenetic emergence of linguistic behavior *constrained by the phenotype* as described in the last chapter. This is in principle not different from the "universality" of human shape or of the morphogenesis in a particular species that results from inherent genetic bounds on epigenetic events.[19] There appears to be little justification for Cartesianism as an explanation either of consciousness or of language.

It has not been my intention here or in the preceding chapter either to explain the actual details of grammar in terms of the detailed activities of brain structures[20] or to propose an extensive psycholinguistics. Instead, I have suggested that, in addition to the evolution of phonetic capabilities and systems of gestural recognition, a conceptual means of modeling self-nonself relations in terms of actions is a primitive basis for both the evolution of language and the emergence of higher-order consciousness. Such a development allows the emergence of an autonomous (i.e., symbolic) long-term memory in which the dissociation of conceptual categorization from ongoing short-term temporal successions makes possible a distinction between past, present, and future.

These developments require a gradual[21] evolutionary emergence of systems of phonation. But they also require the relatively rapid emergence of repertoires of neuronal groups for modeling self-nonself relations, systems that demand increasing brain size. I have discussed elsewhere[22] how such developmental events could occur in relatively short evolutionary times on the basis of molecular heterochrony and how the increased size of the repertoires of neuronal groups required for an extensive symbolic memory could have proved adaptive in terms of learning.

The matter of the evolutionary advantages conferred by primary consciousness and higher-order consciousness has been discussed by many authors.[23] In chapter 5, I mentioned that the categorical association of multimodal inputs to adaptive internal states provided by primary consciousness would increase the behavioral range, flexibility, and learning of a species. Primary consciousness supplies the ability to determine by *internal criteria* the salience of particular patterns among multiple parallel signals arising in complex environments. This extends the adaptive value of learning and makes it enormously more flexible. Higher-order consciousness, with its self-nonself distinction and freedom from immediate time constraints and with its increased richness of social communication,[24] eventually led to capabilities allowing the anticipation of future states and planned behavior (see table 5.1). The adaptive flexibility of hunter-gatherers and the subsequent explosive emergence of human populations over the whole globe testify to the short-term advantages conferred by forms of consciousness incorporating linguistic abilities. Whether those advantages will or will not be rapidly lost in the near future remains to be seen.

12

The Conscious and
the Unconscious

It has been a tenet of this book that an adequate theory of consciousness necessarily must be a set of theories. This follows from the idea that consciousness resulted from a series of evolutionary events leading to different brain morphologies and functions. These reentrantly connected morphologies eventually gave rise to primary consciousness and then to higher-order consciousness concomitant with the acquisition of language. To explain the emergence of consciousness, one needs, at the least, a cogent theory of morphologic evolution, a related developmental theory, and a global brain theory.[1]

That global brain theory must account for a variety of processes that are independent of, prior to, or necessary for consciousness. It must therefore distinguish conscious processes from nonconscious and unconscious processes. Without going into great detail, I wish in this chapter to comment on some matters that are important to this discriminatory task. First, I consider how the proposed models of primary and higher-order consciousness can be related to various types of categorization, memory, and intentionality. I follow with a brief discussion of attention and propose a specific model of attention. This hypothesis relating consciousness to attention is useful in seeing how conscious states can affect performance in explicit anatomical and physiological terms. The model leads directly to a consideration of conscious, nonconscious, and unconscious states. Finally, I consider the utility of psychological language in discussing these various issues. All of these subjects will be important in the next chapter, where we examine diseases of consciousness.

UNITY AND HETEROGENEITY OF CONSCIOUS EXPERIENCE

I shall speak here only of conscious experience in humans. The TNGS takes it as fundamental that perceptual categorization[2] can (and must) occur prior to consciousness as a result of the action of reentrant systems. When perceptual (and conceptual)[3] categorization occur, it is clear that they can become accessible to consciousness in terms of their objects. Perception is intentional (i.e., it is of objects), whereas phenomenal experience and sensation lack this intentionality. It is not possible to proceed by introspection to the *mechanisms* of consciousness, only to perceived intentional objects and sensations. Moreover, direct awareness ("consciousness of consciousness," or consciousness$_4$ of Natsoulas)[4] is of perception, not sensation. Consciousness, while it may have a phenomenal unity, is thus a heterogeneous state, accounting perhaps for Malcolm's[5] distinction between intransitive and transitive uses of the word "consciousness."

Having spoken of the problem of the phenomenal aspects of consciousness in chapter 9, I shall not add much more here. But it is clear that "subjective" features relating to self-awareness, first-person usage, meaning, and the like are just that—subjective processes going on in a person who has higher-order consciousness. The *apparent* contrast with so-called objective features of mental experience—spatiotemporal localization, the capacity to perceive and act, the causal relations between physical and mental events—can be understood in terms of the heterogeneity of consciousness arising as a special form of memory connected with the self-nonself distinctions that are related by reentry to perceived events. In chapters 5 and 9, I mentioned the limitations of our ability to determine certain relational properties [C(I)] of internal homeostatic systems about which we must forever remain unconscious in order to *be* conscious!

Consciousness in any one chunk of time is also *causally* heterogeneous inasmuch as it arises from a variety of systems with different histories and access to real-world signals. It depends on perceptual categorization, conceptual categorization, and memory as recategorization, as well as on a set of homeostatic systems defining hedonic states and goals. A conscious state (consciousness during one time period) is subject to different time scales, ranging from those governing rapid external movements to those of short- and long-term memory (see figure 14.2). Different structures must therefore have access to the special self-nonself memory essential to primary consciousness, and this access can be simultaneous or successive. The same holds for higher-order consciousness, although, in this case, the temporal scales are not necessarily defined by those of external events.

The heterogeneity of consciousness in terms of structures carrying out perceptual and conceptual categorization as well as language is illustrated schematically in figure 12.1. Given the heterogeneity of consciousness, the occurrence, particularly in *Homo sapiens,* of metacognition, "consciousness of remembering," the experience of imagery (as a result of internal stimulation of global mappings), and a sense of change and duration (see figure 14.2) is perhaps not surprising.

The notion that any thought process occurs *exclusively* in terms of either imagery or propositions is made irrelevant by this picture—both or either can occur in *Homo sapiens.*[6] In animals without language, reentrant engagement of perceptual categorical systems even down to primary receiving areas should yield a "mental image" to primary consciousness. The occurrence of this process can be tested neurophysiologically by means of modern techniques, for example, in the visual system of various animals. When the resolution of brain-scanning methods is improved, the activity of areas related to imaging may also be tested in human subjects. The salient prediction is that, in tasks requiring imagery,[7] a large number of neuronal groups in several reentrant areas will be engaged, including those in secondary sensory areas.

Furthermore, because concepts are considered to require the mapping (and therefore the classification) of global mappings, the use of image schemata related to bodily states in the organization of thought and language is an expected characteristic in conscious organisms. Image schemata involve concepts connected to positions or states of the body as it relates to objects or events—for example, "obstacle," "resistance," "object," "motion," "containment," and "blockage." The evidence that image schemata are developed in humans comes from the classic studies of Head and from more recent analyses like those of Johnson and of Spelke.[8] Such schemata, frequently reflected as *metaphors* in the language of *Homo sapiens,* may already function in animals with conceptual capabilities and primary consciousness.

Before considering the issue of attention as it bears on conscious awareness, we should point out the obvious relation of conscious aware-

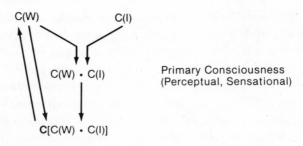

Primary Consciousness
(Perceptual, Sensational)

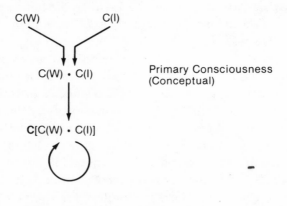

Primary Consciousness
(Conceptual)

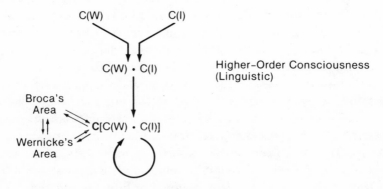

Higher–Order Consciousness
(Linguistic)

Figure 12.1

Heterogeneity of consciousness. All or any of these various systems may be active in a given time period. (See figures 9.1 and 9.2.) The curved bold line beneath **C[C(W)·C(I)]** *in the middle and bottom panels refers to conceptual recombinations in the value-category memory (frontal, temporal, parietal, and cingulate lobes).*

ness to volition. Volition requires the awareness of a goal and the ability to direct action (and thus sensation and perception). Its underpinnings include various value systems (ethological or acquired), perceptual and conceptual categorizations, and learning. In terms of the TNGS, it may be seen as the ability to facilitate the selection of a series of global mappings that are aimed at the satisfaction of needs. Clearly, the ability to focus attention is central to sustaining this activity. But attention depends on a variety of factors, some of which do not or cannot emerge into awareness. Given that this is so, I shall defer further considerations of free will and causal sequences to chapter 14 and turn directly to the matter of attention itself.

ATTENTION

Attention, like consciousness itself, is difficult to define. In descriptive terms it has been associated with notions of intensity, alertness, and vigilance. James considered attention to be a "taking possession by the mind in clear and vivid form of one of what seem simultaneously possible objects or trains of thought."[9] The main issue for him and others of his time was related mainly to the contents of consciousness.

Attention can be focal or diffuse. Indeed, its most remarkable property is its selectivity—the singling out of particular stimuli or patterns for perceptual, conceptual, or motor processing while ignoring other stimuli either from within or without. Attention can persist or be short-lived and phasic; it can modulate an animal's responsiveness to the environment and lend a directional component to behavior. Attention must be discriminated from overall wakefulness ("arousal" or "activation"), although it obviously can be altered by such state-dependent variables.

Processes that we may term attentional arise in the most peripheral sampling of signals as well as in selections from a number of central conscious states. Some attempts to explain the selectivity of attention as a central process have suggested that it occurs *early,* that is, prior to categorization events. A classical version is that of Broadbent,[10] who dealt with the selection of signals from simultaneously received dense inputs to sensory systems. His selection mechanism was embedded in a filter theory—a single channel of input could be selected at frequencies of no more than 2 Hz, and this implied that processing had a limited capacity. In dichotic listening, for example, a message in one ear would be selected at one time while that in the other ear would be rejected.

In contrast to such *early*-selection hypotheses are those that propose that selection occurs *late,* after or at the same time as categorization.[11] Late-selection ideas have in general been associated with the notion that sensory input processing occurs in parallel, with no limit on its capacity. In contrast, most early-selection ideas have tended to suggest (as in the filter theory) that processing resources and capacity are limited.

More recently, the utility of all of these conceptions has been challenged,[12] and attention has come to be regarded as the outcome of a group of mechanisms needed to cope with a variety of selection problems in the control of action. Such views are concerned with how skills can be related to output systems and with how particular constraints are exercised in determining any action that ensues in the light of a goal taken prior. Allport[13] has emphasized that the observable criterion for attentional awareness of an environmental event depends upon a subject's ability to act in response to that event, whether immediately or in recall. This very often comes down to selecting either an object or a location of an object; the final selection for action may occur as a result of competition among varying categorizations of objects. From an evolutionary point of view, this makes sense. Even among the earliest evolved vertebrates, both browsing herbivores or preying carnivores, the ability to restrict food-collecting movements to single objects among a homogeneous collection of potential distractions could contribute significant adaptive advantage. The decision to be made is, Which object? Which action?

Consistent with such ideas is the notion suggested by Neumann[14] that the choice of an output involves behavioral inhibition and action planning, a notion not too different from that of motor plans (see chapter 7, particularly the discussion of the basal ganglia). In humans, largely as a result of prefrontal cortical activity, motor plans can combine skills without training. The important point, in any case, is that the choice of an action leads in turn to the *appearance* of capacity limitation. In general, attentional selection prevents interruption of any single action. This is adaptive inasmuch as any simultaneous *independent* action would interfere with the achievement of a goal, particularly as that goal is arranged in space.

It must not be thought that such ideas of selectional restriction for output are limited to the actual *carrying out* of action, that changes in a motor plan cannot occur, or even that there *must* be a motor output. Conceptual systems may carry out imagined actions without engaging an actual motor output. Moreover, a variety of novel inputs may cause a change in plans, and the practice of various skills in actual motor sequences may lead to automatization and a dropping out from attentive focus of such sequences (e.g., in driving a car, riding a bicycle, or playing scales on the piano). Indeed, it is possible that the ability to coordinate movements in this way evolved from mechanisms that originally emerged chiefly to unify body movements by inhibiting all those that failed to contribute to an immediate goal.

It is becoming more and more obvious that attention comprises *multiple* mechanisms acting at a variety of levels, ranging from the perceptual to the deliberately volitional. Pattern selection, selection of motor plans, and selection of conscious strategies may all be involved. Recent studies by Treisman[15] suggest that the effects of distracting elements, such as emotionally loaded terms and contextually relevant words, can be perceived, even when present in a rejected message. These results clearly require that the filter theory be revised, in regard not only to sensory input but also to categorical classes, color, and other perceptual combinations. Crick[16] has put forward a "searchlight theory," in which various thalamic arousal systems are used to reinforce the hierarchical or vertical association of neural elements in response to particular cues. Neither subsequent experimental evidence nor theoretical considerations have, however, lent any support to his theory.

A variety of other theories incompatible with the filter hypothesis and the notion of restricted capacity have also been proposed. Many take into account that conscious attention can be accompanied by unconscious or preconscious processes that alter recall. For example, work by Julesz on preattentive vision indicates that decisions can be made in the discrimination of texture differences, closure, line ending, and color in very short time intervals, before conscious attention can operate.[17]

Attention is not the same as consciousness, but both are multifarious and neither is likely to be accounted for by a single, simple theory. Rather, attention is best analyzed within a theory of consciousness in terms of particular *hypotheses* concerned with interacting systems. If the functional view of attention[18] as related to output that I described above is maintained, for example, a number of subsidiary relations and mechanisms must be accounted for. In the functional view, attention is related to the formation of motor plans and programs and to the kind of mappings of sensory and perceptual input to motor output that we have presumed to be in part the function of the basal ganglia (see chapter 7).

Any hypothesis that invokes these functions must obviously first explain the selectivity of attentional phenomena. In addition, if one adheres to the ideas of selectivity and motor blockade, one must explain the automatization of skills and the interruption of motor plans and programs after the encounter with novelty or potentially nociceptive stimuli. Such an explanation must also be consistent with the evidence supporting the occurrence of divided consciousness, as reviewed by Hilgard[19] (see chapter 13).

I will not consider the formulation of detailed hypotheses for the various mechanisms of attention in any detail. Nevertheless, it is important to show that the more recent views of attention are consistent with the extended TNGS and that a model related to motor plans and choice is in accord with the idea that attentional responses are related to the construction of global mappings.

In the case of input to the local maps of a global mapping, for example, a certain statistical factor related to motor exploration must enter (see figure 3.4, and compare with figure 14.2). With learning (responding to novelty and surprise) and particularly with the accession of primary consciousness, a balance must be struck between internally determined salience and external accident or novelty. Moreover, with the accession of higher-order consciousness, volitional states related to plans, values, and temporal projections can all affect the choice of maps. In this case, contrary to the early-selection, limited-capacity theories, a *single* sensory or perceptual channel is, in general, quite *unlikely* to be the pivot of attentional shift. Large portions of the nervous system and a metastable hierarchy of needs, values, and cognitive plans are involved. It may very well be that this fact alone accounts for the narrowness and fragility of conscious attention: it is difficult to sustain more than a few *complex* global mappings at any one time and still achieve adaptive motor performance. Perhaps of equal importance in selectional restriction is the role of conscious attention in directing action toward a defined goal, which, in order to *be* defined, must be single at any one time.

Attention, according to this view, can be driven by any level of a system of multiple reentrant maps in a global mapping; it would usually be expected simultaneously to involve several such levels. In the case of volitional states, past learning (conscious and unconscious), as well as present perceptual input, must all be contributory elements. Indeed, it is tempting to consider the possibility that a good deal of conscious attention depends upon *negative* influences, including the gating of sensory input, the suppression of perceptual input by stimulation of concept systems and imagery, and the inhibition of motor activity other than that related to the carrying out of a given motor plan. Let us turn to a model based on these ideas.

A MODEL FOR THE CONSCIOUS CONTROL OF ATTENTION

One of the most striking properties of systems of attention is how they vary before and after the acquisition of motor or cognitive skills. In the initial learning of tasks (particularly complex ones), conscious attention plays a key role—rehearsal in terms of a goal and the linking of various motor or cognitive routines are critical to achievement of that goal. But successful learning leads to automatization, as is seen for humans in speaking, writing, riding a bicycle, playing a musical instrument, or carrying out calculations. After such learning, conscious attention is often *not* required for performance and is only called up if novelty appears or if a goal is not reached. Otherwise, performance can remain unconscious, and at all stages it involves brain operations that are non-conscious. Both primary and higher-order consciousness can be called upon in the exercise of choices during the early learning of such tasks. Indeed, as we shall see later, this appears to be a major function of the conscious state.

The question is, How can conscious states operate to alter attention? We will attempt to sketch a framework within which that question may be answered. Let us first describe a model for a motor program and consider how it may be related to the formation of motor plans, the automatization of skills, and their alteration by surprise, novelty, or nociceptive input.

To account for how motor programs may be carried out and how they might be linked to motor plans, my colleague Joseph Gally has suggested the attentional model (compatible in part with that of Penney and Young)[20] illustrated in figure 12.2. The basic notion is that input to motor cortex leads to output to the spinal cord, which causes particular movements in accordance with motor plans. At the same time, the output from the motor cortex is also routed to the basal ganglia. As we saw in chapter 7, this disinhibits the output of the intralaminar and other nuclei of the thalamus. This in turn leads to an anticipatory arousal of specific cortical areas and results in enhanced sensitivity to proprioceptive and sensory feedback to the cerebral cortex (in appropriate portions of the global mapping, as is shown in figure 12.2). This

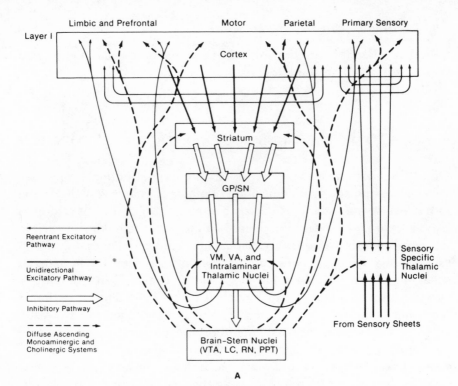

Reentrant Excitatory
Pathway

Unidirectional
Excitatory Pathway

Inhibitory Pathway

Diffuse Ascending
Monoaminergic and
Cholinergic Systems

A

Figure 12.2

A model relating attention and consciousness. A: Neuronal connections in the vertebrate central nervous system that may mediate attention and motor programming. Motor and premotor cortices project to inhibitory neurons in the striatum. These can then prevent the spontaneous firing of pallidal and nigral neurons, which send inhibitory signals to VM, VA, and intralaminar thalamic nuclei. Cortically projecting neurons in these nuclei send axons to layer I and layer VI over large areas of all cortical lobes. The disinhibition of these thalamocortical neurons may enhance the sensitivity of neurons in primary and sensory cortical areas. This enables proprioceptive or other sensory feedback to these areas to signal motor areas quickly and efficiently, thus altering impulses to motor neurons and disinhibiting the cortical areas needed to attend to the next reentrant signal, and so on. All components of the system are innervated by the diffuse ascending monoaminergic and cholinergic neurons present in the brain stem. GP/SN, globus pallidus/substantia nigra; LC, locus ceruleus; PPT, pedunculopontine tegmental nucleus; RN, raphe nucleus; VTA, vertical tegmental area. B: Neuroanatomical connections in the mammalian cortex that may underlie the reentrant neuronal circuits involved in motor programs, attention, and consciousness. Three different neuronal loops are schematically diagrammed; reentrant reciprocal excitatory connections between multiple cortical areas are present in each. These loops, distinguished by the subcortical structures involved, are mutually compatible and can function concurrently and synergistically. Any or all are candidates for mediating the reentrant pathway that gives rise to primary consciousness (see chapter 9). Higher-order consciousness similarly involves analogous cortical areas related

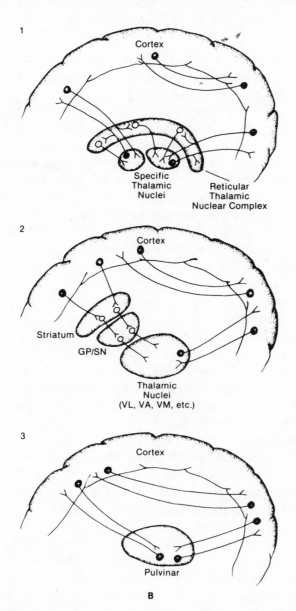

to speech. 1: *Reentrant excitatory connections between specific thalamic nuclei and specific central areas make collateral contacts with neurons in the reticular nucleus of the thalamus. These, in turn, make diffuse, semitopographic contacts with both relay and local circuit neurons in several different thalamic nuclei. 2: A simplified diagram of the "attentional" loop illustrated in A. 3: The medial pulvinar nucleus of the thalamus is reentrantly connected with prefrontal, cingulate, and parietal cortical areas and hence can correlate activity in all three areas. These neuronal loops can send output to the basal ganglia (see A) affecting and modulating attentional search or focus in terms of a preconceived goal.*

reinforced cortical sensory input will then be carried by cortical U loops back to motor cortex. In this model, the basal ganglia serve to specify which cortical areas will be reinforced.

It is the mechanism for generating an anticipatory (expectant) sustained enhancement of neuronal sensitivity that may have been the chief contribution of the attention system in early vertebrates to the subsequent evolution of higher brain functions. We have already discussed neurons whose activity signals readiness to respond (see table 6.1). Besides leading to animals capable of utilizing increasingly complex motor programs, this mechanism may have been essential to the development of the ability to conceptualize and to manipulate concepts in a serial order. Presyntax, for example, may involve the fact that certain concepts "anticipate" others, particularly in the prefrontal cortex (see chapter 8).

Global mappings carrying out a motor program can be modified by two sources—one related to motor plans and the other to automatization and response to novelty. Frontal and prefrontal areas appear necessary for the formation of concepts related to motor plans (see chapter 9). Input from these areas to the appropriate portions of the basal ganglia could affect adjacent overlapping parallel circuits (see chapter 7) in the ganglia. In this fashion, conceptual alterations could modify an incipient motor program mediated via the basal ganglia, as is indicated in the model (figure 12.2).

Such inputs related to motor plans do not account, however, for automatization and responses to novelty. To account for these phenomena, we invoke midbrain and limbic inputs to the basal ganglia and cortex. Given the complexity, multilayered character, and extensive phenomenology of attention, I shall not consider the ramifications of this idea in great detail. I nonetheless present it here briefly because of its strong connection with issues related to the efficacy of consciousness (see table 5.1). It is also pertinent to our discussion, in the next section, of the interactions among the various brain components mediating nonconscious, unconscious, and conscious activities.

The key notion is based on our previous hypothesis: a major mechanism of attention is the ability to shift allocations in a global mapping (figure 12.2). This involves selection events among a number of reentrant local maps in classification couples or n-tuples. In unattended events, or diffusely attended events (events on the "fringe"), these allocations are determined by the nature of the input, the degree of earlier categorization or memory, and the animal's overall state (or wakefulness). Because of changes in goals, intrusion of novelty, altered appetites, or various conceptual states, a choice of relations among input patterns and output patterns may have to be made.

After formulation or determination of a goal, however, a global mapping of the kind shown in figure 12.2, *A* must be *constructed* on the basis of present perceptual input and motor state. The selection of neuronal groups in components of this mapping is affected by the regions of the brain responsible for concepts and plans related to the goal (figure 12.2, *B*). This is so because such concepts *recombine activated portions* of previous global mappings related to categories and acts. Concept formation and image formation activate neuronal groups, and that activation may become part of a successful motor program.

If learning guided by attention has *already* occurred, it facilitates the construction of the appropriate global mapping in less than some critical time period (< 0.5 sec). Under these circumstances, the acts leading to the goal (whether they involve motor skills or conceptual skills) are carried out *without* stimulation of the reentrant loops relating value-category memory to current perceptual categorization in primary consciousness, or the reentrant loops involved in higher-order consciousness. These loops (figure 12.2, *B*) include the thalamocortical and corticothalamic fibers from different thalamic nuclei, each controlled by activation of the reticular nucleus. Additional circuits include the various longitudinal fasciculi and the corticocortical connections via the medial pulvinar nucleus.

According to the present hypothesis, activation of these loops resulting in conscious attention can occur if frontal activity fails to lead to construction of a complete global mapping or if a novel, surprising, or unrehearsed stimulus pattern supervenes. Under such circumstances, feedback and reentry from midbrain and basal forebrain inputs will occur to the reticular nucleus. This will alter the pattern of correlation of activity in various cortical areas. Simultaneously, inputs from the midbrain will also stimulate the basal ganglia (see chapter 7) and disrupt the ongoing motor program, allowing construction of a new program. Allocation among modalities and actions is made by altering the perceptual or conceptual salience of the inputs, by activating various memory paths related to recategorization, or by setting up a new motor plan. This allocation results in new selection patterns of neuronal groups and constitutes a change in attention.

We may now return to our key question: how could primary consciousness alter the allocation of priorities in such a system? One may suppose that a change of salience among the parallel reentrant loops leading to primary consciousness (see figures 10.1 and 12.2, *B*) may alter the activity of cortical regions responsible for concept formation or imaging. This could change the neural activity in the basal ganglia and in various local maps of a global mapping and alter attentive focus, leading to serial search in terms of a goal. If higher-order consciousness were present, verbal interactions could lead to similar changes and facilitate search or a steady focus on volitional goals.

Besides the basal ganglia, another organ of succession, the hippocampus, may be required to maintain focal attention (i.e., "retrieve a train of thought"), particularly in the presence of potential distractions. It may also be important in the sequencing of attention, in the sense that recovery of a particular episode of attention requires short-term memory.

In this scheme, major portions of actions (including willed actions) are driven by some neural sources not accessible to phenomenal awareness. Nonetheless, conscious states achieved via the circuits in figure 12.2, B allow modeling, rehearsal, and activation of such sources well before a given action, judgment, or thought. The actual triggering of such output states does not necessarily have to be *immediately* preceded by the appropriate conscious state, however.

The foregoing hypotheses relating conscious plans to motor programs, novelty, and automatization are thus compatible with the role of consciousness in affecting the operation of nonconscious neural components. They also connect attention to hedonic states and to peripheral autonomic and central arousal. One of the advantages of these hypotheses is that they remove the need for a *special* tag on novel events—if, in a given context, recategorical memory prompts construction of a global mapping within some time period, no novelty is considered to have occurred. If this mapping fails, however, limbic reentry will engage the key loops leading to primary or higher-order consciousness. Barring preemption by nociceptive inputs and unexpected signals, allocation of specific loops will then be determined by "majority vote" in local maps or by prior conceptual states.

Such a view of attention is consistent with the proposal that the direction of learning is also strongly influenced by novelty and hedonic needs.[21] It concedes priority to the dominance of nonconscious behavior and orienting responses in emergencies as established during evolution (see figure 9.3). Nonetheless, because having intentional states depends on values, categorizations, and memories in a system capable of action, this selectional hypothesis of attention is compatible with the "intention to attend" in animals having higher-order consciousness. It allows for parapraxes and actions not as planned[22] insofar as prior conscious, nonconscious, and unconscious elements can *all* causally interact, compete, and contribute to a particular outcome. We now turn to such elements.

CONSCIOUS, NONCONSCIOUS, AND UNCONSCIOUS STATES

Most conscious states show intentionality—they are about things, events, or other states.[23] They reveal the interdependence between an active continuing individual or subject and a particular content involving objects or events. This is entirely consistent with the proposed models of primary and higher-order consciousness. In thinking about this interdependence, it is useful to distinguish conscious states from nonconscious and unconscious states. Nonconscious states can contribute to conscious states, but their mechanisms can never be brought to awareness. Unconscious mental processes resemble conscious ones in many ways but cannot attain direct access to consciousness; as I shall discuss in the next section, they can be defined only in contrast to, and in terms of, conscious states.[24]

These various states of perceptual, conceptual, and memorial function and the structures that give rise to them depend strongly upon evolutionary and ethological variables. This is so because of the natural selection for animals having combinations of set points in their limbic and hedonic systems that advance particular adaptive goals. Such systems alter learning, memory, and (given the appropriate structures) consciousness. Extraordinary dissociations can occur in performance and in various neuropsychological disorders.[25] In these disorders, loss of domain-specific input to awareness can occur while the individual can maintain some degree of performance "unknowingly." Such cases, including blindsight and unilateral neglect, were discussed in chapter 2 and will be considered further in the next chapter. Insofar as they are irreversible, they consign certain performances forever to the nonconscious domain.

If we examine the machinery of perceptual categorization[26] (classification couples and global mappings), we see that it is exercised primarily as a nonconscious process. By its nature, it must be intentional and can act immediately. No form of "unconscious inference"[27] is required, however, for perceptual categorization to occur (see chapter 4, for an example). In contrast, conceptual categorization, while also intentional, is not tied strictly to single objects and events—it is recombinatorial and relational.[28] The *mechanism* underlying concept formation is also nonconscious, although, as the model for attention presupposes, consciousness may be required in the *formation* of some new concepts. But memory as recategorization in its various forms can be either conscious ("metacognitive") or nonconscious, depending upon the state of the animal and the time course of events. There are many types of recategorical memory sharing properties related to internal, self-defining hedonic (or homeostatic) states, or to imagery,[29] and in our species, to language. The first kind of memory is nonconscious; the latter two kinds can become conscious.

Prior to discussing unconscious states, we should consider a few issues concerning the epistemic nature and causal efficacy of consciousness as well as some further matters related to attention. Consciousness depends on a special form of memory and therefore, if it has any efficacy, must depend on the extent of that memory. Primary consciousness also depends on immediate perceptual categorization and thus on the content of that categorization (this defines its intentionality). The various neural activities integrated by primary consciousness can certainly lead to integrated responses between a variety of parallel input systems, and thus they may be causally efficacious in behavior and learning (see table 5.1).

The variation in the causal role of consciousness is a matter of degree, and changes in attentional states of the animal can alter it. This is so because attention is considered in the present theory to arise from the redistribution of reentry among the various different mapped systems that give rise to primary and higher-order consciousness. The heterogeneity in time and space of consciousness (figures 12.1 and 12.2) fits this notion. The accompanying phenomenal experiences—sensation, particular percepts and images, as well as feelings—should not be confused, however, with the activity of any of the parts that give rise to the *output* of such a system. Rather, they represent a particular state of the entire system. The addition of language to this picture complicates it greatly because of the enormously enhanced memorial and creative aspects that it allows. But aside from the increased number of states that language permits, its main importance is its reinforcement of the ability to develop a concept of past and future and thus permit modeling of plans in terms of intentions. As is illustrated in the list presented in table 5.1, higher-order consciousness is *obviously* efficacious in this respect.

It is useful to stress two additional points. First, the efficacy of consciousness is most clearly marked in dealing with *initial aspects* of novelty, planning, and thought.[30] Once learning and the proper patterning and automatization of responses have occurred, there is no need for any conscious integrative process, as was emphasized in the preceding section. Second, because its contributing structures can also act independently to achieve patterned behavior,[31] consciousness is neither epistemically privileged nor necessarily even *fundamentally* epistemic. Moreover, a conscious state can be of a "mood" with no external consequences whatsoever.

Time, exterior signals, plan and initial intent, emotional state, and disease can all alter the reentrant relations between consciousness and the nonconscious components of the brain (see figure 12.2 and chapter 13). They can also alter the relation of inputs and memories that are presently accessible to those that are inaccessible.[32] This brings us directly to the question of unconscious mental states.

REPRESSION AND THE UNCONSCIOUS

The positing of an unconscious is the essential binding principle of all of Freud's psychological theories.[33] Whatever the controversies concerning his dependent and derivative theories,[34] the existence of human motives and memories not always epistemically available to consciousness seems well supported by the evidence derived from studies of parapraxes, hypnotism, and neuroses.[35] Unlike the *fundamental unavailability* of nonconscious to conscious states, however, the position of Freud was that unconscious states, although inaccessible at a particular time, could be made accessible. It is important to notice that the unconscious states derive originally from the interactions of basic value-dependent hedonic systems, perception, and language. It is as a set of *conceptual categories* that their contents are subject[36] to recategorization in memory.

Erdelyi[37] has pointed out some of the definitional difficulties associated with Freud's use of the term "unconscious." In its *descriptive* use, the term applies to all psychological materials not currently present in consciousness. In its *dynamic* use, Freud refers to those elements that can easily and frequently be transformed into conscious states (Freud's so-called preconscious) and to those that can be transformed only with great difficulty or not at all (the "unconscious proper," or dynamic unconscious). The unconscious proper can be the result of repression, but, as we have indicated by our previous use of the term "nonconscious," there are many inaccessible states that do *not* result from repression. Freud's additional systemic usage of the term "unconscious" to designate "the *system unconscious,*" or the id, need not detain us here. We are concerned only with his dynamic use of the term.

What is valuable in understanding this use is Erdelyi's[38] distinction between the hypermnesia (or recovery) paradigm of the unconscious, and the dissociation paradigm. Hypermnesia implies an initially unconscious component from which information is recovered, so that the individual at one time is unaware and at a succeeding time is aware of that information. In the dissociation paradigm, an event indicating available information may occur (e.g., blushing that is appropriate to context) but is denied and is not accessible to awareness of the individual. Whereas hypermnesia involves comparison of a *single* indicator of information over two *successive occasions,* dissociation involves a *concurrent* contrast between *two different indicators.* Dissociation depends on semantic and conceptual contexts in a relativistic fashion, as we shall discuss in the last section of this chapter.

The fact that certain states can remain repressed is not inconsistent with the present models. The TNGS and the extended theory strongly implicate value-dependent systems in learning and in consciousness. Indeed, the very existence of consciousness depends upon the existence of self-nonself memory systems whose internal inputs must themselves remain forever inaccessible ("nonconscious") to direct awareness. Moreover, these nonconscious internal systems can be dominant over world input (see figure 9.3). Unconscious states are capable of altering responses in a similar fashion but are not always inaccessible. They reflect a *selective* inability to recall in the self-nonself memory. We shall discuss such dissociative reactions in some detail in the next chapter.

Unconscious states are perforce selective: according to the extended theory, loss of the entire memory system itself would obviously result in complete loss of consciousness. The abilities of recall depend upon cue, attentional state, and the gating of the various conceptual classifications of global mappings back through the cortical appendages. Alterations of the synaptic connections of such appendages during the *initial* formation of long-term memory could affect the ease with which they are subsequently engaged. The connection of these appendages to hedonic inputs and value systems provides a mechanism for this, as we discussed in chapter 9. Earlier conscious states involving other values can also affect the degree of association of such long-term memories by affecting conceptually and linguistically driven areas. Repression can be the result.

But what would be the adaptive advantage of repression? One possible answer is related to the efficacy and continuity of higher-order conscious states. These states occupy a large number of neuronal groups and systems at any one time. For efficacy, it is important that concepts of the self be developed without disruption. Alterations of that self-concept that require too large or abrupt a change in conceptual or value-derived systems would be maladaptive.[39] In a linguistically equipped animal, the rich means of reducing access to states considered threatening is in place: symbols *do* matter, and they matter to the efficacy of consciousness as well.

One interesting consequence of the TNGS that restricts the excessive application of Freudian theories of repression[40] emerges from the idea that memory is an *ability*—the ability to recategorize (chapter 6). The veridicality of what is remembered cannot be described in terms of information theory, because a given memory is not replicative. Instead, it is an ability that depends upon a vast network of other memories and neuronal states. Perceptual and conceptual memories are subject to many influences. Thus, it is likely that not all variability in memorial capacity is a result of repression or defense. To the extent that these variable properties of memory affect consciousness itself, the same remarks apply a fortiori.

If we accept the Freudian position on the unconscious, not only do deep problems related to the epistemic reliability of self-knowledge arise, but it is clear that introspection may be subject to grave error. Incorrigibility in the Cartesian sense is incompatible with these assertions and with Freud's theories.[41] Recent experiments[42] on split-brain patients reveal, for example, that the left brain maintains linguistic personal contact and introspection, whereas the right brain's activities are not subject to the person's direct awareness. Nevertheless, emotionally charged material presented to the right brain, which may have primary consciousness, can cause emotional responses and rationalizations on the part of that person. While this does not prove Freud's contentions, it is consistent with them.

About the other theories of Freud, I have little to say here.[43] But inasmuch as dream states represent a state of consciousness in which there is a sharp decrease in world (W) inputs, it may be illuminating to comment on some recent conclusions made by Hobson.[44] Because recent research on REM sleep indicates that it may be initiated by reciprocal functions of giant cell activity (REM-on) and locus ceruleus cell activity (REM-off), Hobson has rejected Freud's proposal that dreams reflect wishes. Moreover, in the so-called synthesis model, he suggests that the content of dreams is *simply* the result of such physiological activity and of the reduced cognitive activities of the brain in the absence of the W input that would otherwise organize such activity.

While REM sleep may be initiated chemically and while *some* dreams may merely be fragmentary activities of a system of consciousness with reduced W inputs, it is difficult to rule out the mechanisms of repression proposed by Freud and to rule in the synthesis model[45] suggested in its place. It is clear that repressive mechanisms operate in the waking state, where conscious cognitive integration helps make sense of the world. There is no reason to expect, however, that such mechanisms are completely canceled during sleep. In any case, dreams occur in all phases of sleep, not just REM sleep. It is a long way from acetylcholine to the incest taboo, and great care must be exercised in relating physiological states to the contents of conscious states in language-bearing animals.

LEVELS OF DESCRIPTION: THE CHOICE OF LANGUAGE IN PSYCHOLOGICAL SYSTEMS

This last discussion brings us close to an important methodological issue. Freud, in his *Project for a Scientific Psychology*,[46] espoused type-type identity[47] for neurons and thoughts and espoused eliminative reductionism of an extreme degree. In his later rejection of this formulation, he assumed an equally strong position of property dualism, asserting the impossibility of the reduction of psychology to neuroscience, while remaining a materialist in his philosophy. This not only requires a language based in psychological terms but *insists* on it.[48] As has been pointed out by Flanagan,[49] this probably derived from his studies with Brentano, who insisted on the meaninglessness for psychological explanation of any languages that had no terms descriptive of intentional states.

Quine has made a related point: "Thinking about Vienna may be a neural event which might be described in strict neural terms if we had access to the mechanism. But one can never translate the predicate 'Thinking about Vienna' into neural terms. Mental events are classified by mentalistic language in ways that are incommensurable with the classifications expressible in psychological language."[50] He equates this position with the doctrine of anomalous monism, as it is termed by Davidson.

This difficulty arises because of the complexity, degeneracy, and historical aspects of brain states and the nature of linguistic convention in establishing meaning. *More is involved than a brain state*—this more has to do with external signals and the diverse mapping onto language functions of conscious states. A mentalistic term and its relation to memory imply a history, an environment, and possibly other persons as well.[51] At any one time, therefore, perception of a particular object and its naming may depend on one set of neuronal groups and at another time on another. Yet its name and mapping through language remain invariant, according to the categorization mode. There can also exist a large set of degenerate neural states giving the same mapping, which is also context-dependent. A many-many relation therefore exists between a description of neural states and a particular agreed-upon category. The complexity of this situation obviously recommends talking in terms of intentionality if it serves adequately for description and communication.[52] But this is not symmetric: neural states definitely underlie intentional states, and the direct ascription of mentalistic terms to the operations of the brain itself rather than to a person can only lead to confusion.[53]

In addition to these interactive external factors, there is an internal one related to accompanying sensation. A particular set of neural interactions can lead to a describable or reportable *phenomenal* state and an output or set of outputs. Any future set of neural states that produces *a similar phenomenal state* (and in some cases an enhanced probability of activation of these outputs) has the possibility of yielding the same kind of output *regardless of whether previous specific perceptual contents and categories related to intentionality are present.*[54] The relation of the causal efficacy of conscious and unconscious mental states within the animal to the analysis of causality in general will be considered further in chapter 15. It will emerge that none of these complexities force us to abandon a brain-based model of consciousness.

In the present chapter, I have tried to show how the models of consciousness that I have advanced are consistent with an explicit hypothesis on attention and with various notions of intentionality and of unconscious mental states. In the next, I want to consider the implications of these models for a variety of neuropsychological and psychiatric disorders.

13

Diseases of Consciousness

A central theme of preceding chapters of this book is that consciousness is the key function of human brains. The questions I want to address in the present chapter are, first, how diseases affect consciousness and, second, whether one may speak of diseases of consciousness.

Addressing these questions in the context of the extended theory is an enormous challenge. The models that have been proposed to account for primary and higher-order consciousness include the activities of complex brain regions at many different levels of organization. Not only are the reentrant loops leading to consciousness very complex, but their functions involve historical change, and individual and social development both play important roles in the emergence of higher-order consciousness. Furthermore, brain disorders affecting lower levels such as synapses may be expected to affect other levels and various brain areas in very diverse ways.

Despite these difficulties, the extended TNGS provides an opportunity to examine diseases of the nervous system from a unified point of view. The theory can be used as a heuristic framework in which to explore how consciousness might be affected by different diseases involving the various brain areas that play a role in the models. In the ideal case, an analysis of various diseases would itself provide evidence for the dependence of primary and higher-order consciousness on particular anatomical and biochemical properties of the networks that have been proposed to underlie them. It would reveal the heterogeneity of the components underlying conscious states and show how their functions can be fractionated by different disorders. It might be used to show the bases for the commonalities and the overlapping

symptoms occurring in a variety of diseases that are nevertheless different in etiology and pathogenesis. It would be expected to reveal subtle
relations between the parallel channels linking consciousness and attention. In certain cases, it might shed light on the connection between
memory and language and between individuality and personhood. Finally, the theory might be extremely helpful in showing how partially
functioning or locally compromised portions of neural systems underlying consciousness could reintegrate and adapt to disorder. In actual
cases, of course, we can expect that these aims will be realized only in
part.

In addition to laying the grounds for the understanding of complex
causal chains in brain disorders, the TNGS provides a framework for
relating commonalities of symptoms regardless of their etiology. Instead of talking about psychoses and neuroses or about organic and
functional disorders, one is invited by this view to talk about diseases
of attention, diseases of motion, diseases of categorization, diseases of
reentry, diseases of succession, and diseases of qualia and of self. A
consideration of these disorders in terms of the framework of the TNGS
may reveal common patterns and show connections between particular
brain functions and the origins of consciousness. Let us erect this framework and then turn to a series of examples to illustrate these notions.

A General Framework

The framework provided by the extended theory is not to be considered a substitute for various nosological or etiological systems of diagnosis.[1] Rather, it offers a basis for the interpretation of symptoms, a means
of connecting disorders across various levels of disturbance (ranging
from molecular alteration to gross tissue loss), and a reference against
which to test various ideas about consciousness itself. I shall present this
framework cursorily here, mainly in terms of the diagrams in figure
13.1. Various disorders are placed into a common-framework diagram
for primary and higher-order consciousness by showing disruptions of
reentrant circuits at particular points, by placing darkened or dashed
arrows to indicate asymmetries of reentry, or by splitting or duplicat-
ing a particular functional region, such as the one subserving value-
category memory.

The locations of these perturbations in the basic diagram reflect only
crudely the dynamic disturbances in each pathological condition, and

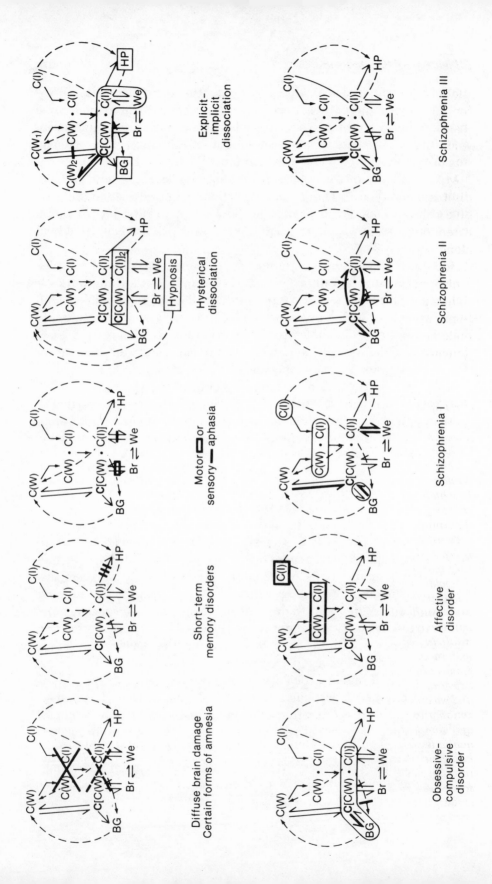

the individual diagrams can be viewed merely as metonyms standing for the overall process leading to conscious states. Nonetheless, the diagrams serve as useful comparative devices and, above all, emphasize again that consciousness is a result of the interaction of quite specific sets of brain regions.

My plan is simply to list at this point the various sites and related disorders and then to discuss some of them in greater detail in order to give substance to the assignments. The examples[2] picked for more extended consideration are diffuse brain damage and memory disorders along with aphasia; hysteria and dissociative states; neuropsychological dissociations; obsessive-compulsive disease; affective disorders; and schizophrenia. An examination of diffuse brain damage gives some insight into the global control of consciousness. A study of hysteria and hypnosis shows the possibility of fractionation of personhood by symbolic and semantic means. Neuropsychological syndromes show how domain-specific dissociations of inputs to consciousness lead to interpre-

Figure 13.1

A set of schematic drawings illustrating major brain sites and reentrant paths involved in the establishment of conscious states, indicating possible disturbances in various neuropsychiatric diseases. These diagrams are intended only as heuristic devices for discussions of diseases of consciousness and do not necessarily have either etiological or pathogenic significance. Diffuse brain damage leading to certain amnesias is supposed to affect midbrain sites, areas in which C(I) and C(W) are compared, and cortical regions subserving value-category memory. Short-term memory loss is supposed to occur as a result of disruption (bars across arrows) of medial temporal and hippocampal (HP) regions, and motor or sensory aphasia in disruption of reentry to or from Broca's (Br) or Wernicke's (We) areas. Hysterical dissociation involves temporary reordering ("splitting") of the value-category memory, and hypnosis is a dissociation of this memory via semantic input. Both conditions alter attentional pathways involving the basal ganglia (BG). Explicit-implicit dissociations result in a disruption [bars across arrows to C(W)] of key reentrant pathways for primary consciousness in a domain-specific fashion. This can result in semantic reordering (outlined area). Obsessive-compulsive disorder may involve an alteration [outlined area and bar across C(I) inputs] in circuits from cortex to basal ganglia relating conceptual assessments in the value-category memory to motor programs. These disorders are diseases of attention and succession in which the affective state alters the balance between automatization and novelty. Affective disorders are considered to alter value states C(I) and comparisons of C(I) with C(W) and are diseases of altered assessment of qualia with secondary effects on intentionality. Schizophrenia is considered to be a generalized disease of reentry taking on protean forms (labeled arbitrarily in examples I, II, and III) as it affects all parts of brain sites leading to consciousness. It is a disease of qualia and of intentionality. Darkened reentrant arrows indicate altered transmitter logic.

tive and semantic reordering of the patient's view of himself and the world. Obsessive-compulsive disorder gives some insight into the relation between plans and attentional states. Affective diseases reveal how alterations in value states and qualia can affect the assessment of reality. Schizophrenia provides a view of the multicentric and reentrant nature of conscious systems and shows how far these systems are from a direct registration of "reality," even in the normal.

The current state of our knowledge is such that these various diseases can be related to our heuristic framework in only a marginally satisfactory fashion. The framework may nevertheless be useful in focusing our thoughts on the various levels at which brain areas subserving consciousness interact. Let us begin with one of the more vexing examples, diffuse brain damage leading to alterations in consciousness.

Brain Damage, Amnesia, and Aphasia

Clinicians are likely to evaluate consciousness in terms of three sets of criteria: alertness or state of arousal, orientation (or awareness and self-awareness), and motivational or "executive" control. In general, diseases that affect one or another of these characteristics can also affect memory. In any given case, it is a challenge to decide whether such memory disturbances cause particular alterations of consciousness or are the results of these alterations. The various etiologies of the conditions (concussion, epilepsy, fever, anoxia and toxicoses, and encephalitis) often result in diffuse brain damage, making it particularly difficult to trace a specific locus responsible for the alterations in states corresponding to any of the three criteria used for evaluation (see table 13.1).

As a consequence of any of these disorders,[3] consciousness can become "clouded." Perceptual acuity and memorial capacity are diminished. In more severe cases, there is a fragmentation of the Jamesian properties of consciousness and a loss of coherency in the "flights and perchings" of conscious content. These may appear to be random, and there may be either perseveration of activity, automatized activity, or random performances of old habits. Speech may be incoherent and full of alliterations or rhymes. There is little or no evidence of introspection. Conscious attention to novelty is gone, and it appears that there is responsiveness to perceptual channels only, while conceptual and semantic fragments are produced without meaningful reference to self.

After recovery, there is usually no clear memory or even no memory

TABLE 13.1

Responses to Diffuse Brain Injuries Affecting Consciousness*

Primary Disorders	*Presumed Sites of Disturbances*
Disturbances of Alertness	
Confusion	Damage to value-category memory (prefrontal, parietal, cingulate, temporal cortex)
Reduced alertness	Brain-stem arousal systems
Somnolence	Reticular nucleus of thalamus
Disturbances of Awareness or Self-Awareness	
Akinetic mutism	Small diencephalic lesion
Persistent vegetative state (PVS)	Disconnection of cortex (including both the key reentrant loop and value-category memory)
Dysphasia with loss of higher-order consciousness	Loss of connections to frontal and temporal cortex (reduction to a state of primary consciousness)
Transient awareness disorders, *déjà vu, jamais vu,* derealization, depersonalization	Temporal and frontolimbic cortex
Longer-Term Secondary Disorders	*Presumed Sites of Disturbances*
Dissociative States	
Hysteria	See figure 13.1 and text
Unilateral neglect	Parietal cortex or VA nucleus of the thalamus
Attentional Disorders	
Distractibility	Reentrant loops between orbitofrontal cortex and basal ganglia
Reduction of attention span	
Memory Disorders	
Amnesia (long-term, late)	Value-category memory (frontal, temporal, etc.)
Korsakoff (short-term)	Value-category memory and diencephalon
Bitemporal (short-term)	Hippocampus, amygdala

*The contents are based on R. L. Wood, in Stevens, ed., *Aspects of Consciousness,* vol. 4, *Clinical Issues,* 1–39.

at all of the period during which these symptoms were displayed. In cases of injury, there may be severe retrograde or anterograde amnesia. Cortical lesions can lead to either a selective short-term or long-term memory defect.

Amnesic disorders of a more global kind, such as Korsakoff's syndrome and medial temporal or diencephalic disorders, show complex alterations. I will not discuss these in detail[4] but will mention a few key features. A major difficulty in assessing amnesic symptoms is to determine to what extent the patients have conceptual or semantic disorders. Patients with midbrain lesions generally show retrograde amnesia but not anterograde amnesia. In contrast, patients who have undergone complete removal of the hippocampus (along with some medial temporal tissue)—such as the celebrated case HM—show more or less normal long-term memory up to some period before the lesion and a complete failure of short-term memory. Such amnesics have a clear "Jamesian" consciousness, indicating that the hippocampus is truly a cortical appendage serving consciousness but is not directly required for it. The patient may, of course, complain of the strangeness of his state, but his consciousness is not clouded. As I mentioned in chapter 2, certain amnesic patients can show dissociation—while unaware, they may reveal priming effects in learning tests and retain many motor skills.

I will mention aphasia even more briefly, only to make the point that the analysis of these disturbances is consistent with the proposal (chapter 9) that the language areas mediate a special form of recategorical memory.[5] In general, in such cases conceptual capability is more or less intact. These disorders are traceable to an interruption of the function of reentrant pathways to and from Broca's and Wernicke's areas.

In diffuse brain damage and amentia, it is likely that *several* key centers are affected. The key ones are likely to be those correlating value (in the brain stem, septum, basal forebrain, etc.) and category, and the value-category memory itself, located mainly in the cortex. It is also likely that reentrant paths to and from the basal ganglia and hippocampus are malfunctioning. The failure of these linkages would lead to the fragmentation that is seen in those disturbances in which the Jamesian flow (see figure 9.2) is interrupted. Moreover, misfunctioning of the value-category memory or imbalances in connections to the key reentrant paths for primary consciousness would lead to a perceptually driven but incoherent set of responses with no opportunity to direct attention or mobilize conceptual constructs of the self. The patient would be in a degraded state in which both primary and higher-order consciousness are fragmented and mixed and his behavior is "randomly automatized."

The discussion here has concentrated on diffuse brain damage and its sequelae, and I have deliberately avoided focal disorders in the present section, but it may be revealing to consider briefly one special set of focal disturbances classically called the frontal lobe syndrome.[6] I shall not discuss the disorders of affect and emotional behavior resulting from lesions of the medial or orbital prefrontal cortex. A more focused set of symptoms results from lesions of the dorsolateral convexity of the prefrontal cortex in humans. Luria[7] has pointed out the inability of patients with this kind of lesion to make plans and the disintegration of complex programs of behavior in this disorder. He has suggested that this part of the cortex might be involved in a prelinguistic function essential to the formulation in language of a plan of action. As a result of all these disturbances, the patient's behavior repeatedly shows errors of action and attention and his responses are inconsistent.

This description is consonant with our attribution of a portion of the conceptual value-category memory to the prefrontal cortex (see chapter 9) and to its role in attentional states (chapter 12). The studies of Milner and Petrides[8] clearly show that patients with these disorders have diminished performance in delayed matching tests. Milner and her coworkers found that patients with prefrontal lesions perform badly on tests involving a short-term memory, particularly as it relates to ordering. She has also indicated the difficulties that ensue from the failure of these patients to control interferences that arise from distracting internal or external stimuli.

These observations suggest that while the Jamesian flow can be experienced by patients with these lesions, they are conceptually impaired in their abilities to free themselves from that flow by the construction of planned actions consequent to a goal. Their higher-order consciousness exists but is fragmented by this inability. They are not as free as normal persons from the immediate claims of the present and the bondage of real time.

The foregoing discussion is, of course, necessarily inadequate to the task of analyzing the complex states that follow acute or chronic diffuse brain damage. Perhaps when brain-imaging techniques are brought to bear and a statistical analysis of many cases has been carried out, we can place these disorders into our scheme in a more satisfactory fashion. The same remarks hold a fortiori for cases of coma, complete loss of consciousness, and persistent vegetative states. Despite these difficulties, it is possible to link these disturbances to our heuristic framework in a general fashion. In other neuropsychiatric diseases, we can show a bit more specificity. Let us now turn to them.

DISSOCIATIVE DISEASES: SPECIFIC BLOCKADE OF REENTRANT LOOPS

Consciousness may undergo dissociative alterations in a number of different ways. These range from the alterations induced by hypnoses to those of various forms of hysteria, fugues, and multiple personalities. There are also striking cases of domain-specific alterations that involve the dissociations of implicit and explicit knowledge seen in various neuropsychological disorders and after split-brain surgery.

Dissociation can be determined by repressed wishes in hysteria, by external suggestion in hypnosis, or by the interruption of neural pathways after lesions or surgery. Symbolic, semantic, or conceptual alterations occur in all of these instances. In hysteria and hypnosis, semantic and symbolic factors affect consciousness and attention. In neuropsychological disorders, alterations in concepts about the body can be reflected in a reorganization of higher-order consciousness as indicated by altered reports about body image or altered response to limbs. In all these cases, a dissociation can occur between forms of "implicit knowledge," according to which the patient performs, and "explicit knowledge," involving his conscious awareness.

Let us briefly consider the neuroses and hypnotic states. As we saw in chapter 12, Freud's early concern with hysteria provided a remarkable insight into the dissociative unconscious.[9] One of the most striking features of the symptoms induced in hysteria is their symbolic nature. The symbolic nature of glove and stocking anesthesia (in which the patient does not feel the areas that would be covered by these articles) obviously reflects conceptual knowledge that is implicit but barred from explicit, semantically driven awareness in higher-order consciousness. The fact that this anesthesia does not respect neuroanatomical boundaries only accentuates this point. Similarly, the occurrence of paralysis in conversion hysteria reflects the patient's *concepts*—according to Freud, concepts that carry symbolic freight related to repressed unconscious wishes.

In more recent times, investigations of hypnosis, of multiple personalities, and of what Hilgard[10] has aptly termed divided consciousness have left us with little doubt that there are, as he puts it, "multiple controls of human thought and action." As we shall see, these are consistent with the model of attention presented in chapter 12. Hilgard uses information processing approaches to account for such controls. For example, he views the normal subject as exercising executive and monitoring functions over voluntary motion and sensation. These two functions interact with each other. He suggests that, in hypnosis, the executive functions are shared by the hypnotist and the subject. The executive then affects the monitor to reduce its critical scanning (as it ordinarily would do in the unhypnotized subject), leading in this case to a certain degree of distortion of reality. Some part of the monitoring function seems to exist behind an amnesic barrier—the "hidden observer," who is available for communication only through automatic writing or talking. Another part is completely uncritical, accepting distorted reality as if it were undistorted. Hilgard correctly emphasizes, I believe, that this picture is one of parallel processing—of two experiences occurring at once—one of which is open to the awareness of the subject and the other of which is not.

The extended TNGS provides a more specific and less homuncular view of how these dissociations come to pass. If we consider the model of attention presented in the last chapter, it is clear that higher-order consciousness can alter various motor plans, conceptual goals, and image schemata. It is a reasonable hypothesis that a socially constructed self based on semantic exchange and learning can be altered by external intervention. Compliance with the hypnotist based on past rewards and on images related to gratification of authority can be exercised at a number of different levels. The engagement of a motor program (a sequence of responses that selects and restricts potential or actual outputs in a system that otherwise has few capacity limits) is consistent with this view of dissociation. Such a program can be activated by a motor plan, which in turn is under the influence of conceptual and linguistic responses, internal or external (see chapter 12).

It is not difficult to imagine that control of such motor plans and programs can be relinquished to unconscious structures built by semantic and social interaction with the hypnotist. The dissociative reactions involving changes in responses to qualia (obtained by, for example, placing a subject's hand in ice water with hypnotic suggestions that this is comfortable, while eliciting messages such as "ouch" written by the other hand) may seem to pose greater problems. But it is well known that pain responses are strongly related to context and to peripheral and central states as well as to goals and actions. Their *identification* as pain strongly depends upon the mix of these variables. In this matter, as Wall[11] has pointed out, there is no contradiction: pain, like other phenomenal states of consciousness, is relative to background—it is a relation.

The notion that higher-order consciousness is the result of an elaborated interaction between linguistic and concept-forming parts of the brain, with C(I) dominant in the latter (see chapter 9), is consistent with the dissociations seen in hysteria and hypnosis. The model is consistent with unconscious allocation of symbolic structures relating to the self or to unconscious wishes. A dissociation between the two, fractionating the value-category memory (see figure 13.1), would still reflect implicit knowledge (and as the examining physician or an observer of a hypnotized subject soon discovers, this knowledge is not neuroanatomically accurate). These instances reveal how symbolic exchange may lead to dissociations in higher-order consciousness. Such dissociations are consistent with the idea that higher-order consciousness is semantically driven and that the areas responsible for concept formation can drive action after attentional reallocation of semantic resources.

The neuropsychological syndromes (reviewed briefly in chapter 2) also show how lesion-induced dissociation can alter symbolic and semantic responses in the conscious patient.[12] Sometimes patients with these syndromes give what appear to be unrealistic or distorted responses. There is no convincing evidence, however, that patients with disorders of bodily awareness such as unilateral neglect and anosognosia suffer from either neurotic dissociation or psychosis.[13] Anosognosics can actively deny the existence of a paralysis and will on occasion attribute the affected parts to others or attempt to throw them out of bed as strange. A patient with no serious weakness, but who suffers from unilateral neglect, can achieve good performance in spontaneous automatic acts on the neglected side but be unable to carry out commands involving that side (usually the left). The amnesic or prosopagnosic who shows implicit but not explicit knowledge of particular domain-specific stimuli provides an anatomically based counterpart to the reorganization of consciousness that occurs in the dissociative states induced by hypnosis or hysteria. But, in accord with our hypothesis, in these anatomically based cases, the neurology and psychology are consistent with each other.

Other, more focal disorders exist, such as finger agnosia, in which the patient cannot identify or execute commands relating to his fingers (and, very rarely, toes). Phantom limb is experienced not only by amputees but, more interestingly from the present point of view, also occasionally by hemiplegics. In the latter cases, the phantom limbs—

fingers, arms, or, more rarely, lower extremities—tend to be experienced as *supernumerary*. In these focal disorders of the body image, an explanation invoking alterations in the plasticity or the alteration of map boundaries of somatosensory maps seems plausible. Indeed, this plasticity has been cited as a major piece of evidence in support of the TNGS (see *Neural Darwinism*). There is no particular reason to hold that processes other than alterations in primary receiving areas are a sufficient cause for these disorders. They may be considered disorders of local mapping.

Matters are otherwise for the more general disorders of body image as seen in hemineglect and anosognosia.[14] Several theories have been advanced to account for the patient's responses in these conditions. The neurologically consistent laterality of these disorders makes it difficult to accept the psychodynamic explanation—that the patient is simply denying the illness. The attribution of the disorder to a difficulty in verbalization may have some support in certain cases. Perceptual awareness and right-left orientation occur in preverbal children, however, and they therefore do not necessarily depend on linguistic performance. This lessens the force of explanations based solely on the existence of verbal disorders.

In general, cortical lesions underlying disturbances of body image are limited to the parietal area. Since this area is one of the four regions of the cortex considered to be essential for the value-category memory that is central to consciousness, it is a reasonable hypothesis that these syndromes reflect not disturbances of the body image the patient already has *had* but rather failures to integrate his actual body in conscious experience. But what is really quite striking is the fact that the patient reintegrates his entire semantic interpretation often without emotional disturbance. One would have thought that, if a body image were "reliably" or replicatively "stored" in memory, the discrepancy with his present state would be found extremely disturbing. In fact, the patient is not so disturbed—he cannot attend to parts of his personal space, and his semantic reintegration seems to be dependent on this.

In the light of the extended TNGS, these observations have several significant implications, which we may briefly summarize:

1. The patient's reintegration of his present state into a cogent verbal account that involves denial graphically illustrates that memory is recategorical and not replicative. The patient's conceptual categories adjust to his present capabilities.
2. Among other possible disturbances, the loss of parietal functions alters his ability to attend.

3. As in other implicit-explicit dissociations, some affected patients can
   carry out acts involving implicit knowledge, demonstrating that consciousness is not always necessary for performance, even rather complicated performance.

These conclusions are consistent with the idea that these neuropsychological disorders are diseases of consciousness and that they affect •
key reentrant loops to domain-specific maps while leaving most of the
value-category memory intact. Rather than involving specific linguistic
disturbance, most of them are accompanied by striking *conceptual*
rearrangements and integrations.

Unlike their superficially similar counterparts in conversion hysteria
or hypnosis, however, some of these disorders are irreversible. Moreover, they do not display a divided consciousness but rather a radically
reintegrated one. Nonetheless, both sets of situations are consistent
with the models of primary and higher-order consciousness proposed
here. Each gives sharp insights into how new integrations of the structures and processes leading to consciousness can occur as a result of
alterations in categorizations, and how alterations of categorizations
can result from domain-specific losses in reentrant loops.

I have already mentioned one of the most extreme forms of dissociation in previous chapters: split-brain patients. I shall not consider them
in any detail here.[15] But it is clear from studies of various cases that
higher-order consciousness and the subjective self and speech are
served by the left hemisphere. It is a moot point whether there is any
trace of higher-order consciousness in an isolated right hemisphere that
possesses some speech capacity. But it is tempting to suggest that the
right hemisphere mediates a form of primary consciousness: it can
respond to complex cues in terms of internal values and salience, can
carry out visually presented verbal commands, and can have access to
certain long-term memories.

OBSESSIVE-COMPULSIVE DISORDER AS A DISEASE OF
SUCCESSION AND ATTENTION

I referred in chapter 7 to some evidence suggesting that obsessive-
compulsive disorder is related to basal ganglion dysfunction. Wise and
Rappaport[16] have pointed out the association of obsessive-compulsive
symptoms with various syndromes involving the basal ganglia. As they
indicate, brain-imaging studies and responses to certain psychosurgical

treatments are consistent with the idea that these structures are involved in obsessive-compulsive disorders. These researchers suggest a
simple model in which there are "stimulus detectors" in the striatum
that can act innately or be modified by learning. They also posit "motivation detectors" in the striatum. Both of these kinds of detectors can
inhibit tonically discharging pallidal cells, leading to disinhibition of a
thalamic cell group. The striatal serotonin system is supposed to modulate inputs from the anterior cingulate cortex to the "motivation detectors." If, for example, a striatal input signals dirty hands, the "stimulus
detectors" recognize this as such, discharge, and block the tonic discharge of pallidal cells, releasing thalamocortical circuits and leading to
the normal behavioral response, hand washing. A hyperactive striatal
input from the anterior cingulate may alter this pattern, however, leading to so-called vacuum behavior or displacement activity (similar to
those proposed by ethologists for innate releasing mechanisms). These
responses would then constitute obsessive-compulsive rituals.

These authors point out, however, that some clinical data do not fully
support this model. For example, Huntington's disease and idiopathic
Parkinsonism can be associated with depression and psychotic symptoms but not with obsessive-compulsive disorder. The model also does
not account for the relatively long time course of obsessive disorder, the
behavioral specificity for performance of only one or two actions at a
time, or the efficacy of behavior therapy in the disease.

These difficulties may be avoided by taking a different view of the
function of the basal ganglia, one more consistent with the interactions
between higher-order consciousness and selective attention. In the attentional model discussed in the preceding chapter, the basal ganglia
connect the motor plans formulated by cortical action to motor programs. The basal ganglia contain no specific innate patterns but *modulate* the relations between different cortical areas mediating conceptual
categorization and motor output. According to the attentional model,
restriction in attention occurs because of the selection of a particular
motor program (see figure 12.2 and chapter 12). If we assume that the
lesion in obsessive-compulsive disorder relates to limbic alterations that
block conscious attention while facilitating the basal ganglion activity
that executes a motor program, we have a picture of a disease of attention and succession. There is a failure to alter the relation between
automatization and novelty, and the same motor plan is repeatedly
executed. It is the semantic-conceptual element in the frontal cortex
and speech centers, combined with the selective restriction of the attentional mechanism giving rise to the behavioral specificity for a plan,

that can account for the fixation on one or two behaviors at a time.

An individual with such a disorder is not conscious of reaching the goal of the repetitious ritual as such. He thus has a defect in explicit knowledge. In this view of the disease, unconscious and repressed fears can still underlie the *triggering* of the rituals that ensue, and alterations in synaptic strengths linking the basal ganglia to the cortex can be induced by such trigger factors. This would account in some cases for the chronicity of the disease and at the same time for its distinctiveness from Parkinson's and Huntington's diseases. This interpretation is also consistent with the response of some cases to behavior therapy. In any event, obsessive-compulsive disorder is a disease of succession and attention and certainly is also appropriately described as a disease of consciousness.

AFFECTIVE DISORDER: VALUE DISTURBANCE AND ALTERED QUALIA

Depression is a normal human emotion and probably serves an adaptive role during times of threat. As one of the subjective aspects of emotional experience, it can serve communicative roles in addition to ensuring withdrawal from threat. But certain disturbances of unknown origin can lead to primary affective disorder accompanied by incapacitating depression. Affective disorders can take the form shown by patients who are depressed but also have manic episodes (bipolar disease) or that shown by patients who have only recurrent episodes of depression (unipolar disease). The variability and the individual reactions in these diseases are striking; nonetheless, positive family history is greater in the bipolar group of patients, and the two groups differ in their response to drugs.

These patients may have such severe impairment that they become socially withdrawn and unable to work. But only 10 percent or so of the cases show hallucinations, delusions, confusion, or impaired memory. Some psychiatrists have found it useful to distinguish between endogenous and reactive forms of depression. In endogenous disease, the patients are likely to have had no previous history of neuroses, are older at onset, lack a clear history of precipitation by stressful events, and show strong correlation among a group of symptoms—early morning awakening, weight loss, motor retardation, guilt, and unreactivity, as well as a lack of pleasure-seeking behavior. In the manic phase, patients show elation, hyperactivity, flight of ideas, and grandiosity.

Following Klein,[17] Carroll[18] has suggested that depression can be understood in terms of a series of defects: (1) inhibition of a central pleasure-reward system, (2) disinhibition of a central pain regulatory system, and (3) inhibition of psychomotor facilitatory systems. Alterations in the first system lead to a loss of internal image and anhedonia, as well as loss of satisfaction in work and social interactions. In manic episodes, a disinhibition of this pleasure-reward system leads to omnipotent and grandiose ideas and to an overly optimistic view of future pleasure and reward.

Quite separate in some cases (though overlapping in others) is the alteration of thresholds for central pain, leading to morbid fears, weeping, unhappiness, overreaction to unpleasant stimuli, and hopelessness. As in schizophrenia, the content of ideas in the disease episodes is determined by individual social and historical factors, but the form is determined by the disorder. The obverse alteration, inhibition of the perception of psychic pain in manics, leads to elation, reckless risk taking, and misassessment of future possibilities of disappointment.

The third element (inhibition of psychomotor activity) in the descriptions by Klein and by Carroll[19] relates to motor retardation, retarded speech, paucity of thoughts, and a loss of energy. The manic shows the opposite: psychomotor acceleration, flights of ideas, and pressured speech without interruption. In particular cases, expressions of these three major groups of symptoms are seen in varying degrees.

The pleasure-reward disturbance suggests the possibility of alteration in appetitive centers connected to limbic circuits of the forebrain.[20] Similarly, midbrain and limbic circuits connected to aversive responses seem reasonable candidates for the site of the central pain disturbance. Alterations in the limbic connections of the basal ganglia may be responsible for the psychomotor symptoms. In all cases, there is a suggestion that the midbrain circuits affecting these regions have been disturbed. In no case, however, can a single neurotransmitter be identified as the cause. It seems much more likely that there is a defect in the interactive coordination of a variety of neurotransmitters, including dopamine, norepinephrine, acetylcholine, and enkephalin.

In most cases of affective disorder, there is apparently no gross disturbance of consciousness per se. Nonetheless, one main component (the midbrain-limbic circuits) of the value-category memory that is central to consciousness appears to be disturbed. The ensuing lack or excess of "hedonic drive" certainly would affect the patient's conscious evaluative capacities. In this sense, affective disease is a disease of the evaluation of qualia rather than primarily a disease of intentionality. In those cases in which true delusions and hallucination occur, however, one may reasonably assume that systems akin to those involved in schizophrenia have become affected. Indeed, the borderline between such cases and so-called schizoaffective disorders is not sharply drawn.

Schizophrenia as a Generalized Disease of Reentry

I shall close this account of particular examples by considering certain aspects of schizophrenia, a disorder that several authors have considered a disease of consciousness.[21] To a newcomer, nothing is so striking and baffling as the florid variety and individuality and the remarkable diagnostic and etiological problems posed by this disorder.[22] Furthermore, nothing is so revealing of the challenge to interpretation offered by this disease as a look at various attempts to classify it. One has only to glance at *ICD 9* (the ninth revision of the *International Classification of Diseases*)[23] or at the *Diagnostic and Statistical Manual of Mental Disorders* (*DSM III*, of the American Psychiatric Association)[24] to see the difficulties of description. When one considers the evidence for and against a genetic component[25] in this disorder, the problem of constructing a reasonable explanation of the varied yet individual symptoms on a biochemical basis becomes intimidating.

One cannot help being struck by the bizarre features of the nuclear syndrome. Thought echo, thought broadcast, thought insertion, thought block, thought withdrawal, third-person auditory hallucinations, and various delusions of control of alien forces and of certainty can all mix in varying proportions, accompanying emotional blunting, low motivation, and poor interpersonal rapport. Despite the thought disorders in the disease, it has sometimes been described as a disorder characterized by "clear consciousness." Although clarity of consciousness has been ascribed to schizophrenics, there is evidence that acute episodes of the disease are actually accompanied by a "dream-like state and slight clouding of consciousness with perplexity" (*ICD 9*). The patient can be easily distracted, has difficulty maintaining attention, misjudges perceptual signals, can have visual illusions, and can show difficulties in comprehension. He can be slow in response, perseverate, show poor judgment, and have difficulty in sharply discriminating gestalten.

In schizophrenia, the patient is subject to a barrage of signals that make a kind of sense but only in fragments and across various islands of perceptuomotor awareness. At the same time, he may demonstrate a blunting of affect. It is as if, at one time or another, all of the components we have considered to be important for primary and higher-order consciousness are affected by this disease.

Furthermore, following recovery from acute episodes, patients can have poor recollection of the contents of the acute experience. One must agree with Weller[26] and others that, while schizophrenia is a disease of consciousness affecting qualia, veridical perception, and thought, it is also frequently one in which the patient is confused—that is, his consciousness is *not* clear.

What can account for the diversity of symptoms, the individual flavor, and the bizarre features of this disorder? Clearly, any hypothesis is at hazard. While there appears to be a genetic component[27] underlying predisposition to the disease, environmental factors also clearly play a role. Current evidence[28] suggests that there is no *simple* neurotransmitter abnormality that could account for the symptoms, even though drugs that bind specifically to dopamine receptors can dramatically alter the symptoms of the disease.

One proposal consistent with the TNGS that may account for the diversity and the bizarre features of schizophrenia is that it is a disease of reentry with greater or lesser degrees of influence on various areas leading to higher-order consciousness. How could reentry be affected? In *Neural Darwinism,* I pointed out that pairs of channels responsive to different transmitters or voltage levels could cooperate or not, depending on the *time* at which they were in a particular state. Outside of a particular time window, they would no longer act together.[29] This dependency can lead to completely different selectional correlations. An alteration in the interactions between several neurotransmitters could lead by these means to a general disorder of communication between reentrant maps.

Suppose that schizophrenia is caused by an alteration at the synaptic level of "transmitter logic" and that, because of an imbalance in the action of multiple transmitters, there is a failure in heterosynaptic inhibition or facilitation that varies among different maps. While neuronal groups in a given region might function in such a way as to retain the synaptic efficacies underlying memory, the reentrant pathways to and from this region might show asynchronous behavior or a failure in appropriate mapping. As a result of inappropriate reentry between maps carrying out perceptual categorizations, imaging may predominate over perceptual input or mix with it, or different modalities might no longer be coordinated. This could lead to hallucination and a breakdown of connection with real-world signals. The fear and confusion induced by such a predicament are not difficult to imagine.

Now consider what would happen if the conceptual systems themselves failed to reenter or to engage organs of succession in a sequential fashion. At such a point, one would expect to see a rearrangement of the otherwise close relation between the lexicon and conceptual systems. Finally, imagine that in the chronic state of the disease, the linkage to the language centers themselves is compromised. It is not difficult to see that confusion of speech and "word salad" might result.

In any particular case, the actual form and sequence of the symptoms induced by these derangements of reentry would depend upon the composition of the repertoires in which neuronal group selection had already occurred in normal life. In a selective system, historical factors and the nature of preexisting variation both play strong roles in determining individuality. The sequence of alterations in reentrant mapping postulated as an element in this disease would itself vary from individual to individual. The combined result would be that each patient's actual symptomatology would be unique insofar as different mappings would be altered at different times. Moreover, in each person, a given change could have a different significance. This result follows directly from the fact that symbolic exchange and changes in synaptic efficacy follow a many-many relation unique to each individual.

The idea of schizophrenia as a generalized disease of reentry is obviously an explanation neither of the etiology nor of the pathogenesis of schizophrenic disease. But, inasmuch as all brain maps have very many biochemical features in common, it is not difficult to see how a common etiology could variably affect different combinations based on an individual history of synaptic change. This hypothesis does suggest that, whatever the etiology of the disease, it is likely to be one that can potentially affect a large variety of different maps—above all, those linking the value-category memory to perceptual categorization. The fundamental (and possibly testable) idea is that most of the neurons in many of these maps are normal but that the sequences of reentry leading to neuronal group selection are disturbed by an alteration affecting "transmitter logic" and timing.

SOME EVALUATIVE REMARKS

I am aware of the highly conjectural and preliminary nature of even the few sketches I have provided here. They are meant not as a well-

change a particular combinatorial pattern of synaptic efficacies in even two different individuals and achieve the same results as a semantic exchange. (Obviously, if our theory is correct, these two individuals have different detailed neural arrangements. No known drug can be delivered across variant anatomy and synaptic patterns to yield an effective selection of isofunctional neuronal groups, resulting in identical inputs or outputs in different individuals.)

Drugs, of course, *can* alter particular synaptic conditions across patterns of transmitter logic.[30] These important effects can yield complementary changes in brain activity that will often mitigate various symptoms and responses. Nevertheless, such effects, even if dramatic, cannot in general be traced to a simple or linear causal chain. We must expect causal chains to be complex in reentrant systems.

If the view we have put forth in this book is correct, the relation of perceptual categorization to conscious concept formation may be acutely rearranged after the intervention of various pathogenic disturbances. The fact that in normal persons the means for perceptual categorization is disjunct, involves polymorphous sets, and also samples an open-ended environment that offers no clear-cut instructions and has potentially vague boundaries should prompt us to view psychiatric disorder in a new light. Our worldview is a matter of individual and social convention as well as of lawful scientific descriptions. By social consent, it is "crazy" to attempt to defy the restrictions imposed on us by these lawful descriptions, particularly if it endangers ourselves or others. But, in fact, the TNGS provides a somewhat different view of how we arrive at a "safe and sane" position in society even as normal individuals. The idea of disease is relative to the norms of that society and to the disease in question. Derangement and diseases of consciousness represent adaptation to alterations in the reentrant maps, homeostatic regions, and cortical appendages that are responsible for perceptual awareness. In a nervous system functioning by means of neuronal group selection, these disorders would be expected to lead to highly individual constellations of symptoms. Different diseases, of course, have different causes and involve different portions of the systems leading to consciousness. Yet, despite the individual nature of symptoms in each disease, one would expect to see similar types of symptoms even in widely different diseases if given portions of the reentrant systems are similarly affected. Some of the accounts we have given here tend to support this view.

With further study of the relations between neurotransmitter action and the mechanisms of reentry, it may be possible to trace more accurately the origins and background of particular symptoms in diseases of consciousness. In the meanwhile, the extended TNGS provides a brain-based framework within which it is possible to understand how such a wide range of etiologies and pathologies can lead to neuropsychiatric disorder. This analysis does not diminish the importance of social factors in leading to pathology. On the contrary, it provides a means of understanding how such factors may lead to alterations in patterns of synaptic selection and how such changes may be reconciled with the consequences of more obvious neuroanatomical and neuropathological disturbances.

PART FIVE

BIOLOGICALLY
BASED
EPISTEMOLOGY

14

Physics, Evolution, and Consciousness: A Summary

I have attempted in three books—*Topobiology, Neural Darwinism,* and the present volume—to construct a global brain theory that is compatible with physics and evolutionary theory. Of necessity, this has been a complex and demanding task. It may be useful to retrace some of its key steps and to point out again some methodological limitations that must be transcended for its continuing value to be assured.

In the first place, we cannot begin with consciousness and proceed to physics and evolutionary theory, although this is obviously the order in which these subjects arose in the history of human interests. For historical reasons and given the conceptual priorities, we must travel in a loop in order to comprehend the physical means that gave rise to consciousness. We must begin by assuming the grand theories of two advanced scientific arenas: physics and biological evolution. Having reconciled their premises with those of our brain theory, we can, if we wish, reconstruct the history and origination of the *objects* of such theories without any loop. In this way, as Armstrong[1] puts it, we may bring the being who puts forward the scientific worldview within that worldview.

My summary will assume that the reader is more or less familiar with these two grand theories. I shall use some schematic diagrams to summarize the extended brain theory in the hope that they may simplify the task of relating it to these grand theories. But I must also warn that these diagrams do not include the various qualifications that are necessary for an understanding of all aspects of the extended TNGS without distortion.

This theory assumes that the world is structured as described by quantum field theory, relativity theory, and statistical mechanics. Many portions of that world are far from equilibrium in the thermodynamic sense. In addition to these physical constraints, the theory also assumes that all aspects of brains, structural and functional, may be attributed ultimately to evolution as described by the theory of natural selection. In constructing the brain theory, no additional attributes are assumed for matter or its interactions.[2]

A key argument that follows from these assumptions is that the functional properties of brains, including consciousness, result from phenotypic properties, notably morphology. In other words, the constraints operating on various psychological phenomena arise because of the involvement of functions that are made possible only by particular anatomies. Thus, a central problem that must be solved to allow an understanding of brain function is the problem of morphologic evolution.[3] In *Topobiology*, I argued that to solve this problem, evolutionary theory requires an appropriate developmental theory. The latter theory must accomplish two things: (1) reconcile developmental genetics with the mechanochemical events that give rise to form, and (2) show how evolutionary and ecological change can be reconciled with the developmental mechanisms that give rise to changing forms in different species.

TOPOBIOLOGY AND THE MORPHOREGULATOR HYPOTHESIS

As a basis for such a developmental theory, the morphoregulator hypothesis was formulated. According to this hypothesis, genetically regulated development of form rests on topobiological events—molecular events at cell surfaces occurring as a function of place and regulating or altering the primary processes of development. These processes include cell division, movement, death, adhesion, and differentiation (figure 14.1). The hypothesis proposes that morphoregulatory molecules (particularly cell adhesion molecules, or CAMs, and substrate adhesion molecules, or SAMs) are key elements in topobiologically controlled events because they are under strict genetic regulation and because they are essential both for the formation of cell collectives and

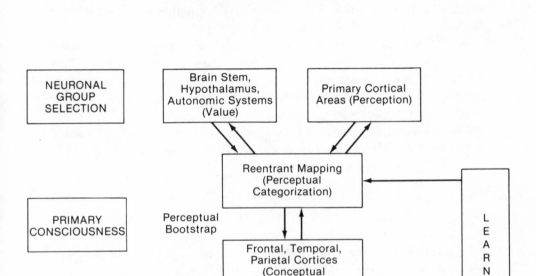

Figure 14.1
Consciousness and morphology. (Compare to figure 15.1.)

for cell migration and communication in development. Alteration of signals to the control loops affecting morphoregulatory genes (which control the structural genes for such molecules) leads dynamically to developmental changes in shape. This leads in turn to new boundaries between cells and their collectives and alters various other gene signaling events. A heritable change in morphoregulatory genes followed by natural selection for fitness based on the changed morphology may lead to molecular heterochrony. This term refers to alterations in the timing of action of morphoregulatory genes governing key developmental events that are the basis of a given form. Obviously and a fortiori, all of these remarks apply to the evolution and development of brains.

The morphoregulator hypothesis is important for our present concerns because it provides an obligate basis for the generation of neuronal diversity and individual variation in neural connections that underlie the TNGS. Because form depends upon place-dependent dynamics that are epigenetic, extensive diversity is developmentally generated in each brain within neuronal populations, particularly at their finest ramifications, as they form synapses.

With this background, we are in a position to survey the extended TNGS, especially its proposals for the origins of consciousness. This survey will not recapitulate the many detailed mechanisms of the theory but instead will emphasize the linkages among the key ideas. I will not hesitate to range from neurons up to issues concerned with language, meaning, and social interactions. As I pursue this task, the reader may find it useful to relate the discussion to the diagram in figure 14.1.

THE TNGS PROPER

The TNGS makes the following three proposals. (1) During development, dynamic processes of morphogenesis lead selectively to the formation of anatomy specific for a species but *obligatorily* possessing enormous anatomical variation at its finest levels and ramifications. A population of groups of neurons in a given brain region, consisting of variant neural networks arising by such processes of somatic selection, is known as a primary repertoire. (2) During behavior, and as a result of neural signaling, a second means of selection occurs—without alteration of anatomy, various synaptic connections are selectively strengthened or weakened to give a secondary repertoire consisting of variant functioning neural circuits. (3) As a result of evolution and through interaction between sensory and motor systems, many of these repertoires are arranged in maps. Such maps are connected by parallel and reciprocal connections that provide the basis of the third tenet of the theory—the occurrence of reentrant signaling. As a result of input from the environment and phasic reentrant signaling during behavior, some groups in local maps are competitively selected over others.

As we saw in chapter 4, reentry involves the exchange of signals between different repertoires in a parallel and recursive manner. In addition to its other functions, it allows a variety of connected maps containing these repertoires to reflect the spatiotemporal continuity of events and signals in the world. The unlabeled world (which follows the laws of physics but in which biologically adaptive patterns occur that are not described by physics) is disjunctively sampled by various parallel sensorimotor channels. At any moment, not all features or correlations of features are sampled. This sampling results in the selection of combinations of neuronal groups (closely connected sets of neurons forming particular variant circuits) that are mapped in various ways. Selections of groups within different maps are *correlated* by reentry. For perceptual activity, at least one local map in a reentrant set must receive signals from a given sensory receptor sheet in a fashion that maintains some conformal relation to the spatiotemporal distributions of the real-world things and events that give rise to those signals. This mapping is not necessarily in fine grain (or cell-to-cell), but it is point-to-area or area-to-area.

A series of such local maps reentrantly connected to each other and driven continuously by motor and sensory sampling of the environment through behavior and undergoing continuous synaptic selection of its neuronal groups constitutes a global mapping. Global mappings are dynamic and metastable. They provide the basis for the sampling by parallel sensory channels of those stimulus features and their correlations that are essential for perceptual categorization. They involve large portions of the nervous system and sensorimotor ensembles and are continuously driven, maintained, or obliterated by motor activity.

In general, metastable global mappings, arising from continuous motor exploration and involving many reentrant maps and sensorimotor loops, are the minimal basis for perceptual categorization. Pair-wise or higher-order interactions of reentrant maps in these mappings form so-called classification couples or *n*-tuples, which combine the results of independent disjunctive samplings to yield categorization. The nature of the features sampled is in turn related to particular phenotypic constraints of sensory and motor organs that evolved in a given species because they were adaptive. The neuronal group selection leading to particular interactions of maps is degenerate—more than one combination of neuronal groups can give a particular output. It is as a result of degenerate selection within global mappings that properties of generalization and association arise.

Inasmuch as neuronal group selection occurs by synaptic change, more or less stable alterations in synaptic efficacy provide the basis for storage in memory. Storage is not replicative and not mediated by codes. Rather, it is dynamic and represents an enhancement of the ability to categorize on the basis of past behavior and current context. It is therefore dependent upon correlations in global mappings. In this view, memory is a form of recategorization with obligatory associative properties made possible by synaptic changes within local maps.

Local maps linked by reentry to form global mappings are part of a system of interactive neural populations undergoing selection that constitute important parts of the cerebral cortex. Such cortical mappings alone are insufficient, however, either to deal with temporal ordering of signals or to provide indications of "value" based on the self-adaptive or homeostatic functions of the nervous system. For the first of these needs (temporal ordering), cerebellar structures and basal ganglia evolved to correlate movement sequences, and hippocampal structures evolved to order sequences of classification couples or n-tuples in the short term. The second of these needs (relating category to value) requires the linkage of the cortex and cortical appendages such as the hippocampus and basal ganglia to structures of the limbic system involved with value and hedonic satisfaction. It also requires learning.

Learning relates various perceptual categorizations to those behaviors that result in adaptive value. According to the TNGS, perceptual categorization is necessary for learning, which is a specific linkage between categorization and value to yield an adaptive response. Value is established by evolutionarily determined patterns in the phenotype. These patterns emerge from the activities of self-regulating portions of the brain that govern homeostatic regulation, satiation, or protective responses and that contribute inputs to the limbic system. Value is thus an evolutionarily determined assignment of adaptive or homeostatic function, and it can be altered by synaptic changes resulting in preference of one state over another. States related to value may be internal and ethologically fixed (e.g., hypothalamic discharge or endocrine levels) or may be dependent upon external occasions (light is favored over darkness, etc.). In the course of behavior, selective interaction and linkage occur between limbic and brain-stem structures having adaptive homeostatic functions and the global mappings that mediate perceptual categorization. This linkage opens the possibility of discrimination between self and nonself.

CONSCIOUSNESS AND THE EXTENDED TNGS

Organisms capable only of perceptual categorization via multiple sensory modalities and submodalities lack flexible means to provide internally determined decisions on the salience of signals arriving in parallel, except as determined by fixed evolutionarily determined schemata of behavior. With the evolution of structures allowing the emergence of primary consciousness, however, immediate means for richly relating salience to past adaptations of an *individual* animal became available.[4] This is so because primary consciousness allows inner states resulting from memories of *previous* perceptual categorizations that were linked to value to be connected with *current* perceptual input.

The development of primary consciousness required the evolution of mapped cortical areas in conjunction with that of various organs of succession. The categorization of smooth movements and the development of short-term memory are the bases of ordering in space and time (figure 14.2). Such a system of primary consciousness depends strongly upon topographic mappings. Simultaneously, however, there evolved cortical regions able to categorize the types of global mappings carried out by the brain itself. Such regions (presumably frontal, temporal, and parietal) form the basis for concept formation. In such regions, recombinations of categories and higher-order generalizations become possible, and with them *conceptual* categorization and memory as a prerequisite for forming a model of the world. The sequencing of such conceptual states emerged from systems involved with motor plans and motor sequences. This provided a presyntax, which is a main basis for thought in animals with primary consciousness.

For primary consciousness to appear, two sets of structures were required: (1) a special memory system conceptually relating past categorizations to value had to be developed; (2) reentrant connections relating the conceptual system to the current immediately categorized signals had to be established. Primary consciousness emerges from the interaction of the value-category memory and ongoing (current or present) perceptual categorization.

Possessed with primary consciousness alone, animals are bound to the small time intervals mediated by short-term memory; they have no concept of the past. With the evolution in hominids of the vocal tract, of the supralaryngeal space, and of Broca's and Wernicke's areas, however, a means for symbolic categorization emerged (figures 14.1 and 14.2). Symbolic categorization and speech permitted concepts of past

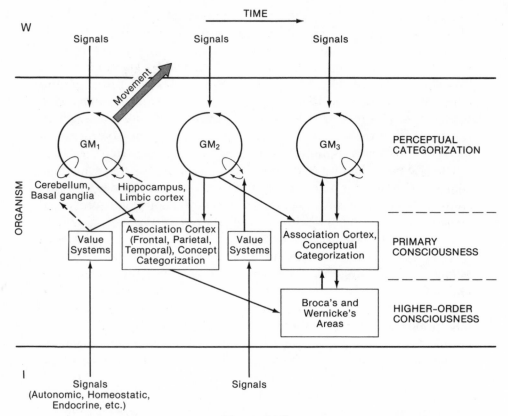

Figure 14.2

Ordering in space and time. The notion of consciousness is permeated with ideas of time and continuity. According to the theory, this occurs first because of action and the need for movement in perceptual categorization achieved by means of global mappings. Such mappings succeed each other in various ways, depending on the salience of signals and on attention. Second, the development of a special conceptual memory in animals with higher-order consciousness leads to the development of notions of the past and future. The workings of both primary and higher-order consciousness thus depend strongly upon discriminative reentrant events that have a variety of time constraints. GM_1, GM_2, GM_3 = different global mappings; W = world; I = internal states.

and future to be developed along with time-independent models of self and world. With such models, the more developed forms of higher-order consciousness became possible.

The entire speech system evolved by way of affective and observational learning in a social scene. The actual signs and symbols of language are arbitrary, but they serve to link conceptual categorization to a specialized system of phonological recognition and memory. According to the extended TNGS, there is a semantic bootstrapping via linkage of phonological and lexical systems to already existent conceptual systems. Syntax arises as a result within the constraints and special memory provided by areas such as Broca's area and its reentrant connections. The development of a sufficiently large lexicon leads to the possibility of its further categorization by the concept system. This form of conceptual categorization of both lexicon and grammar, independent of current perceptual input, leads in turn to an increasingly rich set of meaning relations. The various interactions are schematized in figure 14.3.

The theory holds that both during evolution and in the individual, concepts precede language and meaning. They are driven by the perceptual apparatus and are constructed by the brain as it models its own classes of activity. Concepts are nonetheless coherent and can correspond to things and motions. In their most elaborate form, they may serve as bases for image schemata ("object," "motion," "barrier," "container," etc.) summarizing a variety of general physical situations. Once embellished and fortified by the enhanced powers of a lexicon, they retain these "metaphorical" properties[5] but can also recombine and modify each other in an explosive fashion. One of the chief concepts to emerge along with language is that of the "self" not merely as a biological individual but as a subjective identity demarcated from conspecifics.

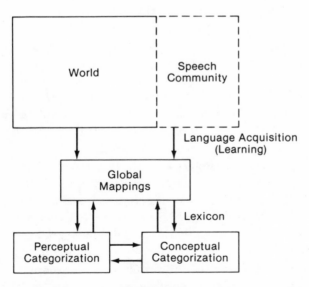

Figure 14.3
Relations leading to language as the extended basis for higher-order consciousness. (See figure 14.2 for dynamics of global mappings.)

Together, these properties and characteristics expand the possibilities of higher-order consciousness.

This epigenetic view of language as it relates to consciousness is consistent with various properties of grammar, including universality. It denies the occurrence of a preexisting module encoding a universal grammar and is inconsistent with ideas of deep and superficial structures. The proposal that language arises epigenetically is consistent, however, with the idea of meaning holism.[6] Meaning and reference are both relative and normative, and no meaning can in general be built in by evolution.

The extended TNGS asserts that consciousness arose as an evolutionary outcome of certain morphologies, and ultimately, in its higher forms, of certain social organizations. Its efficacy and evolutionary value were first related to the enhanced reactions of an animal capable of the assignment of salience to various novelties in order to carry out more adaptive behavior. Later, with higher-order consciousness, the ability to plan a series of actions, *more or less* free of immediate time constraints, must have enhanced fitness. In hominids, at least, primary consciousness must have had evolutionary efficacy, insofar as it is required for the development of a self concept and of language.

At this point, it may be useful to return briefly to the issue of consciousness and time. In chapter 7, I stressed the fundamental importance of the organs of succession. Having developed the ideas of primary consciousness and higher-order consciousness, we may now connect the important functions of these organs in assuring smooth movements, memory, and choice to the properties of continuity and flow in conscious events (figure 14.2). The properties of motion converted by global mapping and reentry to adaptive action are fundamental to the building of perceptual experience via short- and long-term memory. This continual activity (which might be called the rhythm of reentry) is the substrate for continuity in primary consciousness. Changes in this dynamic substrate by shifts in attention will change the direction and content of this Jamesian flow but will not halt it.

With the accession of higher-order consciousness and language, models of the past and future can be constructed by means of the rich interaction of conceptual categories and linguistic memory. The continuity of consciousness is not broken by this construction—instead, it becomes possible to compare the simultaneous perceptual flow of primary consciousness with the content of these models. The resultant "sense" of duration is sharply modifiable by sensory input, by attentional and arousal states, and by alterations of motor activity. The apparent flow of external and internal events may be emphasized or suppressed and coupled or decoupled to a greater or lesser degree, but it is never fully suppressed in conscious states. The parallel comments[7] of Augustine and James about knowing what time is and what consciousness is, but not being able to express their nature in words, are both likely to be rooted in this curious coupling and decoupling of the flow and sampling of inner and outer states (figure 14.2). It is not surprising that the eventual development of an adequate *scientific* description of time in relativistic terms required conventions of measurement and an extraordinary set of rational constructions.[8]

CONCLUSIONS

The summary remarks in this chapter may serve to show the major connections between evolution, development, morphology, and consciousness in a physical and social world. I have tried to provide the outlines of a biological theory of consciousness. My aim has been to show how the properties of consciousness can be linked to the structure and physiology of the brain and thus to offer a reasonable picture of how those properties may have evolved. Furthermore, I have attempted to suggest how consciousness might control behavior and thus contribute to survival value and fitness.

Many of the properties of consciousness can be derived more or less directly from the properties of the processes and structures from which they stem. Given the extended theory, we can account for the subjective nature of consciousness and for its relation to volition. We can also account for the observation that consciousness is neither a simple copy of experience nor a direct transfer from memorial states. In the case of linguistically competent animals such as ourselves, the theory can account for direct awareness, the extension and richness of conceptual categorization, and the ability to free the construction of plans from the bondage of present time while continuing to behave in an adaptive manner. Of course, as in every theory, there are many unexplored areas and incompletely developed ideas. But I hope I have shown that it is at least feasible to construct a self-consistent brain-based theory of consciousness without making any assumptions in addition to those already implicit in the TNGS.

It may be of some additional value to point out again how the present constructions differ from those assumed in a cognitive or information processing model[9] and by functionalism. According to the extended TNGS, the brain is a selective system and is not a Turing machine. In the brain, the mappings and states are highly degenerate and, in some cases, stochastic. There is no case to be made for "machine functionalism" in such a system, and there is no need for such a case (see chapter 2). Proceeding from a completely different set of premises, Putnam (who was perhaps the most trenchant of its expositors) has recently made clear the difficulties of such a view.[10]

Acting in the world, a conscious animal of a given phenotype is no philosopher. It need pay no attention to "actual" causes, to entailment, or to the construction of logical analyses; it must pursue only pragmatic goals. This claim is not vitiated by the fact that humans, with language and higher-order consciousness, can construct powerful artificial systems of rationality. Indeed, the foregoing analysis relaxes the set of requirements that a conceptual and even verbally competent animal *must* meet in order to survive. Rationality is not always, or even often, required. Many elements enter into behavior, success is relative, entailment is not a primary issue, and induction as a mode of thought is prevalent in guiding behavior even if it is not logically justified.[11] Pragmatism and relativism prevail, and changes in the environment, in the speech community, and in history often play greater roles than logic.

A final word of exorcism may be in order. In such a system, the homunculus is unnecessary. The TNGS indicates that it is the individual phenotype and its brain that is the unit of change and exchange. No overall explicit program drives an animal's behavior, although its phenotype is limited by evolutionary and developmental constraints that are the basis of "universality," be that of faces or of grammars. While strongly governed by constraints related to value, such an individual is open to novel experience. Because of the degenerate nature of its repertoires, that individual can generalize on that experience at various levels—perceptual, conceptual, and linguistic. In our case, observational learning and social exchange allow us to develop linguistic conventions that are more or less arbitrary. But the constraints of physics and the structure of the world nonetheless ultimately impose certain uniformities on our conceptual schemes. Obviously, while relative, these uniformities have allowed us to build a scientific worldview in which we ourselves can be placed. It is fortunate that the ontological relativity of meaning and reference[12] do not entail total confusion.[13]

It is on these imperfect means and on the rich affective exchange based on an inner life that personhood is built. In such a construct, values constrain behavior, action modulates it, and memory alters it and is altered in turn. Any future scientific synthesis relating psychology, biology, and physics is likely to continue to depend on just such "irrational" but necessary variables.

15

Philosophical Issues: Qualified Realism

In the end, we must return to the "scientific observer" and to his creator, the person who perceives, feels, and thinks. I have presented a biological theory to account in some detail for how neural systems in certain phenotypes can give rise to conscious experience. Such a theory obviously has strong implications for specific branches of neuroscience, as I have already discussed. But it also has suggestive implications for larger scientific issues as well as for philosophy, particularly the philosophy of mind.[1] To espouse such a scientific theory is not necessarily to espouse a particular philosophical view, although the tenets of the theory, if proven true, may rule out many classical views.

Philosophy is concerned with how we represent the world. It is therefore concerned with identity, causality, and meaning—relations between the mind and reality (including the body whose structure underlies the mind). Given that these are some of its concerns, in order to sustain a metaphysical view of the world, it is necessary to understand the nature of the mind and its limits. As McGinn puts it, "An acceptable metaphysics must yield a credible epistemology."[2]

In this chapter, I wish to expand on these issues, expressing some personal views about some rather large questions. They include the following:

1. What is the impact of the theory of consciousness, as embedded in the extended TNGS, on attempts to make a world description that is scientifically based?

2. What can be said about the relation of brain states to mental states, and about the evolutionary emergence and efficacity of consciousness?
3. What is the impact of the theory on the notion of knowledge and the origins of the contents of thoughts?
4. What can be said about other philosophical issues of human importance that go beyond these descriptions, such as those related to values?

In this account, I have leaned heavily on Russell's *A History of Western Philosophy* and Ayer's *Philosophy in the Twentieth Century,* not because I agree with their positions but because they provide a clear and cogent framework for those of us who are not trained philosophers.[3] My intent is to offer some personal responses to the above questions, stimulated by the theory to which this book has been addressed. The dedicated working out of deeper responses to these questions is a matter for professional philosophers, who would certainly be well advised to wait and see whether the theory survives close scientific scrutiny. In all cases, when I reject a particular philosophical position, it is on the assumption that the present theory is correct. The risks of that assumption have not escaped me.

THE MATTER OF WORLD DESCRIPTION: CAUSALITY AND CONSCIOUSNESS

Science asks for a description of reality. As long as that description is expressed in physicalist and objectivist terms subject to criteria of verifiability, falsifiability, and predictiveness, we need not consider any additional claim concerned with *how* any single scientific observer actually represents reality. But when this objectivist position is applied to the psychology and biology of consciousness, that claim, central to the philosophy of mind, demands to be addressed (see chapter 1).

This poses a problem of recursion related to the various efforts of the scientific observer. A theory of consciousness rests on a not inconsiderable *number* of other scientific theories, physical and biological. Such a theory must be based on theories of physics, of evolution, and of development and, in its furthest reaches, on a theory of language, each of which makes different demands on our idea of the scientific observer. What should we assume to be primitive, and what should we take to be derivative?

In this book, I have assumed that physics and biology (including evolutionary theory) are primitive and essential.[4] On these bases, I have proposed a theory of primary and higher-order consciousness as an extension of a developmental brain theory, the TNGS.[5] In constructing the extended theory, I have rejected all the claims of classical dualism and, while respecting certain insights brought to the subject by cognitive psychologists, have abjured the idea that a satisfactory account of consciousness can be derived from the notion of mental representations without reference to brain structure.[6]

It is clear that any such assumed order of priority of theories underlying a consciousness theory cannot be related to the historical order in which its real referents and its constituent ideas actually emerged. This is hardly a surprise, but it is an amusing exercise to plot on a logarithmic scale the supposed times of emergence of these components, starting with the origin of life and proceeding through the evolution of hominids to present-day culture. Although this sequence has no intrinsic significance, it does serve to remind us that our nomothetic descriptions have arrived recently and that a scientific description of the world is a very late cultural acquisition.[7]

I stress this order because of certain reductionist or panpsychist claims concerning the origin of consciousness that are sometimes made on the basis of physics alone. Physics applies to the boundaries and uniformities of the world and formally describes certain correlations of its properties as selected by a scientific observer. Accepting a quantum field theory and statistical mechanics, one can imagine a basis (through the occurrence of irreversible heterogeneous events) for the evolution of the macroscopic material arrangements that drive perception and that led through further evolution to the emergence of a conscious perceiver. But historically and creatively, that perceiver is prior to the science of physics as well as to any theory of consciousness. The sequence is matter → evolution → vertebrates → primary consciousness → man → social communication and language → natural science. The theory espoused here insists that the evolution of neuronal group selection and of special forms of memory were required for consciousness to emerge. This dissociates the actual history and nature of consciousness from any dependence upon *close* physical analysis. Admitting quantum field theory as a basic *description* of the structure of the material world, we have no need to assume that its *laws* are identical with those governing consciousness. Extreme reductionist positions that expect to *account* for consciousness on the basis of quantum mechanics and that ignore the facts of evolution seem overambitious and empty.[8] It goes without saying that, given this position, all panpsychist and idealist accounts of consciousness are excluded.

According to the analysis of consciousness presented here, all perceptual events on which concepts and thinking are based occur as a result of continual interactions with the physical world. Events in this world detected without the aid of instruments are "at scale" with percipient organisms and are parallel, numerous, and dense. Furthermore, according to the TNGS, such events can be partitioned in terms of possible patterns in an infinite number of ways. The "density" of perceptual impressions is in part a reflection of the density of world events and in part a property of the phenotype. In any case, neural responses are much less dense than world events, despite the complexity of the brain.

This position accords well with some of the philosophical analyses put forward by Quine,[9] but to understand behavior we cannot, as he does, stay only with the stimulation of receptor sheets and the analysis of language, leaving the inner psychological workings untouched. A somatic selective system embedded in the world in the fashion described in *Neural Darwinism* (figure 15.1) shows an enormous range of stochastic variables, many levels of interaction, strong density dependence of population variables, and complex causal relations. An adequate theory of consciousness must account for how signals and sense are combined well before the accession of language. I attempted to sketch the outlines of such a theory in chapters 7 through 10.

Although that consciousness theory is realistic and naturalistic in its assumptions, by its very nature its realism is qualified and conditional. The qualifications result not only from the limits of our sensory systems but also from the nature of selective systems and the inherent constraints on their capacity to sample from the density of world events. This has implications for physics as well as biology. In particular, the presence of many-one mappings, and the degeneracy of hereditary properties, as well as of the special kinds of memory yielding consciousness in selective systems,[10] require a revision of the conventional physical analysis of chains of causation because, in a selective system, some degree of variation occurs *independently* within a population. This is particularly true in nervous systems to which the TNGS applies. The selective systems underlying perceptual categorization contain a source of variation or diversity that is more or less independent of the causal interactions that will lead eventually to those selectional responses resulting in differential amplification.

In the case of organisms with rich nervous systems subject to the mechanisms described by the TNGS, genetic mutation and somatic epigenetic variation provide potent sources of variance that can interact indirectly with each other by means of natural selection, as is indicated by the morphoregulator hypothesis. This is schematized in figure 15.1. In the world (considered here as the econiche), independent chains of events can occur that are far from equilibrium or irreversible. Not only can interactions of such events with evolving populations cause changes in gene frequencies, but their interactions in individuals capable of perceptual categorization can lead to changes in efficacies of synaptic populations. These historical changes can in turn change individual behavior, further altering the likelihood of phenotypic selection in evolution.

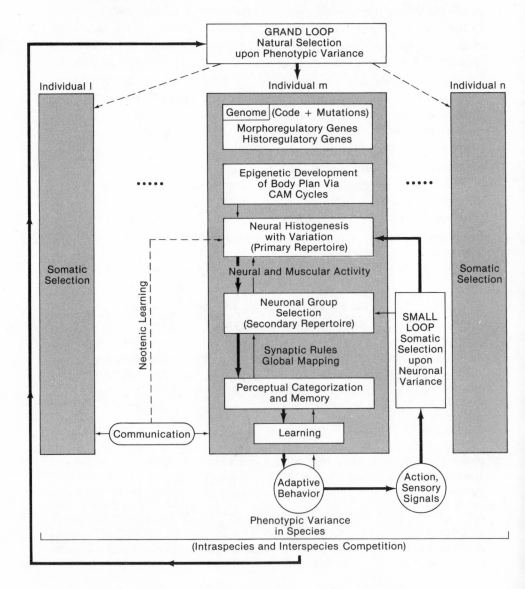

For the purposes of the present discussion, the most important property of selective neural systems is that they have recategorical memory. If an organism has primary consciousness and a concept system, however primitive, past experiences (as well as ethologically determined variables) will lead to storage of changes that alter future behavior (figure 15.2). This will change patterns of action so that *local* world events may occur in ways that would *never* have spontaneously arisen in the world in the absence of such organisms.

A causal mapping of such changes, while to some extent globally predictable, has *at least two independent* stochastic elements—one set in the irreversible events of the world and the other in the variances of the somatic selectional system affecting individual behavior through memory. The historical interactions between these two systems and the selectional events that modify behavior are nonlinear and complex in the extreme. The fact that variance in the two systems can be independent, that the system of neuronal group selection has the property of degeneracy, and that the interaction of the two systems is historical leads to a large degree of unpredictability and indeterminacy at the macroscopic level.

Now let us add to this picture the acquisition of higher-order consciousness. In this case, the causal relations are altered once more, this time in terms of planned acts as well as past memories. Intentionality can become higher-order,[11] and actions will definitely occur in fashions that would not otherwise spontaneously arise in a world without conscious organisms. It is as if a small set of patterns of *past* events in the

Figure 15.1

A schematic illustrating some interactions between evolution (the "grand loop") and various developmental constraints imposed by embryological events and by somatic neuronal group selection in individuals (the "small loop"). All processes within the vertical rectangular boxes are assumed to take place within different individuals (l, m, n) in a species. Adaptive behavior and learning depend upon perceptual categorization established in the small loop. This leads to somatic variance that is unique to each individual. Phenotypic variants that are most adapted on the average undergo differential reproduction. Resultant changes in gene frequencies occur in a large collection of historegulatory genes and in a smaller collection of morphoregulatory genes (the morphoregulator hypothesis; see figure 14.1), setting up new evolutionary opportunities for somatic selection in the small loop. Communication in species with changes leading to delays in completion of parts of the primary repertoire can lead to neotenic learning (see chapter 11 in Neural Darwinism*) that can be fixated in a population. Species developing true social transmission can carry out information processing. This is obviously highly developed in* Homo sapiens, *the only species with true language and our reference for higher-order consciousness.*

Figure 15.2

Complex causal interactions in selectional systems. Two kinds of physical events occur—one in the niche, one in the brain. Fluctuations in these events can be independent. Selection in the brain has a "hereditary property"—a recategorical memory. When this takes the form of C[C(W)·C(I)], *it can eventually alter the degree of its relation to C(W) by changing sensory channels, attentional states, and so on. If such changes then occur, the state of* C[C(W)·C(I)] *and other brain systems is changed. If there is an alteration in value [C(I)], this can lead to a change in action and therefore to altered causation. But "thoughts" do not drive molecules; states of systems alter other states. The* C[C(W)·C(I)] *system is reentrant to areas affected by past states and present states. The resultant behavior can be orderly or emotional—in either case, it is caused. But it can definitely change causal chains in the niche, changes that would not have occurred in the absence of such conscious animals (see* dotted line *in left-hand side of diagram representing such an alternative, events* w ——> z *instead of* w ——> y). *The complex relation of causation results from the hereditary and interactive properties of memory, relating past events, categories, and values to present physiological states. These states allow effects on the environment (which contains no such complex categorical assignments), effects that would not otherwise have occurred. The mapping between the events in the niche and those in the brain leading to ex post facto selection is historical and to some extent indeterminate, largely because of the degeneracy present in various neural repertoires.*

world were transformed relationally and then used in some *present* time for the effecting of further pattern. This "slippage" in time of the consequences of patterns of world events transformed by complex selectional, categorical, and intentional systems to yield additional directed consequences is unique to conscious systems. While none of this analysis leads to freedom from the constraints of thermodynamic laws, no simple thermodynamic analysis in terms of particle physics or statistical mechanics alone is likely to be adequate to the analysis of the evolving causal chains that emerge as a result of consciousness and memory.

I have elaborated on the themes of density dependence, variance, and causality in selective systems because I wish to draw a conclusion regarding functionalism, information processing, and computation[12] as a source of behavior and thinking. Given the conclusions of the foregoing analyses, there is no effective procedure by which *all* possible events and relations in a world consisting of the interacting conscious animal and econiche can be represented in a computer or a Turing machine. Even if the requirement were reduced to embodying some *smaller subset* of possible events and relations and not all, the existence of irreversibility, uncertainty, high density, and novelty would still preclude construction of an appropriate set of computational abstractions.[13] The stochastic elements and historical properties of the two

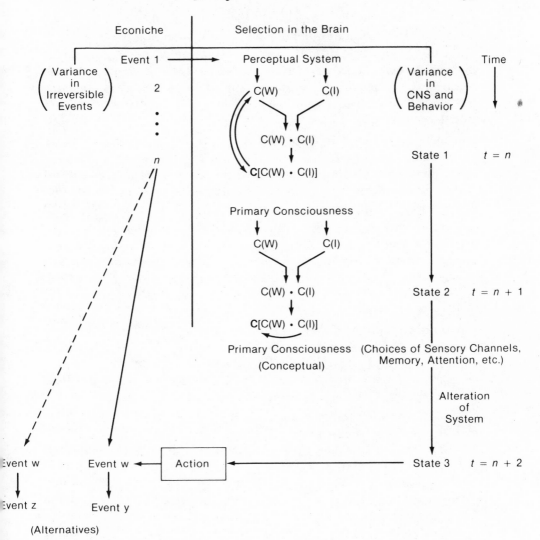

separate but interacting systems would also complicate such an effort at representation. Effective procedures for present situations (and certainly those that might occur in the future) are simply not available. If this is so, a closed solution of the philosophical problem of induction is also likely to remain unavailable, and talk of entailment as a criterion for *scientific* descriptions is in vain (see the section on scientific heuristics later in the present chapter). We may agree with Quine[14] (but for reasons different from his) that there is no first philosophy.

More specifically, according to the TNGS, the brain and its processes of perceptual categorization do not represent a Turing machine[15]—to account for higher brain functions, there is no need to posit a "tape" describing a sufficient number of effective procedures as existing either in the observed world or in the genetic structure of the organism, and there is no evidence that such a tape exists. Genetic and epigenetic constraints, the laws of physics, and natural and somatic selection are sufficient. The emergence of consciousness as an evolutionary event and the subsequent emergence of language have led to the *idea* of information. But we should not reify it as a prior or immanent property of the world.

Although consciousness emerging in selective systems can lead to special causal alterations in the world, our analysis leads us to conclude that no special addition to physics is required for the emergence of consciousness. The same laws apply to matter in inanimate and animate organization, and idealism, dualism, *res cogitans,* mentalism, or unusual material states are rejected as unnecessary. As we saw in our discussion of causality and will see when we further consider states of consciousness, so is rationalism as a *primary* basis for establishing perceptual categories.

A connected point may be worth a few remarks in addition to those made in the last three chapters. This concerns the correlation between "brain" states and "mental" states. This correlation is clearly degenerate—many different brain states can lead to a single, particular conscious state. There is token identity in the sense that a mental event is a physical event, although as a process it has properties that cannot be identical to those of the structural components of the brain that give rise to it. However, mental properties cannot vary in the absence of variation in brain states, and thus they are supervenient properties. From the previous discussion on causality and from the above remarks on Turing's theorem, it is clear that simple functionalism[16] will not account for the picture developed in the extended TNGS. Mental states do not consist solely of causes, and, in any case, as I have just pointed out, the causal picture supported by a selectional theory does not resemble that of a Turing machine (see chapter 2).

Whatever their present relations, it is obvious that during evolution a great variety of brain states have historically preceded conscious states, which appeared rather late in evolutionary history. There was a long time in the history of the world when it was free of consciousness and certainly of thought. It is not likely that, prior to the emergence of language, there were any "selves" or "persons" inhabiting the world either. Biological individuality is not simply equatable with personhood.[17]

DETERMINISM, VOLITION, AND FREE WILL

How does the previous discussion on causal relation bear on the classical dilemma of physical determinism versus free will? Many philosophers support one or another form of soft determinism or compatibilism, as advocated by Locke, Hume, and Mill. It is argued that conscious individuals can choose various goals by preference as well as the means to reach them. These goals can be the result of deliberate thought and rehearsal and can override even strong desires. As long as such an agent is not coerced or compelled, he has many choices for his behavior, despite the fact that the ultimate capabilities existing in a behavioral repertoire are determined and constrained by certain microproperties of physical systems. Even more than the ability to plan, the ability to engage in immediate voluntary intentional actions gives rise to the conviction that there is some degree of free will. While some restrictive bounds for behavior may exist (such as those determined by unconscious and external events), they do not fully constrain the capabilities of a conscious rational agent. As Searle puts it, we are free, but our freedom is not radical.[18]

Our previous analysis (see figure 15.2) casts new light on the issue, lending support to compatibilism. Selective systems (such as those posed by the TNGS) breach the deadlock imposed by bottom-up determinism. Just as the order of nucleotides in a given gene depends on higher-order selection of phenotypes in the evolutionary past,[19] so a selectionistic brain theory allows alterations of particular synaptic populations that then become stable. In both cases, the molecular *constraints* are highly determined, but the particular historical and differential amplifications acting on a hereditary or autocorrelated system resulted in various unpredictable but definite events and structures. The building up of a system of higher-order consciousness capable of rehearsal and planning based on value-laden memory and goals adds one more level of selection capable of acting on particular synaptic subpopulations. Moreover, this selection is plastic: while it depends upon a number of internal and external events, in a degenerate system such as that postulated by the TNGS, multiple choices always remain (figure 15.3). The self based on consciousness needs no homunculus and can nonetheless exercise a voluntary choice within a microdeterministic frame. Although we can agree with Honderich[20] that quantum indeterminacy is not at the heart of the issue, we can disavow his remorselessly determinist account (which denies both compatibilism and

Figure 15.3

Multilevel Determination in Selectional Systems

Determinant Conditions	Causal Sequences		
Historical change in an econiche	Natural selection $\rightarrow$ Phenotype	$\rightarrow$ Altered gene frequencies in population $\downarrow$ Particular base sequences (nonetheless chemically determined)	
Nonconscious behavior with memory related to value	Somatic selection $\rightarrow$ Particular synaptic populations	$\rightarrow$ Altered activity or firing (constrained by chemistry and anatomy) $\downarrow$ Particular behavior	
Conscious behavior	Memory based on $\rightarrow$ Rehearsal of values, goals, and possible outputs plans with conceptual components interacting with perceptual categorization	$\rightarrow$ Selection of particular combinations of synaptic subpopulations (constrained as above, but also by external and unconscious events and attentional shifts)	

incompatibilism) because it ignores the population properties of selective systems.

BIOLOGICALLY BASED EPISTEMOLOGY AND QUALIFIED REALISM

Quine has developed a realistic and naturalistic position of philosophical behaviorism that provides large insights into the relations between things and thoughts, accounting nicely for how certain features of scientific theories can emerge.[21] But this philosophical behaviorism is not enough. How, as Ayer[22] puts it, can a system of *perceptions* be developed and serve as a basis for *belief* in the physical world of common sense?

According to the analysis of consciousness given here, this question can be answered, at least in the sense that the scientific position of materialism and realism can be reconciled with the evolution of structures leading to perceptual categorization, memory, and perceptual experience. The evolutionary sequence of events following the emergence of nervous systems was roughly as follows. Perceptual categorization with rich possibilities probably originated with reptiles and birds inasmuch as homoiothermy provided a reliable basis for homeostasis of internal environments. The appearance of the biological individual allowed the development of a neurally based self-nonself distinction that was to a certain degree independent of environmental change. Consciousness of the first kind, or primary consciousness, arose in such vertebrate species (probably with birds, but almost certainly with mammals) as a function of newly evolved reentrant brain structures. The resulting consciousness is a property or capacity conferred on the organism by particular evolved parts of a brain, *not* by properties of material particles or of the whole brain. Direct awareness, "consciousness of consciousness," consciousness$_4$, or higher-order consciousness gradually developed along with emerging self-awareness through the evolution of brain areas capable of mediating concepts and primitive symbolic precursors to language. Higher-order consciousness became sharply defined with true speech in man.

Consciousness is thus *a property of morphology* or, more precisely, of certain morphological structures in a given phenotype.[23] It is based on their material and molecular order, on the developmental interaction of the phenotype with objects and events in an econiche, and on the continually updated relation to immediate perceptual categories of remembered self-nonself categories that are based on value. Prior states of primary consciousness were required for the evolution of language and higher-order consciousness, which then provided a basis for enhanced social transmission and intersubjective communication.[24] The establishment by these means of shared commonsense conventions[25] (despite the private and individual neuronal bases of categories) and finally the development of scientific procedures have led to our present worldview[26] of physics and biology.

What further philosophical implications does this set of conclusions hold for our notion of the scientific observer? To answer this question, we must consider not only several issues concerned with the relation

between mind and matter but also certain spoken or unspoken attitudes of modern science toward these issues.

There are two large areas concerned with mind and matter—metaphysics and epistemology. With Ayer,[27] we may consider the key questions connecting these areas to be, What are we justified in taking there
to be? And how far is what there is of our own making? What is objective and what is subjective? I consider here only the relations of the
present theory to some larger philosophical positions, deferring to the
next two sections a description of those aspects related to mental
events.

Historical discussions[28] of the first question have centered on the
problem of objectivity and have separated realists from idealists. Although much remains to be said about the issue of objectivity, I shall
only reiterate that the theory of evolution and the TNGS in its extended
form support the position of scientific realism and are not compatible
with idealism. Regarding the second question, empiricists and rational-
ists have argued about the basis of our capacity for knowledge. Since
Plato, this debate has been concerned with the problem of universals—
and opinions have ranged from medieval debates about nominalism
versus realism to modern debates about empiricism versus rationalism.
From all that I have said in this book and in *Neural Darwinism,* it is
clear that while an aware animal can go beyond the information given,
unconscious inference as a primary or necessary mode of *perceptual*
categorization is rejected by the TNGS. Nonetheless, realism based on
perception is *qualified* by the various means of perception, such as
sensory receptors and reentrant systems, and is not direct. Naive realism, in the sense that the world affords a direct transfer of *information*
that suffices for perception and action, is untenable. As we shall see, the
theory of consciousness and of concept formation developed here nevertheless provides scientific realism and empiricism with an opportunity to incorporate the possibility of the *development within culture* of
relational systems such as logic and mathematics.

Ayer[29] has noted that the position of modern science on these matters
is not clearly spelled out; in effect, science takes neither monist nor
pluralist positions. Its theories are loose and face the verdict of experience as a whole. They are "adjusted" in the face of "facts." Metaphysi-
cally, however, the physical scientist as observer is a subtle materialist
and his conclusions are provisional upon experiment. While his metaphysics is materialist, his epistemology is less clear-cut. As trenchantly
stated by Schrödinger,[30] after removing the observer and his mind from
nature by assent (the position of the Galilean observer as described in

chapter 1), a physical scientist cannot expect to find "mind" in nature. Moreover, he cannot find direct indications or evidence of perceptions, or sensations, or consciousness in the scientific theories that this postulated observer formulates for communication with, and instruction of, other such observers. The epistemological position of modern science (at least physical science) is thus either noncommittal or implicitly dualistic.

As I have repeatedly emphasized in this book, ever since the opening chapter, a biological scientist forced to deal with psychology and physics together cannot rest content with either of these positions. He must resolve the problem first clearly posed by Descartes that has led science to a potential and unacceptable split—a materialist metaphysics combined with an implicitly dualist, rationalist, or idealist epistemology. It is clear that without a robust theory of consciousness, the issue cannot be resolved. An adequate theory must shed light on the nature and the physical and evolutionary origins of consciousness *without* abandoning the materialism and hypothetical realism that the physical scientist applies to the world outside the observer. This is the goal of the extended theory presented here.

By taking evolutionary biology into the area of brain development and function, the TNGS and the theory of consciousness based on its assumptions lead to the view that I have called qualified realism— realism admittedly affected by phenotypic limits on sensory qualities and perceptual categorizations. Perceptual categories based on neural structures and phenotypes and the emergence of linguistic communication *can* lead by social transmission to relational systems of thought that can in turn be used for the scientific investigation of the world. But we may conclude that these systems can also lead either to "fantasies" or to systems of logic and mathematics without denying that these disparate "nonnatural" cultural systems have biological origins in perceptual relations that are based in turn on the physical order. As we shall see in the next several sections, our realism is also qualified by the characteristics and limits of these culturally developed systems as well.

THE PROBLEM OF KNOWLEDGE AND ITS RELATION TO LANGUAGE

If our theory is correct, we can rule out several philosophical positions concerned with how we acquire knowledge. The TNGS asserts that signals are not prior information and that perceptual categorization is fundamental, unconscious, and prior to sensation. Naive realism is not consistent with the TNGS, nor is any form of reductionism or phenomenalism that implies the deduction of pattern from "sense data."

What about personal knowledge? We have seen not only that the scientific approach to physics and biology that derives from the extended TNGS is inductive and skeptical but also that, aside from its rigor in descriptive analysis, it does not differ very much from a commonsense position on personal knowledge. At the commonsense level, we may say with Moore[31] that at the macroscopic human scale all things are located in a single space and time, that men have minds but things do not (and can exist independently of minds), and that men know the difference between material objects and acts of consciousness.

Commonsense philosophy and a consideration of matters of everyday life also must be reconciled with the view presented by science. Sellars[32] sharply posed the problem of how we might reconcile the ultimate homogeneity of "manifest sensation" or the manifest image of common sense with the ultimate nonhomogeneity of the system of scientific objects. The role of memory as recategorization in both primary and higher-order consciousness and the nonlinear global interactions of reentrant maps provide an answer to this problem. Molecular constitution does not impose "grain" on such systems.

To know, as Ayer[33] puts it, is to be able to perform, and to remember is to be able to reproduce a performance. This is consistent with memory as recategorization as postulated in the present theory. We can check individually and mutually whether a conscious thought corresponds to a real-world state. The present account of consciousness leaves little room for the notions of infallible or incorrigible mental states, however, be they thoughts *or* sensations. Unconscious and nonconscious states can govern some of our actions, and both can alter knowledge. We can be in error even about a given phenomenal state— hallucinations can have contents but no objects. Moreover, we can occasionally misconstrue or misrepresent the color of an object or be deluded. While we can continually check our constructions, the Cartesian quest for certainty is, in any extreme form, hopeless. We must take a more humble view of the solidity and completeness of what we can know.

What can we say about the relations of the theory to the language and concepts that support our thoughts? One of the most important consequences of the theory is that it leads to a rejection of meaning rationalism[34] and the notion of a language of thought. In its view of concepts as arising from a categorization of global mappings, and in the notion of presyntax, it provides a general theory of the content of thought *prior to* language. It also relates that content to objects and events in the world and at the same time provides a natural bridge to the evolution of language. The position taken is more or less consistent with a form of realism proposed on philosophical grounds by Millikan.[35]

In this view, concepts are nonlinguistic and can be achieved as a result of interactions with the world and other members of a species in the absence of speech. Unlike language (or at least speech), concepts are not conventional or arbitrary, are not linked to a speech community, and do not depend upon sequential presentation. But in an animal with presyntax and recategorical memory, concepts can be used both combinatorially and recursively to some extent (see chapter 8). At the same time, concepts are strongly tied to the world via the relation of global mappings to perceptual categorization.

The conceptual categorization that emerges prior to language is obviously richer than perceptual categorization but is also enormously enhanced by language. Nonetheless, *concepts are about the world,* and the present view is consistent with the notion of higher-order conceptual categories as relations between such cognitive constructs and the world.[36] This is also consistent with the idea that so-called image schemata[37] are at the base of metaphorical relations. Such schemata follow naturally from the connection between sensorimotor components of global mappings and concepts; as language emerges, they would be expected to persist and affect linguistic development.

The extended theory provides a strong basis for a noncircular connection between concepts and language. There is no "language of thought,"[38] for concepts have none of the properties of language (see above and chapter 8). There is thought and there is language. Language systems evolved through the development of phonology, which by reentrant means could allow semantic bootstrapping and syntactic development. The rich reentrant connectivity between phonological, syntactic, and semantic levels is not so different in its consequences from that which allows object "images" to form from functionally segregated areas in the visual system (see chapter 4). The resulting development of a rich lexical functional grammar[39] involves the realization of syntax during language acquisition.

This view is not consistent with the idea that a universal grammar is genetically specified or with the notions of deep structures or Cartesian linguistics.[40] Instead, it is epigenetic—the structures postulated by neural Darwinism (which are, of course, genetically *constrained*) are considered to be fundamental for those analyzed by the philosophy of mind, which are in turn considered fundamental to the philosophy of language. In espousing this view, we must nevertheless concede that there is a very large realm of linguistics proper about which the TNGS has little to say, given the additional local and historical features of languages in real speech communities. A brain theory cannot replace accounts of real events.

One conclusion consistent with qualified realism is obvious: given the ability of the conceptual system to treat the lexicon in a categorical fashion, it is perhaps not surprising that the statements we make are often about more than the experiences on which they are based. In this lies the possibility of error as well as of creation.

SCIENCE AND HEURISTICS

While science can serve as our best means for verification, it cannot replace either our commonsense view or philosophy, whatever the initial errors we risk in either of these enterprises. Perceptual experiences along with consciousness and linguistic communication (based on evolution of particular brain structures capable of categorization) are all required to develop thoughts *prior to* a scientific procedure. Scientific procedure serves to correct perceptual and conceptual errors by communal action and agreement. At the heuristic level, the "realism" that provides an epistemological means for reconciling modern physics with modern psychology still remains qualified—even absurd (or counterfactual) ideas may lead to a scientific insight; in any case, a scientific description cannot be deduced a priori. Rationalism alone fails as a basis for such a description.

Nor can verification by scientific means alone warrant either the value or the authenticity of an idea. Assumption of the opposite position, as proposed by Monod,[41] for example, leads to anachronism and a vicious circle. We must have thoughts before doing experiments and can never do enough experiments to verify all of them—not all verifiable ideas can actually be verified. Moreover, certain unverifiable ideas can have enormous heuristic value. Monod's assertion (which itself can never be scientifically verified) can appear reasonable only if one adopts the position of an ideal Galilean observer who has removed mind from nature. Such a procedure *is* reasonable in certain physical frames of inquiry (see chapter 1), but it is neither exhaustive nor fit for other frames, particularly those concerned with mental properties.

Mind in nature is a property of particular brains with particular histories, that is, of particular phenotypes with particular brain areas and structures capable of the kind of memory that leads to consciousness. Given the selectional nature of the systems supporting consciousness, knowledge of science alone is no guarantee of a good idea. Nonetheless, an idea shown to be robust under scientific test is as good as we can get, however strange it may appear to be.

I end this section with some further comments on common sense and the so-called[42] "strangeness" of scientific constructions. The scientific worldview that applies to the very large and the very small (on the scale of the observer) has frequently been described as "strange." Relativity and quantum physics certainly do not obey common sense. But neither do events of perception at the macroscopic scale of the observer. A detailed *scientific* analysis of the "primary processes" of vision,[43] for example, reveals many odd and unexpected properties of the organization of perceptual responses. The use of the word "illusion" or the adoption of an excessively rationalistic, inferential, or cognitivist position hides this strangeness. To the extent that science, in its attempt to unify knowledge, goes beyond familiar perceptual experience and corrects habitual commonsense perceptions by large theoretical constructs, its conclusions must always appear strange, regardless of scale. The structure of the world is obviously different from that of conscious experience—our realism must be qualified not only by our phenotypic limits but also by the influence of our conscious experience and history on our ways of knowing.

PERSONHOOD AND HUMAN CONCERNS

Philosophy (aside from professional philosophy in the strict sense of the word) is supposed to have a bearing on everyday life and on our sense of the whole of experience.[44] What can we say of the worldview that seems to follow from the picture outlined in the present analysis of consciousness? Does a biologically based view of consciousness alter our view of immortality? Does it have any significant bearing on our desires, beliefs, and values?

I have taken the position that matter following physical laws is independent of consciousness and have concluded that the phenomenon of consciousness is the result of a particular order of animate matter that arose relatively recently in evolution. Thus, it arose as a result of a very particular world history. According to this view, a machine with similar orderings and functions would have primary consciousness. But, also according to this view, it would not be a Turing machine. And, in any event, unless it had language, it could not have higher-order consciousness.

Consciousness is a process occurring separately in each individual; it is historical, changing, partial, and linked to the perception of objects. It is therefore not a property of particles of matter or even of most biological arrangements of matter. Matter exists prior to mind, and on death individual minds are doomed to extinction in the sense that the conscious processes and thoughts possessed by those individuals are no longer possible. With the death of each individual, that particular memory and consciousness is lost—if personal identity depends on morphology undergoing a particular history, it cannot persist in a disembodied state. There is, as such, no individual immortality.[45]

Nevertheless, although the world is not of our making, and although we must disappear in death, while alive we may alter both it and ourselves causally by conscious means. Given the historical nature of creation, it follows that those socially cooperative interactions based on creative skepticism (but not on dogma) that lead to an increasingly rich culture are the most valuable heritage we have. While our consciousness is based on an ethologically determined set of values, the acquisition of higher-order consciousness and the interactions in a culture allow us to achieve new values. In a culture, each person can have the freedoms of grammar, of private imagination, and of subjective individuality—and still enjoy the harmonious constraints of art and communal belief as well as the final satisfaction of a shared scientific worldview. That view will someday allow us securely to understand the origins of consciousness in the relations between matter, evolution, and brain development. When finally substantiated by scientific means, such a view will allow an individual to see his place in the world with greater clarity—how he came from the world, and how he may contribute to his fellows while he enjoys for a brief time the privilege of consciousness and communication.

Science is the greatest of communal cultural achievements and is among the highest achievements of human consciousness. Nevertheless, it must be said that, however grand, the scientific view *derives* from other cultural ingredients and does not compel them. Science is only a partial experience of the consciousness that, once born and developed in human culture, has a potentially endless sweep in subjective personal experience, in art,[46] and in the creation of myths. What spins up out of consciousness, language, and culture is necessarily full of novelty. From this point of view, whatever we establish scientifically to be true, there is much in our experience that is of our own making and much of it the most precious part of our life. That this is so, however, should not be allowed to obscure our knowledge of the structural conditions of the world's being, and of our being, and of how we know them, all of which can come reliably only from scientific inquiry itself.

EPILOGUE

These concluding remarks suggest that the elaboration and verification of theories of brain function will have an increasingly significant bearing on philosophical matters and human concerns. The fundamental subject underlying all theories of brain function is morphologic evolution. I discussed that subject in *Topobiology.* In *Neural Darwinism,* I applied the developmental principles of topobiology to the origin and evolution of brain structure and function. Those two theoretical enterprises are subject to test. In the present effort to construct the extended theory, I have gone one step further, a step not so easily subject to test. Nonetheless, the constraints of the two previous theories (which are considerable) provide strong grounds for this attempt to explain consciousness in terms of the material structures and functions of the brain.

I have tried to show, however imperfectly, the feasibility of a principled biological theory of consciousness and to consider some of its consequences. The theory is both genetic and epigenetic. To the extent that it rests on the theory of natural selection, it is to that extent a nativist theory. The theory is a parsimonious one as well. It rests only on the application of notions of developmental and experiential selection and of mechanisms of reentry: in other words, its constraints are just those applied to the TNGS.

In the view that has emerged from this effort, consciousness may be seen as the haughty and restless second cousin of morphology. Memory is its mistress, perception its somewhat abused wife, logic its housekeeper, and language its poorly paid secretary. Whether this view of the household will collapse, to be replaced by a more respectable one, remains to be seen.

At the end of his *Psychology: Briefer Course,* James remarked,

> Something definite happens when to a certain brain-state a certain "scious-
> ness" corresponds. A genuine glimpse into what it is would be *the* scientific
> achievement, before which all past achievements would pale. But at present,
> psychology is in the condition of physics before Galileo and the laws of
> motion, of chemistry before Lavoisier and the notion that mass is preserved
> in all reactions. The Galileo and the Lavoisier of psychology will be famous
> men indeed when they come, as come they some day surely will, or past
> successes are no index to the future. When they do come, however, the
> necessities of the case will make them "metaphysical." Meanwhile the best
> way in which we can facilitate their advent is to understand how great is the
> darkness in which we grope, and never to forget that the natural-science
> assumptions with which we started are provisional and revisable things.[1]

Although we are not much further along after almost a century, it is
my hope that the present thoughts, showing that it is at least feasible
to construct a detailed and principled brain-based theory of consciousness, may speed the arrival of these scientist-metaphysicians. The vigor
of present-day research in biology and neuroscience strongly encour-
ages me in that hope.

NOTES

Abbreviations of Scholarly Journals

Am. Philos. Q.	American Philosophical Quarterly
Am. Psychol.	American Psychologist
Am. Sci.	American Scientist
Ann. Neurol.	Annals of Neurology
Annu. Rev. Cell Biol.	Annual Review of Cell Biology
Annu. Rev. Neurosci.	Annual Review of Neuroscience
Arch. Gen. Psychiatry	Archives of General Psychiatry
Arch. Neurol. Psychiatry	Archives of Neurology and Psychiatry
Behav. Brain Sci.	Behavioral and Brain Sciences
Bibl. Biotheor.	Bibliotheca Biotheoretica
Biol. Cybern.	Biological Cybernetics
Brain Behav. Evol.	Brain Behavior and Evolution
Brain Res.	Brain Research
Brit. J. Psychol.	British Journal of Psychology
Bull. Psychon. Soc.	Bulletin of the Psychonomic Society
Child Dev.	Child Development
Cognit. Psychol.	Cognitive Psychology
Exp. Brain Res.	Experimental Brain Research
Hum. Neurobiol.	Human Neurobiology
Int. Rev. Physiol.	International Review of Physiology
J. Clin. Exp. Neuropsychol.	Journal of Clinical and Experimental Neuropsychology
J. Comp. Neurol.	Journal of Comparative Neurology
J. Exp. Psychol. Anim. Behav. Processes	Journal of Experimental Psychology: Animal Behavior Processes
J. Nerv. Ment. Dis.	Journal of Nervous and Mental Diseases
J. Neurophysiol.	Journal of Neurophysiology
J. Neurosci.	Journal of Neuroscience

J. Philos.	*Journal of Philosophy*
J. Physiol. (Lond.)	*Journal of Physiology (London)*
J. Psycholinguist. Res.	*Journal of Psycholinguistic Research*
J. R. Soc. Med.	*Journal of the Royal Society of Medicine*
J. Theoret. Biol.	*Journal of Theoretical Biology*
Math. Biosci.	*Mathematical Biosciences*
Perspect. Biol. Med.	*Perspectives in Biology and Medicine*
Philos. Q.	*Philosophical Quarterly*
Philos. Rev.	*Philosophical Review*
Philos. Trans. R. Soc. [*Biol.*]	*Philosophical Transactions of the Royal Society of London B* [*Biological Sciences*]
Physiol. Rev.	*Physiological Review*
Proc. Natl. Acad. Sci. USA	*Proceedings of the National Academy of Sciences of the United States of America*
Proc. R. Soc. Lond. [*Biol.*]	*Proceedings of the Royal Society of London B* [*Biological Sciences*]
Psychol. Rev.	*Psychological Review*
Q. J. Exp. Psychol.	*Quarterly Journal of Experimental Psychology*
Rev. Metaphys.	*Review of Metaphysics*
Rev. Neurol. (Paris)	*Revue Neurologique (Paris)*
Sci. Am.	*Scientific American*
Trends Neurosci.	*Trends in Neuroscience*
Vision Res.	*Vision Research*

Chapter 1. Consciousness and the Scientific Observer

1. G. Galilei, *Dialogue Concerning the Two Chief World Systems* (1632), trans. S. Drake (Berkeley: Univ. of California Press, 1962); G. Galilei, *The Assayer* (1623), in *Discoveries and Opinions of Galileo,* trans. S. Drake (New York: Doubleday, 1957). See also E. Schrödinger, *Mind and Matter* (Cambridge, Eng.: Cambridge Univ. Press, 1958); A. N. Whitehead, *Science and the Modern World* (New York: Macmillan, 1925).

2. R. Descartes, *Passions of the Soul* (1649) and *Meditations* (1641), in *The Philosophical Works of Descartes,* vols. 1 and 2, ed. E. Haldane and G. Ross (Cambridge, Eng.: Cambridge Univ. Press, 1978). See also A. Kenny, *Descartes: A Study of His Philosophy* (New York: Random House, 1968); B. Williams, *Descartes: The Project of Pure Inquiry* (New York: Humanities, 1978); M. Wilson, *Descartes* (Boston: Routledge and Kegan Paul, 1978).

3. Whitehead, *Science and the Modern World,* chap. 9.

4. C. Darwin, *On the Origin of Species by Means of Natural Selection or the Preservation of Favoured Races in the Struggle for Life* (London: Murray, 1859).

5. P. H. Barrett, P. J. Gautrey, S. Herbert, D. Kohn, and S. Smith, eds., *Charles Darwin's Notebooks, 1836–1844: Geology, Transmutation of Species, Metaphysical Enquiries* (Ithaca: Cornell Univ. Press, 1987), 539, n. 84E. See also

R. J. Richards, *Darwin and the Emergence of Evolutionary Theories of Mind and Behavior* (Chicago: Univ. of Chicago Press, 1987).

6. W. James, "Does consciousness exist?" in *The Writings of William James*, ed. J. J. McDermott (Chicago: Univ. of Chicago Press, 1977), 169–83.

7. Whitehead, *Science and the Modern World*, chap. 9.

8. James, "Does consciousness exist?"

9. Whitehead, *Science and the Modern World*, chap. 9, 203.

10. W. Sellars, *Science, Perception, and Reality* (New York: Humanities, 1963).

11. Schrödinger, *Mind and Matter.*

12. W. James, *The Principles of Psychology*, vol.1 (reprint; New York: Dover, 1950), 225. See also W. James, *Psychology: Briefer Course* (New York: Henry Holt, 1893), 152.

13. Ibid.

14. D. R. Griffin, *Animal Thinking* (Cambridge: Harvard Univ. Press, 1984). See also D. R. Griffin, ed., *Animal Mind–Human Mind* (Berlin: Springer-Verlag, 1982). The inability to study behavior, neural activity, and mental images directly is one of the origins of James's "psychologist's fallacy." See James, *The Principles of Psychology*, vol. 1, 196–98.

15. This term was revived by F. Brentano, *Psychologie vom empirischen Standpunkt* (1874), vol. 1, ed. O. Kraus (Leipzig: F. Meiner, 1924–28). See also J. R. Searle, *Intentionality: An Essay on the Philosophy of Mind* (Cambridge, Eng.: Cambridge Univ. Press, 1983), and E. S. Reed, "Two theories of the intentionality of perceiving," *Synthese* 54 (1983):85–94.

16. W. V. Quine, *Word and Object* (Cambridge: MIT Press, 1960); W. V. Quine, *Ontological Relativity and Other Essays* (New York: Columbia Univ. Press, 1969); W. V. Quine, *Roots of Reference* (Peru, Ill.: Open Court, 1973). See also G. D. Romanos, *Quine and Analytic Philosophy* (Cambridge: MIT Press, 1983).

17. See A. Grünbaum, "The philosophical retention of absolute space in Einstein's general theory of relativity," in *Problems of Time and Space*, ed. J. J. C. Smart (New York: Macmillan, 1964), 313–17. The removal of issues of mind versus matter from the scientific domain was specifically endorsed by Ernst Mach; see his *Die Analyse der Empfindungen*, 8th ed. (Jena: Fischer, 1919), esp. 29–30. An amusing and penetrating account of the exaggerated application of physicalism to psychology is given by S. K. Langer, "Idols of the laboratory," in *Mind: An Essay on Human Feeling*, vol. 1 (Baltimore: Johns Hopkins Press, 1967), chap. 2.

18. Whitehead, *Science and the Modern World*. See also B. Russell, *A History of Western Philosophy* (New York: Simon & Schuster, 1945); B. Russell, *The Problems of Philosophy* (Oxford: Oxford Univ. Press, 1959); A. J. Ayer, *Philosophy in the Twentieth Century* (East Hanover, N.J.: Vintage Books, 1984).

19. G. M. Edelman, *Neural Darwinism: The Theory of Neuronal Group Selection* (New York: Basic Books, 1987).

20. See note 14 above.

21. See D. Broadbent, *Behavior* (New York: Basic Books, 1961); J. B. Watson, *Psychology from the Standpoint of a Behaviorist* (Philadelphia: F. Pinter, 1919); B. F. Skinner, *About Behaviorism* (Englewood Cliffs, N.J.: Prentice-Hall, 1957).

22. See, for example, Z. W. Pylyshyn, *Computation and Cognition* (Cambridge: MIT Press, 1984); J. A. Fodor, *The Modularity of Mind* (Cambridge: MIT Press, 1983); R. Jackendoff, *Consciousness and the Computational Mind* (Cambridge: MIT Press, 1987); J. R. Anderson, *Cognitive Psychology and Its Implications* (San Francisco: Freeman, 1980). A good account of the difficulties resulting from ignoring consciousness in cognitive psychology may be found in T. Shallice, "Dual functions of consciousness," *Psychol. Rev.* 79 (1972):383–93.

23. Ibid.

24. See R. L. Gregory, *Mind in Science* (Cambridge, Eng.: Cambridge Univ. Press, 1981); Schrödinger, *Mind and Matter.* See also G. C. Globus, G. Maxwell, and I. Savodnik, eds., *Consciousness and the Brain: A Scientific and Philosophical Inquiry* (New York: Plenum, 1976).

25. I shall not attempt an exhaustive survey of these models, however rare. Some examples may be seen in *Consciousness and Self-Regulation,* vols. 1 and 2, ed. G. E. Schwartz and D. Shapiro; vols. 3 and 4, ed. R. J. Davidson, G. E. Schwartz, and D. Shapiro (New York: Plenum, 1976–86). Specific examples may be seen in the articles by E. R. John and by K. H. Pribram in vol. 1. Another series of volumes with wide-ranging discussion is *Aspects of Consciousness,* vol. 1, *Psychological Issues,* ed. G. Underwood and R. Stevens; vol. 2, *Structural Issues,* ed. G. Underwood and R. Stevens; vol. 3, *Awareness and Self-Awareness,* ed. G. Underwood; vol. 4, *Clinical Issues,* ed. R. Stevens (New York: Academic, 1979–84). See also R. W. Thatcher and E. R. John, eds., *Functional Neuroscience: Foundations of Cognitive Processes* (Hillsdale, N.J.: Lawrence Erlbaum Associates, 1977); R. W. Sperry, "A modified concept of consciousness," *Psychol. Rev.* 76 (1969): 532–36; R. W. Sperry, "An objective approach to subjective experience: Further explanation of an hypothesis," *Psychol. Rev.* 77 (1970): 585–90; R. W. Sperry, "Neurology and the mind-body problem," *Am. Sci.* 40 (1952): 291–312; R. W. Sperry, "Changing concepts of consciousness and free will," *Perspect. Biol. Med.* 20 (1976): 9–19.

An example lacking any Cartesian shame is seen in K. R. Popper and J. C. Eccles, *The Self and Its Brain* (Berlin: Springer-Verlag, 1981), which is an explicit dualist-interactionist account. See also P. A. Buser and A. Rougeul-Buser, eds., *Cerebral Correlates of the Conscious Experience* (Amsterdam and New York: North Holland, 1978). K. S. Pope and J. L. Singer, *The Stream of Consciousness* (New York: Plenum, 1978), and M. Horowitz, ed., *Psychodynamics and Cognition* (Chicago: Univ. of Chicago Press, 1988), both contain further articles.

26. This requirement is embodied in M. Delbrück's posthumous *Mind from Matter* (Boston: Blackwell Scientific, 1985).

27. See Edelman, *Neural Darwinism.*

28. See E. S. Reed, "Descartes's corporeal ideas hypothesis and the origin of scientific psychology," *Rev. Metaphys.* 35 (1982): 731–52.

29. See note 1 above.

30. Edelman, *Neural Darwinism.*

31. Ibid. See also Delbrück, *Mind from Matter.*

32. See note 22 above.

33. G. M. Edelman, *Topobiology: An Introduction to Molecular Embryology* (New York: Basic Books, 1988).

34. This subject is touched on in *Neural Darwinism,* but only briefly.

35. See James, *The Principles of Psychology* and *Psychology: Briefer Course,* and Whitehead, *Science and the Modern World.*

36. Excellent brief accounts may be found in J. R. Searle, *Minds, Brains, and Science* (Cambridge: Harvard Univ. Press, 1984), and in C. McGinn, *The Character of Mind* (Oxford: Oxford Univ. Press, 1982).

37. See D. M. Armstrong and N. Malcolm, *Consciousness and Causality* (Oxford: Blackwell, 1984), and Jackendoff, *Consciousness.*

38. See Griffin, *Animal Thinking.*

39. For an abstract argument, see J. R. Lucas, "Minds, machines and Gödel," in K. M. Sayre and F. J. Crosson, eds., *The Modeling of Mind* (Indiana: Univ. of Notre Dame Press, 1963), 255–72. The argument I shall pursue in later chapters is different. For a brief description of Turing machines, see chapter 2.

40. Sellars, *Science, Perception, and Reality.*

41. See notes 15 and 22 above and also Edelman, *Neural Darwinism.*

42. Edelman, *Neural Darwinism.*

43. Quine, *Word and Object;* Quine, *Ontological Relativity;* Quine, *Roots of Reference.*

44. S. W. Hawking, *A Brief History of Time* (New York: Bantam Books, 1988).

45. Schrödinger, *Mind and Matter.*

Chapter 2. Proposals and Disclaimers

1. T. Natsoulas, "Consciousness," *Am. Psychol.* 33 (1974): 906–14. See also T. Natsoulas, "Toward a model for consciousness in the light of B. F. Skinner's contribution," *Behaviorism* 6 (1978): 139–75. I leave out a seventh category considered by Natsoulas. See also G. H. Mead, *Mind, Self and Society* (Chicago: Univ. of Chicago Press, 1934).

2. Mead, *Mind, Self and Society.*

3. The properties of consciousness$_4$ are discussed at length by Natsoulas in his article in *Behaviorism.* See also Natsoulas, "Consciousness," and an excellent essay by A. J. Marcel, "Phenomenal experience and functionalism," in Marcel and E. Bisiach, eds., *Consciousness in Contemporary Science,* 121–58.

4. N. Malcolm in D. M. Armstrong and N. Malcolm, *Consciousness and Causality* (Oxford: Blackwell, 1984), 30.

5. See note 3 above.

6. D. Premack and A. J. Premack, *The Mind of an Ape* (New York: Norton, 1983). See also G. G. Gallup, Jr., "Self-recognition in primates: A comparative approach to the bidirectional properties of consciousness," *Am. Psychol.* 32 (1977): 329–33.

7. D. C. Dennett, "Quining Qualia," in Marcel and Bisiach, eds., *Consciousness in Contemporary Science,* 42–77. For other examples of very rigorous definitional approaches, see A. Allport, "What concept of consciousness?" ibid., 159–82.

8. Ibid.

9. Searle, *Minds, Brains, and Science.*

10. J. A. Gray, "The mind-brain identity theory as a scientific hypothesis," *Philos. Q.* 21 (1971): 247–52; G. Mandler, *Cognitive Psychology: An Essay in Cognitive Science* (Hillsdale, N.J.: Lawrence Erlbaum Associates, 1985).

11. See chapters 12 and 13 for a discussion of these matters.

12. T. Nagel, *The View from Nowhere* (New York: Cambridge Univ. Press, 1986). For an argument indicating that the only meaningful statements about qualia are those that are intrasubjective and also claiming that an adequate empirical basis for an analysis of intentionality will allow us to decide reliably that the qualia of others are comparable, see S. Shoemaker, "The inverted spectrum," in his *Identity, Cause, and Mind: Philosophical Essays* (Cambridge, Eng.: Cambridge Univ. Press, 1984), 327–57.

13. Quine, *Word and Object* and *From a Logical Point of View: Nine Logico-philosophical Essays,* 2d ed. (Cambridge: Harvard Univ. Press, 1980).

14. See D. Premack, "Minds with and without language," in *Thought without Language,* ed. L. Weiskrantz (Oxford: Clarendon, 1988). Of course, the absence of evidence in animals other than chimpanzees does not allow us to consider that they are not self-conscious.

15. See Griffin, *Animal Mind–Human Mind.* See also A. P. Georgopoulos, J. T. Lurito, M. Petrides, A. Schwartz, and J. T. Massey, "Mental rotation of the neuronal population vector," *Science* 243 (1989): 234–36, and P. E. Haenny, J. H. R. Maunsell, and P. H. Schiller, "State-dependent activity in monkey visual cortex. II. Retinal and extraretinal factors in V4," *Exp. Brain Res.* 69 (1988): 245–59, for some evidence that imaging is in some sense reflected in neuronal populations. An account of the neuropsychology of imaging may be found in M. J. Farah, "Is visual imagery really visual? Overlooked evidence from neuropsychology," *Psychol. Rev.* 95 (1988): 305–17.

16. D. L. Schacter, M. P. McAndrews, and M. Moscovitch, "Access to consciousness: Dissociations between implicit and explicit knowledge in neuropsychological syndromes," in Weiskrantz, ed., *Thought without Language,* 242–78. For an account of hemineglect as a disturbance of attention, see M. M. Mesulam, "A cortical network for directed attention and unilateral neglect," *Ann. Neurol.* 10 (1981): 309–25.

17. See L. Weiskrantz, *Blindsight: A Case Study and Implications* (Oxford: Clarendon, 1986).

18. For a brief account of neuropsychological disorders like hemineglect, see M. Williams, *Brain Damage, Behavior, and the Mind* (New York: Wiley, 1979).

19. E. Bisiach, "Language without thought," in Weiskrantz, ed., *Thought without Language,* 465–91.

20. Schacter et al., "Access to consciousness."

21. See H. Putnam, *Mind, Language, and Reality (philosophical papers)* (Cambridge, Eng.: Cambridge Univ. Press, 1975). There are various forms of functionalism that I do not discuss here. See Shoemaker, *Identity, Cause, and Mind;* N. Block, "Troubles with functionalism," in C. W. Savage, ed., *Cognition: Issues in the Foundations of Psychology,* Minnesota Studies in the Philosophy of Science, vol. 9 (Minneapolis: Univ. of Minnesota Press, 1978), 261–325; W. G. Lycan, *Consciousness* (Cambridge: MIT Press, 1987). Note also that the term "functionalism" as used here is not to be confused with the same term as it has

been applied to psychological operations by followers of William James (see the introductory remarks to chapter 3).

22. H. Putnam, *Representation and Reality* (Cambridge: MIT Press, 1988), chap. 5.

23. See J. R. Searle, "What is an intentional state?" *Mind* 88 (1979): 72–94, and his "Minds, brains, and programs," *Behav. Brain Sci.* 3 (1980): 417–24, as well as his *Minds, Brains, and Science.*

24. See R. Van Gulick, "Consciousness, intrinsic intentionality, and self-understanding machines," in Marcel and E. Bisiach, eds., *Consciousness in Contemporary Science,* 78–100, as well as Block, "Troubles with functionalism."

25. Putnam, *Representation and Reality,* 73, 36.

26. See Romanos, *Quine and Analytic Philosophy.*

27. Edelman, *Neural Darwinism.*

28. G. N. Reeke, Jr., and G. M. Edelman, "Real brains and artificial intelligence," *Daedalus* 117, no. 1 (1987): 143–73.

29. Ibid.

30. Edelman, *Topobiology* and *Neural Darwinism.* See also C. J. Lumsden and E. O. Wilson, *Genes, Mind, Culture: The Co-evolutionary Process* (Cambridge: Harvard Univ. Press, 1981), 334–40.

31. See note 28 above.

32. James, *The Principles of Psychology.*

33. This may seem to have a bit of the flavor of the claims of ecological psychology, and indeed it does have. But it is not in agreement with direct perception as proposed by J. J. Gibson. See J. J. Gibson, *The Ecological Approach to Visual Perception* (Boston: Houghton Mifflin, 1979) and E. S. Reed, *James J. Gibson and the Psychology of Perception* (New Haven: Yale Univ. Press, 1988), as well as Edelman, *Neural Darwinism,* chap. 8, for a disclaimer. The entire argument may be suspect because of the possibility that we cannot detect incongruities, such as abrupt discontinuities, even when they exist.

Chapter 3. Neural Darwinism

1. See, for example, J. E. Hochberg, *Perception,* 2d ed. (Englewood Cliffs, N.J.: Prentice-Hall, 1979), and Gibson, *Ecological Approach.*

2. F. A. Hayek, *The Sensory Order: An Inquiry into the Foundations of Theoretical Psychology* (Chicago: Univ. of Chicago Press, 1952).

3. S. Freud, *Project for a Scientific Psychology* (1895), in *The Standard Edition of the Complete Psychological Works of Sigmund Freud,* vol. 1, ed. J. Strachey (London: Hogarth, 1976), 283–411. See also F. J. Sulloway, *Freud, Biologist of the Mind* (New York: Basic Books, 1983), and R. C. Solomon, "Freud's neurological theory of the mind," in *Freud: A Collection of Critical Essays,* ed. R. Wollheim (Garden City, N.Y.: Anchor Books, 1974), 25–52.

4. James, *The Principles of Psychology.*

5. D. O. Hebb, *The Organization of Behavior: A Neuropsychological Theory*

(New York: Wiley, 1949). For Hebb's later thoughts, see his *Essay on Mind* (Hillsdale, N.J.: Lawrence Erlbaum Associates, 1980).

6. D. Bindra, *A Theory of Intelligent Behavior* (New York: Wiley, 1976).

7. G. M. Edelman and V. B. Mountcastle, *The Mindful Brain: Cortical Organization and the Group Selective Theory of Higher Brain Function* (Cambridge: MIT Press, 1978); Edelman, *Neural Darwinism.*

8. Ibid.

9. K. S. Lashley, "Structural variation in the nervous system in relation to behavior," *Psychol. Rev.* 54 (1947): 325–34.

10. For example, see the references in note 22, chapter 1. A detailed account of the deficiencies of the information processing approach may be found in Edelman, *Neural Darwinism.* See also C. von Hofsten, "Catching," in *Perspectives on Perception and Action,* ed. H. Heuer and A. F. Sanders (Hillsdale, N.J.: Lawrence Erlbaum Associates, 1987), 33–46, for the deficiencies of this approach in relation to perception and motion. It should be noted that so-called neural networks or parallel distributed processing methods (see J. L. McClelland, D. E. Rumelhart, and the PDP Research Group, *Parallel Distributed Processing: Explorations in the Microstructure of Cognition,* vol. 1, *Foundations,* vol. 2, *Psychological and Biological Models* [Cambridge: MIT Press, 1986]) do not avoid the difficulties of the information processing approach, inasmuch as they require specification of both input and output of a system. See also J. A. Fodor and Z. W. Pylyshyn, "Connectionism and cognitive architecture: A critical analysis," *Cognition* 28 (1988): 3–71.

11. Edelman and Mountcastle, *Mindful Brain;* Edelman, *Neural Darwinism* and *Topobiology.*

12. Edelman, *Neural Darwinism.*

13. See J. Kaas, M. M. Merzenich, and H. P. Killackey, "The reorganization of somatosensory cortex following peripheral nerve damage in adult and developing mammals," *Annu. Rev. Neurosci.* 6 (1983): 325–56.

14. R. J. Herrnstein, "Acquisition, generalization, and discrimination of a natural concept," *J. Exp. Psychol. Anim. Behav. Processes* 5 (1979): 116–29; R. J. Herrnstein, "Riddles of natural categorization," *Philos. Trans. R. Soc.* [*Biol.*] 308 (1985): 129–44; R. J. Herrnstein and P. A. de Villiers, "Fish as a natural category for people and pigeons," in *The Psychology of Learning and Motivation,* vol. 14, ed. G. H. Bower (New York: Academic, 1980), 59–95.

15. D. C. Van Essen, "Visual areas of the mammalian cerebral cortex," *Annu. Rev. Neurosci.* 2 (1979): 227–63; S. M. Zeki, "The mapping of visual functions in the cerebral cortex," in *Brain Mechanisms of Sensation: Third Taniguchi Symposium on Brain Sciences,* ed. Y. Katsuki, R. Norgren, and M. Sato (New York: Wiley, 1981), 105–28. S. M. Zeki, "Uniformity and diversity of structure and function in macaque monkey pre-striate visual cortex," *J. Physiol. (Lond.)* 277 (1978): 273–90.

16. This kind of categorization must be distinguished from conceptual categorization (for which, see U. Neisser, ed., *Concepts and Conceptual Development: Ecological and Intellectual Factors in Categorization* [Cambridge, Eng.: Cambridge Univ. Press, 1987]), and from categorical perception, which is concerned with the qualitative decisions on sensory signals occupying a continuous domain (see S. Harnad, ed., *Categorical Perception: The Groundwork of Cogni-*

tion [Cambridge, Eng.: Cambridge Univ. Press, 1987]). I have made this and other pertinent distinctions in *Neural Darwinism.*

17. See note 7 above.

18. W. M. Cowan, "Aspects of neural development," *Int. Rev. Physiol.* 17 (1978): 149–91. Cowan assesses the balance of factors judiciously, without prejudicing the issue. Recent misinterpretations have arisen, however. For example, D. Purves, *Body and Brain: A Trophic Theory of Neural Connections* (Cambridge: Harvard Univ. Press, 1988), lumps the claims of neural Darwinism with those of early attempts to use selectional thinking in understanding neuromuscular connections (J.-P. Changeux and A. Danchin, "Selective stabilization of developing synapses as a mechanism for the specifications of neuronal networks," *Nature* 264 [1976]: 705–12), or octopus learning (J. Z. Young, "The organization of a memory system," *Proc. R. Soc. Lond.* [*Biol.*] 163 [1965]: 285–320). While recognizing the value of these contributions, I explicitly noted that eliminative selection resulting only in the removal of preexisting connections was inadequate for a rich selective brain theory (see Edelman, *Neural Darwinism,* 14–16). Purves's use of the term "regressive theories" to label the conflation of these ideas is prejudicial. His analogizing of somatic selection and Haeckelian recapitulation (*Body and Brain,* 172) is completely inappropriate, as is made clear by detailed arguments presented in *Topobiology* and *Neural Darwinism.*

19. Edelman, *Topobiology.*

20. Edelman and Mountcastle, *Mindful Brain,* and Edelman, *Neural Darwinism* and *Topobiology.*

21. Edelman, *Topobiology;* G. M. Edelman, "Cell adhesion molecules in the regulation of animal form and tissue pattern," *Annu. Rev. Cell Biol.* 2 (1986): 81–116; G. M. Edelman, "Morphoregulatory molecules," *Biochemistry* 27 (1988): 3533–43; G. M. Edelman, "Cell surface modulation and marker multiplicity in neural patterning," *Trends Neurosci.* 7 (1984): 78–84.

22. Cowan, "Aspects of neural development."

23. Ibid.

24. Heterosynaptic interactions take account of multiple inputs to a cell from many neurons and also of chemical and electrical changes that do not require the actual firing of a neuron. See L. H. Finkel and G. M. Edelman, "Population rules for synapses in networks," in *Synaptic Function,* ed. G. M. Edelman, W. E. Gall and W. M. Cowan (New York: Wiley, 1987), 711–57.

25. See note 5 above.

26. See note 24 above.

27. See note 15 above.

28. See Edelman, *Neural Darwinism,* chaps. 3 and 10. Two additional remarks may be useful. First, as I suggested in these chapters, sampling in different classification couples in nonlinguistic animals may yield polymorphous sets. These are sets inclusion in which requires neither necessary nor sufficient conditions but instead requires the fulfillment of various disjunctions. For further discussion, see I. Dennis, J. A. Hampton, and S. E. G. Lea, "New problems in concept formation," *Nature* 243 (1973): 101–7, and the works of R. J. Herrnstein cited in the bibliography. Second, movement may be essential for categorization. See R. J. Held, "History as a factor in maintaining stability of perception

and coordination," *J. Nerv. Ment. Dis.* 132 (1961): 26–32, and M. Jeannerod, *The Brain Machine: The Development of Neurophysiological Thought* (Cambridge: Harvard Univ. Press, 1985).

29. See F. O. Schmitt, F. G. Worden, G. Adelman, and S. G. Dennis, eds., *The Organization of the Cerebral Cortex* (Cambridge: MIT Press, 1981).

30. Edelman, *Topobiology.*

31. J. C. Pearson, L. H. Finkel, and G. M. Edelman, "Plasticity in the organization of adult cerebral cortical maps: A computer simulation based on neuronal group selection," *J. Neurosci.* 7 (1987): 4209–23.

32. See note 13 above.

33. P. Landry and M. Deschênes, "Intracortical arborizations and receptive fields of identified ventrobasal thalamocortical afferents to the primary somatic sensory cortex in the cat," *J. Comp. Neurol.* 199 (1981): 345–71.

34. See note 31 above.

35. D. H. Hubel and T. N. Wiesel, "Functional architecture of the macaque monkey visual cortex," *Proc. R. Soc. Lond.* [*Biol.*] 198 (1977): 1–59.

36. C. M. Gray and W. Singer, "Stimulus-specific neuronal oscillation columns of cat visual cortex," *Proc. Natl. Acad. Sci. USA* 86 (1989): 1698–1702; C. M. Gray, P. O. Konig, A. K. Engel, and W. Singer, "Oscillatory responses in cat visual cortex exhibit inter-columnar synchronization which reflects global stimulus properties," *Nature* 338 (1989): 334–37. See also R. Eckhorn, R. Bauer, W. Jordon, M. Brosch, W. Kruse, M. Munk, and H. J. Reitboeck, "Coherent oscillations: A mechanism of feature linking in the visual cortex," *Biol. Cybern.* 60 (1988): 121–30.

37. Ibid. The whole phenomenon has been modeled in terms of reentrant groups. See O. Sporns, J. A. Gally, G. N. Reeke, Jr., and G. M. Edelman, "Reentrant signaling among simulated neuronal groups leads to coherency in their oscillatory activity," *Proc. Natl. Acad. Sci. USA* 86 (1989): 7265–69.

38. H. P. Barlow, "Neuroscience: A new era?" *Nature* 331 (1988): 571.

39. See note 24 above. See also R. E. Michod, "Darwinian selection in the brain," *Evolution* 4 (1989): 694–96. Of course, this amplification must be more or less stable over time to yield autocorrelation or a hereditary property.

40. See note 24 above.

41. See note 38 above.

42. See notes 24 and 31 above.

43. H. P. Barlow, "Single units and sensation: A neuron doctrine for perceptual psychology?" *Perception* 1 (1972): 371–94.

44. D. I. Perrett, E. T. Rolls, and W. Caan, "Visual neurons responsive to faces in the monkey temporal cortex," *Exp. Brain Res.* 47 (1982): 329–42; D. I. Perrett, P. A. Smith, D. D. Potter, A. J. Mistlen, A. S. Head, A. D. Milner, and M. A. Jeeves, "Neurons responsive to faces in the temporal cortex: Studies on functional organization, sensitivity to identity, and relation to perception," *Hum. Neurobiol.* 3 (1984): 197–208. See also Sporns et al., "Reentrant signaling."

45. See note 13 above.

46. See note 37 above.

47. For an extensive discussion of global mapping, see *Neural Darwinism,* chap. 8; the related subject of memory is covered in ibid., chap. 9.

48. Ibid.

49. J. E. R. Staddon, *Adaptive Behavior and Learning* (Cambridge, Eng.: Cambridge Univ. Press, 1983).

50. See *Neural Darwinism,* chaps. 3 and 11, for more discussion.

51. For a general summary of this procedure, see G. N. Reeke, Jr., L. H. Finkel, O. Sporns, and G. M. Edelman, "Synthetic neural modeling: A new approach to the analysis of brain complexity," in *Signal and Sense: Local and Global Order in Perceptual Maps,* ed. G. M. Edelman, W. E. Gall, and W. M. Cowan (New York: Wiley, in press). For accounts of the automata, see, for Darwin I, G. M. Edelman, "Group selection as the basis for higher brain function," in Schmitt et al., eds., *Organization of the Cerebral Cortex* (Cambridge: MIT Press, 1981), 535–63; for Darwin II, G. M. Edelman and G. N. Reeke, Jr., "Selective networks capable of representative transformations, limited generalizations, and associative memory," *Proc. Natl. Acad. Sci. USA* 79 (1982): 2091–95; for Darwin III, Reeke, Jr., et al., "Synthetic neural modeling."

52. Reeke, Jr., and Edelman, "Real brains."

53. S. R. Graubard, ed., "Artificial intelligence," *Daedalus* 17, no. 1 (1988).

54. See note 51 above and also Reeke, Jr., and Edelman, "Real brains."

55. Ibid.

56. James, *The Principles of Psychology,* vol. 1, 196–98. This fallacy consists in, among other things, attributing causal explanations based on introspection to another's behavior. It arises, of course, because we cannot in general correlate world, behavior, and an animal's neural activity simultaneously.

57. Graubard, "Artificial intelligence."

58. See note 24 above.

59. See note 51 above.

Chapter 4. Reentrant Signaling

1. Edelman, *Neural Darwinism;* J. Szentágothai, "The brain-mind relation: A pseudoproblem?" in *Mindwaves: Thoughts on Intelligence, Identity, and Consciousness,* ed. C. Blakemore and S. Greenfield (Oxford: Blackwell, 1987), 323–38.

2. L. H. Finkel and G. M. Edelman, "The integration of distributed cortical systems by reentry," *J. Neurosci.* (in press).

3. Edelman, *Neural Darwinism;* Edelman, "Group selection"; G. M. Edelman and L. H. Finkel, "Neuronal group selection in the cerebral cortex," in *Dynamic Aspects of Neocortical Function,* ed. G. M. Edelman, W. E. Gall, and W. M. Cowan (New York: Wiley, 1984), 653–95. For an apposite account on feedback, see W. R. Ashby, *An Introduction to Cybernetics* (New York: Wiley, 1966), 54: "[The] concept of 'feedback,' so simple and natural in certain elementary cases, becomes artificial and of little use when the interconnexions between the parts become more complex. When there are only two parts joined so that each affects the other, the properties of the feedback give important and useful information about the properties of the whole. But when the parts fuse to even as few as four, if every one affects the other three, then twenty circuits can be traced through them; and knowing the properties of all the twenty

circuits does *not* give complete information about the system. Such complex systems cannot be treated as an interlaced set of more or less independent feedback circuits, but only as a whole."

4. E. A. DeYoe and D. C. Van Essen, "Concurrent processing streams in monkey visual cortex," *Trends Neurosci.* 11 (1988): 219–26; S. M. Zeki and S. Shipp, "The functional logic of cortical connections," *Nature* 335 (1988): 311–17.

5. D. Marr, *Vision: A Computational Investigation into the Human Representation and Processing of Visual Information* (San Francisco: Freeman, 1982).

6. D. H. Ballard, G. E. Hinton, and T. J. Sejnowski, "Parallel visual computation," *Nature* 306 (1983): 21–26; P. K. Kienker, T. J. Sejnowski, G. E. Hinton, and L. E. Schumacher, "Separating figure from ground with a parallel network," *Perception* 15 (1986): 197–216.

7. See note 2 above.

8. See notes 2 and 4 above.

9. See note 4 above.

10. See note 3 above and Pearson et al., "Plasticity." A model of reentry with group dynamics which exhibits coherency of oscillatory behavior complements the RCI model and may be found in Sporns et al., "Reentrant signaling among simulated neuronal groups leads to coherency in their oscillatory activity," *Proc. Natl. Acad. Sci. USA* 86 (1989): 7265–69.

11. J. A. Movshon, E. H. Adelson, M. S. Grizzi, and W. T. Newsome, "The analysis of moving visual patterns," in *Pattern Recognition Mechanisms*, ed. C. Chagas, R. Gattass, and C. Gross, *Exp. Brain Res. Suppl.* 11 (1985): 117–51.

12. G. F. Poggio, B. C. Motter, S. Squatrito, and Y. Trotter, "Responses of neurons in visual cortex (V1 and V2) of the alert macaque to dynamic random-dot stereograms," *Vision Res.* 25 (1985): 397–406; see also G. F. Poggio and T. Poggio, "The analysis of stereopsis," *Annu. Rev. Neurosci.* 7 (1984): 379–412, and K. A. Stevens, "Evidence relating subjective contours and interpretations involving occlusion" (AI Memo 637, MIT Artificial Intelligence Laboratory, 1981).

13. D. C. Van Essen, "Functional organization of primate visual cortex," in *Cerebral Cortex*, vol. 3, *Visual Cortex*, ed. A. Peters and E. G. Jones (New York: Plenum, 1985), 259–320; D. H. Hubel and T. N. Wiesel, "Receptive fields, binocular interaction and functional architecture in the cat's visual cortex," *J. Physiol. (Lond.)* 160 (1962): 106–54; G. H. Henry, "Streaming in the striate cortex," in *Visual Neuroscience*, ed. J. D. Pettigrew, K. J. Sanderson, and W. R. Levick (New York: Cambridge Univ. Press, 1986), 260–79; Zeki, "Mapping of visual functions"; DeYoe and Van Essen, "Concurrent processing streams"; M. S. Livingstone and D. H. Hubel, "Psychophysical evidence for separate channels for the perception of form, color, movement, and depth," *J. Neurosci.* 7 (1987): 3416–68.

14. V. S. Ramachandran, "Capture of stereopsis and apparent motion by illusory contours," *Perception and Psychophysics* 39 (1986): 361–73; V. S. Ramachandran and P. Cavanaugh, "Subjective contours capture stereopsis," *Nature* 317 (1985): 527–30; V. S. Ramachandran, V. M. Rao, and T. R. Vidyasagar, "Apparent movement with subjective contours," *Vision Res.* 13 (1973): 1399–

401. See also K. Nakayama, "Biological motion processing: A review," *Vision Res.* 25 (1985): 625–40. G. Kanizsa, *Organization in Vision: Essays on Gestalt Perception* (New York: Praeger, 1979), makes a clear argument relating gestalt phenomena to illusory contours and other perceptual effects. See also S. J. Petry and G. E. Meyer, eds., *Perception of Illusory Contours* (New York: Springer-Verlag, 1987). For accounts of "unconscious inference," see H. von Helmholtz, *Treatise on Physiological Optics* (1925), ed. J. P. C. Southall (reprint; New York: Dover, 1962), and Gregory, *Mind in Science.*

15. Poggio et al., "Responses of neurons in visual cortex"; Poggio and Poggio, "Analysis of stereopsis"; Stevens, "Evidence relating subjective contours"; Edelman, *Topobiology;* K. Koffka, *Principles of Gestalt Psychology* (New York: Harcourt Brace World, 1935). See also notes 12, 13, and 14.

16. Zeki, "Mapping of visual functions"; DeYoe and Van Essen, "Concurrent processing streams"; Livingstone and Hubel, "Psychophysical evidence." See also note 14 above.

17. See note 4 above.

18. Ramachandran, "Capture of stereopsis"; Ramachandran and Cavanaugh, "Subjective contours capture stereopsis"; Ramachandran et al., "Apparent movement with subjective contours."

19. Koffka, *Principles of Gestalt Psychology.*

20. Kanizsa, *Organization of Vision.*

21. Helmholtz, *Treatise on Physiological Optics;* Gregory, *Mind in Science.*

22. Koffka, *Principles of Gestalt Psychology.*

Chapter 5. Perceptual Experience and Consciousness

1. See Sperry, "Neurology and the mind-body problem,"; R. W. Sperry, "Brain bisection and consciousness," in *Brain and Conscious Experience,* ed. J. C. Eccles (New York: Springer-Verlag, 1966), 298–313.

2. See R. Granit, *The Purposive Brain* (Cambridge: MIT Press, 1977). This subject is obviously related to the issue of the efficacy of consciousness, about which opinions range widely, depending largely upon various philosophical views of the mind-body problem. James, in *The Principles of Psychology* and *Psychology: Briefer Course,* pressed strongly for the idea of consciousness as an agency. Sperry, in his articles "A modified concept," "An objective approach to subjective experience," and "Mental phenomena as causal determinants in brain function," in Globus et al., eds., *Consciousness and the Brain,* 163–78, supports a similar idea. But those favorably disposed to epiphenomenalism or certain computer views of the brain argue against such efficacy. See, for example, Jackendoff, *Consciousness.* Clearly, the admission of unconscious processes (see chapter 12) does *not* dispose of consciousness as efficacious.

3. This will be pursued in greater depth in chapters 9–11.

4. All of these elements are described in *Neural Darwinism,* but the last one (4) only superficially. In the present context, I use the word *value* to refer to evolutionarily or theologically derived constraints favoring behavior that fulfills

homeostatic requirements or increases fitness in an individual species. See the description of Darwin III in chapter 3 for some instantiations at different levels.

5. Immunologists are aware of this sense. See, for example, F. M. Burnet, *The Clonal Selection Theory of Acquired Immunity* (Nashville: Vanderbilt Univ. Press, 1959). To a lesser extent, so are biochemists—see R. Williams, *Biochemical Individuality* (London: Chapman and Hall, 1956). Here, I am stressing the physiological side—the brain as a gland, as a homeostatic or regulative organ influenced by such microscopic processes and largely dominant over perturbations that might upset the performance of vital or sexual functions.

6. N. Tinbergen, *The Study of Instinct* (Oxford: Clarendon, 1951); N. Tinbergen, "An objective study of the innate behavior of animals," *Bibl. Biotheor.* 1 (1942): 39–98; J. L. Gould, *Ethology* (New York: Norton, 1982). For the relation to evolution and "closed programs," see E. Mayr, "Behavior programs and evolutionary strategies," *Am. Sci.* 62 (1974): 650–59.

7. See D. W. Pfaff and C. V. Mobbs, "Some concepts deriving from the neural circuit for a hormone-driven mammalian reproductive behavior," in H. McLennan, J. R. Ledsome, C. H. S. McIntosh, and D. R. Jones, eds., *Advances in Physiological Research* (New York: Plenum, 1987), 233–51.

8. Detailed anatomical proposals will be given in chapters 7–9.

9. Edelman, *Neural Darwinism;* Pfaff and Mobbs, "Some concepts deriving from the neural circuit." See also Staddon, *Adaptive Behavior.*

10. Pfaff and Mobbs, "Some concepts deriving from the neural circuit."

11. Ibid.; Edelman, *Neural Darwinism;* note 2 above.

12. James, *The Principles of Psychology.*

13. This is discussed in chapters 2 and 12. A variety of clinical syndromes as well as psychological results suggests that complex processes can occur without awareness. See, for example, Schacter et al., "Access to consciousness," and A. J. Marcel, "Conscious and unconscious perception: Experiments on visual masking and word recognition," *Cognit. Psychol.* 15 (1983): 197–237. See also chapter 13.

14. See A. Kenny, "Homunculus fallacy," in *Interpretations of Life and Mind,* ed. M. Grene (New York: Humanities, 1971).

15. Indeed, while being conscious is not a matter of degree (see N. Malcolm in Armstrong and Malcolm, eds., *Consciousness and Causality),* there are many states of consciousness. To the extent that an increasing store of categorical memories has not accumulated, the states of consciousness would be severely limited, for example, in a newborn. For a relevant discussion in humans, see C. E. Izard, "The emergence of emotions and the development of consciousness in infancy," in *The Psychobiology of Consciousness,* ed. J. M. Davidson and R. J. Davidson (New York: Plenum, 1980), 193–216.

16. See chapter 15 for comments on the density of world events. Phenomenal experience is not identical to the categorizations yielded by perceptual processes. See A. J. Marcel, "Conscious and unconscious perception: An approach to the relations between phenomenal experience and perceptual processes," *Cognit. Psychol.* 15 (1983): 238–300, and also chapter 9.

17. See P. Zubec, *Sensory Deprivation: Fifteen Years of Research* (New York: Irvington, 1969). A particularly clear brief account of work in this area is given

by G. F. Reed, "Sensory deprivation," in Underwood and Stevens, eds., *Aspects of Consciousness*, vol. 1, *Physiological Issues*, 155–78. The chief effects of this state are inability to maintain attention, heightened and bizarre imagery, decreased ability to reason logically, and impaired temporal discrimination.

18. See note 13 above.

19. See Premack and Premack, *Mind of an Ape*, and C. A. Ristau and D. Robbins, "Language of the great apes: A critical review," *Advances in the Study of Behavior*, vol. 12, ed. J. S. Rosenblatt, R. A. Hinde, C. Beer, and M. C. Busnel (New York: Academic, 1982), 141–255.

20. See J. S. Bruner, *Beyond the Information Given: Studies in the Psychology of Knowing* (New York: Norton, 1973) and F. C. Bartlett, *Thinking: A Study of Humans* (New York: Basic Books, 1958). For a view consistent with the present one, stressing categorization and pattern recognition, see H. Margolis, *Patterns, Thinking, and Cognition: A Theory of Judgment* (Chicago: Univ. of Chicago Press, 1987).

21. For some philosophical views, see P. F. Strawson, *Individuals: An Essay in Descriptive Metaphysics* (New York: Methuen, 1964); D. Parfit, *Reasons and Persons* (Oxford: Oxford Univ. Press, 1984); J. R. Perry, *Personal Identity* (Berkeley: Univ. of California Press, 1975); S. Shoemaker, *Self-Knowledge and Self-Identity* (Ithaca: Cornell Univ. Press, 1963); B. Williams, *Problems of the Self* (Cambridge, Eng.: Cambridge Univ. Press, 1973). For potential interactions between biology and concepts of self, see H. J. Eysenck and M. W. Eysenck, *Personality and Individual Differences* (New York: Plenum, 1985). For developmental views, see B. E. McKenzie and R. H. Day, *Perceptual Development in Early Infancy: Problems and Issues* (Hillsdale, N.J.: Lawrence Erlbaum Associates, 1987); A. Yonas, ed., *Perceptual Development in Early Infancy*, Minnesota Symposia on Child Psychology, vol. 20; M. Lewis and J. Brooks-Gunn, *Social Cognition and the Acquisition of Self* (New York: Plenum, 1979); M. S. Mahler, F. Pine, and A. Bergman, *The Psychological Birth of the Human Infant: Symbiosis and Individuation* (New York: Basic Books, 1975.)

22. P. Lieberman, *The Biology and Evolution of Language* (Cambridge: Harvard Univ. Press, 1984).

23. I shall discuss this at length in chapter 10. The interested reader may consult J. Bresnan, ed., *The Mental Representation of Grammatical Relations* (Cambridge: MIT Press, 1982), and S. Pinker, *Language Learnability and Language Development* (Cambridge: Harvard Univ. Press, 1984), for discussions of semantic bootstrapping.

24. See R. W. Sperry, M. S. Gazzaniga, and J. E. Bogen, "Interhemispheric relations: The neocortical commissures; syndromes of hemispheric disconnection," in *Handbook of Clinical Neurology*, vol. 4, ed. P. J. Vinken and G. W. Bruyn (Amsterdam: North Holland, 1969), 273–90, and M. S. Gazzaniga, *The Bisected Brain* (New York: Appleton-Century-Crofts, 1970). The more recent views of Gazzaniga may be found in his articles "Brain modularity: Toward a philosophy of conscious experience," in Marcel and Bisiach, eds., *Consciousness in Contemporary Science*, 218–38, and "The dynamics of cerebral specialization and modular interactions," in Weiskrantz, ed., *Thought without Language*, 430–50.

25. See note 2 above.

Chapter 6. Memory as Recategorization

1. Edelman, *Neural Darwinism,* points out that the word "memory" has been used in a great variety of ways. For a sampling of different views, the interested reader may consult L. G. Nilsson, *Perspectives in Memory Research: Essays in Honor of Uppsala University's 500th Anniversary* (Hillsdale, N.J.: Lawrence Erlbaum Associates, 1979); D. A. Norman, *Memory and Attention* (New York: Wiley, 1969); U. Neisser, *Memory Observed: Remembering in Natural Contexts* (San Francisco: Freeman, 1982); J. R. Anderson and G. H. Bower, *Human Associative Memory,* 2d ed. (Washington, D.C.: Hemisphere, 1974); L. R. Squire and N. Butters, *Neuropsychology of Memory* (New York: Guilford, 1984); E. Tulving, *Elements of Episodic Memory* (New York: Oxford Univ. Press, 1983); and F. C. Bartlett, *Remembering: A Study in Experimental and Social Psychology* (Cambridge, Eng.: Cambridge Univ. Press, 1964). Memory has also been conflated with its synaptic bases (see R. F. Thompson, T. W. Berger, and J. Madden IV, "Cellular processes of learning and memory in the mammalian CNS," *Annu. Rev. Neurosci.* 6 [1983]: 447–91, and R. F. Thompson, "The neurobiology of learning and memory," *Science* 233 [1986]: 941–47). Memory occurs in different modalities and across different stretches of time. The problem of definition certainly rests in part on the ease with which memorial events are observed in linguistic animals and analogized with electronic storage, and in part on the likelihood that there are multiple means by which synaptic changes affect different brain areas with segregated functions.

2. For a clear-cut distinction between perceptual categorization and conceptual categorization, compare the treatment in *Neural Darwinism,* which is concerned mainly with the first, with Neisser, ed., *Concepts and Conceptual Development.*

3. Finkel and Edelman, "Population rules for synapses in networks." This article makes the point that memory cannot be conflated with some of its mechanisms.

4. See Staddon, *Adaptive Behavior and Learning,* for a discussion of the role of surprise in changing the direction of learning.

5. The term "recategorization" thus does not necessarily mean the recall of a categorical response only. It also includes the constantly changing associative context that can result in a response *similar* to a given previous categorical response but enriched by ongoing changes.

6. James emphasized that he considered this to be the foremost fact about consciousness (*Psychology: Briefer Course,* chap. 11): "Thought goes on." According to him, the conscious state of mind is personal, in constant change, continuous, and selective. It is amusing and possibly revealing to compare James's notions on consciousness with St. Augustine's on time: "What then is time? If no one asks me, I know what it is. If I wish to explain him who asks me, I do not know." See St. Augustine, *Confessions* (401), trans. R. Warner (New York: Mentor Books, 1963), 267. Consciousness is something "we know as long as no asks us to define it," James wrote in *The Principles of Psychology,* 152. As is pointed out in J. Pelikan, *The Mystery of Continuity: Time and History, Memory and Eternity in the Thought of St. Augustine* (Charlottesville: Univ.

Press of Virginia, 1986), the element of temporal continuity was central to Augustine's thought.

7. N. Bernstein, *The Coordination and Regulation of Movements* (Oxford: Pergamon, 1967).

8. Ibid. See also S. Grillner, "Locomotion in vertebrates: Central mechanisms and reflex interaction," *Physiol. Rev.* 55 (1975): 247–304; S. Grillner, "On the neural control of movement: A comparison of basic rhythmic behaviors," in *Function and Formation of Neural Systems,* ed. G. S. Stent (New York: Springer-Verlag, 1977), 197–224.

9. Finkel and Edelman, "Population rules for synapses in networks."

10. A useful short history of memory research based directly or indirectly on ideas of coding may be found in C. N. Cofer, "Human learning and memory," in *The First Century of Experimental Psychology,* ed. E. Hearst (Hillsdale, N.J.: Lawrence Erlbaum Associates, 1979), 323–69.

11. Finkel and Edelman, "Population rules for synapses in networks."

12. There seems to be little doubt that modality-specific forms of memory exist. Neuropsychological data showing defects specific to particular modalities reveal some of the necessary components of these forms but not their overall mechanisms. This is also true for language, as witness the various forms of aphasias, agnosias, and the like. See A. R. Luria, *Higher Cortical Functions in Man,* trans. B. Haigh (New York: Basic Books, 1984); M. B. Arnold, *Memory and the Brain* (Hillsdale, N.J.: Lawrence Erlbaum Associates, 1984); E. Goldberg, "The gradiential approach to neocortical functional organization," *J. Clin. Exp. Neuropsychol.* (in press).

Chapter 7. Time and Space: Cortical Appendages and Organs of Succession

1. Although local maps and global mappings are central to the ideas in this book, I do not discuss their relation to the psychological question of the origin of spatial sense or its connections to physical theories of space-time. For an amusing historical account, see M. J. Morgan, *Molyneux's Question: Vision, Touch and the Philosophy of Perception* (Cambridge, Eng.: Cambridge Univ. Press, 1977); for physical bases and philosophical accounts, see M. D. Akhundov, *Conceptions of Space and Time: Sources, Evolution, Directions* (Cambridge: MIT Press, 1986). H. Schöne, *Spatial Orientation: The Spatial Control of Behavior in Animals and Man* (Princeton: Princeton Univ. Press, 1984), is a valuable ethological and physiological account. G. E. Myers, *William James: His Life and Thought* (New Haven: Yale Univ. Press, 1986), has a useful survey of James's thoughts on various aspects. Finally, J. J. Gibson's various writings provide important views (see references). The monograph *James J. Gibson,* by E. S. Reed, gives a clear account.

2. Bernstein, *Coordination.*

3. See G. Bock, M. O'Connor, and J. Marsh, eds., *Motor Areas of the Cerebral Cortex,* Ciba Foundation Symposium, no. 132 (New York: Wiley, 1987).

4. Edelman, *Neural Darwinism,* chap. 8; Bernstein, *Coordination.*

5. Edelman, *Neural Darwinism,* chap. 8; J. A. S. Kelso and B. Tuller, "A dynamical basis for action systems," in *Handbook of Neuroscience,* ed. M. S. Gazzaniga (New York: Plenum, 1984), 321–56.

6. M. Jeannerod, *The Neural and Behavioral Organization of Goal-Directed Movements* (New York: Oxford Univ. Press, 1988).

7. M. Ito, *The Cerebellum and Neural Control* (New York: Raven Press, 1984); M. Glickstein, C. Yeo, and J. Stein, eds., *Cerebellum and Neuronal Plasticity* (New York: Plenum, 1986); J. S. King, ed., *New Concepts in Cerebellar Neurobiology* (New York: Alan R. Liss, 1987); R. R. Llinás, "Functional significance of the basic cerebellar circuit in motor coordination," in *Cerebellar Functions,* ed. J. R. Bloedel, J. Dichgans, and W. Precht (Berlin: Springer-Verlag, 1984), 170–85; R. R. Llinás and J. I. Simpson, "Cerebellar control of movement," in *Handbook of Behavioral Neurobiology,* vol. 5, ed. A. L. Towe and E. S. Luschei (New York: Plenum, 1981), 231–302.

8. J. W. Joseph, G. M. Shambes, J. M. Gibson, and W. Welker, "Tactile projections to granule cells in caudal vermis of the rat's cerebellum," *Brain Behav. Evol.* 15 (1978): 141–49; G. M. Shambes, J. M. Gibson, and W. Welker, "Fractured somatotopy in granule cell tactile areas of rat cerebellar hemispheres revealed by micromapping," ibid., 94–140; J. Kassel, G. M. Shambes and W. Welker, "Fractured cutaneous projections to the granule cell layer of the posterior cerebellar hemisphere of the domestic cat," *J. Comp. Neurol.* 225 (1984): 458–68.

9. G. Andersson and O. Oscarsson, "Climbing fiber microzones in cerebellar vermis and their projections to different groups of cells in the lateral vestibular nucleus," *Exp. Brain Res.* 32 (1978): 565–79; O. Oscarsson, "Functional units of the cerebellum-sagittal zones and microzones," *Trends Neurosci.* 2 (1979): 143–45; K. Logan and L. T. Robertson, "Somatosensory representation of the cerebellar climbing fiber system in the rat," *Brain Res.* 372 (1986): 290–300.

10. W. T. Thach, "Cerebellar inputs to motor cortex," in Bock et al., eds., *Motor Areas of the Cerebral Cortex,* 201–20.

11. See note 8 above.

12. See note 9 above.

13. J. M. Bower and D. C. Woolston, "Congruence of spatial organization of tactile projections to granule cell and Purkinje cell layers of cerebellar hemispheres of the albino rat: Vertical organization of the cerebellar cortex," *J. Neurophysiol.* 49 (1983): 745–66.

14. For example, D. Marr, "A theory of cerebellar cortex," *J. Physiol.* 202 (1969): 437–70, and J. S. Albus, "A theory of cerebellar function," *Math Biosci.* 10 (1971): 25–61. R. R. Llinás gives a good review of various models in "Electrophysiology of cerebellar networks," in *Handbook of Physiology,* section 1, *The Nervous System,* vol. 2, ed. V. B. Brooks (Bethesda, Md.: American Physiological Society, 1981), 831–976.

15. Edelman, *Neural Darwinism.*

16. R. L. Isaacson and K. H. Pribram, eds., "The hippocampus," *Neurophysiology and Behavior,* vol. 2 (New York: Plenum, 1975); L. Weiskrantz, "A comparison of hippocampal pathology in man and other animals," in *Functions of the Septo-Hippocampal System,* Ciba Foundation Symposium, no. 58, ed. K.

Elliott and J. Whelan (Amsterdam: Elsevier–North Holland, 1978), 373–87; J. O'Keefe and L. Nadel, *The Hippocampus as a Cognitive Map* (Oxford: Clarendon, 1978); B. Milner, "Memory and the human brain," in *How We Know: The Inner Frontiers of Cognitive Science,* Proceedings of Nobel Conference 20, ed. M. Shafto (San Francisco: Harper & Row, 1985), 31–59; M. Mishkin, "A memory system in the monkey," *Philos. Trans. R. Soc. [Biol.]* 298 (1982): 85–95; M. Mishkin, B. Malamut, and J. B. Chevalier, "Memories and habits: Two neural systems," in *Neurobiology of Learning and Memory,* ed. G. S. Lynch, J. L. McGough, and N. M. Weinberger (New York: Guild, 1984), 65–77.

17. D. L. Rosene and G. W. Van Hoesen, "Hippocampal efferents reach widespread areas of cerebral cortex and amygdala in the rhesus monkey," *Science* 198 (1977): 315–17.

18. Ibid.; G. W. Van Hoesen, "The parahippocampal gyrus: New observations regarding its cortical connections in the monkey," *Trends Neurosci.* 5 (1982): 345–50.

19. L. W. Swanson and W. M. Cowan, "An autoradiographic study of the organization of the efferent connections of the hippocampal formation in the rat," *J. Comp. Neurol.* 172 (1977): 49–84.

20. J. W. Papez, "A proposed mechanism of emotion," *Arch. Neurol. Psychiatry* 38 (1937): 725–43.

21. P. O. Andersen, B. H. Bland, and J. D. Dudar, "Organization of the hippocampal output," *Exp. Brain Res.* 17 (1973): 152–68; J. N. P. Rawlins and K. F. Green, "Lamellar organization in the rat hippocampus," *Exp. Brain Res.* 28 (1977): 335–44.

22. For studies on long-term potentiation, see G. S. Lynch, V. K. Gribkoff, and S. A. Deadwyler, "Long-term potentiation is accompanied by a reduction in dendritic responsiveness to glutamic acid," *Nature* 263 (1976): 151–53; G. S. Lynch, R. Dunwiddie, and V. K. Gribkoff, "Heterosynaptic depression: A postsynaptic correlate of long-term potentiation," *Nature* 266 (1977): 737–39; G. S. Lynch, S. Halpain, and M. Baudry, "Effects of high frequency synaptic simulation on glutamate receptor binding studies with a modified *in vitro* hippocampal slice preparation," *Brain Res.* 244 (1982): 101–11; G. S. Lynch and M. Baudry, "The biochemistry of memory: A new and specific hypothesis," *Science* 224 (1984): 1057–63; P. O. Andersen, "Possible mechanisms for long-lasting potentiation of synaptic transmission in hippocampal slices from guinea-pigs," *J. Physiol. (Lond.)* 302 (1980): 463–82; P. O. Andersen, "Specific long-lasting potentiation of synaptic transmission in hippocampal slices," *Nature* 266 (1977): 736–37.

23. Ibid.

24. E. V. Evarts, Y. Shinoda, and S. P. Wise, *Neurophysiological Approaches to Higher Brain Functions* (New York: Wiley, 1984).

25. C. D. Marsden, "The mysterious motor function of the basal ganglia: The Robert Wartenberg lecture," *Neurology* 32 (1981): 514–39; M. R. DeLong, G. E. Alexander, A. P. Georgopoulos, M. D. Crutcher, S. J. Mitchell, and R. T. Richardson, "Role of basal ganglia in limb movements," *Hum. Neurobiol.* 2 (1984): 235–44; S. J. Mitchell, R. T. Richardson, F. H. Baker, and M. R. DeLong, "The primate globus pallidus: Neuronal activity related to direction of movement," *Exp. Brain Res.* 68 (1987): 491–505; C. D. Marsden, "What do the basal

ganglia tell premotor cortical areas?" in Bock et al., eds., *Motor Areas of the Cerebral Cortex,* 282–95.

26. G. E. Alexander, M. R. DeLong, and P. L. Strick, "Parallel organization of functionally segregated circuits linking basal ganglia and cortex," *Annu. Rev. Neurosci.* 9 (1986): 357–81; G. E. Alexander and M. R. DeLong, "Microstimulation of the primate neostriatum: I. Physiological properties of striatal microexcitable zones," *J. Neurophysiol.* 53 (1985): 1401–16; M. D. Crutcher and M. R. DeLong, "Single cell studies of primate putamen: I. Functional organization," *Exp. Brain Res.* 53 (1984): 233–43; "II. Relations to direction of movement and pattern of muscular activity," ibid., 244–58.

27. R. Malach and A. M. Graybiel, "Mosaic architecture of the somatic sensory-recipient sector of the cat's striatum," *J. Neurosci.* 6 (1986): 3436–58; G. Fishell and D. van der Kooy, "Pattern formation in the striatum: Developmental changes in the distribution of striatonigral neurons," *J. Neurosci.* 7 (1987): 1969–78; C. R. Gerfen, "The neostriatal mosaic compartmentalization of corticostriatal input and striatonigral output systems," *Nature* 311 (1984): 461–64; P. M. Groves, M. Martone, S. J. Young, and D. M. Armstrong, "Three-dimensional pattern of enkephalin-like immunoreactivity in the caudate nucleus of the cat," *J. Neurosci.* 8 (1988): 892–908.

28. See note 26 above.

29. See note 25 above and R. E. Passingham, "Two cortical systems for directing movement," in Bock et al., eds., *Motor Areas of the Cerebral Cortex,* 151–64.

30. See note 25 above.

31. R. Barker, "How does the brain control its own activity? A new function for the basal ganglia," *J. Theoret. Biol.* 131 (1988): 497–507.

32. S. P. Wise and J. L. Rappaport, "Obsessive-compulsive disorder: Is it basal ganglia dysfunction?" in *Obsessive-Compulsive Disorder in Children and Adolescents,* ed. J. L. Rappaport (Washington, D.C.: American Psychiatric Press, 1989), 327–44.

33. See E. T. Rolls and G. V. Williams, "Sensory and movement-related activity in different regions of the primate striatum," in *Basal Ganglia and Behavior: Sensory Aspects of Motor Functioning,* ed. J. S. Schneider and T. I. Lidsky (Toronto: Hans Huber, 1987), 37–59.

34. See note 25 above.

35. See Schneider and Lidsky, eds., *Basal Ganglia and Behavior.*

36. See note 7 above.

37. D. E. Haines and E. Dietrichs, "On the organization of interconnections between the cerebellum and hypothalamus," in *New Concepts in Cerebellar Neurobiology,* ed. J. S. King (New York: Alan R. Liss, 1987), 113–49.

38. G. M. Edelman, W. E. Gall, and W. M. Cowan, eds., *Dynamic Aspects of Neocortical Function* (New York: Wiley, 1984).

Chapter 8. Concepts and Presyntax

1. The temptation follows, I believe, from the more general nature of concepts, from language's *dependence* on them (see chapter 10), and from the fact

that in order to *talk* about concepts in prelinguistic animals, we must use metaphors. The only test of a concept in such an animal is by means of its behavior. From that behavior, we must *infer* a process that goes beyond perceptual categorization. A good source of reviews dedicated to the idea that thought (and obviously concepts) may occur without language is L. Weiskrantz, ed., *Thought without Language.* Two very strong positions are taken by A. Kertesz, "Cognitive function in severe aphasia," ibid., 451–63, and E. Bisiach, "Language without thought," ibid., 465–91.

2. The position I shall take is in accord with that of R. G. Millikan, in *Language, Thought, and Other Biological Categories: New Foundations for Realism* (Cambridge: MIT Press, 1984), which asserts that a conceptual transaction is between an organism and the world. Insofar as there are things in the world and an ability to generalize upon such things, relations are generated that could be called ontological.

3. In order to derive conceptual relations from perceptual categorizations, an animal must use its phenotype in a variety of ways in *relation* to real-world events, which it perceptually categorizes, as well as in relation to its memory. This relation depends upon building a body schema in terms of motion and motor sensory interactions. This was well recognized by H. Head in *Studies in Neurology,* vol. 2 (London: Hodder and Stoughton, 1920). See also R. C. Oldfield and O. L. Zangwill, "Head's concept of the schema and its application in contemporary British psychology: I. Head's concept of the schema," *Brit. J. Psychol.* 32 (1942): 267–86; "II. Critical analysis of Head's theory," ibid., 33 (1942): 58–64; "III. Bartlett's theory of memory," ibid., 111–29; "IV. Walter's theory of thinking," ibid., 33 (1943): 143–49. This notion was derived from neuropsychological experience with traumatized humans, not animals. In *Neural Darwinism,* I tried to show that the idea that memory is an enhanced ability to recategorize and generalize rests to some degree on the idea of a body schema.

4. Indeed, the difficulty in assessing *how* we have concepts is conjugate to that of deciding *that* animals have concepts. Given the rich dependence of language acquisition and formation on conceptual ability, and the notion that conceptual centers of the brain can categorize the lexicon itself, it is no wonder that concepts and symbols for concepts are conflated. See F. C. Keil, *Semantic and Conceptual Development: An Ontological Perspective* (Cambridge: Harvard Univ. Press, 1979), for an analysis of how ontological categories emerge in speech-using humans and what constraints appear to be exercised on the predicates formed. The evidence (outside that of neuropsychology and the clinic) that image schemata are important in humans is pursued by M. Johnson in *The Body in the Mind: The Bodily Basis of Meaning, Imagination, and Reason* (Chicago: Univ. of Chicago Press, 1987). His methodology involves the examination of language for propositional structures that can emerge only because of a complex web of nonpropositional schematic structures that themselves emerge from our bodily experience. The metaphors or topics include notions of objects, motion, containment, in-out, superimposition, force, balance, blockage, compulsion, diversion, attraction, and the like. Clearly, these must involve tying perceptual categories with conceptual categories or modes of modeling

the world. (See Neisser, ed., *Concepts and Conceptual Development,* for ideas about conceptual categories.)

The difficulty in accepting the validity of image schemata from this analysis alone lies in the indirectness of the method, but if the data are taken together with neuropsychological data (see note 3 above), there is some reason to support this notion. No method other than behavioral analysis is applicable to nonverbal animals, although, as we shall see, chimpanzee behavior and communication with humans gives some additional support to the idea that nonhumans can have concepts.

A very important and more tangible analysis can be seen in the studies of Spelke and her associates on the determination of nature of objects by preverbal children. See E. Spelke, "The origins of physical knowledge," in Weiskrantz, ed., *Thought without Language,* 168–84.

5. See Ristau and Robbins, "Language of the great apes"; Premack and Premack, *Mind of an Ape;* D. Premack, "Minds with and without language."

6. Perhaps imaging and imagination should be added to this list.

7. Notice that recursive reentry as demonstrated in the early visual system (chapter 4) can be enormously powerful in resolving conflict, in figural synthesis, and the like. But it cannot *recombine* various mappings or their parts without a large constraint by primary perceptual input.

8. As was shown in chapter 7, some global mappings may be linked by the hippocampus, others by the basal ganglia, and still others by the cerebellum. These dynamic structures depend for their initial creation upon motor sensory coordination and correlation as well as continued motion. The potential relation to concepts concerned with image schemata (see note 4 above) is obvious.

9. This assumption follows from the fact that global mappings begin with action itself, whereas concepts must arise within certain brain areas, activating only certain portions of such mappings.

10. Spelke, "Origins of physical knowledge."

11. The evolution of reentrant mappings that map brain functions themselves, rather than spatial or topographic features, should not require any exotic additions to developmental mechanisms. Natural selection upon variants with such structures is all that is required.

12. This is perhaps one of the most significant means for extending primary consciousness to higher-order consciousness. See chapter 11.

13. See, for example, J. A. Fodor, *Representations: Philosophical Essays on the Foundations of Cognitive Science* (Cambridge: MIT Press, 1981), and J. A. Fodor, *Psychosemantics: The Problem of Meaning in the Philosophy of Mind* (Cambridge: MIT Press, 1987). P. W. Jusczyk and B. Earhard, "The lingua mentis and its role in thought," in *The Nature of Thought: Essays in Honor of D. O. Hebb,* ed. P. W. Jusczyk and R. M. Klein (Hillsdale, N.J.: Lawrence Erlbaum Associates, 1980), 155–86, approach the subject from a different direction.

14. See note 1 above.

15. See Millikan, *Language, Thought, and Other Biological Categories.* But one must be careful not to fall into a version of naive realism. Studies of the responses of young infants to visual illusions of various kinds show that a cognitive and conceptual transformation of input signals occurs. See L. B. Cohen,

"An information processing approach to infant cognitive development," in Weiskrantz, ed., *Thought without Language*, 211–36.

16. I have already mentioned Bartlett, *Thinking*, which relates these capacities to a skill. For views on induction, see J. H. Holland, K. J. Holyoak, R. E. Nisbett, and P. R. Thagard, *Induction: Processes of Inference, Learning, and Discovery* (Cambridge: MIT Press, 1987); for an analysis of judgment, see Margolis, *Patterns, Thinking, and Cognition*. Both are unfortunately limited (perforce) to humans.

17. This capacity, like concept formation itself, must be strongly tied to motor plans and sequences. Indeed, the problem is related to that of serial order in behavior. See K. S. Lashley, "The problem of serial order in behavior," in *Cerebral Mechanisms in Behavior*, ed. L. A. Jeffress (New York: Wiley, 1951). For more on motor plans and sequences, see the discussion of attention in chapter 12.

18. See note 1 above.

19. See also D. Rosenbaum, "Hierarchical organization of motor programs," in *Higher Brain Function: Recent Explorations of the Brain's Emergent Properties*, ed. S. P. Wise (New York: Wiley, 1987), 45–66. J. H. Abbs and K. J. Cole, "Neural mechanisms of motor equivalence and goal achievement," ibid., 25–43, makes the tie to potential speech mechanisms. J. C. Fentress, "Hierarchical motor control," in *Psychobiology of Language*, ed. M. Studdert-Kennedy (Cambridge: MIT Press, 1983), 40–61, gives a good account related to mouse grooming.

I use this example of temporal cortical circuits to emphasize that short-term memory for succession of sounds (presumably involving hippocampal loops) already must be a major evolutionary achievement, particularly in nocturnal animals.

20. See note 16 above.

Chapter 9. A Model of Primary Consciousness

1. As I stressed in *Neural Darwinism*, this linkage and matching is essential for learning in which global mappings linked to hedonic systems are crucial elements.

2. I consider the possible anatomical loci for these circuits later. A differentiation of different memory states and consciousness is made by E. Tulving, "Multiple memory systems and consciousness," *Hum. Neurobiol.* 6 (1987): 67–80.

3. See, for example, Lycan, *Consciousness*, and D. C. Dennett, *Brainstorms* (Montgomery, Vt.: Bradford Books, 1978).

4. It is important to note that this model is dynamic, because it is driven by global mappings and conceptual activity, and that it depends critically upon the recursive properties of reentry. Obviously, this implies that the nature of self is constantly being transformed.

5. This, it must be remarked again, refers to biological individuality, not personhood. See chapter 5, note 5.

6. See Staddon, *Adaptive Behavior and Learning;* R. A. Rescorla, "Pavlovian excitability and inhibitory conditioning," in *Handbook of Learning and Cognitive Processes: Conditioning and Behavior Theory,* vol. 2, ed. W. K. Estes (Hillsdale, N.J.: Lawrence Erlbaum Associates, 1976), 7–35. R. A. Rescorla, "Behavioral studies of Pavlovian conditioning," *Annu. Rev. Neurosci.* 11 (1988): 329–52; R. A. Rescorla and R. A. Wagner, "A theory of Pavlovian conditioning: Variations in the effectiveness of reinforcement and nonreinforcement," in *Classical Conditioning II,* ed. A. Black and W. R. Prokasy (New York: Appleton-Century-Crofts, 1972), 64–99; A. Dickenson, *Contemporary Animal Learning Theory* (Cambridge, Eng.: Cambridge Univ. Press, 1980).

7. This refers to various proprioceptive and kinesthetic aspects.

8. See P. Marler and H. S. Terrace, eds., *The Biology of Learning* (Berlin: Springer-Verlag, 1984).

9. A striking example relates to sexually dimorphic behavior. See D. B. Kelley, "Sexually dimorphic behaviors," *Annu. Rev. Neurosci.* 11 (1988): 225–51.

10. J. M. Fuster, "The prefrontal cortex, mediator of cross-temporal contingencies," *Hum. Neurobiol.* 4 (1985): 169–79. See also J. M. Fuster, "The profrontal cortex and temporal integration," in *Cerebral Cortex: Association and Auditory Cortices,* vol. 4., ed. A. Peters and E. G. Jones (New York: Plenum, 1985): 151–77.

11. W. Walter, R. Cooper, V. Aldridge, W. McCallum, and A. Winter, "Contingent negative variation: An electric sign for sensory-motor association and expectancy in the human brain," *Nature* 203 (1964): 380–84.

12. See note 10 above.

13. D. H. Ingvar, "Memory of the future: An essay on the temporal organization of conscious awareness," *Hum. Neurobiol.* 4 (1985): 127–36.

14. P. E. Roland, "Cortical organization of voluntary behavior in man," *Hum. Neurobiol.* 4 (1985): 155–67.

15. For a good review of frontal lobe syndromes, see J. W. Brown, "Frontal lobe syndromes," in *Handbook of Clinical Neurology,* vol. 45, ed. P. J. Vinken, G. W. Bruyn, and H. Klawans (Amsterdam: North Holland, 1985), 23–41. See also E. Perecman, ed., *The Frontal Lobes Revisited* (New York: IRBN Press, 1987); D. T. Stuss and D. F. Benson, *The Frontal Lobes* (New York: Raven Press, 1986); P. S. Goldman-Rakic, "Topography of cognition: Parallel distributed networks in primate association cortex," *Annu. Rev. Neurosci.* 14 (1988): 137–56.

16. Some particularly useful summaries related to this task are M. Steriade and R. R. Llinás, "The functional states of the thalamus and the associated neuronal interplay," *Physiol. Rev.* 68 (1988): 649–742; J. A. Hobson and M. Steriade, "Neuronal basis of behavioral state control," in *Handbook of Physiology,* section 1, *The Nervous System,* vol. 4 (Bethesda, Md.: American Physiological Society, 1986), 701–823; Schmitt et al., eds., *Organization of the Cerebral Cortex;* Edelman et al., eds., *Dynamic Aspects of Neocortical Function.* I have already mentioned E. Perecman, ed., *Frontal Lobes Revisited,* and Goldman-Rakic, "Topography of cognition." The role of frontal and particularly prefrontal cortex in choice, inhibition, and delayed cognitive responses is well spelled out by A. Diamond, "Differences between adult and infant cognition: Is the

crucial variable presence or absence of language?" in Weiskrantz, ed., *Thought without Language*, 337–70. See also the discussion of the anatomy of the hippocampus and basal ganglia in chapter 7 and associated references.

17. Ibid.

18. See E. G. Jones, *The Thalamus* (New York: Plenum, 1985), and the review by Steriade and Llinás, "Functional states." The idea that disturbances of the various thalamic nuclei reentrantly connected to the cortex may underlie the losses seen in various neuropsychological disorders is consistent with the observations of Schacter et al., "Access to consciousness." See also Marcel, "Phenomenal experience."

19. Hobson and Steriade, "Neuronal basis of behavioral state control."

20. See note 18 above.

21. Schacter et al., "Access to consciousness."

22. See B. Libet, "Cortical activation in conscious and unconscious experience," *Perspect. Biol. Med.* 9 (1965): 77–86; B. Libet, "Neuronal versus subjective timing for a conscious sensory experience," in *Cerebral Correlation of Conscious Experience*, ed. P. A. Buser and A. Rougeul-Buser (Amsterdam and New York: North Holland, 1965), 69–82. If these figures are correct, the temporal delays in establishing the *very first* traces of primary consciousness in a developing animal may not be much longer than seconds.

23. The model is consistent with the interpretation that phenomenal experience is neither identical to nor a direct reflection of representations yielded by perceptual processes. See Marcel, "Conscious and unconscious perception." Perhaps the best presentation of various views on the issue of qualia and phenomenal states as contrasted with functionalism is Marcel and Bisiach, eds., *Consciousness in Contemporary Science*. Marcel's article in that book, entitled "Phenomenal experience and functionalism," makes a cogent case for treating such experience as a central psychological fact. I shall eschew here any extended discussion of arguments made by phenomenologists as well as any detailed consideration of the problem of qualia. The interested reader may consult P. Tibbets, ed., *Perception: Selected Readings in Science and Phenomenology* (New York: Times Books, 1969), esp. pt. 3; C. V. Borst, *The Mind-Brain Identity Theory* (London: Macmillan, 1970); H. Feigl, M. Scriven, and G. Maxwell, eds., *Concepts, Theories, and the Mind-Body Problem*, Minnesota Studies in the Philosophy of Science, vol. 2 (Minneapolis: Univ. of Minnesota Press, 1958); J. J. C. Smart, *Philosophy and Scientific Realism* (London: Routledge and Kegan Paul, 1963); S. Hook, ed., *Dimensions of Mind* (New York: New York Univ. Press, 1960). See also M. Bunge, *The Mind-Body Problem: A Psychobiological Approach* (Oxford: Pergamon, 1980). The subject of bodily sensations is well treated by D. M. Armstrong, *A Materialist Theory of the Mind* (New York: Humanities, 1968). A lively discussion of qualia may be found in Lycan, *Consciousness*. For a discussion of the subjective and objective (much scorned by Lycan), see T. Nagel, "What is it like to be a bat?" *Philos. Rev.* 83 (1974): 435–50.

24. See note 2 above.

25. See Lycan, *Consciousness*. The position taken in the present book is not a denial of qualia, however, and is more or less in accord with that of A. J. Marcel, "Phenomenal experience and functionalism." For a total denial of qualia, see Dennett, "Quining qualia."

26. James, *The Principles of Psychology*, vol. 1, 196–98.

27. See notes 18 and 23 above.

28. One such gedankenexperiment is the mediation paradigm between two automata given below; obviously, these are not animals.

29. See J. P. Zubec, *Sensory Deprivation;* Reed, "Sensory deprivation"; and W. Heron, "The pathology of boredom," *Sci. Am.* 196, no. 1 (1957): 52–56.

30. For various accounts, see A. Borbély, *Secrets of Sleep* (New York: Basic Books, 1986); J. A. Hobson, *The Dreaming Brain* (New York: Basic Books, 1988); and the review by Hobson and Steriade, "Neuronal basis of behavioral state control."

31. Note that this is not a notion of exhaustion and replenishment. Rather, it has to do with varying the matching of states of cells with different functions.

32. This position was actually extended to verbal animals by B. F. Skinner, *Verbal Behavior* (Englewood Cliffs, N.J.: Prentice-Hall, 1957).

33. See note 23 above.

34. The gedankenexperiment is not similar to experiments on infant imitation and memory in which the infant sees the adult performing the task *and* the task. See A. N. Meltzoff, "Infant imitation and memory: Nine-month-olds in immediate and deferred tests," *Child Dev.* 59 (1988): 217–25, for a nice example. Nevertheless, the performance of nine-month-old infants is impressive. Some imitation, such as contagious yawning, is likely to be pseudoimitative, possibly the result of ethological fixed action patterns. See R. R. Provine, "Contagious yawning and infant imitation," *Bull. Psychon. Soc.* 27 (1989): 125–26. This is why the gedankenexperiment insists on *novelty*.

35. E. H. Lenneberg, "Of language, knowledge, apes, and brains," *J. Psycholinguist. Res.* 1 (1971): 1–29. Crude as it is, the automaton gedankenexperiment of mediated performance would be enormously difficult to arrange. Difficult or not, it would be even more persuasive if A_2 were prevented from its activity and then threw a tantrum! See D. C. Dennett, *The Intentional Stance* (Cambridge: MIT Press, 1987), for more fantasy. Possibly pertinent are studies of joint reference or "deictic gaze" in which infants became increasingly adept at turning and fixating visual targets to which their mothers gaze or point (or both). See G. Butterworth and L. Grover, "The origins of referential communication in human infancy," in Weiskrantz, ed., *Thought without Language*, 5–24.

36. Premack and Premack, *Mind of an Ape;* D. Premack and G. Woodruff, "Does the chimpanzee have a theory of mind?" *Behav. Brain Sci.* 4 (1978): 515–26; Premack, "Minds with and without language."

37. G. Gottlieb, "Comparative psychology and ethology," in *The First Century of Experimental Psychology*, ed. E. Hearst (Hillsdale, N.J.: Lawrence Erlbaum Associates, 1979), 147–73.

38. See notes 16, 18, and 23 above.

Chapter 10. Language

1. The literature on these important subjects is vast. For a general introduction, see V. Fromkin and R. Rodman, *An Introduction to Language*, 4th ed.

(New York: Holt, Rinehart & Winston, 1974); A. Akmajian, R. Demers, and R. M. Harnish, *Linguistics,* 2d ed. (Cambridge: MIT Press, 1984). For an early survey of the biological aspects, see E. H. Lenneberg, *Biological Foundations of Language* (New York: Wiley, 1967).

2. See N. Chomsky, *Cartesian Linguistics* (New York: Harper & Row, 1966); N. Chomsky, *Language and Mind* (New York: Harcourt Brace World, 1972); N. Chomsky, *Rules and Representations* (New York: Columbia Univ. Press, 1980); N. Chomsky, *Knowledge and Language: Its Nature, Origin, and Use* (New York: Praeger, 1986).

3. See Edelman, *Neural Darwinism,* chap. 8. For an extended and varied discussion of evidence that concepts and thinking can occur prior to and independently of language, see Weiskrantz, ed., *Thought without Language.* See particularly the articles by E. Spelke and L. Cohen concerning early concepts in young infants. The articles in that volume by Kertesz, "Cognitive function in severe aphasia," and by Bisiach, "Language without thought," provide an extreme position on this issue. For a discussion of neotenic learning, which may have a bearing upon language acquisition, see Edelman, *Neural Darwinism,* chap. 11.

4. Lieberman, *Biology and Evolution of Language.*

5. I. G. Mattingly and A. M. Liberman, "Specialized perceiving systems for speech and other biologically significant sounds," in *Auditory Function: Neurobiological Bases of Hearing,* ed. G. M. Edelman, W. E. Gall, and W. M. Cowan (New York: Wiley, 1988), 775–93. The connection of these comments on reentry and coarticulation to such speech dysfunctions as stuttering is obvious.

6. Lieberman, *Biology and Evolution of Language.*

7. Bresnan, ed., *Mental Representation of Grammatical Relations.* See especially S. Pinker, "A theory of the acquisition of lexical interpretive grammars," ibid., 655–726, for a discussion of semantic bootstrapping. A small review of phonological and semantic behaviors in infancy and early childhood may be found in P. Mounoud, "The ontogenesis of different types of thought: Language and motor behaviors as nonspecific manifestations," in Weiskrantz, ed., *Thought without Language,* 25–45.

8. See note 3 above.

9. Pinker, *Language Learnability and Language Development* (see his notes, chap. 2).

10. R. Brown, *A First Language: The Early Stages* (Cambridge: Harvard Univ. Press, 1973). See also J. Macnamara, *Names for Things: A Study of Human Learning* (Cambridge: MIT Press, 1982), and J. G. de Villiers and P. A. de Villiers, *Language Acquisition* (Cambridge: Harvard Univ. Press, 1978).

11. Lieberman, *Biology and Evolution of Language.*

12. See Neisser, *Concepts and Conceptual Development.*

13. Jackendoff, *Consciousness,* has a clear discussion of such levels (although his theories bear no resemblance to those proposed here). See also R. Jackendoff, *Semantics and Cognition* (Cambridge: MIT Press, 1985).

14. See notes 7 and 9 above.

15. This position (following Chomsky) is revealed in D. Lightfoot, *The Language Lottery: Toward a Biology of Grammars* (Cambridge: MIT Press, 1982),

in the works of Jackendoff cited in note 13 above, and in N. Hornstein, *Logic as Grammar* (Cambridge: MIT Press, 1984). For an extreme Platonic realist view, see J. J. Katz, *Language and Other Abstract Objects* (Totowa, N.J.: Rowman and Littlefield, 1981).

16. See note 13 above.

17. Finkel and Edelman, "Integration of distributed cortical systems by reentry." Chapter 4 of the present book contains a synopsis. But note that only after such mappings are linked to systems for primary consciousness can one expect to see correlation leading to an "image."

18. Lieberman, *Biology and Evolution of Language.*

19. Premack and Premack, *Mind of an Ape;* Premack, "Minds with and without language."

20. See note 7 above.

21. See note 5 above.

22. See note 3 above.

23. See Lenneberg, *Biological Foundations.*

24. For a discussion of related matters and other views and models, see M. Studdert-Kennedy, ed., *Psychobiology of Language* (Cambridge: MIT Press, 1983), and M. A. Arbib, D. Caplan, and J. C. Marshall, *Neural Models of Language Processes* (New York: Academic, 1982). For an excellent account of signing, see E. Klima and U. Bellugi, *The Signs of Language* (Cambridge: Harvard Univ. Press, 1978).

25. H. Keller, *The Story of My Life* (New York: Doubleday, 1902).

26. See note 10 above.

27. See note 3 above. Neotenic learning is discussed in chapter 11 of *Neural Darwinism.*

28. See notes 2 and 15 above.

29. See note 7 above.

30. Lieberman, *Biology and Evolution of Language.*

31. Mattingly and Liberman, "Specialized perceiving systems for speech."

32. J. Bresnan and R. M. Kaplan, "Introduction: Grammars as mental representations of language," in Bresnan, ed., *Mental Representation of Grammatical Relations,* xvi–lii.

33. See notes 2 and 15 above.

34. Bresnan and Kaplan, "Introduction."

35. Edelman, *Neural Darwinism,* chap. 9. See also chapter 5 of the present work.

36. Bresnan, ed., *Mental Representation of Grammatical Relations;* Bresnan and Kaplan, "Introduction."

37. Ibid.

38. See notes 2 and 15 above.

39. See Lieberman, *Biology and Evolution of Language.*

40. See notes 2 and 15 above.

41. Pinker, *Language Learnability and Language Development,* 371 n. 11.

42. This problem of constraints is treated extensively in Edelman, *Topobiology,* and also in *Neural Darwinism.*

43. See Neisser, ed., *Concepts and Conceptual Development,* and J. R. Searle, *Speech Acts: An Essay in the Philosophy of Language* (Cambridge, Eng.: Cam-

bridge Univ. Press, 1969). The development of such models relates to problems of meaning and reference described by Quine; see his *Roots of Reference* and *Ontological Relativity.* The position taken in the present theory is consistent with the relativity of meaning and reference that Quine has persuasively demonstrated. But it goes well beyond the starting position of philosophical behaviorism. For an extreme behaviorist view with which I have no sympathy, see Skinner, *Verbal Behavior.* For discussions of concepts of self and personhood, see the references cited in note 21 of chapter 5, and in notes 3 and 5 of chapter 11. Mahler et al., *Psychological Birth of the Human Infant,* provides a psychoanalytic viewpoint.

Chapter 11. Higher-Order Consciousness

1. This notion, of course, relates to an individual. For discussion of the collective and social development of chronologies, see D. J. Wilcox, *The Measure of Times Past: Pre-Newtonian Chronologies and the Rhetoric of Relative Time* (Chicago: Univ. of Chicago Press, 1987); G. J. Whitrow, *Time in History: The Evolution of Our General Awareness of Time and Temporal Perspective* (Oxford: Oxford Univ. Press, 1988); and J. T. Fraser, *Time: The Familiar Stranger* (Amherst: Univ. of Massachusetts Press, 1987). For some views on individual development, see W. J. Friedman, ed., *The Developmental Psychology of Time* (New York: Academic, 1982). For a philosophical analysis, see L. Sklar, *Philosophy and Spacetime Physics* (Berkeley: Univ. of California Press, 1985).

2. Natsoulas, "Consciousness"; Natsoulas, "Toward a model of consciousness."

3. Lewis and Brooks-Gunn, *Social Cognition.* See also chapter 5, note 21.

4. For an account that stresses the role of grooming in various bonding relations in primates, see P. C. Reynolds, *On the Evolution of Human Behavior* (Los Angeles: Univ. of California Press, 1981). For recent studies of infant imitation, see Meltzoff, "Infant imitation and memory."

5. See Ristau and Robbins, "Language of the great apes," and Premack, "Minds with and without language." See also Reynolds, *On the Evolution of Human Behavior;* G. G. Gallup, Jr., "Towards an operational definition of self-awareness," in *Socioecology and Psychology of Primates,* ed. R. H. Tuttle and G. G. Gallup, Jr. (The Hague: Mouton, 1975), 309–41; and Gallup, Jr., "Self-recognition in primates." For a general discussion of conceptual categories as models, see Neisser, ed., *Concepts and Conceptual Development.*

6. See Diamond, "Differences between adult and infant cognition."

7. Lieberman, *Biology and Evolution of Language.*

8. See note 5 above.

9. Diamond, "Differences between adult and infant cognition."

10. P. C. Reynolds makes the case for the strong affective relation in such transmission in *On the Evolution of Human Behavior.* He bases his case on the interaction between affective and instrumental responses in a social scene. He argues for a progressive evolution of mechanisms involved in affective instrumental integration. These give rise to "qualitatively different forms of social coordination" that are nevertheless implemented by affective mechanisms for public display, by internal state, and by motivation of socially directed behavior.

He extends this idea to human language, which he views as a further form of affective-instrumental integration involving the conjunction of vocal effectors and concepts.

This view is consistent with the fundamental relation between affective-hedonic centers and conscious states proposed here. Consciousness in higher forms requires "a delicate responsiveness to the needs and intentions of others" in a social context.

See also E. S. Savage-Rumbaugh, B. J. Wilkerson, and R. Bakerman, "Spontaneous gestural communication among conspecifics in the pygmy chimpanzee *(Pan paniscus)*," in *Progress in Ape Research,* ed. G. H. Bourne (New York: Academic, 1977), 97–116.

11. This argument was pursued in chapters 8 and 10. For a strong position on the social bases of language development, see L. S. Vygotsky, *Thought and Language* (Cambridge: MIT Press, 1962).

12. See note 10 above.

13. See C. F. Hockett, *A Course in Modern Linguistics* (New York: Macmillan, 1958); C. F. Hockett and S. A. Altmann, "A note on design features," in *Animal Communication: Techniques of Study and Results of Research,* ed. T. A. Sebeok (Bloomington: Indiana Univ. Press, 1968), 61–72; C. F. Hockett, "The origin of speech" *Sci. Am.* 203, no. 3 (1960): 88–111; C. F. Hockett and R. Ascher, "The human revolution," *Current Anthropology* 5 (1964): 135–68.

14. Ibid. See also Lieberman, *Biology and Evolution of Language.*

15. See Searle, *Intentionality;* and also Dennett, *Intentional Stance.*

16. See note 10 above.

17. See chapter 10.

18. See Chomsky, *Knowledge and Language,* and associated references in notes 2 and 15 of chapter 10.

19. Edelman, *Topobiology.*

20. See A. Caramazza, "Some aspects of language processing revealed through the analysis of acquired aphasia: The lexical system," *Annu. Rev. Neurosci.* 11 (1988): 395–421, for a review of "cognitive" approaches to this subject as contrasted with more classical neuropsychological approaches.

21. Diamond, "Differences between adult and infant cognition," and Lieberman, *Biology and Evolution.*

22. Edelman, *Neural Darwinism.*

23. See, for example, J. H. Crook, *The Evolution of Human Consciousness* (Oxford: Clarendon, 1980); R. W. Coan, *Human Consciousness and Its Evolution: A Multidimensional View* (Westport, Conn.: Greenwood Press, 1987); Granit, *The Purposive Brain;* and, of course, James, *The Principles of Psychology.* See Marcel and Bisiach, eds., *Consciousness and Contemporary Science,* for discussions of the usefulness of phenomenal awareness in the individual animal.

24. See note 10 above.

Chapter 12. The Conscious and the Unconscious

1. The recognition of this need underlies my connected efforts in *Topobiology, Neural Darwinism,* and the present work.

2. Edelman, *Neural Darwinism.*

3. See Neisser, ed., *Concepts and Conceptual Development.*

4. Natsoulas, "Consciousness."

5. In Armstrong and Malcolm, *Consciousness and Causality.* This heterogeneity and the fact that consciousness is not simply a mirror of the world are discussed in G. Mandler, *Mind and Body: Psychology of Emotion and Stress* (New York: Norton, 1984). See also Marcel, *Cognitive Psychology,* and the items by M. Gazzaniga listed in the bibliography.

6. For a summary and analysis of the so-called imagery debate, see N. Block, ed., *Imagery* (Cambridge: MIT Press, 1981); Pylyshyn, *Computation and Cognition;* and S. M. Kosslyn, *Image and Mind* (Cambridge: Harvard Univ. Press, 1980). See also R. N. Shepard and L. A. Cooper, *Mental Images and Their Transformations* (Cambridge: MIT Press, 1982). For work on animals, see Georgopoulos et al., "Mental rotation of the neuronal population vector." See Farah, "Is visual imagery really visual?" for neuropsychological evidence, and Haenny et al., "State dependent activity in monkey," for physiological evidence in animals. A review of task performance using measurement of regional cortical blood flow and metabolism may be found in Roland, "Cortical organization of voluntary behavior in man."

7. Ibid.

8. Johnson, *Body in the Mind.* Oldfield and Zangwill, in *Brit. J. Psychol.* in 1942 and 1943, reviewed Head's work. See also Spelke, "Origins of physical knowledge."

9. James, *The Principles of Psychology,* vol. 1, 403.

10. D. Broadbent, *Perception and Communication* (London: Pergamon, 1958). See also M. I. Posner, 1980. "Mental chronometry and the problem of consciousness," in Jusczyk and Klein, eds., *Nature of Thought,* 95–115.

11. See A. H. C. Van der Heiden, "Central selection in vision," in *Perspectives on Perception and Action,* ed. H. Heuer and A. F. Sanders (Hillsdale, N.J.: Lawrence Erlbaum Associates, 1987), 421–26. A typical early, limited-capacity theory is in Broadbent, *Perception and Communication.* For a late, unlimited-capacity theory, see J. A. Deutsch and R. Deutsch, "Attention: Some theoretical considerations," *Psychol. Rev.* 70 (1963): 80–90.

12. See, for example, O. Neumann, "Beyond capacity: A functional view of attention," in Heuer and Sanders, eds., *Perspectives on Perception and Action,* 361–94, and A. Allport, "Selection for action: Some behavioral and neurophysiological considerations of attention and action," ibid., 395–419.

13. Allport, "Selection for action."

14. Neumann, "Beyond capacity."

15. A. M. Treisman, "Contextual cues in selective listening," *Q. J. Exp. Psychol.* 12 (1960): 242–48. For her latest work, see A. M. Treisman and G. Gedale, "A feature integration theory of attention," *Cognit. Psychol.* 12 (1980): 97–136. For a general review, see Underwood, "Attention and awareness in cognitive and motor skills."

16. See F. H. C. Crick, "Function of the thalamic reticular complex: The searchlight hypothesis," *Proc. Natl. Acad. Sci. USA* 81 (1984): 4586–90.

17. See D. Kahneman and A. M. Treisman, "Changing views of automaticity," in *Varieties of Attention,* ed. R. Parasuraman and D. R. Davies (New York:

Academic, 1984). For preattentive processes, see B. Julesz, "Toward an axiomatic theory of preattentive vision," in Edelman et al., eds., *Dynamic Aspects of Neocortical Function,* 585–612.

18. See note 12 above.

19. E. R. Hilgard, *Divided Consciousness: Multiple Controls in Human Thought and Action* (New York: Wiley, 1977).

20. J. B. Penney, Jr., and A. B. Young, "Speculations on the functional anatomy of basal ganglia disorders," *Annu. Rev. Neurosci.* 6 (1983): 73–94.

21. Edelman, *Neural Darwinism.* See also Staddon, *Adaptive Behavior.*

22. See J. Reason, 1979. "Actions not as planned: The price of automatization," in Underwood and Stevens, eds., *Aspects of Consciousness,* vol. 1, *Psychological Issues,* 67–89.

23. See Searle, *Intentionality,* and Dennett, *Intentional Stance.*

24. See M. H. Erdelyi, "Hypermnesia and insight," in Marcel and Bisiach, eds., *Consciousness in Contemporary Science,* 200–217, and M. H. Erdelyi, *Psychoanalysis: Freud's Cognitive Psychology* (New York: Freeman, 1985), for a discussion of the difficulties of defining the unconscious. For an extended analysis of dissociative states, see Hilgard, *Divided Consciousness.* For a different categorization, see E. Pöppel, *Mindworks: Time and Conscious Experience* (Boston: Harcourt Brace Jovanovich, 1985). A useful set of reviews may be found in two critical collections: K. S. Bowers and D. Meichenbaum, eds., *The Unconscious Reconsidered* (New York: Wiley, 1984), and Horowitz, ed., *Psychodynamics and Cognition.* As is noted in the text, Freud also referred to the "preconscious," a term that applies to ideas that are descriptively unconscious but can become conscious at any time.

25. I mentioned, in chapters 2 and 10, a variety of neuropsychological disorders that cause selective, domain-specific irreversible losses to consciousness. See Schacter et al., "Access to consciousness," and also chapter 13.

26. Edelman, *Neural Darwinism.*

27. See Gregory, *Mind in Science,* for a discussion of this idea of H. von Helmholtz. See also Helmholtz's own *Treatise on Physiological Optics.*

28. Neisser, ed., *Concepts and Conceptual Development,* chap. 7.

29. See note 6 above.

30. See Staddon, *Adaptive Behavior and Learning,* on surprise in learning. See also Treisman and Gelade, "Feature-integration theory of attention."

31. See U. Neisser, *Cognitive Psychology* (New York: Appleton-Century-Crofts, 1967).

32. See figure 9.3. See also Schacter et al., "Access to consciousness," and Marcel, "Conscious and unconscious perception."

33. See Sulloway, *Freud;* R. Wollheim, ed., *Freud: A Collection of Critical Essays* (Garden City, N.Y.: Anchor Books, 1974); Freud, *Project for a Scientific Psychology.* A good general account is Erdelyi, *Psychoanalysis.* See also I. Rosenfield, *The Invention of Memory: A New View of the Brain* (New York: Basic Books, 1988).

34. B. A. Farrell, *The Standing of Psychoanalysis* (Oxford: Oxford Univ. Press, 1981); S. Fisher and R. P. Greenberg, *The Scientific Credibility of Freud's Theories and Therapy* (New York: Basic Books, 1977). See also Wollheim, *Freud;* A. Grünbaum, "Epistemological liabilities of the clinical appraisal of psychoana-

lytic theory," *Nous* 14 (1980): 307–85; A. Grünbaum, "Is Freudian psychoanalytic theory pseudoscientific by Karl Popper's criterion of demarcation?" *Am. Philos. Q.* 16 (1979): 131–44; B. Von Eckhardt, "The scientific status of psychoanalysis," in *Introducing Psychoanalytic Theory,* ed. S. Gilman (New York: Bruner/Mazel, 1983). An amusing idea, which I shall not pursue here, is that conversion symptoms relate to conceptual distortions and inappropriate use of global mappings in a "metaphorical" sense as image schemata. See Johnson, *Body in the Mind,* for a discussion of the latter.

35. S. Freud, *On Dreams,* ed. J. Strachey (reprint; New York: Norton, 1963); S. Freud, *Introductory Lectures on Psychoanalysis* (New York: Liveright, 1919); S. Freud, *New Introductory Lectures on Psychoanalysis* (New York: Norton, 1933). Modern cognitivist revisions (see, for example, J. F. Kihlstrom, "The cognitive unconscious," *Science* 237 [1987]: 1445–52) do not appear to constitute a significant advance.

36. See note 24 above.

37. Ibid.

38. Ibid.

39. See note 35 above.

40. See notes 33 and 35 above.

41. But see Hilgard, *Divided Consciousness.* See also O. J. Flanagan, Jr., *The Science of the Mind* (Cambridge: MIT Press, 1984). See also Dennett, *Intentional Stance,* for a discussion of some of these issues.

42. Gazzaniga, *Bisected Brain.* See also D. MacKay, "Divided brains–divided minds," in *Mindwaves,* ed. C. Blakemore and S. Greenfield (Oxford: Blackwell, 1987), 5–16. None of the present views are in accord with the position taken by J. Jaynes in *The Origin of Consciousness in the Breakdown of the Bicameral Mind* (Boston: Houghton Mifflin, 1976).

43. See notes 33 and 34 above.

44. Hobson, *Dreaming Brain.* See also works on sleep referred to in chapter 5, particularly Borbély, *Secrets of Sleep.*

45. Ibid.

46. See note 33 above.

47. See note 41 above, particularly Flanagan, Jr., *The Science of the Mind.*

48. Ibid. See also R. Cummens, *The Nature of Psychological Explanation* (Cambridge: MIT Press, 1983). The fiercest linguistic analysis of mentalistic usage from a behaviorist viewpoint is G. Ryle, *The Concept of Mind* (Chicago: Univ. of Chicago Press, 1949).

49. Flanagan, *Science of the Mind.*

50. W. V. Quine, *Quiddities: An Intermittently Philosophical Dictionary* (Cambridge: Harvard Univ. Press/Belknap Press, 1987), entry on "mind versus body," 133; Quine, *Roots of Reference.* See also Putnam, *Representation and Reality.* Quine's and Putnam's positions on meaning holism and the relativity of discourse can be related to the context dependence and relativity of dissociative states. See Erdelyi, *Psychoanalysis,* and Hilgard, *Divided Consciousness.*

51. See Putnam, *Representation and Reality,* and Dennett, *Intentional Stance.* The latter's notion that intentionality is simply a pragmatically valuable *posture* is at odds with the position taken in this book.

52. See notes 23 and 50 above.

53. I have deliberately avoided explicit discussion of classical disputes and categorizations related to the mind-brain problem and its surrounding philosophical hypotheses. The reader who wishes a view of the problems may consult the references in the notes to chapter 9, particularly note 23. Two clear expositions, one a good catalog and the other a good analysis, are P. M. Churchland, *Matter and Consciousness* (Cambridge: MIT Press, 1984), and Searle, *Minds, Brains, and Science.* The limitations of such hypotheses for constructing scientific theories of consciousness are well discussed by Gray, "The mind-brain identity theory."

54. A good analysis may be found in Marcel, *Phenomenal Experience and Functionalism.*

Chapter 13. Diseases of Consciousness

1. For a general survey, see Stevens, ed., *Aspects of Consciousness,* vol. 4, *Clinical Issues.* For an extensive textbook consideration of various neuropsychiatric disorders, see H. I. Kaplan and B. J. Sadock, *Comprehensive Textbook of Psychiatry/IV,* vols. 1 and 2 (Baltimore: Williams and Wilkins, 1985).

2. Ibid.

3. The ordering of this discussion is based on P. Eames and R. LL. Wood, "Consciousness in the brain-damaged adult," in Stevens, ed., *Aspects of Consciousness,* vol. 4, *Clinical Issues,* 1–39.

4. See Squire and Butters, *Neuropsychology of Memory,* for an extended account.

5. A satisfactory analysis of aphasia from the point of view taken in this book would require writing another book. But I am tempted to say here that the consideration of language centers as "reentrant secretaries" for conceptual areas provokes a new set of thoughts about the interpretation of these disorders.

6. Brown, "Frontal lobe syndromes."

7. Luria, *Higher Cortical Functions in Man.* See also A. R. Luria, *The Working Brain: An Introduction to Neuropsychology* (New York: Basic Books, 1973). T. Shallice, *From Neuropsychology to Mental Structure,* (Cambridge, Eng.: Cambridge Univ. Press, 1988), gives a good account of the modern cognitivist approaches to neuropsychology.

8. See B. Milner and M. Petrides, "Behavioral effects of frontal-lobe lesions in man," *Trends Neurosci.* 7 (1984): 403–7, and B. Milner, M. Petrides, and M. L. Smith, "Frontal lobes and the temporal organization of memory," *Hum. Neurobiol.* 4 (1985): 137–42.

9. Freud, *Introductory Lectures on Psychoanalysis* and *New Introductory Lectures.* See Erdelyi, *Psychoanalysis,* and Flanagan, *Science of the Mind,* for evaluative reviews.

10. See Hilgard, *Divided Consciousness.*

11. P. D. Wall, " 'My foot hurts': The analysis of a sentence," in *Essays on the Nervous System,* ed. R. Bellairs and E. G. Gray (Oxford: Clarendon, 1974), 391–406.

12. See Schacter et al., "Access to consciousness."

13. For a brief overview, see Williams, *Brain Damage, Behavior, and the Mind.*

14. Ibid., and Schacter et al., "Access to consciousness."

15. See Gazzaniga, *Bisected Brain* and "Dynamics of cerebral specialization."

16. Wise and Rappaport, "Obsessive-compulsive disorder."

17. D. F. Klein, "Endogenomorphic depression: A conceptual and terminological division," *Arch. Gen. Psychiatry* 31 (1974): 442–54; D. F. Klein and J. M. Davis, *Diagnosis and Drug Treatment of Psychiatric Disorders* (Baltimore: Williams and Edwards, 1969).

18. B. J. Carroll, "Neurobiological dimensions of depression and mania," in *The Origins of Depression: Current Concepts and Approaches,* Dahlem Konferenzen, no. 26, ed. J. Angst (Berlin: Springer-Verlag, 1983), 163–86.

19. See notes 17 and 18 above.

20. Carroll, "Neurobiological dimensions of depression and mania."

21. See C. D. Frith, "Schizophrenia: An abnormality of consciousness?" in Underwood and Stevens, eds., *Aspects of Consciousness,* vol. 2, *Structural Issues,* 150–68, and M. P. I. Weller, "Some problems in the diagnosis of schizophrenia and the concept of clear consciousness," in Stevens, ed., *Aspects of Consciousness,* vol. 4, *Clinical Issues,* 117–65.

22. For a survey of the current status of schizophrenia, see H. Helmchen and F. A. Henn, eds., *Biological Perspectives of Schizophrenia,* Dahlem Konferenzen, no. 40 (New York: Wiley, 1987). Very detailed models based on the neuroanatomy and pharmacology of the striatopallidal and limbic loops have been proposed to account for the alterations in schizophrenia and depression. See, for an extended example, N. R. Swerdlow and G. F. Koob, "Dopamine, schizophrenia, mania, and depression: Toward a unified hypothesis of cortico-striato-pallido-thalamic function," *Behav. Brain Sci.* 10 (1987): 197–245.

23. World Health Organization, *Manual of the International Classification of Diseases,* 9th ed. (Geneva: World Health Organization, 1977).

24. American Psychiatric Association, *The Diagnostic and Statistical Manual of Mental Disorders,* 3d ed. (Washington, D.C.: American Psychiatric Association, 1987).

25. See note 22 above.

26. See note 21 above.

27. See note 22 above.

28. Ibid.

29. See Edelman, *Neural Darwinism,* chap. 7.

30. Ibid.

Chapter 14. Physics, Evolution, and Consciousness: A Summary

1. Armstrong, *Materialistic Theory of the Mind.*

2. It should perhaps also be added that because the theory of consciousness is based on the TNGS, it explicitly excludes information processing models as

a basis. We considered the issue in chapter 2. See Reeke, Jr., and Edelman, "Real brains," and Reeke, Jr., et al., "Synthetic neural modeling," for a discussion. For some theories of consciousness based on information processing models, see D. A. Oakley, *Brain and Mind* (London: Methuen, 1985); P. N. Johnson-Laird, *The Computer and the Mind* (Cambridge: Harvard Univ. Press, 1988); P. N. Johnson-Laird, *Mental Models: Towards a Cognitive Science of Language, Inference and Consciousness* (Cambridge: Harvard Univ. Press, 1983).

3. See Edelman, *Topobiology.*

4. See table 5.1. This adaptive response does not of course rule out the existence of so-called "closed" programs of behavior. See *Neural Darwinism,* chapter 11, and particularly E. Mayr, "Behavior programs and evolutionary strategies," *Am. Sci.* 62 (1974): 650–59.

5. See Johnson, *Body in the Mind.*

6. See the items by Quine in the bibliography.

7. See James, *The Principles of Psychology,* 152, and St. Augustine, *Confessions,* 267, and also note 6 to chapter 6.

8. Of course, I mean the Einsteinian revolution. See Fraser, *Time, the Familiar Stranger,* Wilcox, *Measure of Times Past,* and Whitrow, *Time in History,* for the cultural side. An excellent review of the cognitive aspects may be found in R. A. Block, "Time and consciousness," in Underwood and Stevens, eds., *Aspects of Consciousness,* vol. 1, *Psychological Issues,* 179–217. For a philosophical discussion of continuity in relation to the self, see M. Warnock, *Memory* (London: Faber and Faber, 1987). It is intriguing to note that L. E. J. Brouwer, the proponent of intuitionism in mathematics, has suggested that all mathematical elements arise from the contrast between current conscious experience and the direct awareness of past experience, what he calls "two-icity." See his "Consciousness, philosophy, and mathematics," in *Proceedings of the Tenth International Congress of Philosophy,* vol. 2, ed. E. W. Beth, H. J. Pos, and J. H. A. Hollak (Amsterdam: North Holland, 1949), 1235–49.

9. See Reeke, Jr., and Edelman, "Real brains." The best contrast is in Johnson-Laird, *Computer and the Mind* and *Mental Models.*

10. Putnam, *Representation and Reality.* See Reeke, Jr., and Edelman, "Real brains," for a discussion of the comparison with Turing machines.

11. For an account of induction in humans based on the information processing view, see Holland et al., *Induction.* See also R. Nisbett and L. Ross, *Human Inference: Strategies and Shortcomings of Social Judgment* (Englewood Cliffs, N.J.: Prentice-Hall, 1980). See also Margolis, *Patterns, Thinking, and Cognition.*

12. See the items by Quine in the bibliography.

13. For an attack on Quine's position on ontological relativity, see Searle, *Philosophy.*

Chapter 15. Philosophical Issues: Qualified Realism

1. See McGinn, *Character of Mind;* Searle, *Minds, Brains, and Science;* Churchland, *Matter and Consciousness;* and W. Bechtel, *Philosophy of Mind.*

2. McGinn, *Character of Mind,* 126.

3. For newcomers, Russell's *Problems of Philosophy* offers a gentle and short ride.

4. By physics, I mean quantum field theory, statistical thermodynamics, and their extensions. By evolutionary theory, I mean the modern synthesis—see E. Mayr, *The Growth of Biological Thought: Diversity, Evolution, and Inheritance* (Cambridge: Harvard Univ. Press, 1982). The comments relate to the physics assumption and the evolutionary assumption that I adopted in chapter 3.

5. Edelman, *Topobiology* and *Neural Darwinism.*

6. This does not imply that one must necessarily abjure cognitive models, only that too much must not be claimed for them. See the notes on psychological language, in chapter 12.

7. See I. B. Cohen, *Revolution in Science* (Cambridge: Harvard Univ. Press, 1985), and T. S. Kuhn, *The Essential Tension: Selected Studies in Scientific Tradition and Change* (Chicago: Univ. of Chicago Press, 1977).

8. See, for example, H. Margenau, *The Miracle of Existence* (Boston: Shambaylaya Publications, 1987), and E. P. Wigner, "Remarks on the mind-body problem," in *The Scientist Speculates,* ed. I. J. Good (London: Heinemann, 1979), 284–302.

9. See, for example, Quine, *Roots of Reference,* and his other works listed in the bibliography.

10. Edelman, *Neural Darwinism.*

11. Dennett, *Intentional Stance.*

12. See Johnson-Laird, *Computer and the Mind.* See also Bechtel, *Philosophy of Mind,* for a review of the various forms of functionalism.

13. See Reeke, Jr., and Edelman, "Real brains."

14. See note 9 above.

15. See Reeke, Jr., and Edelman, "Real brains."

16. But for various points of view, see Lycan, *Consciousness;* Putnam, *Representations and Reality;* and also Bechtel, *Philosophy of Mind.* T. Honderich, *A Theory of Determinism* (Oxford: Clarendon, 1988), gives a short, critical analysis of functionalism as well as a view of other such theories of consciousness.

17. I hope that my use of the same term "self-nonself," first for biological individuality and then for evolving personhood, has not beclouded the issue. See also Strawson, *Individuals,* and the works cited in note 21, chapter 5.

18. Searle, *Minds, Brains, and Science.* See also Hebb, *Essay on Mind,* and D. T. Campbell, "Evolutionary epistemology," in *The Philosophy of Karl Popper,* ed. P. A. Schlepp (La Salle: Open Court, 1966). Honderich, *Theory of Determinism,* gives a remorselessly determinist view but does not take into account the unpredictabilities introduced by selective systems.

19. M. Polanyi and H. Prosch, *Meaning* (Chicago: Univ. of Chicago Press, 1975). See also W. C. Wimsatt, "Reductionism, levels of organization, and the mind-body problem," in Globus, Maxwell, and Savodnik, eds., *Consciousness and the Brain,* 205–67.

20. Honderich, *Theory of Determinism.*

21. See note 9 above.

22. Ayer, *Philosophy in the Twentieth Century.*

23. Edelman, *Topobiology.*

24. Reynolds, *On the Evolution of Human Behavior.* See also R. Boyd and P. J. Richerson, *Culture and the Evolutionary Process* (Chicago: Univ. of Chicago Press, 1985).

25. For a philosophical view, see D. Lewis, *Convention: A Philosophical Study* (Cambridge: Harvard Univ. Press, 1969).

26. See notes 4 and 7 above.

27. Ayer, *Philosophy in the Twentieth Century.*

28. Ibid.

29. Ibid.

30. Schrödinger, *Mind and Matter.* Of course, when I refer to the modern scientist as materialist, the term is contrastive and refers to the subtle but important variations imposed by modern field theories and relativity on science as concerned with the observer's description of nature. Such subtle materialism must take account of the alterations of our view of cause imposed by quantum theory. At this level, metaphysics and epistemology can hardly be distinguished from one another.

31. G. E. Moore, *Some Main Problems of Philosophy* (New York: Macmillan, 1953).

32. Sellars, *Science, Perception, and Reality.* See also C. McGinn, *The Subjective View: Secondary Qualities and Indexical Thoughts* (Oxford: Oxford Univ. Press, 1983), for a discussion of "secondary qualities" and of the manifest and scientific images.

33. A. J. Ayer, *The Problem of Knowledge* (Middlesex, N.J.: Penguin Books, 1956).

34. For a heated attack on meaning rationalism, see Millikan, *Language, Thought, and Other Biological Categories.*

35. Ibid.

36. Neisser, *Concepts and Conceptual Development.*

37. Johnson, *Body in the Mind.*

38. For the different views, see Fodor, *Psychosemantics;* Jusczyk and Earhard, "Lingua mentis"; Dennett, *Intentional Stance.* Putnam, *Representations and Reality,* also casts doubts on a lingua mentis.

39. Bresnan, ed., *Mental Representation of Grammatical Relations.*

40. See the works of Chomsky listed in the bibliography.

41. J. Monod, *Chance and Necessity* (New York: Alfred Knopf, 1971).

42. See, for example, Delbrück, *Mind from Matter.*

43. Kanizsa, *Organization in Vision.*

44. See the references related to the subject of personhood, in the notes to chapter 13. See also note 21, chapter 5.

45. A moving analysis of the emergence of the recognition of mortality is given by S. K. Langer, "Dream's ending: The tragic vision," in *Mind: An Essay on Human Feeling,* vol. 3 (Baltimore: Johns Hopkins Press, 1967), chap. 21.

46. Ibid.

Epilogue

1. James, *Psychology: Briefer Course,* 468.

BIBLIOGRAPHY

Abbs, J. H., and K. J. Cole. "Neural mechanisms of motor equivalence and goal achievement." In *Higher Brain Function: Recent Explorations of the Brain's Emergent Properties*, ed. S. P. Wise, 25–43. New York: Wiley, 1987.

Akhundov, M. D. *Conceptions of Space and Time: Sources, Evolution, Directions*. Cambridge: MIT Press, 1986.

Akmajian, A., R. Demers, and M. P. Harnish. *Linguistics*, 2d ed. Cambridge: MIT Press, 1984.

Albus, J. S., "A theory of cerebellar function." *Math. Biosci.* 10 (1971): 25–61.

Alexander, G. E., and M. R. DeLong. "Microstimulation of the primate neostriatum: I. Physiological properties of striatal microexcitable zones." *J. Neurophysiol.* 53 (1985): 1401–16; "II. Somatotopic organization of striatal microexcitable zones and their relation to neuronal response properties." *J. Neurophysiol.* 53 (1985): 1417–30.

Alexander, G. E., M. R. DeLong, and P. L. Strick. "Parallel organization of functionally segregated circuits linking basal ganglia and cortex." *Annu. Rev. Neurosci.* 9 (1986): 357–81.

Allport, A. "Selection for action: Some behavioral and neurophysiological considerations of attention and action." In *Perspectives on Perception and Action*, ed. H. Heuer and A. F. Sanders, 395–419. Hillsdale, N.J.: Lawrence Erlbaum Associates, 1987.

———. "What concept of consciousness?" In *Consciousness in Contemporary Science*, ed. A. J. Marcel and E. Bisiach, 159–82. Oxford: Clarendon, 1988.

American Psychiatric Association. *The Diagnostic and Statistical Manual of Mental Disorders (DSM III)*, 3d ed. Washington, D.C.: American Psychiatric Association, 1987.

Andersen, P. O. "Specific long-lasting potentiation of synaptic transmission in hippocampal slices." *Nature* 266 (1977): 736–37.

———. "Possible mechanisms for long-lasting potentiation of synaptic transmission in hippocampal slices from guinea-pigs." *J. Physiol. (Lond.)* 302 (1980): 463–82.

Andersen, P. O., B. H. Bland, and J. D. Dudar. "Organization of the hippocampal output." *Exp. Brain Res.* 17 (1973): 152–68.

Anderson, J. R. *Cognitive Psychology and Its Implications*. San Francisco: Freeman, 1980.

Anderson, J. R., and G. H. Bower. *Human Associative Memory*, 2d ed. Washington, D.C.: Hemisphere Publishing, 1974.

Andersson, G., and O. Oscarsson. "Climbing fiber microzones in cerebellar vermis and their projections to different groups of cells in the lateral vestibular nucleus." *Exp. Brain Res.* 32 (1978): 565–79.

Arbib, M. A., D. Caplan, and J. C. Marshall. *Neural Models of Language Processes.* New York: Academic, 1982.

Armstrong, D. M. *A Materialist Theory of the Mind.* New York: Humanities, 1968.

Armstrong, D. M., and N. Malcolm. *Consciousness and Causality.* Oxford: Blackwell, 1984.

Arnold, M. B. *Memory and the Brain.* Hillsdale, N.J.: Lawrence Erlbaum Associates, 1984.

Ashby, W. R. *An Introduction to Cybernetics.* New York: Wiley, 1966.

Augustine, St. *Confessions* (401). Trans. R. Warner. New York: Mentor Books, 1963.

Ayer, A. J. *The Problem of Knowledge.* Middlesex, N.J.: Penguin Books, 1956.

———. *Philosophy in the Twentieth Century.* East Hanover, N.J.: Vintage Books, 1984.

Ballard, D. H., G. E. Hinton, and T. J. Sejnowski. "Parallel visual computation." *Nature* 306 (1983): 21–26.

Barker, R. "How does the brain control its own activity? A new function for the basal ganglia." *J. Theoret. Biol.* 131 (1988): 497–507.

Barlow, H. P. "Single units and sensation: A neuron doctrine for perceptual psychology?" *Perception* 1 (1972): 371–94.

———. "Neuroscience: A new era?" *Nature* 331 (1988): 571.

Barrett, P. H., P. J. Gautrey, S. Herbert, D. Kohn, and S. Smith, eds. *Charles Darwin's Notebooks, 1836–1844: Geology, Transmutation of Species, Metaphysical Enquiries.* Ithaca: Cornell Univ. Press, 1987.

Bartlett, F. C. *Thinking: A Study of Humans.* New York: Basic Books, 1958.

———. *Remembering: A Study in Experimental and Social Psychology.* Cambridge, Eng.: Cambridge Univ. Press, 1964.

Bechtel, W. *Philosophy of Mind: An Overview for Cognitive Science.* Hillsdale, N.J.: Lawrence Erlbaum Associates, 1988.

Bennett, J. *Linguistic Behavior.* Cambridge, Eng.: Cambridge Univ. Press, 1976.

Bernstein, N. *The Coordination and Regulation of Movements.* Oxford: Pergamon, 1967.

Bindra, D. *A Theory of Intelligent Behavior.* New York: Wiley, 1976.

Bisiach, E. "Language without Thought." In *Thought without Language,* ed. L. Weiskrantz, 465–91. Oxford: Clarendon, 1988.

Blakemore, C., and S. Greenfield, eds. *Mindwaves: Thoughts on Intelligence, Identity, and Consciousness.* New York: Blackwell, 1987.

Block, N., ed. *Imagery.* Cambridge: MIT Press, 1981.

———. "Troubles with functionalism." In *Cognition: Issues in the Foundations of Psychology.* Minnesota Studies in the Philosophy of Science, vol. 9, ed. C. W. Savage, 261–325. Minneapolis: Univ. of Minnesota Press, 1978.

Block, R. A. "Time and consciousness." In *Aspects of consciousness*. Vol. 1, *Psychological Issues*, ed. G. Underwood and R. Stevens, 179–217. New York: Academic, 1979.

Bock, G., M. O'Connor, and J. Marsh, eds. *Motor Areas of the Cerebral Cortex*, Ciba Foundation Symposium, no. 132. New York: Wiley, 1987.

Borbély, A. *Secrets of Sleep*. New York: Basic Books, 1986.

Boring, E. G. *The Physical Dimensions of Consciousness*. New York: Dover, 1963.

Borst, C. V. *The Mind-Brain Identity Theory*. London: Macmillan, 1970.

Bower, G. H., ed. *The Psychology of Learning and Motivation*. Vols. 3 and 4. New York: Academic, 1982.

Bower, J. M., and D. C. Woolston. "Congruence of spatial organization of tactile projections to granule cell and Purkinje cell layers of cerebellar hemispheres of the albino rat: Vertical organization of the cerebellar cortex." *J. Neurophysiol.* 49 (1983): 745–66.

Bowers, K. S., and D. Meichenbaum, eds. *The Unconscious Reconsidered*. New York: Wiley, 1984.

Boyd, R., and P. J. Richerson. *Culture and the Evolutionary Process*. Chicago: Univ. of Chicago Press, 1985.

Brentano, F. *Psychologie vom empirischen Standpunkt*. Vol. 1, ed. O. Kraus. Leipzig: F. Meiner, 1924–28.

Bresnan, J., ed. *The Mental Representation of Grammatical Relations*. Cambridge: MIT Press, 1982.

Bresnan, J., and R. M. Kaplan. "Introduction: Grammars as mental representations of language." In *The Mental Representation of Grammatical Relations*, ed. J. Bresnan, xvi–lii. Cambridge: MIT Press, 1982.

Broadbent, D. *Perception and Communication*. London: Pergamon, 1958.

———. *Behavior*. New York: Basic Books, 1961.

Brouwer, L. E. J. "Consciousness, philosophy, and mathematics." In *Proceedings of the Tenth International Congress of Philosophy*. Vol. 2, ed. E. W. Beth, H. J. Pos, and J. H. A. Hollak, 1235–49. Amsterdam: North Holland, 1949.

Brown, J. W. "Frontal lobe syndromes." In *Handbook of Clinical Neurology*. Vol. 45, ed. P. J. Vinken, G. W. Bruyn, and H. Klawans, 23–41. Amsterdam: North Holland, 1985.

Brown, R. *A First Language: The Early Stages*. Cambridge: Harvard Univ. Press, 1973.

Bruce, C. J., and M. E. Goldberg. "Primate frontal eye fields: I. Single neurons discharging before saccades." *J. Neurophysiol.* 53 (1985): 603–35.

Bruner, J. S. *Beyond the Information Given: Studies in the Psychology of Knowing*. New York: Norton, 1973.

Bunge, M. *The Mind-Body Problem: A Psychobiological Approach*. Oxford: Pergamon, 1980.

Burnet, F. M. *The Clonal Selection Theory of Acquired Immunity*. Nashville: Vanderbilt Univ. Press, 1959.

Buser, P. A., and A. Rougeul-Buser, eds. *Cerebral Correlates of the Conscious Experience*. Amsterdam and New York: North Holland, 1978.

Butterworth, G., and L. Grover. "The origins of referential communication in human infancy." In *Thought without Language,* ed. L. Weiskrantz, 5–24. Oxford: Clarendon, 1988.

Campbell, D. T. "Evolutionary epistemology." In *The Philosophy of Karl Popper,* ed. P. A. Schlepp. La Salle: Open Court, 1966.

Caramazza, A. "Some aspects of language processing revealed through the analysis of acquired aphasia: The lexical system." *Annu. Rev. Neurosci.* 11 (1988): 395–421.

Carroll, B. J. "Neurobiological dimensions of depression and mania." In *The Origins of Depression: Current Concepts and Approaches,* Dahlem Konferenzen, no. 26, ed. J. Angst, 163–86. Berlin: Springer-Verlag, 1983.

Changeux, J.-P., and A. Danchin. "Selective stabilization of developing synapses as a mechanism for the specifications of neuronal networks." *Nature* 264 (1976): 705–12.

Chapman, C. E., G. Spidalieri, and Y. Lamarre. "Discharge properties of area S neurons during arm movements triggered by sensory stimuli in the monkey." *Brain Res.* 309 (1984): 63–77.

———. "Activity of dentate neurons during arm movements triggered by visual, auditory, and somesthetic stimuli in the monkey." *J. Neurophysiol.* 55 (1986): 203–26.

Chomsky, N. *Cartesian Linguistics.* New York: Harper & Row, 1966.

———. *Language and Mind.* Extended ed. New York: Harcourt Brace World, 1972.

———. *Rules and Representations.* New York: Columbia Univ. Press, 1980.

———. *Knowledge and Language: Its Nature, Origin and Use.* New York: Praeger, 1986.

Churchland, P. M. *Matter and Consciousness.* Cambridge: MIT Press, 1984.

Coan, R. W. *Human Consciousness and Its Evolution: A Multidimensional View.* Westport, Conn.: Greenwood Press, 1987.

Cofer, C. N. "Human learning and memory." In *The First Century of Experimental Psychology,* ed. E. Hearst, 323–69. Hillsdale, N.J.: Lawrence Erlbaum Associates, 1979.

Cohen, I. B. *Revolution in Science.* Cambridge: Harvard Univ. Press, 1985.

Cohen, L. B. "An information processing approach to infant cognitive development." In *Thought without Language,* ed. L. Weiskrantz, 211–36. Oxford: Clarendon, 1988.

Cowan, W. M. "Aspects of neural development." *Int. Rev. Physiol.* 17 (1978): 149–91.

Crick, F. H. C. "Function of the thalamic reticular complex: The searchlight hypothesis." *Proc. Natl. Acad. Sci. USA* 81 (1984): 4586–90.

Crook, J. H. *The Evolution of Human Consciousness.* Oxford: Clarendon, 1980.

Crutcher, M. D., and M. R. DeLong. "Single cell studies of primate putamen: I. Functional organization." *Exp. Brain Res.* 53 (1984): 233–43. "II. Relations to direction of movement and pattern of muscular activity." *Exp. Brain Res.* 53 (1984): 244–58.

Cummens, R. *The Nature of Psychological Explanation.* Cambridge: MIT Press, 1983.

Darwin, C. *On the Origin of Species by Means of Natural Selection or the Preservation of Favoured Races in the Struggle for Life.* London: Murray, 1859.

Davidson, J. M., and R. J. Davidson, eds. *The Psychology of Consciousness.* New York: Plenum, 1980.

Davidson, R. J., G. E. Schwartz, and D. Shapiro, eds. *Consciousness and Self-Regulation.* Vol. 3. New York: Plenum, 1983.

Davidson, R. J., G. E. Schwartz, and D. Shapiro, eds. *Consciousness and Self-Regulation.* Vol. 4. New York: Plenum, 1986.

Delbrück, M. *Mind from Matter.* Boston: Blackwell Scientific, 1985.

DeLong, M. R., G. E. Alexander, A. P. Georgopoulos, M. D. Crutcher, S. J. Mitchell, and R. T. Richardson. "Role of basal ganglia in limb movements." *Hum. Neurobiol.* 2 (1984): 235–44.

Dennett, D. C. *Brainstorms.* Montgomery, Vt.: Bradford Books, 1978.

———. *The Intentional Stance.* Cambridge: MIT Press, 1987.

———. "Quining qualia." In *Consciousness in Contemporary Science,* ed. A. J. Marcel and E. Bisiach, 42–77. Oxford: Clarendon, 1988.

Dennis, I., J. A. Hampton, and S. E. G. Lea. "New problems in concept formation." *Nature* 243 (1973): 101–7.

Descartes, R. *Meditations.* In *The Philosophical Works of Descartes.* Vols. 1 and 2, ed. E. Haldane and G. Ross. Cambridge, Eng.: Cambridge Univ. Press, 1978.

———. *Passions of the Soul.* In *The Philosophical Works of Descartes.* Vols. 1 and 2, ed. E. Haldane and G. Ross. Cambridge, Eng.: Cambridge Univ. Press, 1978.

Deutsch, J. A., and R. Deutsch. "Attention: Some theoretical considerations." *Psychol. Rev.* 70 (1963): 80–90.

de Villiers, J. G., and P. A. de Villiers. *Language Acquisition.* Cambridge: Harvard Univ. Press, 1978.

DeYoe, E. A., and D. C. Van Essen. "Concurrent processing streams in monkey visual cortex." *Trends Neurosci.* 11 (1988): 219–26.

Diamond, A. "Differences between adult and infant cognition: Is the crucial variable presence or absence of language?" In *Thought without Language,* ed. L. Weiskrantz, 337–70. Oxford: Clarendon, 1988.

Dickenson, A. *Contemporary Animal Learning Theory.* Cambridge, Eng.: Cambridge Univ. Press, 1980.

Drake, S. *Discoveries and Opinions of Galileo.* New York: Doubleday, 1957.

———. *Galileo.* Oxford: Oxford Univ. Press, 1980.

Dretske, F. I. *Knowledge and the Flow of Information.* Cambridge: MIT Press, 1981.

Eames, P., and R. L. C. Wood. "Consciousness in the brain-damaged adult." In *Aspects of Consciousness.* Vol. 4, *Clinical Issues,* ed. R. Stevens, 1–39. New York: Academic, 1984.

Eccles, John C., ed. *Brain and Conscious Experience.* New York: Springer-Verlag, 1966.

Eckhorn, R., R. Bauer, W. Jordan, M. Brosch, W. Kruse, M. Munk, and H. J. Reitboeck. "Coherent oscillations: A mechanism of feature linking in the visual cortex?" *Biol. Cybern.* 60 (1988): 121–30.

Edelman, G.M. "Group selection as the basis for higher brain function." In *Organization of the Cerebral Cortex,* ed. F. O. Schmitt, F. G. Worden, G. Adelman, and S. G. Dennis, 535–63. Cambridge: MIT Press, 1981.

———. "Cell surface modulation and marker multiplicity in neural patterning." *Trends Neurosci.* 7 (1984): 78–84.

———. "Cell adhesion molecules in the regulation of animal form and tissue pattern." *Annu. Rev. Cell Biol.* 2 (1986): 81–116.

———. *Neural Darwinism: The Theory of Neuronal Group Selection.* New York: Basic Books, 1987.

———. "Morphoregulatory molecules." *Biochemistry* 27 (1988): 3533–43.

———. *Topobiology: An Introduction to Molecular Embryology.* New York: Basic Books, 1988.

Edelman, G. M., and L. H. Finkel. "Neuronal group selection in the cerebral cortex." In *Dynamic Aspects of Neocortical Function,* ed. G. M. Edelman, W. E. Gall, and W. M. Cowan, 653–95. New York: Wiley, 1984.

Edelman, G. M., W. E. Gall, and W. M. Cowan, eds. *Dynamic Aspects of Neocortical Function.* New York: Wiley, 1984.

Edelman, G. M., and V. B. Mountcastle. *The Mindful Brain: Cortical Organization and the Group Selective Theory of Higher Brain Function.* Cambridge: MIT Press, 1978.

Edelman, G. M., and G. N. Reeke, Jr. "Selective networks capable of representative transformations, limited generalizations, and associative memory." *Proc. Natl. Acad. Sci. USA* 79 (1982): 2091–95.

Elliot, K., and J. Whelan, eds. *Functions of the Septo-hippocampal System,* Ciba Foundation Symposium, no. 58. Amsterdam: Elsevier–North Holland, 1978.

Erdelyi, M. H. *Psychoanalysis: Freud's Cognitive Psychology.* New York: Freeman, 1985.

———. "Hypermnesia and insight." In *Consciousness in Contemporary Science,* ed. A. J. Marcel and E. Bisiach, 200–17. Oxford: Clarendon, 1988.

Evarts, E. V., Y. Shinoda, and S. P. Wise. *Neurophysiological Approaches to Higher Brain Functions.* New York: Wiley, 1984.

Eysenck, H. J., and M. W. Eysenck. *Personality and Individual Differences.* New York: Plenum, 1985.

Farah, M. J. "Is visual imagery really visual? Overlooked evidence from neuropsychology." *Psychol. Rev.* 95 (1988): 305–17.

Farrell, B. A. *The Standing of Psychoanalysis.* Oxford: Oxford Univ. Press, 1981.

Feigl, H., M. Scriven, and G. Maxwell, eds. *Concepts, Theories, and the Mind-Body Problem.* Minnesota Studies in the Philosophy of Science. Vol. 2. Minneapolis: Univ. of Minnesota Press, 1958.

Fentress, J. C. "Hierarchical motor control." In *Psychobiology of Language,* ed. M. Studdert-Kennedy, 40–61. Cambridge: MIT Press, 1983.

Finkel, L. H., and G. M. Edelman. "Population rules for synapses in networks." In *Synaptic Function,* ed. G. M. Edelman, W. E. Gall, and W. M. Cowan, 711–57. New York: Wiley, 1987.

———. "The integration of distributed cortical systems by reentry." *J. Neurosci.* In press.

Fishell, G., and D. van der Kooy. "Pattern formation in the striatum: Developmental changes in the distribution of striatonigral neurons." *J. Neurosci.* 7 (1987): 1969–78.

Fisher, S., and R. P. Greenberg. *The Scientific Credibility of Freud's Theories and Therapy.* New York: Basic Books, 1977.

Flanagan, O. J., Jr. *The Science of the Mind.* Cambridge: MIT Press, 1984.

Fodor, J. A. *Representations: Philosophical Essays on the Foundations of Cognitive Science.* Cambridge: MIT Press, 1981.

———. *The Modularity of Mind.* Cambridge: MIT Press, 1983.

———. *Psychosemantics: The Problem of Meaning in the Philosophy of Mind.* Cambridge: MIT Press, 1987.

Fodor, J. A., and Z. W. Pylyshyn. "Connectionism and cognitive architecture: A critical analysis." *Cognition* 28 (1988): 3–71.

Fraser, J. T. *Time: The Familiar Stranger.* Amherst: Univ. of Massachusetts Press, 1987.

Freud, S. *Project for a Scientific Psychology (Entwurf einer Psychologie).* In *The Standard Edition of the Complete Psychological Works of Sigmund Freud.* Vol. 1, ed. J. Strachey, 283–411. London: Hogarth, 1976.

———. *Introductory Lectures on Psychoanalysis.* New York: Liveright, 1919.

———. *New Introductory Lectures on Psychoanalysis.* New York: Norton, 1933.

———. *On Dreams,* ed. J. Strachey. Reprint. New York: Norton, 1963.

Friedman, W. J., ed. *The Developmental Psychology of Time.* New York: Academic, 1982.

Frith, C. D. "Schizophrenia: An abnormality of consciousness?" In *Aspects of Consciousness.* Vol. 2, *Structural Issues,* ed. G. Underwood and R. Stevens, 150–68. New York: Academic, 1981.

Fromkin, V., and R. Rodman. *An Introduction to Language.* 4th ed. New York: Holt, Rinehart & Winston, 1974.

Fuster, J. M. "Unit activity in the prefrontal cortex during delayed response performance: Neuronal correlates of short-term memory." *J. Neurophysiol.* 36 (1973): 61–78.

———. "The prefrontal cortex, mediator of cross-temporal contingencies." *Hum. Neurobiol.* 4 (1985): 169–79.

———. "The prefrontal cortex and temporal integration." In *Cerebral Cortex: Association and Auditory Cortices.* Vol. 4, ed. A. Peters and E. G. Jones, 151–77. New York: Plenum, 1985.

Galilei, G. *The Assayer.* 1623. Trans. S. Drake. In *Discoveries and Opinions of Galileo.* New York: Doubleday, 1957.

———. *Dialogue concerning the Two Chief World Systems.* 1632. Trans. S. Drake. Berkeley: Univ. of California Press, 1962.

Gallup, G. G., Jr. "Towards an operational definition of self-awareness." In *Socioecology and Psychology of Primates,* ed. R. H. Tuttle and G. G. Gallup, Jr., 309–41. The Hague: Mouton, 1975.

———. "Self-recognition in primates: A comparative approach to the bidirectional properties of consciousness." *Am. Psychol.* 32 (1977): 329–33.

Garner, W. R. *The Processing of Information and Structure.* Hillsdale, N.J.: Lawrence Erlbaum Associates, 1974.

Gazzaniga, M. S. *The Bisected Brain.* New York: Appleton-Century-Crofts, 1970.

———. "The dynamics of cerebral specialization and modular interactions." In *Thought without Language,* ed. L. Weiskrantz, 430–50. Oxford: Clarendon, 1988.

———. "Brain modularity: Toward a philosophy of conscious experience." In *Consciousness in Contemporary Science,* ed. A. J. Marcel and E. Bisiach, 218–38. Oxford: Clarendon, 1988.

Georgopoulos, A. P., J. T. Lurito, M. Petrides, A. Schwartz, and J. T. Massey. "Mental rotation of the neuronal population vector." *Science* 243 (1989): 234–36.

Gerfen, C. R. "The neostriatal mosaic compartmentalization of corticostriatal input and striatonigral output systems." *Nature* 311 (1984): 461–64.

Gibson, J. J. *The Ecological Approach to Visual Perception.* Boston: Houghton Mifflin, 1979.

Glickstein, M., C. Yeo, and J. Stein, eds. *Cerebellum and Neuronal Plasticity.* New York: Plenum, 1986.

Globus, G. C., G. Maxwell, and I. Savodnik, eds. *Consciousness and the Brain: A Scientific and Philosophical Inquiry.* New York: Plenum, 1976.

Goldberg, E. "The gradiential approach to neocortical functional organization." *J. Clin. Exp. Neuropsychol.* In press.

Goldman-Rakic, P. S. "Topography of cognition: Parallel distributed networks in primate association cortex." *Annu. Rev. Neurosci.* 14 (1988): 137–56.

Gottlieb, G. *Behavioral Embryology: Studies on the Development of Behavior and the Nervous System.* New York: Academic, 1973.

———. "Comparative psychology and ethology." In *The First Century of Experimental Psychology,* ed. E. Hearst, 147–73. Hillsdale, N.J.: Lawrence Erlbaum Associates, 1979.

Gould, J. L. *Ethology.* New York: Norton, 1982.

Granit, R. *The Purposive Brain.* Cambridge: MIT Press, 1977.

Graubard, S. R., ed. "Artificial intelligence." *Daedalus* 117, no. 1 (1988).

Gray, C. M., and W. Singer. "Stimulus-specific neuronal oscillation columns of cat visual cortex." *Proc. Natl. Acad. Sci. USA* 86 (1989): 1698–1702.

Gray, C. M., P. Konig, A. K. Engel, and W. Singer. "Oscillatory responses in cat visual cortex exhibit inter-columnar synchronization which reflects global stimulus properties." *Nature* 338 (1989): 334–37.

Gray, J. A. "The mind-brain identity theory as a scientific hypothesis." *Philos. Q.* 21 (1971): 247–52.

Gregory, R. L. *Mind in Science.* Cambridge, Eng.: Cambridge Univ. Press, 1981.

———. *Odd Perceptions.* London: Methuen, 1986.

Grene, M., ed. *Interpretations of Life and Mind.* New York: Humanities, 1971.

Grice, H. P. *Logic and Conversation.* In *Studies in Syntax.* Vol. 3, ed. P. Cole and J. L. Morgan, 41–58. New York: Academic, 1967.

Griffin, D. R., ed. *Animal Mind–Human Mind.* Berlin: Springer-Verlag, 1982.

———. *Animal Thinking.* Cambridge: Harvard Univ. Press, 1984.

Grillner, S. "Locomotion in vertebrates: Central mechanisms and reflex interaction." *Physiol. Rev.* 55 (1975): 247–304.

———. "On the neural control of movement: A comparison of basic rhythmic behaviors." In *Function and Formation of Neural Systems*, ed. G. S. Stent, 197–224. New York: Springer-Verlag, 1977.

Groves, P. M., M. Martone, S. J. Young, and D. M. Armstrong. "Three-dimensional pattern of enkephalin-like immunoreactivity in the caudate nucleus of the cat." *J. Neurosci.* 8 (1988): 892–902.

Grünbaum, A. "The philosophical retention of absolute space in Einstein's general theory of relativity." In *Problems of Time and Space*, ed. J. J. Smart, 313–17. New York: Macmillan, 1964.

———. "Is Freudian psychoanalytic theory pseudoscientific by Karl Popper's criterion of demarcation?" *Am. Philos. Q.* 16 (1979): 131–44.

———. "Epistemological liabilities of the clinical appraisal of psychoanalytic theory." *Nous* 14 (1980): 307–85.

Gunderson, K. *Mentality and Machines.* 2d ed. Minneapolis: Univ. of Minnesota Press, 1985.

Haenny, P. E., J. H. R. Maunsell, and P. H. Schiller. "State-dependent activity in monkey visual cortex. II. Retinal and extraretinal factors in V4." *Exp. Brain Res.* 69 (1988): 245–59.

Haines, D. E., and E. Dietrichs. "On the organization of interconnections between the cerebellum and hypothalamus." In *New Concepts in Cerebellar Neurobiology*, ed. J. S. King, 113–49. New York: Alan R. Liss, 1987.

Haldane, E., and G. Ross, eds. *The Philosophical Works of Descartes.* Cambridge, Eng.: Cambridge Univ. Press, 1978.

Harnad, S., ed. *Categorical Perception: The Groundwork of Cognition.* Cambridge, Eng.: Cambridge Univ. Press, 1987.

Hawking, S. W. *A Brief History of Time.* New York: Bantam Books, 1988.

Hayek, F. A. *The Sensory Order: An Inquiry into the Foundations of Theoretical Psychology.* 1952. Reprint. Chicago: Univ. Chicago Press, 1976.

Head, H. *Studies in Neurology.* Vol. 2. London: Hodder and Stoughton, 1920.

Hebb, D. O. *The Organization of Behavior: A Neuropsychological Theory.* New York: Wiley, 1949.

———. *Essay on Mind.* Hillsdale, N.J.: Lawrence Erlbaum Associates, 1980.

Held, R. J. "History as a factor in maintaining stability of perception and coordination." *J. Nerv. Ment. Dis.* 132 (1961): 26–32.

———. "Plasticity in sensory motor systems." *Sci. Am.* 213, no. 5 (1965): 85–94.

Helmchen, H., and F. A. Henn, eds. *Biological Perspectives of Schizophrenia.* Dahlem Konferenzen, no. 40. New York: Wiley, 1987.

Helmholtz, H. von. *Treatise on Physiological Optics*, ed. J. P. C. Southall. New York: Dover, 1962.

Helson, H. *Adaptation Level Theory: A Symposium.* New York: Academic, 1971.

Henry, G. H. "Streaming in the striate cortex." In *Visual Neuroscience*, ed. J. D. Pettigrew, K. J. Sanderson, and W. R. Levick, 260–79. New York: Cambridge Univ. Press, 1986.

Heron, W. "The pathology of boredom." *Sci. Am.* 196, no. 1 (1957): 52–56.

Herrnstein, R. J. "Acquisition, generalization, and discrimination of a natural concept." *J. Exp. Psychol. Anim. Behav. Processes* 5 (1979): 116–29.

———. "Riddles of natural categorization." *Philos. Trans. R. Soc. Lond.* [*Biol.*] 308 (1985): 129–44.

Herrnstein, R. J., and P. A. de Villiers. "Fish as a natural category for people and pigeons." In *The Psychology of Learning and Motivation.* Vol. 14, ed. G. H. Bower, 59–95. New York: Academic, 1980.

Hikosaka, O., and R. Wurtz. "Visual and oculomotor functions of substantia nigra pars reticulata III memory-contingent visual and saccade response." *J. Neurophysiol.* 49 (1983): 1268–84.

Hikosaka, O., and M. Sakamoto. "Cell activity in monkey caudate nucleus preceding saccadic eye movements." *Exp. Brain Res.* 63 (1986): 659–62.

Hilgard, E. R. *Divided Consciousness: Multiple Controls in Human Thought and Action.* Expanded ed. New York: Wiley, 1977.

Hobson, J. A. *The Dreaming Brain.* New York: Basic Books, 1988.

Hobson, J. A., and M. Steriade. "Neuronal basis of behavioral state control." In *Handbook of Physiology.* Section 1, *The Nervous System.* Vol. 4, 701–823. Bethesda, Md.: American Physiological Society, 1986.

Hochberg, J. E. *Perception.* 2d ed. Englewood Cliffs, N.J.: Prentice-Hall, 1979.

Hockett, C. F. *A Course in Modern Linguistics.* New York: Macmillan, 1958.

———. "The origin of speech." *Sci. Am.* 203, no. 3 (1960): 88–111.

Hockett, C. F., and S. A. Altmann. "A note on design features." In *Animal Communication: Techniques of Study and Results of Research,* ed. T. A. Sebeok, 61–72. Bloomington: Indiana Univ. Press, 1968.

Hockett, C. F., and R. Ascher. "The human revolution." *Current Anthropology* 5 (1964): 135–68.

Hofsten, C. von. "Catching." In *Perspectives on Perception and Action,* ed. H. Heuer and A. F. Sanders, 33–46. Hillsdale, N.J.: Lawrence Erlbaum Associates, 1987.

Holland, J. H., K. J. Holyoak, R. E. Nisbett, and P. R. Thagard. *Induction: Processes of Inference, Learning, and Discovery.* Cambridge: MIT Press, 1987.

Honderich, T. *A Theory of Determinism.* Oxford: Clarendon, 1988.

Hook, S., ed. *Dimensions of Mind.* New York: New York Univ. Press, 1960.

Hornstein, N. *Logic as Grammar.* Cambridge: MIT Press, 1984.

Horowitz, M., ed. *Psychodynamics and Cognition.* Chicago: Univ. of Chicago Press, 1988.

Hubel, D. H., and T. N. Wiesel. "Receptive fields, binocular interaction and functional architecture in the cat's visual cortex." *J. Physiol. (Lond.)* 160 (1962): 106–54.

———. "Functional architecture of the macaque monkey visual cortex." *Proc. R. Soc. Lond. [Biol.]* 198 (1977): 1–59.

Ingvar, D. H. "Memory of the future: An essay on the temporal organization of conscious awareness." *Hum. Neurobiol.* 4 (1985): 127–36.

Isaacson, R. L., and K. H. Pribram, eds. *The Hippocampus.* Vol. 2, *Neurophysiology and Behavior.* New York: Plenum, 1975.

Ito, M. *The Cerebellum and Neural Control.* New York: Raven Press, 1984.

Izard, C. E. "The emergence of emotions and the development of consciousness in infancy." In *The Psychobiology of Consciousness,* ed. J. M. Davidson and R. J. Davidson, 193–216. New York: Plenum, 1980.

Jackendoff, R. *Semantics and Cognition.* Cambridge: MIT Press, 1985.

———. *Consciousness and the Computational Mind.* Cambridge: MIT Press, 1987.

James, W. *The Principles of Psychology.* 1890. Reprint. New York: Dover, 1950.

———. "Does consciousness exist?" In *The Writings of William James,* ed. J. J. McDermott, 169–83. Chicago: Univ. of Chicago Press, 1977.

———. *Psychology: Briefer Course.* New York: Henry Holt, 1893.

Jaynes, J. *The Origin of Consciousness in the Breakdown of the Bicameral Mind.* Boston: Houghton Mifflin, 1976.

Jeannerod, M. *The Brain Machine: The Development of Neurophysiological Thought.* Cambridge: Harvard Univ. Press, 1985.

———. *The Neural and Behavioral Organization of Goal-Directed Movements.* New York: Oxford Univ. Press, 1988.

John, E. R. "A model of consciousness." In *Consciousness and Self-Regulation,* ed. G. Schwartz and D. Shapiro, 1–50. New York: Plenum, 1976.

Johnson, M. *The Body in the Mind: The Bodily Basis of Meaning, Imagination, and Reason.* Chicago: Univ. of Chicago Press, 1987.

Johnson-Laird, P. N. *Mental Models: Towards a Cognitive Science of Language, Inference and Consciousness.* Cambridge: Harvard Univ. Press, 1983.

———. *The Computer and the Mind.* Cambridge: Harvard Univ. Press, 1988.

Jones, E. G. *The Thalamus.* New York: Plenum, 1985.

Joseph, J. W., G. M. Shambes, J. M. Gibson, and W. Welker. "Tactile projections to granule cells in caudal vermis of the rat's cerebellum." *Brain Behav. Evol.* 15 (1978): 141–49.

Julesz, B. "Toward an axiomatic theory of preattentive vision." In *Dynamic Aspects of Neocortical Function,* ed. G. M. Edelman, W. E. Gall, and W. M. Cowan, 585–612. New York: Wiley, 1984.

Jusczyk, P., and B. Earhard. "The lingua mentis and its role in thought." In *The Nature of Thought: Essays in Honor of D. O. Hebb,* ed. P. W. Jusczyk and R. M. Klein, 155–86. Hillsdale, N.J.: Lawrence Erlbaum Associates, 1980.

Kaas, J., M. M. Merzenich, and H. P. Killackey. "The reorganization of somato-sensory cortex following peripheral nerve damage in adult and developing mammals." *Annu. Rev. Neurosci.* 6 (1983): 325–56.

Kahneman, D., and A. M. Treisman. "Changing views of automaticity." In *Varieties of Attention,* ed. R. Parasuraman and D. R. Davies, 29–61. New York: Academic, 1984.

Kanizsa, G. *Organization in Vision: Essays on Gestalt Perception.* New York: Praeger, 1979.

Kaplan, H. I., and B. J. Sadock. *Comprehensive Textbook of Psychiatry/IV.* Vols. 1 and 2. Baltimore: Williams and Wilkins, 1985.

Kassel, J., G. M. Shambes, and W. Welker. "Fractured cutaneous projections to the granule cell layer of the posterior cerebellar hemisphere of the domestic cat." *J. Comp. Neurol.* 225 (1984): 458–68.

Katz, J. J. *Language and Other Abstract Objects.* Totowa, N.J.: Rowman and Littlefield, 1981.

Keil, F. C. *Semantic and Conceptual Development: An Ontological Perspective.* Cambridge: Harvard Univ. Press, 1979.

Keller, H. *The Story of My Life.* 1902. Reprint. New York: Doubleday, 1954.

Kelley, D. B. "Sexually dimorphic behaviors." *Annu. Rev. Neurosci.* 11 (1988): 225–51.

Kelso, J. A. S., and B. Tuller. "A dynamical basis for action systems." In *Handbook of Neuroscience,* ed. M. S. Gazzaniga, 321–56. New York: Plenum, 1984.

Kenny, A. *Descartes: A Study of His Philosophy.* New York: Random House, 1968.

———. "Homunculus fallacy." In *Interpretations of Life and Mind: Essays around the Problem of Reductionism,* ed. M. Grene, 65–74. New York: Humanities, 1971.

Kertesz, A. "Cognitive function in severe aphasia." In *Thought without Language,* ed. L. Weiskrantz, 451–63. Oxford: Clarendon, 1988.

Kienker, P. K., T. J. Sejnowski, G. E. Hinton, and L. E. Shumacher. "Separating figure from ground with a parallel network." *Perception* 15 (1986): 197–216.

Kihlstrom, J. F. "The cognitive unconscious." *Science* 237 (1987): 1445–52.

King, J. S., ed. *New Concepts in Cerebellar Neurobiology.* New York: Alan R. Liss, 1987.

Klein, D. F. "Endogenomorphic depression: A conceptual and terminological division." *Arch. Gen. Psychiatry* 31 (1974): 442–54.

Klein, D. F., and J. M. Davis. *Diagnosis and Drug Treatment of Psychiatric Disorders.* Baltimore: Williams and Edwards, 1969.

Klima, E., and U. Bellugi. *The Signs of Language.* Cambridge: Harvard Univ. Press, 1978.

Koffka, K. *Principles of Gestalt Psychology.* New York: Harcourt Brace World, 1935.

Kosslyn, S. M. *Image and Mind.* Cambridge: Harvard Univ. Press, 1980.

Kuhn, T. S. *The Essential Tension: Selected Studies in Scientific Tradition and Change.* Chicago: Univ. of Chicago Press, 1977.

Landry, P., and M. Deschênes. "Intracortical arborizations and receptive fields of identified ventrobasal thalamocortical afferents to the primary somatic sensory cortex in the cat." *J. Comp. Neurol.* 199 (1981): 345–71.

Langer, S. K. *Mind: An Essay on Human Feeling.* Vol. 1. Baltimore: Johns Hopkins Univ. Press, 1967.

Langer, S. K. *Mind: An Essay on Human Feeling.* Vol. 3. Baltimore/London: Johns Hopkins Univ. Press, 1982.

Lashley, K. S. "Structural variation in the nervous system in relation to behavior." *Psychol. Rev.* 54 (1947): 325–34.

———. "The problem of serial order in behavior." In *Cerebral Mechanisms in Behavior,* ed. L. A. Jeffress. New York: Wiley, 1951.

———. *The Neuropsychology of Lashley: Selected Papers.* New York: McGraw-Hill, 1960.

Lenneberg, E. H. *Biological Foundations of Language.* New York: Wiley, 1967.

———. "Of language, knowledge, apes, and brains." *J. Psycholinguist. Res.* 1 (1971): 1–29.

Lewis, D. *Convention: A Philosophical Study.* Cambridge: Harvard Univ. Press, 1969.

Lewis, M., and J. Brooks-Gunn. *Social Cognition and the Acquisition of Self.* New York: Plenum, 1979.

Libet, B. "Cortical activation in conscious and unconscious experience." *Perspect. Biol. Med.* 9 (1965): 77–86.

———. "Neuronal versus subjective timing for a conscious sensory experience." In *Cerebral Correlates of Conscious Experience,* ed. P. A. Buser and A. Rougeul-Buser, 69–82. Amsterdam and New York: North Holland, 1965.

Lieberman, P. *The Biology and Evolution of Language.* Cambridge: Harvard Univ. Press, 1984.

Lightfoot, D. *The Language Lottery: Toward a Biology of Grammars.* Cambridge: MIT Press, 1982.

Livingstone, M. S., and D. H. Hubel. "Psychophysical evidence for separate channels for the perception of form, color, movement and depth." *J. Neurosci.* 7 (1987): 3416–68.

———. "Segregation of form, color, movement and depth: Anatomy, physiology and perception." *Science* 240 (1988): 740–49.

Llinás, R. R. "Electrophysiology of cerebeller networks." In *Handbook of Physiology.* Section 1, *The Nervous System.* Vol 2, ed. V. B. Brooks, 831–976. Bethesda, Md.: American Physiological Society, 1981.

———. "Functional significance of the basic cerebellar circuit in motor coordination." In *Cerebellar Functions,* ed. J. R. Bloedel, J. Dichgans, and W. Precht, 170–85. Berlin: Springer-Verlag, 1984.

Llinás, R. R., and J. I. Simpson. "Cerebellar control of movement." In *Handbook of Behavioral Neurobiology.* Vol. 5, ed. A. L. Towe and E. S. Luschei, 231–302. New York: Plenum, 1981.

Lloyd, J. E. "Bioluminescence and communication." In *How Animals Communicate,* ed. T. A. Sebeok, 164–83. Bloomington: Indiana Univ. Press, 1977.

Logan, K., and L. T. Robertson. "Somatosensory representation of the cerebellar climbing fiber system in the rat." *Brain Res.* 372 (1986): 290–300.

Lucas, J. R. "Minds, machines, and Gödel." In *The Modeling of Mind,* ed. K. M. Sayre and F. J. Crosson, 255–72. Indiana: Univ. of Notre Dame Press, 1963.

Lumdsden, C. J., and E. O. Wilson. *Genes, Mind, Culture: The Co-evolutionary Process.* Cambridge: Harvard Univ. Press, 1981.

Luria, A. R. *The Working Brain: An Introduction to Neuropsychology.* New York: Basic Books, 1973.

———. *Higher Cortical Functions in Man.* Trans. B. Haigh. New York: Basic Books, 1984.

Lycan, W. G. *Consciousness.* Cambridge: MIT Press, 1987.

Lynch, G. S., and M. Baudry. "The biochemistry of memory: A new and specific hypothesis." *Science* 224 (1984): 1057–63.

Lynch, G. S., R. Dunwiddie, and V. K. Gribkoff. "Heterosynaptic depression: A postsynaptic correlate of long-term potentiation." *Nature* 266 (1977): 737–39.

Lynch, G. S., V. K. Gribkoff, and S. A. Deadwyler. "Long term potentiation is accompanied by a reduction in dendritic responsiveness to glutamic acid." *Nature* 263 (1976): 151–53.

Lynch, G. S., S. Halpain, and M. Baudry. "Effects of high-frequency synaptic simulation on glutamate receptor binding studies with a modified *in vitro* hippocampal slice preparation." *Brain Res.* 244 (1982): 101–11.

Mach, E. *Die Analyse der Empfindungen.* 8th ed. Jena: Fischer, 1919.

MacKay, D. "Divided brains–divided minds." In *Mindwaves,* ed. C. Blakemore and S. Greenfield, 5–16. Oxford: Blackwell, 1987.

Macnamara, J. *Names for Things: A Study of Human Learning.* Cambridge: MIT Press, 1982.

Mahler, M. S., F. Pine, and A. Bergman. *The Psychological Birth of the Human Infant: Symbiosis and Individuation.* New York: Basic Books, 1975.

Malach, R., and A. M. Graybiel. "Mosaic architecture of the somatic sensory-recipient sector of the cat's striatum." *J. Neurosci.* 6 (1986): 3436–58.

Mandler, G. *Mind and Body: Psychology of Emotion and Stress.* New York: Norton, 1984.

———. *Cognitive Psychology: An Essay in Cognitive Science.* Hillsdale, N.J.: Lawrence Erlbaum Associates, 1985.

Marcel, A. J. "Conscious and unconscious perception: Experiments on visual masking and word recognition." *Cognit. Psychol.* 15 (1983): 197–237.

———. "Conscious and unconscious perception: An approach to the relations between phenomenal experience and perceptual processes." *Cognit. Psychol.* 15 (1983): 238–300.

———. "Phenomenal experience and functionalism." In *Consciousness in Contemporary Science,* ed. A. J. Marcel and E. Bisiach, 121–58. Oxford: Clarendon, 1988.

Marcel, A. J., and E. Bisiach, eds. *Consciousness in Contemporary Science.* Oxford: Clarendon, 1988.

Margeneau, H. *The Miracle of Existence.* Boston: Shambaylaya Publications, 1987.

Margolis, H. *Patterns, Thinking, and Cognition: A Theory of Judgment.* Chicago: Univ. of Chicago Press, 1987.

Marler, P., and H. S. Terrace, eds. *The Biology of Learning.* Berlin: Springer-Verlag, 1984.

Marr, D. "A theory of cerebellar cortex." *J. Physiol.* 202 (1969): 437–70.

———. *Vision: A Computational Investigation into the Human Representation and Processing of Visual Information.* San Francisco: Freeman, 1982.

Marsden, C. D. "The mysterious motor function of the basal ganglia: The Robert Wartenberg lecture." *Neurology* 32 (1981): 514–39.

———. "What do the basal ganglia tell premotor cortical areas?" In *Motor Areas of the Cerebral Cortex.* Ciba Foundation Symposium, no. 132, ed. G. Bock, M. O'Connor, and J. Marsh, 282–95. New York: Wiley, 1987.

Mattingly, I. G., and A. M. Liberman. "Specialized perceiving systems for speech and other biologically significant sounds." In *Auditory Function: Neurobiological Bases of Hearing,* ed. G. M. Edelman, W. E. Gall, and W. M. Cowan, 775–93. New York: Wiley, 1988.

Mayr, E. "Behavior programs and evolutionary strategies." *Am. Sci.* 62 (1974): 650–59.

———. *The Growth of Biological Thought: Diversity, Evolution, and Inheritance.* Cambridge: Harvard Univ. Press, 1982.

McClelland, J. L., D. E. Rumelhart, and the PDP Research Group. *Parallel Distributed Processing: Explorations in the Microstructure of Cognition.* Vol. 1, *Foundations.* Vol. 2, *Psychological and Biological Models.* Cambridge: MIT Press, 1986.

McDermott, J. J., ed. *The Writings of William James.* Chicago: Univ. of Chicago Press, 1977.

McGinn, C. 1982. *The Character of Mind.* Oxford: Oxford Univ. Press, 1982.

————. *The Subjective View: Secondary Qualities and Indexical Thoughts.* Oxford: Oxford Univ. Press, 1983.

McKenzie, B. E., and R. H. Day. *Perceptual Development in Early Infancy: Problems and Issues.* Hillsdale, N. J.: Lawrence Erlbaum Associates, 1987.

Mead, G. H. *Mind, Self and Society.* Chicago: Univ. of Chicago Press, 1934.

Meltzoff, A. N. "Infant imitation and memory: Nine-month-olds in immediate and deferred tests." *Child Dev.* 59 (1988): 217–25.

Mesulam, M. M. "A cortical network for directed attention and unilateral neglect." *Ann. Neurol.* 10 (1981): 309–25.

Michod, R. E. "Darwinian selection in the brain." *Evolution.* In press.

Millikan, R. G. *Language, Thought, and Other Biological Categories: New Foundations for Realism.* Cambridge: MIT Press, 1984.

Milner, B. "Memory and the Human Brain." In *How We Know: The Inner Frontiers of Cognitive Science.* Proceedings of Nobel Conference 20, ed. M. Shafto, 31–59. San Francisco: Harper & Row, 1985.

Milner, B., and M. Petrides. "Behavioral effects of frontal-lobe lesions in man." *Trends Neurosci.* 7 (1984): 403–7.

Milner, B., M. Petrides, and M. L. Smith. "Frontal lobes and the temporal organization of memory." *Hum. Neurobiol.* 4 (1985): 137–42.

Mishkin, M. "A memory system in the monkey." *Philos. Trans. R. Soc.* [*Biol.*] 298 (1982): 85–95.

Mishkin, M., B. Malamut, and J. B. Chevalier. "Memories and habits: Two neural systems." In *Neurobiology of Learning and Memory,* ed. G. S. Lynch, J. L. McGough, and N. M. Weinberger, 65–77. New York: Guild, 1984.

Mitchell, S. J., R. T. Richardson, F. H. Baker, and M. R. DeLong. "The primate globus pallidus: Neuronal activity related to direction of movement." *Exp. Brain Res.* 68 (1987): 491–505.

Miyashita, Y., and H. S. Chang. "Neuronal correlate of pictorial short-term memory in the primate temporal cortex." *Nature* 331 (1988): 68–70.

Monod, J. *Chance and Necessity.* New York: Alfred Knopf, 1971.

Moore, G. E. *Some Main Problems of Philosophy.* New York: Macmillan, 1953.

Morgan, M. J. *Molyneux's Question: Vision, Touch and the Philosophy of Perception.* Cambridge, Eng.: Cambridge Univ. Press, 1977.

Mounoud, P. "The ontogenesis of different types of thought: Language and motor behaviors as nonspecific manifestations." In *Thought without Language,* ed. L. Weiskrantz, 25–45. Oxford: Clarendon, 1988.

Mountcastle, V. B. "Brain mechanisms for directed attention." *J. R. Soc. Med.* 71 (1978): 14–28.

Movshon, J. A., E. H. Adelson, M. S. Grizzi, and W. T. Newsome. "The analysis of moving visual patterns." In *Pattern Recognition Mechanisms,* ed. C. Chagas, R. Gattass, and C. Gross. *Exp. Brain Res. Suppl.* 11 (1985): 117–51.

Myers, G. E. *William James: His Life and Thought.* New Haven: Yale Univ. Press, 1986.

Nagel, T. "What is it like to be a bat?" *Philos. Rev.* 83 (1974): 435–50.

————. *The View from Nowhere.* New York: Cambridge Univ. Press, 1986.

Nakayama, K. "Biological motion processing: A review." *Vision Res.* 25 (1985): 625–40.

Natsoulas, T. "Consciousness." *Am. Psychol.* 33 (1974): 906–14.

———. "Toward a model for consciousness in the light of B. F. Skinner's contribution." *Behaviorism* 6 (1978): 139–75.

Neisser, U. *Cognitive Psychology.* New York: Appleton-Century-Crofts, 1967.

———. *Memory Observed: Remembering in Natural Contexts.* San Francisco: Freeman, 1982.

———, ed. *Concepts and Conceptual Development: Ecological and Intellectual Factors in Categorization.* Cambridge, Eng.: Cambridge Univ. Press, 1987.

Neumann, O. "Beyond capacity: A functional view of attention." In *Perspectives on Perception and Action,* ed. H. Heuer and A. F. Sanders, 361–94. Hillsdale, N.J.: Lawrence Erlbaum Associates, 1987.

Niki, H., and W. Watanabe. "Prefrontal and cingulate unit activity during timing behavior in the monkey." *Brain Res.* 171 (1979): 213–24.

Nilsson, L. G. *Perspectives in Memory Research: Essays in Honor of Uppsala University's 500th Anniversary.* Hillsdale, N.J.: Lawrence Erlbaum Associates, 1979.

Nisbett, R., and L. Ross. *Human Inference: Strategies and Shortcomings of Social Judgment.* Englewood Cliffs, N.J.: Prentice-Hall, 1980.

Norman, D. A. *Memory and Attention.* New York: Wiley, 1969.

Oakley, D. A. *Brain and Mind.* London: Methuen, 1985.

O'Keefe, J., and L. Nadel. *The Hippocampus as a Cognitive Map.* Oxford: Clarendon, 1978.

Oldfield, R. C., and O. L. Zangwill. "Head's concept of the schema and its application in contemporary British psychology: I. Head's concept of the schema." *Brit. J. Psychol.* 32 (1942): 267–86.

———. "Head's concept of the schema and its application in contemporary British psychology: II. Critical analysis of Head's theory." *Brit. J. Psychol.* 33 (1942): 58–64.

———. "Head's concept of the schema and its application in contemporary British psychology: III. Bartlett's theory of memory." *Brit. J. Psychol.* 33 (1942): 111–29.

———. "Head's concept of the schema and its application in contemporary British psychology: IV. Walter's theory of thinking." *Brit. J. Psychol.* 33 (1943): 143–49.

Oscarsson, O. "Functional units of the cerebellum-sagittal zones and microzones." *Trends Neurosci.* 2 (1979): 143–45.

Papez, J. W. "A proposed mechanism of emotion." *Arch. Neurol. Psychiatry* 38 (1937): 725–43.

Parfit, D. *Reasons and Persons.* Oxford: Oxford Univ. Press, 1984.

Passingham, R. E. "Two cortical systems for directing movement." In *Motor Areas of the Cerebral Cortex.* Ciba Foundation Symposium, no. 132, ed. G. Bock, M. O'Connor, and J. Marsh, 151–64. New York: Wiley, 1987.

Pearson, J. C., L. H. Finkel, and G. M. Edelman. "Plasticity in the organization of adult cerebral cortical maps: A computer simulation based on neuronal group selection." *J. Neurosci.* 7 (1987): 4209–23.

Pelikan, J. *The Mystery of Continuity: Time and History, Memory and Eternity in the Thought of St. Augustine.* Charlottesville: Univ. Press of Virginia, 1986.

Penney, J. B., Jr., and A. B. Young. "Speculations on the functional anatomy of basal ganglia disorders." *Annu. Rev. Neurosci.* 6 (1983): 73–94.

Perecman, E., ed. *The Frontal Lobes Revisited.* New York: IRBN Press, 1987.

Perrett, D. I., E. T. Rolls, and W. Caan. "Visual neurons responsive to faces in the monkey temporal cortex." *Exp. Brain Res.* 47 (1982): 329–42.

Perrett, D. I., P. A. Smith, D. D. Potter, A. J. Mistlen, A. S. Head, A. D. Milner, and M. A. Jeeves. "Neurons responsive to faces in the temporal cortex: Studies on the functional organization, sensitivity to identity, and relation to perception." *Hum. Neurobiol.* 3 (1984): 197–208.

Perry, J. R. *Personal Identity.* Berkeley: Univ. of California Press, 1975.

Petry, S. J., and R. Gannon. "Time, motion, and objectness in illusory contours." In *Perception of Illusory Contours,* ed. S. J. Petry and G. E. Meyer, 193–200. New York: Springer-Verlag, 1987.

Petry, S. J., and G. E. Meyer, ed. *Perception of Illusory Contours.* New York: Springer-Verlag, 1987.

Pettigrew, J. D., ed. *Visual Neuroscience.* New York: Cambridge Univ. Press, 1986.

Pfaff, D. W., and C. V. Mobbs. "Some concepts deriving from the neural circuit for a hormone-driven mammalian reproductive behavior." In *Advances in Physiological Research,* ed. H. McLennan, J. R. Ledsome, C. H. S. McIntosh, and D. R. Jones, 233–51. New York: Plenum, 1987.

Pichod, P. "DSM-III: The third edition of the diagnostic and statistical manual of mental disorders from the American Psychiatric Association." *Rev. Neurol.* 142 (1986): 489–99.

Pinker, S. *Visual Cognition.* Cambridge: MIT Press, 1954.

———. "A theory of the acquisition of lexical interpretive grammars." In *The Mental Representation of Grammatical Relations,* ed. J. Bresnan, 655–726. Cambridge: MIT Press, 1982.

———. *Language Learnability and Language Development.* Cambridge: Harvard Univ. Press, 1984.

Poggio, G. F., and T. Poggio. "The analysis of stereopsis." *Annu. Rev. Neurosci.* 7 (1984): 379–412.

Poggio, G. F., B. C. Motter, S. Squatrito, and Y. Trotter. "Responses of neurons in visual cortex (V1 and V2) of the alert macaque to dynamic random-dot stereograms." *Vision Res.* 25 (1985): 397–406.

Poizner, H., E. S. Klima, and U. Bellugi. *What the Hands Reveal about the Brain.* Cambridge: MIT Press, 1988.

Polanyi, M., and H. Prosch. *Meaning.* Chicago: Univ. of Chicago Press, 1975.

Pope, K. S., and J. L. Singer. *The Stream of Consciousness.* New York: Plenum, 1978.

Pöppel, E. *Mindworks: Time and Conscious Experience.* Boston: Harcourt Brace Jovanovich, 1985.

Popper, K. R., and J. C. Eccles. *The Self and Its Brain.* Berlin: Springer-Verlag, 1981.

Posner, M. I. "Mental chronometry and the problem of consciousness." In *The*

Nature of Thought: Essays in Honor of D. O. Hebb, ed. P. W. Jusczyk and R. M. Klein, 95–115. Hillsdale, N.J.: Lawrence Erlbaum Associates, 1980.

Premack, D. "Minds with and without language." In *Thought without Language,* ed. L. Weiskrantz, 46–65. Oxford: Clarendon, 1988.

Premack, D., and A. J. Premack. *The Mind of an Ape.* New York: Norton, 1983.

Premack, D., and G. Woodruff. "Does the chimpanzee have a theory of mind?" *Behav. Brain Sci.* 4 (1978): 515–26.

Pribram, K. H. "Self consciousness and intentionality: A model based on an experimental analysis of the brain mechanisms involved in the Jamesian theory of motivation and emotion." In *Consciousness and Self-Regulation,* ed. G. Schwarz and D. Shapiro, 51–100. New York: Plenum, 1976.

Provine, R. R. "Contagious yawning and infant imitation." *Bull. Psychon. Soc.* 27 (1989): 125–26.

Purves, D. *Body and Brain: A Trophic Theory of Neural Connections.* Cambridge: Harvard Univ. Press, 1988.

Putnam, H. *Mind, Language, and Reality.* Cambridge, Eng.: Cambridge Univ. Press, 1975.

———. *Representation and Reality.* Cambridge: MIT Press, 1988.

Pylyshyn, Z. W. *Computation and Cognition.* Cambridge: MIT Press, 1984.

Quine, W. V. *Word and Object.* Cambridge: MIT Press, 1960.

———. *Ontological Relativity and Other Essays.* New York: Columbia Univ. Press, 1969.

———. *Roots of Reference.* Peru, Ill.: Open Court, 1973.

———. *The Ways of Paradox and Other Essays.* Cambridge: Harvard Univ. Press, 1976.

———. *From a Logical Point of View: Nine Logico-philosophical Essays.* 2d ed. Cambridge: Harvard Univ. Press, 1980.

———. *Theories and Things.* Cambridge: Harvard Univ. Press, 1981.

———. *Quiddities: An Intermittently Philosophical Dictionary.* Cambridge: Harvard Univ. Press/Belknap Press, 1987.

Quine, W. V., and J. S. Ullian. *The Web of Belief.* New York: Random House, 1978.

Ramachandran, V. S. "Capture of stereopsis and apparent motion by illusory contours." *Perception and Psychophysics* 39 (1986): 361–73.

Ramachandran, V. S., and P. Cavanagh. "Subjective contours capture stereopsis." *Nature* 317 (1985): 527–30.

Ramachandran, V. S., V. M. Rao, and T. R. Vidyasagar. "Apparent movement with subjective contours." *Vision Res.* 13 (1973): 1399–401.

Rawlins, J. N. P., and K. F. Green. "Lamellar organization in the rat hippocampus." *Exp. Brain Res.* 28 (1977): 335–44.

Reason, J. "Actions not as planned: The price of automatization." In *Aspects of Consciousness.* Vol. 1, *Psychological Issues,* ed. G. Underwood and R. Stevens, 67–89. New York: Academic, 1979.

Reed, E. S. "Descartes's corporeal ideas hypothesis and the origin of scientific psychology." *Rev. Metaphys.* 35 (1982): 731–52.

———. "Two theories of the intentionality of perceiving." *Synthese* 54 (1983): 85–94.

————. *James J. Gibson and the Psychology of Perception.* New Haven: Yale Univ. Press, 1988.

Reed, G. F. "Sensory deprivation." In *Aspects of Consciousness.* Vol. 1, *Psychological Issues,* ed. G. Underwood and R. Stevens, 155–78. New York: Academic, 1979.

Reeke, G. N., Jr., and G. M. Edelman. "Real brains and artificial intelligence." *Daedalus* 117, no. 1 (1987): 143–73.

Reeke, G. N., Jr., O. Sporns, L. H. Finkel, and G. M. Edelman. "Synthetic neural modeling: A new approach to the analysis of brain complexity." In *Signal and Sense: Local and Global Order in Perceptual Maps,* ed. G. M. Edelman, W. E. Gall, and W. M. Cowan. New York: Wiley. In press.

Rescorla, R. A. "Pavlovian excitability and inhibitory conditioning." In *Handbook of Learning and Cognitive Processes: Conditioning and Behavior Theory.* Vol. 2, ed. W. K. Estes, 7–35. Hillsdale, N.J.: Lawrence Erlbaum Associates, 1976.

————. "Behavioral studies of Pavlovian conditioning." *Annu. Rev. Neurosci.* 11 (1988): 329–52.

Rescorla, R. A., and A. R. Wagner. "A theory of Pavlovian conditioning: Variations in the effectiveness of reinforcement and nonreinforcement." In *Classical Conditioning II,* ed. A. Black and W. R. Prokasy, 64–99. New York: Appleton-Century-Crofts, 1972.

Reynolds, P. C. *On the Evolution of Human Behavior.* Los Angeles: Univ. of California Press, 1981.

Richards, R. J. *Darwin and the Emergence of Evolutionary Theories of Mind and Behavior.* Chicago: Univ. of Chicago Press, 1987.

Ristau, C. A., and D. Robbins. "Language of the great apes: A critical review." In *Advances in the Study of Behavior.* Vol. 12, ed. J. S. Rosenblatt, R. A. Hinde, C. Beer, and M. C. Busnel, 141–255. New York: Academic, 1982.

Roland, P. E. "Cortical organization of voluntary behavior in man." *Hum. Neurobiol.* 4 (1985): 155–67.

Rolls, E. T., M. J. Burton, and F. Mora. "Hypothalamic neuronal responses associated with the sight of food." *Brain Res.* 111 (1976): 53–66.

Rolls, E. T., and G. V. Williams. "Sensory and movement-related activity in different regions of the primate striatum." In *Basal Ganglia and Behavior: Sensory Aspects of Motor Functioning,* ed. J. S. Schneider and T. I. Lidsky, 37–59. Toronto: Hans Huber, 1987.

Romanos, G. D. *Quine and Analytic Philosophy.* Cambridge: MIT Press, 1983.

Rosenbaum, D. "Hierarchical organization of motor programs." In *Higher Brain Function: Recent Explorations of the Brain's Emergent Properties,* ed. S. P. Wise, 45–66. New York: Wiley, 1987.

Rosene, D. L., and G. W. Van Hoesen. "Hippocampal efferents reach widespread areas of cerebral cortex and amygdala in the rhesus monkey." *Science* 198 (1977): 315–17.

Rosenfield, I. *The Invention of Memory: A New View of the Brain.* New York: Basic Books, 1988.

Russell, B. *The Problems of Philosophy.* 1912. Reprint. Oxford: Oxford Univ. Press, 1959.

————. *A History of Western Philosophy.* New York: Simon & Schuster, 1945.

Ryle, G. *The Concept of Mind.* Chicago: Univ. of Chicago Press, 1949.

Savage-Rumbaugh, E. S., B. J. Wilkerson, and R. Bakerman. "Spontaneous gestural communication among conspecifics in the pygmy chimpanzee *(Pan paniscus)."* In *Progress in Ape Research,* ed. G. H. Bourne, 97–116. New York: Academic, 1977.

Sayre, K. M., and F. J. Crosson, eds. *The Modeling of Mind.* Indiana: Univ. of Notre Dame Press, 1963.

Schacter, D. L., M. P. McAndrews, and M. Moscovitch. "Access to consciousness: Dissociations between implicit and explicit knowledge in neuropsychological syndromes." In *Thought without Language,* ed. L. Weiskrantz, 242–78. Oxford: Clarendon, 1988.

Schmitt, F. O., F. G. Worden, G. Adelman, and S. G. Dennis, eds. *The Organization of the Cerebral Cortex.* Cambridge: MIT Press, 1981.

Schneider, J. S., and T. I. Lidsky, ed. *Basal Ganglia and Behavior: Sensory Aspects of Motor Functioning.* Toronto: Hans Huber, 1987.

Schöne, H. *Spatial Orientation: The Spatial Control of Behavior in Animals and Man.* Princeton: Princeton Univ. Press, 1984.

Schrödinger, E. *Mind and Matter.* 1958. Combined reprint, *What Is Life?* and *Mind and Matter.* Cambridge Eng.: Cambridge Univ. Press, 1987.

Schwartz, G. E., and D. Shapiro, eds. *Consciousness and Self-Regulation.* Vol. 1. New York: Plenum, 1976.

————. *Consciousness and Self-Regulation.* Vol. 2. New York: Plenum, 1978.

Searle, J. R. *Speech Acts: An Essay in the Philosophy of Language.* Cambridge, Eng.: Cambridge University Press, 1969.

————. "What is an intentional state?" *Mind* 88 (1979): 72–94.

————. "Minds, brains, and programs." *Behav. Brain Sci.* 3 (1980): 417–24.

————. *Intentionality: An Essay on the Philosophy of Mind.* Cambridge, Eng.: Cambridge Univ. Press, 1983.

————. *Minds, Brains, and Science.* Cambridge: Harvard Univ. Press, 1984.

————. "Indeterminacy, empiricism, and the first person." *J. Philos.* 84 (1987): 123–46.

Sellars, W. *Science, Perception, and Reality.* New York: Humanities, 1963.

Shallice, T. "Dual functions of consciousness." *Psychol. Rev.* 79 (1972): 383–93.

————. *From Neuropsychology to Mental Structure.* Cambridge, Eng.: Cambridge Univ. Press, 1988.

Shambes, G. M., J. M. Gibson, and W. Welker. "Fractured somatotopy in granule cell tactile areas of rat cerebellar hemispheres revealed by micromapping." *Brain Behav. Evol.* 15 (1978): 94–140.

Shepard, R. N., and J. Metzlar. "Mental rotation of three-dimensional objects." *Science* 171 (1971): 701–3.

Shepard, R. N., and L. A. Cooper. *Mental Images and Their Transformations.* Cambridge: MIT Press, 1982.

Shoemaker, S. *Self-knowledge and Self-identity.* Ithaca: Cornell Univ. Press, 1963.

————. *Identity, Cause, and Mind: Philosophical Essays.* Cambridge, Eng.: Cambridge Univ. Press, 1984.

Shoemaker, S., and R. Swinburne. *Personal Identity.* Oxford: Oxford Univ. Press, 1984.

Skinner, B. F. *About Behaviorism.* Englewood Cliffs, N.J.: Prentice-Hall, 1957.

———. *Verbal Behavior.* Englewood Cliffs, N.J.: Prentice-Hall, 1957.

Sklar, L. *Philosophy and Spacetime Physics.* Berkeley: Univ. of Calif. Press, 1985.

Smart, J. J. C. *Philosophy and Scientific Realism.* London: Routledge and Kegan Paul, 1963.

Solomon, R. C. "Freud's neurological theory of the mind." In *Freud: A Collection of Critical Essays,* ed. R. Wollheim, 25–52. Garden City, N.Y.: Anchor Books, 1974.

Spelke, E. "The origins of physical knowledge." In *Thought without Language,* ed. L. Weiskrantz, 168–84. Oxford: Clarendon, 1988.

Sperry, R. W. "Neurology and the mind body problem." *Am. Sci.* 40 (1952): 291–312.

———. "Brain bisection and consciousness." In *Brain and Conscious Experience,* ed. J. C. Eccles, 298–313. New York: Springer-Verlag, 1966.

———. "A modified concept of consciousness." *Psychol. Rev.* 76 (1969): 532–36.

———. "An objective approach to subjective experience: Further explanation of an hypothesis." *Psychol. Rev.* 77 (1970): 585–90.

———. "Changing concepts of consciousness and free will." *Perspect. Bio. Med.* 20 (1976): 9–19.

———. "Mental phenomena as causal determinants in brain function." In *Consciousness and the Brain: A Scientific and Philosophical Inquiry,* ed. G. C. Globus, G. Maxwell, and I. Savodnik, 163–78. New York: Plenum, 1976.

Sperry, R. W., M. S. Gazzaniga, and J. E. Bogen. "Interhemispheric relationships: The neocortical commissures; syndromes of hemispheric disconnection." In *Handbook of Clinical Neurology.* Vol. 4, ed. P. J. Vinken and G. W. Bruyn, 273–90. Amsterdam: North Holland, 1969.

Sporns, O., J. A. Gally, G. N. Reeke, Jr., and G. M. Edelman, "Reentrant signaling among simulated neuronal groups leads to coherency in their oscillatory activity." *Proc. Natl. Acad. Sci. USA* 86 (1989): 7265–69.

Squire, L. R., and N. Butters. *Neuropsychology of Memory.* New York: Guilford, 1984.

Staddon, J. E. R. *Adaptive Behavior and Learning.* Cambridge, Eng.: Cambridge University Press, 1983.

Steriade, M., and R. R. Llinás. "The functional states of the thalamus and the associated neuronal interplay." *Physiol. Rev.* 68 (1988): 649–742.

Stevens, K. A. "Evidence relating subjective contours and interpretations involving occlusion." AI Memo 637, MIT Artificial Intelligence Laboratory, 1981.

Stevens, R., ed. *Aspects of consciousness.* Vol. 4, *Clinical Issues.* New York: 1984.

Psychology to Cognitive Science. Cambridge: MIT Press,

duals: An Essay in Descriptive Metaphysics. New York:

Studdert-Kennedy, M., ed. *Psychobiology of Language.* Cambridge: MIT Press, 1983.

Stuss, D. T., and D. F. Benson. *The Frontal Lobes.* New York: Raven Press, 1986.

Sulloway, F. J. *Freud, Biologist of the Mind.* New York: Basic Books, 1983.

Swanson, L. W., and W. M. Cowan. "An autoradiographic study of the organization of the efferent connections of the hippocampal formation in the rat." *J. Comp. Neurol.* 172 (1977): 49–84.

Swerdlow, N. R., and G. F. Koob. "Dopamine, schizophrenia, mania, and depression: Toward a unified hypothesis of cortico-striato-pallido-thalamic function." *Behav. Brain Sci.* 10 (1987): 197–245.

Szentágothai, J. "The brain-mind relation: A pseudoproblem?" In *Mindwaves: Thoughts on Intelligence, Identity, and Consciousness,* ed. C. Blakemore and S. Greenfield, 323–38. Oxford: Blackwell, 1987.

Tanji, J., and E. V. Evarts. "Anticipatory activity of motor cortex neurons in relation to direction of an intended movement." *J. Neurophysiol.* 39 (1976): 1062–68.

Thach, W. T. "Cerebellar inputs to motor cortex." In *Motor Areas of the Cerebral Cortex.* Ciba Foundation Symposium, no. 132, ed. G. Bock, M. O'Connor, and J. Marsh, 201–20. New York: Wiley, 1987.

Thatcher, R. W., and E. R. John, eds. *Functional Neuroscience: Foundations of Cognitive Processes.* Hillsdale, N.J.: Lawrence Erlbaum Associates, 1977.

Thompson, R. F. "The neurobiology of learning and memory." *Science* 233 (1986): 941–47.

Thompson, R. F., T. W. Berger, and J. Madden IV. "Cellular processes of learning and memory in the mammalian CNS." *Annu. Rev. Neurosci.* 6 (1983): 447–91.

Tibbets, P., ed. *Perception: Selected Readings in Science and Phenomenology.* New York: Times Books, 1969.

Tinbergen, N. "An objective study of the innate behavior of animals." *Bibl. Biotheor.* 1 (1942): 39–98.

———. *The Study of Instinct.* Oxford: Clarendon, 1951.

Treisman, A. M. "Contextual cues in selective listening." *Q. J. Exp. Psychol.* 12 (1960): 242–48.

Treisman, A. M., and G. Gelade. "A feature integration theory of attention." *Cognit. Psychol.* 12 (1980): 97–136.

Tulving, E. *Elements of Episodic Memory.* New York: Oxford Univ. Press, 1983.

———. "Multiple memory systems and consciousness." *Hum. Neurobiol.* 6 (1987): 67–80.

Underwood, G., ed. *Aspects of Consciousness.* Vol. 3, *Awareness and Self-awareness.* New York: Academic, 1982.

———. "Attention and awareness in cognitive and motor skills." In *Aspects of Consciousness.* Vol. 3, *Awareness and Self-awareness,* ed. G. Underwood, 111–45. New York: Academic, 1982.

Underwood, G., and R. Stevens, eds. 1979. *Aspects of Consciousness.* Vol. 1, *Psychological Issues.* New York: Academic, 1979.

———. *Aspects of Consciousness.* Vol. 2, *Structural Issues.* New York: Academic, 1981.

Van der Heiden, A. H. C. "Central selection in vision." In *Perspectives on Perception and Action,* ed. H. Heuer and A. F. Sanders, 421–26. Hillsdale, N.J.: Lawrence Erlbaum Associates, 1987.

Van Essen, D. C. "Visual areas of the mammalian cerebral cortex." *Annu. Rev. Neurosci.* 2 (1979): 227–63.

———. "Functional organization of primate visual cortex." In *Cerebral Cortex.* Vol. 3, *Visual cortex,* ed. A. Peters and E. G. Jones, 259–320. New York: Plenum, 1985.

Van Gulick, R. "Consciousness, intrinsic intentionality, and self-understanding machines." In *Consciousness in Contemporary Science,* ed. A. J. Marcel and E. Bisiach, 78–100. Oxford: Clarendon, 1988.

Van Hoesen, G. W. "The parahippocampal gyrus: New observations regarding its cortical connections in the monkey." *Trends Neurosci.* 5 (1982): 345–50.

Vinken, P. J., and G. W. Bruyn, eds. *Handbook of Clinical Neurology.* Vol. 4. Amsterdam: North Holland, 1969.

Vinken, P. J., G. W. Bruyn, and H. Klawans, eds. *Handbook of Clinical Neurology.* Vol. 45. Amsterdam: North Holland, 1985.

Von Eckhardt, B. "The scientific status of psychoanalysis." In *Introducing Psychoanalytic Theory,* ed. S. Gilman. New York: Bruner/Mazel, 1983.

Vygotsky, L. S. *Thought and Language.* Cambridge: MIT Press, 1962.

Wall, P. D. " 'My foot hurts': The analysis of a sentence." In *Essays on the Nervous System,* ed. R. Bellairs and E. G. Gray, 391–406. Oxford: Clarendon, 1971.

Walter, W., R. Cooper, V. Aldridge, W. McCallum, and A. Winter. "Contingent negative variation: An electric sign for sensory-motor association and expectancy in the human brain." *Nature* 203 (1964): 380–84.

Warnock, M. *Memory.* London: Faber and Faber, 1987.

Watson, J. B. *Psychology from the Standpoint of a Behaviorist.* Philadelphia: F. Pinter, 1919.

Weiskrantz, L. "A comparison of hippocampal pathology in man and other animals." In *Functions of the Septo-hippocampal System,* Ciba Foundation Symposium, no. 58, ed. K. Elliot and J. Whelan, 373–87. Amsterdam: Elsevier–North Holland, 1978.

———. *Blindsight: A Case Study and Implications.* Oxford: Clarendon, 1986.

———, ed. *Thought without Language.* Oxford: Clarendon, 1988.

Weller, M. P. I. "Some problems in the diagnosis of schizophrenia and the concept of clear consciousness." In *Aspects of Consciousness.* Vol. 4, *Clinical Issues,* ed. R. Stevens, 117–65. New York: Academic, 1984.

Whitehead, A. N. *Science and the Modern World.* New York: Macmillan, 1925.

Whitrow, G. J. *Time in History: The Evolution of Our General Awareness of Time and Temporal Perspective.* Oxford: Oxford Univ. Press, 1988.

Wigner, E. P. "Remarks on the mind-body question." In *The Scientist Speculates,* ed. I. J. Good, 284–302. London: Heinemann, 1979.

Wilcox, D. J. *The Measure of Times Past: Pre-Newtonian Chronologies and the Rhetoric of Relative Time.* Chicago: Univ. of Chicago Press, 1987.

Williams, B. *Problems of the Self.* Cambridge, Eng.: Cambridge Univ. Press, 1973.

———. *Descartes: The Project of Pure Inquiry.* New York: Humanities, 1978.

————. *Brain Damage, Behavior, and the Mind.* New York: Wiley, 1979.

————. *Biochemical Individuality.* London: Chapman and Hall, 1956.

Wilson, M. *Descartes.* Boston: Routledge and Kegan Paul, 1978.

Wimsatt, W. C. "Reductionism, levels of organization, and the mind-body problem." In *Consciousness and the Brain: A Scientific and Philosophical Inquiry,* ed. G. C. Globus, G. Maxwell, and I. Savodnik, 205–67. New York: Plenum, 1976.

Wise, S. P., and J. L. Rappaport. "Obsessive-compulsive disorder: Is it basal ganglia dysfunction?" In *Obsessive-Compulsive Disorder in Children and Adolescents,* ed. J. L. Rappaport, 327–44. Washington, D.C.: American Psychiatric Press, 1989.

Wollheim, R., ed. *Freud: A Collection of Critical Essays.* Garden City, N.Y.: Anchor Books, 1974.

World Health Organization. *Manual of the International Classification of Diseases.* 9th ed. Geneva: World Health Organization, 1977.

Yonas, A., ed. *Perceptual Development in Early Infancy.* Vol. 20, Minnesota Symposia on Child Psychology. Hillsdale, N.J.: Lawrence Erlbaum Associates, 1988.

Young, J. Z. "The organization of a memory system." *Proc. R. Soc. Lond. [Biol.]* 163 (1965): 285–320.

Zeki, S. M. "Uniformity and diversity of structure and function in macaque monkey pre-striate visual cortex." *J. Physiol. (Lond)* 277 (1978): 273–90.

————. "The mapping of visual functions in the cerebral cortex." In *Brain Mechanisms of Sensation: Third Taniguchi Symposium on Brain Sciences,* ed. Y. Katsuki, R. Norgren, and M. Sato. 105–28. New York: Wiley, 1981.

Zeki, S. M., and S. Shipp. "The functional logic of cortical connections." *Nature* 335 (1988): 311–17.

Zubec, J. P. *Sensory Deprivation: Fifteen Years of Research.* New York: Irvington, 1969.

CREDITS

Figures 3.2, 4.1, and 15.1 from Gerald M. Edelman, *Neural Darwinism: The Theory of Neuronal Group Selection.* Copyright © 1987 by Basic Books, Inc. Reprinted by permission of the publisher.

Figure 3.5 from George N. Reeke, Jr., and Gerald M. Edelman, "Real brains and artificial intelligence," *Daedalus* (winter 1988): 162. Reprinted by permission of the publisher.

Figures 4.3, 4.5, 4.6, 4.7, 4.8, and 4.9 from the *Journal of Neuroscience* 9 (September 1989): 3188–3208. Copyright © The Society for Neuroscience. Reprinted by permission.

Figure 4.4 from Gaetano Kanizsa, *Organization in Vision: Essays on Gestalt Perception* (New York: Praeger, 1979), 193. Copyright © 1979 by Gaetano Kanizsa. Reprinted by permission.

INDEX

7359
00
02